Population, Gender and Reproductive Health

International Institute for Population Sciences

Mumbai

Vision

To position IIPS as a premier teaching and research institution in population sciences responsive to emerging national and global needs based on values of inclusion, sensitivity and rights protection.

Mission

The Institute will strive to be a centre of excellence on population, health and development issues through high quality education, teaching and research. This will be achieved by (a) creating competent professionals, (b) generating and disseminating scientific knowledge and evidence, (c) collaboration and exchange of knowledge, and (d) advocacy and awareness.

Population, Gender and Reproductive Health

Editors
F. Ram
Sayeed Unisa
T.V. Sekher

International Institute for Population Sciences, Mumbai

RAWAT PUBLICATIONS

Jaipur • New Delhi • Bangalore • Hyderabad • Guwahati

ISBN 81-316-0394-6

Published by
Prem Rawat for **Rawat Publications**
Satyam Apts, Sector 3, Jawahar Nagar, Jaipur 302 004 (India)
Phone: 0141 265 1748 / 7006 Fax: 0141 265 1748
E-mail: info@rawatbooks.com
Website: www.rawatbooks.com

New Delhi Office
4858/24, Ansari Road, Daryaganj, New Delhi 110 002
Phone: 011 2326 3290

Also at Bangalore, Hyderabad and *Guwahati*

Typeset by Rawat Computers, Jaipur
Printed at Chaman Enterprises, New Delhi

Dedicated to a
distinguished demographer
Late Prof. P.N. Mari Bhat

Contents

Preface and Acknowledgements

The International Conference on "Emerging Population Issues in the Asia-Pacific Region: Challenges for the 21st Century" was organized as a part of the golden jubilee celebrations of the International Institute for Population Sciences (IIPS) during December 10–13, 2006 in Mumbai. About 500 participants (one-fourth of them from outside India) attended the conference. The conference provided an ideal platform for population experts, social scientists, policy makers and researchers to discuss and debate the recent developments in the demographic scenario of Asia and their implications for coming decades. The plenary, technical and poster sessions were organized by giving enough scope for exchange of different views and perspectives. Altogether, 174 oral presentations and 114 poster presentations were conducted in this conference. Besides, there were five plenary sessions on important themes in which 20 eminent scholars presented their views, which generated a healthy debate on many contemporary issues on population, health and gender. The themes of the plenary sessions were population and development, gender concerns in health and population, fertility and family planning, managing migration and urbanization, and public health challenges.

This volume contains 21 selected papers which were presented in the conference. These papers broadly deal with issues of population, gender and reproductive health in the Asian region. We hope the readers will find this book useful for the purposes of research, advocacy, policy formulation and programme implementation.

We are grateful to all those who have contributed to the successful organization of the conference. Various organizations and individuals have provided financial, technical and logistic support at different stages. We would like to thank each and every one involved in the conference. The conference was organized under the leadership of

Prof. P.N. Mari Bhat, who was Director of the Institute. His sudden demise in July 2007 was a great loss to IIPS in particular and Indian demography as a whole. He was very keen on publishing the selected papers from the conference in a book form for wider dissemination. We dedicate this book in memory of Prof. Mari Bhat, one of the finest demographers of his generation.

We would also like to thank the Ministry of Health and Family Welfare, Government of India, for its generous financial support. We gratefully acknowledge the technical support and funding provided by UNFPA, Packard Foundation, WHO, Wellcome Trust, UNAIDS and Population Foundation of India. We thank our co-coordinators in organizing the conference—Prof. S. Lahiri, Prof. B. Paswan, Dr K.C. Das and Major B.V. Ram Kumar—for their contribution. Our thanks are also due to faculty, staff and students of the IIPS for their cooperation and active involvement in organizing the golden jubilee conference. Last but not the least, we would like to thank Ms Princy Yesudian and Ms Archana Basu for their support.

— Editors

Population, Gender and Reproductive Health

An Overview

This volume contains 21 selected papers presented in the international conference dealing with issues of population, gender and reproductive health. These include studies from India, Bangladesh, Indonesia, Thailand, Sri Lanka, Iran and Nepal. The papers are categorized into five sections based on their focus themes. Here, in this chapter, we provide a broad overview of the issues involved.

Section I: Gender Issues

Distortion in sex ratio, particularly among children, has been a major concern in the Asian region during the last two decades. Although there are positive indications of improvement in educational and occupational status of women, this is not reflected in gender equality in all spheres of life. One of the targets of Millennium Development Goals (MDGs) is to remove gender gap by 2015. The first section of this book pertains to important gender issues in this region. The six papers included in this section, covering India, Iran, Bangladesh and Nepal, deal with subjects like sex ratio, gender preference, gender gap in socio-economic status, autonomy of women and violence.

Aghayari-Hir et al. in their paper entitled "Sex Preference in Iran: Verbal Statements vs Parity Progression Ratios" discuss the importance of having sons in the Iranian society. This is expected in a traditional society where sons have higher economic value and they are considered as pillar of old age security. Authors have shown that at each parity, percentage of women moving to higher parity without a son is higher than those with a son. Findings suggest that contrary to the verbal statements by mothers, Iranian women prefer male children and this preference plays a crucial role in their decision to move to higher parities. The paper illustrates that sex preference still exists and desire to have at least one child of either sex makes couples to have a large number of children of unwanted sex. In fact, verbal acceptability of gender equity is not translated into fertility pattern in Iran and this may be due to the inherent demand for sons in the traditional societies with not much social security for old age from the state.

The next paper by Pradhan deals with gender perspectives in the division of labour in Nepal. Examining the division of labour of women in comparison to men who are living in joint and nuclear families, using qualitative data, the study shows that average working hours per day for females as compared to males are significantly higher (10.8 and 7.5 hours respectively). It also demonstrates that there is no significant difference in joint and nuclear families when it comes to the division of labour and working hours of women. In both the family systems, women wake up earlier as compared to men. Water fetching, kitchen work, washing clothes and child rearing are completely women's domains. Women in joint family perform significant agriculture work as compared to men. Comparison of unmarried males and females also shows similar pattern of work division. Unmarried males may escape the task, while the unmarried females have to help their mothers or sister-in-laws. Division of labour at household level is constructed through socio-cultural norms from the childhood and it continues throughout the life span without much change.

Story of women in India over the past years has been a mixed bag of hope and despair. The gender gap in respect of literacy and work participation does exist in the north-east region in spite of general perception that the region represents an egalitarian society. The increasing imbalance in sex ratio is the best example for increasing gender discrimination in this region. Das has examined the sex ratio and literacy and employment status of women in India's north-eastern region. It has been demonstrated that a reverse relationship exists between the status of women and sex ratio. However, it may be noted that the falling sex ratio is not the result of deteriorating child sex ratio, but due to the poor health care conditions prevailing in the region. Women are put into childbearing condition frequently, often leading to the deterioration in their health and eventual death. The pre- and post-natal care is almost non-existent in the region.

Biswas' paper on "Status of Women Empowerment at Household Level in Eastern India" is based on National Family Health Survey of 1998–99. The paper concentrates on household level decisions, such as cooking, staying with family, purchasing jewelry, going to market, friend's and relative's house and education of children, etc. Overall, the status of women is not very impressive in the eastern region. Whenever money matter is involved, the male members of the household generally take the final decisions. However, other than financial matters, women enjoy some degree of freedom in taking decisions. Though the status of urban women is better than their rural counterparts as a whole, there were some spheres where the rural women's household decision-making autonomy supersedes the urban women's autonomy. The study demonstrates that women's autonomy increases with education. The author strongly argues for the measures for enhancing the level of women's education.

Gulati and Nanda examine the changes in sex ratio in India's northern states—Haryana, Delhi, Punjab and Chandigarh, from an economic perspective. Demand for a girl or a boy is examined in terms of demand for household amenities and consumer goods. It appears that the forces of economic reform, coupled with rising aspirations of people, could be the reason behind the low demand for girl children. The solution lies in raising the status of women, making the presence of women felt, and actively contributing to raising their status in decision-making both at community and family levels. Youth, who are more open to such progressive ideas, can be motivated and moulded to contribute towards. Authors warn the implications of emerging 'female-deficit regions' in India and the threat to the centuries old institution of marriage in the wake of increasing female foeticide. Another suggestion put forward by the authors is that of society giving sanction to daughters to perform the last rites of their parents in order to reduce the son preference on religious grounds. Even daughters can take care of old parents when needed and parents should really feel proud of this.

In the last chapter of the first section, Ahsan Ullah explores consequences of violence against women in Bangladesh, based on the qualitative and quantitative data collected from the victims of violence and their support givers (health personnel). This study by Ullah shows the devastating impact of violence against women in terms of loss of reproductive capacity, mental disorder, loss of eye sight, abortion and disfigured face and body. There are laws and promising policies for the protection of women's rights, but, the state has to apply them properly to protect women from the growing incidents of violence. Bangladeshi legal system has done little to diminish women's vulnerability to violence. Limited access to economic opportunity, education and health services perpetuates women's subordination to men and susceptibility to violence. The repercussions of violence against women reverberate throughout the family and community. The initiatives launched by the government and NGOs for the advancement of women have gradually made some impact.

Section II: Fertility and Family Planning

Cultural practices, social norms and traditions vary considerably across the Asian region, both between and within countries. Such diversity makes it difficult to generalize a discussion on fertility and family planning. In the last two decades many countries of this region experienced significant fertility decline. However, the total fertility rates (TFR) are still high in many countries and the level of contraception is considerably low. This leads to the discussion on the efficacy of family planning programmes in reducing TFRs. Literature suggests that family planning programmes play a supportive role for women or couples who choose to space, or have fewer children but are unlikely to create the impetus for a reduction in preferences for larger families. Reduction in fertility rates is achieved through changes in attitudes and cultural perspectives as well as by providing the means for contraception. This section tries to provide the perspectives on fertility, family planning and contraception with four papers related to India, Indonesia and Nepal.

Burhan Ali, in his paper, discusses the family planning and population issues in *Jamaah Salafi*, an Islamist Muslim group in Jogjakarta, Indonesia. By interviewing the leaders and followers of this group and through participant observation, the author describes the world view and the reproductive ethics of the members of *Jamaah Salafi*. It may be noted that this group rejected the official family planning programme of Indonesia. This group disseminates the ideas, teachings and policy that support large families and thereby endangers the natural environment and sustainable development of the country. The paper also highlights the role of religious leaders and government programmes. The *Jamaah Salafi* poses a real challenge to the government because of their opposition to family planning, gender equality and women's education. Based on the findings emerging from the study, the author urges the government to give a special treatment to *Jamaah Salafi,* and also *salafism* in general, related to population issues by considering their special ethics, world view and culture. This understanding is very essential for the government if they want the family planning programme to succeed in the country.

Women's contraceptive choices and the gender-power relations in Nepal have been studied by using quantitative and qualitative information in the next chapter by Gubhaju. In case of Nepal, the sterilization was the only method of contraception before 1980. Other methods of family planning were introduced in the 1980s.It was observed that there was rapid change in the trends of contraceptive use in this Himalayan country. Education of husband and wife is playing an important role in the use of contraception in Nepal. However, many women have serious apprehensions about the use of condom being afraid of becoming pregnant. The author also illustrates that the autonomy of women is influencing the purchase of contraceptives from the market. In few cases, husbands also have shown concern for the health of their spouse and preferred male methods of contraception. While there is some evidence that women's increased autonomy and decision-making enables the use of male exclusive method, the pattern is not consistent and systematic. Emphasis should be given on providing women with appropriate information on choices that are available, by taking into consideration the constraints posed by Nepal's patriarchal family structure that often limits their negotiating power in sexual relations. The author also argues for the increased involvement of men in family planning programmes.

Channakki and Hussain Khan also discuss the decision-making pattern of family planning method acceptors by focusing the situation in Karnataka state of India. Information on decision-making process in terms of the methods chosen, time of acceptance, place of seeking services, and the user are collected from the acceptors. The analysis reveals that a higher percentage of couples have decided together before opting for permanent method of family planning in comparison to temporary (spacing) methods. Government facilities are always preferred for getting services for adopting the permanent method of contraception. It is evident from the study that traditional family planning methods like rhythm and withdrawal are perceived to be harmless in comparison to modern contraceptive methods. This aspect has not received enough attention of programme managers. Further, the dissemination of awareness and right information on these traditional methods will increase their use and effectiveness. In order to design an appropriate and suitable reproductive health and family planning programme, which should be context-based and people-specific, the policy makers need to adopt a broader holistic perspective on people's decision-making process and their perceptions.

The nexus between poverty and fertility is always a matter of serious debate. Many demographers and social scientists believe that there is lack of theory to explain the persistent high fertility and mortality in Indian context. It is against this backdrop, Mukherji presents a new demographic field theory as a theoretical and analytical means for explaining high fertility, particularly in the northern states of India. The demographic field theory implies that the demographic behaviour system, socio-economic system of states, and population policies and programmes of the states are causally linked. The change in one brings change in another. By using the data from various sources, a series of canonical equations were generated by the author linking demographic variables with socio-economic and programme variables. The main argument emerging out of this exercise is that unless abject poverty and female illiteracy are not urgently addressed, high fertility will not reduce. This necessary condition for demographic transition is needed to be fulfilled if we want to see any positive results in this direction. The author suggests massive employment generation, poverty reduction programmes and a fight against illiteracy in India. Lack of meaningful planning and programmes to eliminate poverty according to the author, in the post-independent India, by and large, has been the main reason for this situation.

Section III: Reproductive and Child Health

Unfortunately, very little has been done in involving men in reproductive health (RH) process, especially their awareness of pregnancy care. The study by Islam et al. titled as "Men's Awareness of Pregnancy Care in Bangladesh: A Multilevel Data Analysis" explores men's awareness of pregnancy care using the 1999–2000 Bangladesh Demographic and Health Survey. About 83 per cent of the men knew at least one serious complication related to pregnancy. Slightly more than 62 per cent think that pregnant women should have more food than before. A composite indicator 'degree of awareness of pregnancy care' was measured using three types of information mentioned above. Analysis of data suggests that only 48 per cent of the men are highly aware of pregnancy care. Two-level random intercept multinomial logistic regression analysis suggests that age, division, education, access to mass media and number of living children are significant determinants of the degree of awareness of pregnancy care. Significant community effect was found in the data set. The research emphasizes that men should be more involved in the pregnancy care component of the ongoing RH programme, which is recognized as women-oriented to ensure better RH of women. The results also highlight the need for appropriate community-level interventions to improve men's involvement in the RH process.

The paper by Srivastava primarily aims to investigate the determinants of male involvement as supportive partner in their wives' reproductive health. It was carried out in three villages of Udaipur district of Rajasthan. Both quantitative and qualitative techniques were used for data collection. An index of involvement of the husbands regarding reproductive health issues of their wives has been constructed by the author. Around 80 per cent of the husbands had knowledge regarding their wives' reproductive health problems. Index of husbands' involvement in their wives' reproductive health problem suggests that around 5 per cent of husbands had low involvement, 73 per cent had medium involvement, whereas 22 per cent of the husbands were highly involved. A majority of the husbands reported that taking care of their wives reproductive health problems is their responsibility but they are hesitant to accept that responsibility openly because of shame and traditional norms.

The paper in this section, by Gandotra and Dey entitled, "Is slum population better than rural population in terms of MCH indicators?", examines the changes in the MCH parameters in rural and urban slum population of Gujarat state over time. Two multi-indicator cluster surveys, supported by UNICEF, were conducted in the years 1996 and 1999: one for the entire rural population of Gujarat as universe and other taking six municipal corporations of the urban slum as universe. It was observed that the complete immunization status of rural children increased from 59 per cent in 1996 to 72 per cent in 1999. Similarly, complete immunization status of urban slum children also increased from 31 to 70 per cent during the same period. The coverage of vitamin A prophylaxis along with measles increased from 49 to 69 per cent in rural areas and from 28 to 60 per cent in urban slums over time (1996–99). Increase in the proportion undergoing ANC check-up was found to be much higher in the case of urban slum women (77 to 91%) as compared to rural women (82 to 88%). The study concludes that both in child health and maternal health parameters there has been a substantial increase in the utilization of MCH services, especially among the urban population, which in turn may reduce IMR and MMR considerably.

With the legalization of abortion in 2002, Nepal has joined those countries, which have made remarkable progress in reproductive health and rights of women. The law grants women not only control over their unintended pregnancies, but also allows them to seek abortion from authorized providers during the first twelve weeks of pregnancy for any reason, and up to eighteen weeks in case of rape or incest and up to any gestation period in case of fetal deformity or disability or risk to their life or health. The paper "Abortion in Nepal: Knowledge and Attitudes of Married and Unmarried Men" by Sethi et al. observed that although the law grants women absolute right to abortion, majority of the married men are skeptical about it. Most of the married and unmarried males also disagreed on the abortion right of unmarried women. The study suggests that the programme should focus on creating positive attitudes among rural men towards abortion rights. Further, the authors recommend involvement of community-based health providers and volunteers to establish referral linkages.

Thakur's paper on "Fertility Behaviour and Women's Reproductive Health and Reproductive Rights" is a micro level investigation to find out various socio-cultural factors related to fertility behaviour and also to explore the cultural practices and belief systems influencing the fertility. By analysing the information collected from 500 respondents from the rural areas of Ajmer district, the author observes that though couples try contraception with a desire to stop fertility, the regular use of contraception is leading to pain and discomfort for many, which in turn results in discontinuation of the method. Many women report that psychological pain and sexual violence they usually experience in the marital relationship. Some of them even complain that they do not have the right to question the extramarital relationship of their husbands. Improving the health scenario in our villages depends on changing the behaviour of not only individuals but also community leaders and health service providers. NGOs and social workers have an important role to play in portraying the positive images of women consistent with human dignity.

Section IV: Adolescent Health

Audinarayana's paper "Determinants of Risky Behaviour among Young Men Hosiery Workers in an Urban Setting of South India" discusses the magnitude of risky behaviour (lifestyles) and its major determinants among young men hosiery workers of Tirupur city in Tamil Nadu, based on the data collected from 995 workers. About 48 per cent and 33 per cent of the young men workers are said to be in lesser-risky (playing cards for gambling, chewing tobacco and smoking *beedis*/cigarettes) and higher-risky behaviour (drinking alcohol, use of drugs, watching pornographic films/websites) categories, respectively. Multinomial logistic regression results on the level of risky behaviour revealed that young men workers who are slightly older in age (20–24 years), earning higher monthly income and who have large number of peers engaged in higher risky behaviour have exhibited significantly higher odds of embracing lesser as well as higher risky lifestyles than their counterparts. Conversely, self-religiosity and parents' religiosity appear to be decreasing the odds of embracing lesser and higher risky behaviour in a significant way.

The period of potential pre-marital sex has lengthened among adolescents and youth due to the rise in the age at marriage and decline in age at menarche. In order to fulfil their biological needs, youth engage in risky sexual behaviour. A survey in Sri Lanka to elucidate the level of sexual awareness, behaviour and vulnerability experienced by adolescents revealed many interesting findings. De Silva and Karunathilake found that majority of adolescents aged 10–14 and 15–17 do not possess significant knowledge on sexual behaviour and cultural barriers prevent them acquiring such knowledge. In general, females show less knowledge on sexual behaviour. Among them the estate sector females indicate the lowest level of awareness. Highest level of knowledge (36%) is reported by rural males. Higher knowledge is visible among unmarried males aged 18–24, compared to their married counterparts. Among unmarried urban males in the age group 18–24, nearly half of them believed that their peers have already experienced sexual intercourse. The corresponding figure is 19 per cent for females. Hence, a clear positive relation between the increase in the risk-taking period and sexual vulnerability is visible among the youth in the island nation.

Section V: Health Care and HIV/AIDS

This section has four papers. When it comes to HIV/AIDS knowledge, as shown in the first paper by Arca, Jr. and Sethi, the female Hmong youth in Thailand know more than their male counterparts in almost all subjects. While every boy and girl knows that sexual contact is a mode of transmission, only 82 per cent of the boys compared to 100 per cent of the girls know that sharing needles is a potential route for transmission. Regarding condom, the males have better knowledge of its effectiveness and the correct way to use it compared to females, as is evident from one of the statement: "condoms can be used more than once". Meanwhile, some interesting data point to gender constructs that are prevalent in the Hmong culture resulting in marked differences between the ways boys and girls think about HIV/AIDS and how to prevent it. For instance, all married female youth respondents think that having only one sex partner can help prevent HIV/AIDS transmission but only two-thirds of the married male youth think so. The analysis further shows that there is considerable gender difference on knowledge about condom, modes of HIV transmission, and prevention. On the one hand, the study indicates that despite the Hmong male's dominance in many aspects of family life, he has not yet mastered the knowledge needed to protect himself and his partner from HIV/AIDS. On the other hand, it is the female Hmongs who have shown better knowledge about HIV/AIDS, thus, reinforcing the stereotypical dominance of women in the arena of health care.

AIDS is a disease associated with fear and prejudices for a long time, due to obvious reasons. Providers' attitudes about HIV/AIDS are an important dimension in the delivery of quality care to persons suffering with HIV/AIDS. The paper "Level of Prejudices among Health Care Providers" by Sadhwani and Khan measured the level of prejudices among health care providers towards people living with HIV/AIDS. The study was carried out in Vadodara city in Gujarat. A structured tool was prepared to measure prejudices and the level of knowledge about HIV/AIDS. A sample of 50 doctors, 58 paramedics and 25 lab technicians was interviewed. The scale was found to be reliable on Cronbach's Alpha Coefficient at 0.88. The intrinsic validity based on Cronbach's Alpha Coefficient was 0.94. A higher percentage of the paramedics (31%) than doctors (14%) had more prejudices towards people living with HIV/AIDS. Doctors reflected prejudices when it came to treatment/services, whereas paramedics with regard to family and social interaction, besides treatment/services. Also, knowledge about the disease and training about the same seemed to have a lowering impact on level of prejudices. Thus, it may be concluded that health care providers had prejudices in varying degree, indicating that lack of correct information and education perpetuates prejudices.

Basu's paper deals with one of the most vulnerable groups, i.e., injecting drug users (IDUs) of Mumbai. They are the most vulnerable due to high partner exchange, lack of knowledge about HIV transmission, low condom usage with commercial and non-commercial sex partners, lack of exposure to intervention, and relatively high needle sharing behaviour. This paper analyses the gaps in the programme and suggests upscaling of the intervention activities among the IDUs. The data for this study was gathered from the second and third waves of Behavioural Surveillance Survey (BSS) in Mumbai during 2004–05 and 2005–06. Altogether, 568 IDUs were contacted in both the waves at their cruising sites. In spite of increased access to sterile needles (64 to 99%) over the years, there is a significant increase in sharing needles in high equipment sharing situations (51 to 74%). Significant increase in sex with commercial (24 to 38%) and non-commercial (13 to 30%) partners was reported. Three-fifths of the IDUs had exposure to any interventions related HIV/AIDS. The risk perceptions among the IDUs need to be changed by creating awareness through interpersonal communication.

Lastly, the paper on household health spending characteristics in India by Arokiasamy et al. utilized the data from the World Health Survey conducted in 2003 in six states of India, namely, Assam, Karnataka, Maharashtra, Rajasthan, Uttar Pradesh and West Bengal, to provide valuable insights. According to the study, a household in India on an average spent Rs 117 in a month for health treatment. A major share of health expenditure was on drugs and out-patient care. The households on an average spent Rs 52 on drugs, Rs 35 for out-patient treatment and Rs 18 on other expenses related to treatment. Household health expenditure on in-patient treatment, out-patient treatment, drugs and other related expenses rose with increasing income quintiles. Average household health expenditure is the highest (Rs 203) in Maharashtra and lowest (Rs 90) in Karnataka. The study observes that less than one per cent of the households relied on health insurance for their medical payments. About 7 per cent of the households financed their health expenditure through sale of assets such as furniture, cattle, jewellery, etc. The study revealed that 12 per cent of households in India come under the catastrophic health spending category.

Section I

Gender Issues

CHAPTER 1

Sex Preference in Iran

Verbal Statements vs Parity Progression Ratios

Tavakkol Aghayari-Hir, Aliyar Ahmadi, Abbas Askari Nadoushan and A.H. Mehryar

Taking into account males' higher economic status, higher and well-defined socio-political position, and their better contribution to old-age security of parents beside others, it is neither surprising nor unexpected that the Iranian society, traditionally, has put more emphasis on male than female. However, a recent study (Ministry of Health and Medical Education, 2003) has revealed a sharp decline in sex preference in the country. In fact, knocking at the door of Iranian couples and asking from ever married women of childbearing ages about the desired sex of the next child, they reveal no evidence of preference for male children!

Iranian DSH-type survey conducted in 2000, using a question on women's viewpoint on the sex of their current pregnancy reveals that 15–49 ever married women prefer their expected child to be female rather than male! According to findings of the survey, 20.2 per cent of women prefer to have daughters, compared to 17.7 per cent preferring son as their expected child. Around 62.1 per cent show no preference towards either sex, however.

Furthermore, results of a prospective question referring to sex preference for the future child indicate that daughters are more preferred than sons in urban areas, while the situation is reverse in rural areas, differences are small in both of the cases, however. Around 11.3 per cent of urban women desire to bear a son in their possible child-bearing in the future, while the corresponding figure for their rural counterparts is 12.2 per cent. In contrast, daughter preference was observed around 14.1 per cent among urban women and 11.1 per cent among rural women of childbearing ages (ibid.).

These findings encouraged the research team to investigate the issue more in detail and to ensure whether these findings go with all parities and any sex (compositions) of previous child(ren). Taking into consideration the advantages that a traditional society may assign to male than female, the recent finding regarding the non-existence of the sex preference, looks mostly accidental and clearly could not be regarded as taken for granted. Though, Islamic thoughts and principles that have dominated the country for so many years have emphasized on the value of girls, socio-cultural changes that undergo in the country in line with those in the rest of the world, and governmental family planning programmes that placed the same value for either sex by the motto of "two is enough, whether boy or girl", could weaken somewhat the preference of boys, nevertheless, it seems males are much more preferred than females. This must have stemmed from those traditional values and some of religion-driven laws and rules, which practically are in favour of males than females, which are living to the present times.

This paper addresses the assumed controversy between stated preferences towards female children by the ever married women of childbearing ages (verbal statement) and their actual behaviour, Parity Progression Ratios (PPRs), coming from the birth histories. Since it was expected that the existing preference for a given sex could mainly be derived from the sex compositions of the previous children, preferences in any case have been estimated for different sex (compositions) of the previous child(ren). The study challenges the existing view among administrators around the sex preference in the country.

Sex preference, as it is becoming too easy to diagnose the sex of the foetus by the use of newly introduced medical technologies, cannot only affect people's resort to abortion in the cases of unwanted sex, but also childbearing experiences and fertility levels especially when fertility declines (Bairagi, 2001).

Data and Method

Data for the analyses come from a wide and nationally representative DHS-type survey, administered mainly by the Ministry of Health and Medical Education (MOHME) with the financial and technical assistance and support from some other national and international organizations including; Statistical Centre of Iran (SCI), United Nations Children's Fund (UNICEF), and United Nations Population Fund (UNFPA) in 2000.

Samples for urban and rural areas of 28 provinces plus one additional sample for Tehran metropolitan city are drawn by the use of single-stage cluster sampling technique, using the household as the main sampling unit, provided the required data to investigate the verbal statements of Iranian women and parity progression ratios.

The multi-section questionnaire of the survey includes comprehensive information in various areas such as; background information for all members of the selected households, child labour, accident and disability information for all household members, household amenities and conveniences, mortality data for the household members, fertility, pregnancy, and childbearing, birth histories, family planning and contraceptive use, childcare, breastfeeding, and child health information for all ever married women of childbearing ages inside the household.

Generally, around 2,000 households in each of urban and rural areas of a given province (around 4,000 households in each province) were included in the survey. Since raw data are presented in separate files for urban and rural areas of different provinces, all were merged and analysed after checks were made for possible errors and inconsistencies with the data, especially for those of content errors.

Analyses were carried out examining the questions about sex preference among pregnant (around 5,500) and all ever married 15–49 (around 87,000) women considering the sex composition of the previous child(ren) at each parity. The PPRs were calculated based on birth histories of ever married women with respect to sex composition of their previous children as well.

Since parity refers to number of live births that a woman has, "Parity Progression Ratio from parity i to parity $i + 1$ is the proportion of a cohort who had at least i live births who went to have at least one more" (Preston et al., 2001). Putting this statement into formula, it yields:

$$PRI_{(i,\, i+1)} \frac{\text{Number of women at party } i+1 \text{ or more}}{\text{Number of women at party } i \text{ or more}} = \frac{P_{i+1}}{P_i}$$

In addition, a further step is taken to examine the effects of sex preference on contraceptive use as a proxy for fertility regulation among Iranian ever married women. To do this, Arnold's Method was employed. Although the method has some problems with it (Bairagi, 1987), still it gives *accurate quantitative estimates* of the sex preference on fertility and family planning in most of circumstances (Arnold, 1987)[1].

According to Arnold (1985), "in general, the measure is defined as $\Sigma C_i \times P_i / \Sigma P_i$, where C_i equals the maximum contraceptive use rate at each parity i, and P_i equals the number of persons at each parity i". Applying this formula, the proportion not using contraceptive because of preference towards either sex can be determined.

In this method, to investigate the possible effects of sex preference on fertility or some proxies of fertility such as contraceptive use, it is needed to calculate the fertility level or contraceptive use on two conditions: when the sex preference is present in fertility regulations or contraceptive experiences; and when it is eliminated from those regulations or experiences. In this paper, we have used the contraceptive prevalence as a proxy to investigate the possible effects of sex preference on fertility.

Findings

Verbal Statement

As mentioned earlier, summary report of Iran DHS-type survey (Ministry of Health and Medical Education, 2003) indicates preference in favour of daughters for already pregnant women of childbearing ages. Regarding viewpoints of all women on desired sex of the next child, daughters are more preferred than sons in urban areas. Nevertheless, the story changes significantly when the sex composition of previous parities is taken into account.

Examining preference for the sex of the expected child among those women who were pregnant at the time of the survey (Graph 1) with reference to different sex compositions of various parity levels reveals the *changed* story around sex preference. Horizontal axis in the graph includes parities with different sex compositions (1 representing a son and 2 representing a daughter). The vertical axis shows the proportion of women with parity i or more who progressed to have the children of parity $i+1$ or more with reference to different parities and their different sex compositions.

Although at parity zero there is only a negligible difference between preference for male and female children, it has immediately introduced by taking the sex of previous child at parity 1 into account. Only about 10.2 per cent of mothers with one son preferred to have another in their current pregnancy, while around 40.7 per cent of them expressed a preference for a daughter. About half of first parity women showed uncertainty about their preferred sex for the expected baby. Among mothers of one female child, around 43.6 per cent of them were waiting for a son, while only 2.7 per cent preferred to have one more daughter at their second childbearing. About 53.8 per cent of them did not know which sex they preferred.

Mothers of higher parities have the same pattern of sex preference for their current pregnancy, as illustrated by Graph 1 in more detail. Only around 4.4 per cent of those who had two boys wanted to bear the third boy in their next childbearing that is comparable to mothers with two daughters waiting for the third daughter, which is 2.1 per cent. In contrast, 32.4 per cent of mothers with two sons were expecting a daughter. Corresponding figure for mothers with two daughters expecting for a son is 28.5 per cent. For the mothers of one son and one daughter, around 20.2 and 7.5 per cent prefer to have their next child as son and daughter, respectively. Despite this son preference, the majority (72.3%) showed no preference towards any sex.

Taking the mothers of three children into account, the same pattern of preference is evident. Where only 3.7 per cent of expectant mothers with three sons preferred another son, the majority, 75.9 per cent, preferred to add another daughter to their families. Only 20.4

Graph 1

Sex Preference for Pregnant Women According to Sex (Composition) of Previous Child(ren)

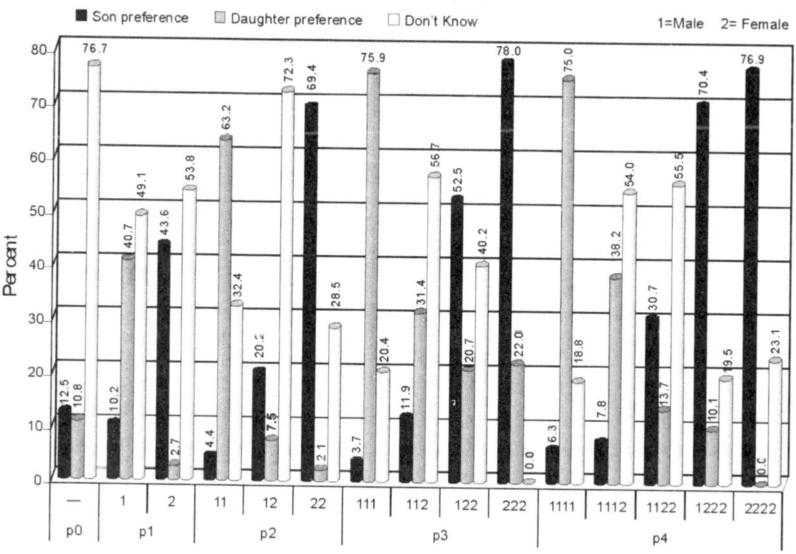

per cent of them do prefer children of either sex or are not sure which sex they prefer. Compared to mothers of three sons preferring to have a daughter in their next childbearing, a large proportion (78%) of mothers with three daughters are enthusiastic to have their next baby as son. The uncertain proportion for mothers with three daughters is about 22 per cent. Regarding the mothers of three children who have children of either sexes, not surprisingly, the proportion desiring to have their next baby as male or female both is well lower than that of mothers with only three boys or three girls. About 11.9 and 31.4 per cent of mothers with two boys and one girl prefer another boy and another girl, respectively. Majority (56.7%) have no idea about the sex they prefer. Approximately, 52.5 per cent of mothers with two daughters and one son desired to bear another son, while the corresponding value for another daughter approaches 21 per cent. About 40.2 per cent of them have no preference in favour of any sex.

Results for the 4th parity show even stronger preference towards either sex with respect to sex composition of previous children. In the case of mothers with 4 male children, where only 6.3 per cent of them preferred to have another son, the percentage of mothers who desired to have their next child as daughter was pretty high, around 75 per cent. Correspondingly, among mothers with 4 daughters, 76.9 per cent preferred to bear another son and, interestingly, none of them hoped to have another daughter. Among mothers with 3-sons-1-daughter and 3-daughter-1-son desire to have another son were 7.9 and 70.4, respectively. Corresponding ratios for another daughter were 38.3 and 10.1 per cent. With respect to mothers with 2 sons and 2 daughters (equal number of sons and daughters), preference for any sex declines. However, desire to have another son is well higher than that of daughter (30.7 comparing to 13.7%).

Moving from unequal positions of sex compositions at different parities to more equal compositions of previous children, majority preferring the child of one sex is replaced by those who show no preference towards either sex. This is not surprising, however, since mothers who have already got the children of both sexes and especially the equal number of boys and girls, the sex of the expected baby is not too much important. In any parity, though the sex that already has not joined the family or its number is lower comparing to children of other sex, is more preferred, everything being equal males are more preferred than females. Therefore, it could be concluded that women's preference towards a child of a given sex mainly is explained by the sex (compositions) of their previous child(ren).

Graphs 2 and 3 illustrate results of a prospective question on preference of all 15–49 ever married women on the desired sex of the future child in terms of sex composition at different parities. Among 0 parity women desire to have a female child was trivially higher than that of male's (15.9% vs 14.5%). However, a very large proportion (close to 63%) of women plaçed no preference for children of either sex. Since in the country where childbearing is one of the initial and important functions of the marriage and all of the couples are expected to have the least number of children and wanted childlessness is not a socially favourable decision, it is not surprising that only 0.9 per cent of ever married 0 parity women did not want to bear any children. Nevertheless, taking the sex of previous child(ren) into account, women mostly preferred the sex that they have not already had.

As illustrated by Graph 2, among mothers with only one child (p1 in the graph), preference for any sex is directly under the influence of the sex that has been born already to the mother or woman. Among mothers with one son, around 42.5 per cent preferred to have a daughter in their future childbearing, while the corresponding figure for

Graph 2

Women's Attitude about the Sex of the Future Child with Respect to the Sex Composition of Previous Children, Parities 0–4

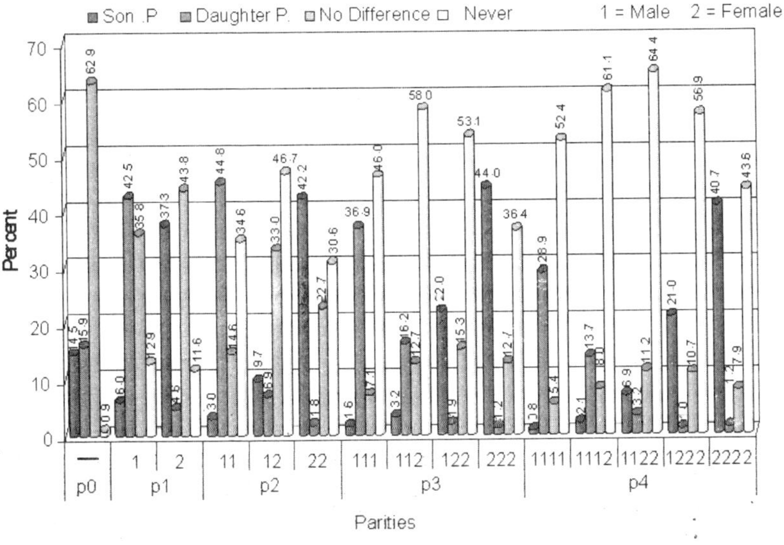

mothers of one daughter preferring to have a son in their future childbearing is 37.3 per cent. About 35.8 per cent of mothers with one son and 43.8 per cent of mothers with one daughter regarded the children of any sex desirable. Interestingly enough are the proportions of mothers of only one child that wanted to stop childbearing at parity one. Around 12.9 per cent of mothers with one son and 11.6 per cent of mothers with only one daughter (*never* categories in the graph at any parity) do not want to have their second child at all.

The same pattern of sex preference is evident when the childbearing experiences of second parity women are considered. Regarding mothers with two children, among those had two sons 44.8 per cent preferred to have their next baby as daughter and only 3 per cent wanted to have another son. In comparison, among mothers with two daughters 42.2 per cent desired to bear a son in their next childbearing and only 1.6 per cent wanted to have their third daughter. Mothers with one son and one daughter mostly (46.7% of them) liked to stop childbearing and for 33 per cent of them the sex of the next child was making no sense. Among them, nevertheless, 9.7 and 6.9 per cent desired to have another son and daughter, respectively.

What is not in line with other parities and at the same time attention-grabbing in the cases of parities one and two is the higher preference towards daughters than sons, though the differences do not seem significant. Sex preference pattern of three and higher parities is distinguishable from those of previous parities in the sense that among higher parity women the preference for sons is clearly evident. The higher preference for daughters among lower parity women could be in part responsible for the Iran DHS findings regarding non-existence of sex preference in the country.

Not as an indisputable or comprehensive but a partial explanation to this could be the new emerging values around childbearing and sex preference in the country. While most of the lower parity (most probably younger) mothers, who have been under the influences of modern times' values and behavioural standards, it could be assumed that the recent generations of mothers may not really put emphasis on male children, what is generally present among mothers of higher parities that mostly are among old-age mothers, who are socialized mostly by the traditional values and ideals. However, further studies are needed to investigate the accuracy of this assumed explanation.

According to Graphs 2 and 3, it is also evident that moving from lower to higher parities, the percentage of women who preferred to stop childbearing (*never* categories) increases. This is never surprising according to the desired or ideal number of children that mainly stated to be two children by ever married women of childbearing ages (Ministry of Health and Medical Education, 2003). Therefore, it is expected that moving to higher parities, some women receive their desired family size and sex composition at any parity and preferred to stop childbearing. Besides, regarding any parity, the percentage of women who expressed no desire for additional children turn out to be larger when they have equal number of sons and daughters. In other words, the more balanced the sex composition of previous children, the higher the likelihood for women to stop childbearing.

However, with reference to almost all parities, it is evident that even in the cases women have equal number of sons and daughters, desire to have male children was higher than that of female (9.8 vs 6.9 at parity 2; 6.9 vs 3.2 at parity 4; and 5.4 vs 2.3 at parity 6). Desire to have a son was even stronger in the cases of parities 5 and 6 that are represented by Graph 3.

At parity 5, among women with 5 sons, around 25.9 per cent preferred to have at least a daughter, while among women with 5 daughters a large proportion (39.9%) desired to have at least one son.

Graph 3

Women's Attitude about the Sex of the Future Child with Respect to the Sex Composition of Previous Children, Parities 5–6

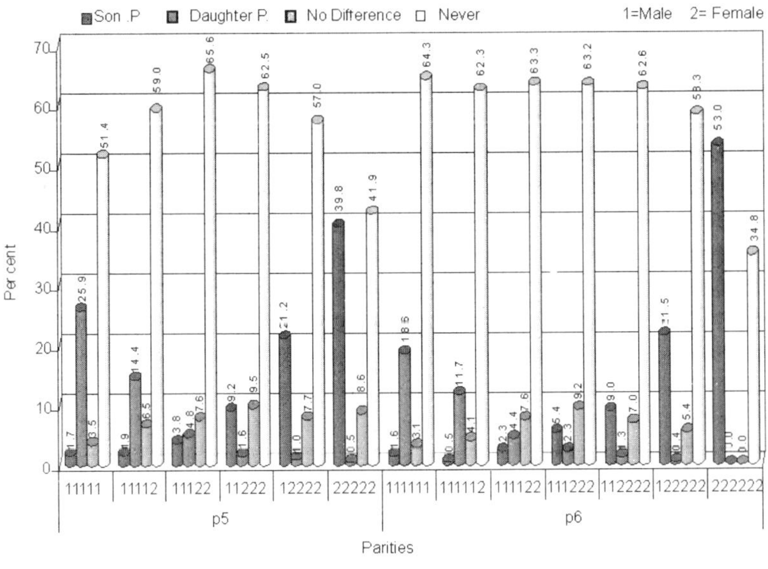

At parity 6, the difference is even larger; i.e., 18.8 per cent of women with 6 sons desired to have their next baby as daughter, while among women of 6 daughters more than half, 53 per cent, desired at least a son.

Illustrations given by the Graphs 2 and 3 generally are indicative of the fact that sex preference among Iranian women is mostly derived from the sex composition of their previous children. However, contrary to the existing view about the sex preference, especially when the third and higher parities are considered, the preference is still in favour of sons than daughters in most of the cases. To compare these stated preferences to that of women's actual behaviour, PPRs with respect to sex composition of previous children are discussed in the next section.

Parity Progression Ratios

Graph 4 shows the PPRs for 15–49 ever married women considering the sex (composition) of the previous child(ren). Curves of the graph from above stand for PPRs from parity i to $i+1$ and beginning points at each curve from the left side show the PPRs for women with only son(s), whereas the end points show the PPRs for women with daughter(s) only. Mid-points are PPRs for women who have both son(s) and daughter(s). To appreciate the graph, one needs to reduce the number of sons and add the number of daughters by one, moving from the left side of the curves towards the right.

The first curve from the above reveals the PPRs for those who have one child (1=son and 2=daughter) to next parity. Beginning point of this curve from the left stands for PPR for women with a son: (1) to next parity, which is almost 79 per cent. The second (in this case last) point of the curve shows the PPR for women with only one daughter (2) to next parity, which is 86 per cent.

The second curve from the above belongs to women with two children who went to have the third. In this case there are three points indicating progression ratios for mothers of different sex compositions, regarding existing children. The first point in this curve from the left, is PPR for women with 2 sons (indicated by two 1s), which is about 76 per cent. The second and middle point of the curve shows the PPR for women with a son and a daughter (12), which is around 75 per cent, and the last point of the curve indicates the PPR for women with two daughters (shown by two 2s), being around 79 per cent.

In the case of mothers of third parity, around 76 per cent of those who have 3 sons (111) progressed to the 4th parity, whereas corresponding figure for the mothers of 3 daughters (222) is close to 80 per cent.

The interpretation of the next all curves are the same. The only difference is that any lower curve refer to PPRs for women of a higher parity. Therefore, as an illustration, the last curve belongs to women with 7 children who progressed to have the 8th child. Starting point of the curve from the left side indicates PPR for women with 7 sons (1 1 1 1 1 1 1) and the last point illustrates the PPR for women with 7 daughters (2 2 2 2 2 2 2). The points show the PPRs for women with different sex compositions of their 7 previous children (including both sexes).

Taking different sex compositions of previous children, progression ratios from parity 3 to parity 4, 4 to 5, 5 to 6, 6 to 7, and from 7 to 8 among mothers with only male children, are found to be 75.8, 76.1, 72.17, 68.82, and 67.61 per cent, respectively. Corresponding progression ratios for women with only female children, are 79.82, 81.2, 78.7, 80.73, and 74.32 per cent. For women who had the children of both sexes, PPRs are found to fall between the two sets of figures given above, albeit much closer to values observed in the case of mothers with no female children.

It should be noted here that preference among Iranian women, taking different parities into account, are stronger towards male

Graph 4

Parity Progression Ratios According to Sex Composition of Previous Children at Different Parity Levels

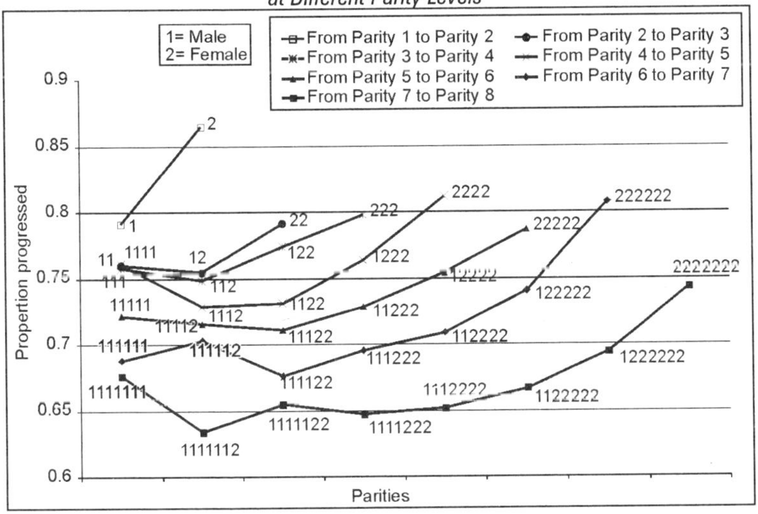

children in almost all parities and at any sex composition. Interestingly, progression ratio for mothers of 6 female children (as illustrated in Graph 4) is comparable with (or even higher than) that of women with only one son! It seems mothers with 6 daughters are still trying to have at least one desired sex, in this case a male child. This is indicative of the strong desire of mothers of higher parities, who only have daughters in their previous childbearing, to have at least one son. Desire to have at least one daughter among daughterless mothers is not as strong as desire for at least one son among sonless mothers, however.

Conventionally, PPRs from a given parity: (i) to a higher parity ($i+1$ or more) show a declining trend with respect to all parities and all sex compositions of previous children. Receiving the desired family size or sex composition or having disappointed to come with the desired family size or sex composition, could be a partial explanation to this trend.

The Effects of Sex Preference on Contraceptive Use

Taking Arnold's view that "most of families receive their wanted family size and desired sex composition mostly by chance", the effect of sex preference on contraceptive use may not be too large. Only those women who cannot receive their desired sex composition by chance, plan to have another child(ren) with the hope of having wanted sexes. However, some of women and couples might stop childbearing while the future baby also can be an unwanted sex (Arnold, 1987). These situations make only small number of women go further through higher parities to examine their chance to get their wanted sex.

Application of Arnold's Method to examine the effect of sex preference on contraceptive use among Iranian women yields the expected small effect. Calculating contraceptive prevalence at different parity levels and various sex compositions of previous parities for two conditions (i.e., current use of contraception and contraception use when sex preference is eliminated from fertility arrangements) showed that the effect of sex preference on contraceptive use is not too large, though considerable in some senses.

While the current use of contraception is estimated to be around 72.50 per cent among ever married women of childbearing ages, it can only be raised to 75.03 per cent if sex preference is removed from childbearing arrangements. Therefore, removing sex preference from fertility arrangements contributes to 3.49 per cent increase in contraceptive use. Although the absolute effect is fairly small, taking the high rate of contraceptive prevalence in the country, it could be assumed as considerable.

Discussion and Conclusion

No son preference—the idea that is mostly derived from Iranian DHS-type survey results, is a relatively supported idea among demographers and administrators. However, the idea seems mostly contrary to traditional emphasis on male because of their higher social, political and economic positions in the society and the advantages that they are benefited in almost all arenas of social life. Examining the verbal statements of women and their actual behaviour (Parity Progression Ratios) could shed more light on the existence or non-existence of sex preference in the country.

Examining the verbal statements or stated preferences of ever married pregnant women of childbearing ages towards their expected babies' sex, makes it clear that their preference towards the sex of their expected child is mostly determined by the sex composition of previous children that they had. Mothers with son(s) mostly like or desire to have daughter(s) too, and mothers with only daughter(s) desire to have son(s) in contrast. Though, both sexes are preferred in this regard, however, in almost all parities males are more preferred than females, indicating that still preference is more in favour of male in childbearing experiences of Iranian ever married women in the year 2000.

Taking into consideration the stated preferences of all 15–49 ever married women towards the sex of the future child(ren) with respect to sex composition of previous children yielded comparable results to those of ever married pregnant women's preferences. In this case also it is found that preference for the sex of next child is mostly determined by the sex (compositions) of previous child(ren). Although at any parity mothers having only children of one sex mostly desired to have the children of other sex, sons are more preferred than daughters again at any given parity (parities 1 and 2 could be regarded as exceptions to this account).

Parity progression ratios for Iranian ever married women of childbearing ages indicate that in spite of that sonless mothers tried to have sons progressing to higher parites and daughterless mothers have tried their chance to bring daughters, in all parities, progression to next parity is higher when women are sonless or the number of sons is less than that of daughters.

As a concluding remark, verbal statement of ever married pregnant and non-pregnant women and parity progression ratios for all ever married women of childbearing ages, actually are indicative of the same fact; preference to have children of the sex that is non-existent and, everything being equal, higher preference towards male child compared to female. Although results are indicative that both the sexes are desired, however, sons are more preferred than daughters. This finding goes with different sex compositions of most of parity levels that were considered. Findings are clearly contrary to reported preference which was somewhat higher for female children by the Iran DHS-type survey results.

Nevertheless, as expected, sex preference plays a marginal role in the country's contraceptive practice. Despite the fact that sex preference is responsible for the birth of *many* children and son preference is responsible for the birth of *many* daughters, however, these two *many* do not have remarkable contribution to contraceptive practice of Iranian ever married women 15–49. Applying the Arnold's Method to estimate the effects of sex preference on contraceptive use revealed that removing sex preference from the childbearing experiences of Iranian 15–49 ever married women can increase the contraceptive use by 3.5 per cent to above 75 per cent, while being 72.5 at presence of sex preference.

Note

1. Interested readers may consult Arnold, 1985; Bairagi, 1987 and Arnold, 1987 for more detailed information on the biases and also possible solutions for the Arnold's Method.

References

Arnold, F. 1985. Measuring the Effect of Sex Preference on Fertility: The Case of Korea. *Demography* 22(2): 280–8.

——. 1987. The Effect of Sex Preference on Fertility: A Reply to Bairagi. *Demography* 24(1): 139–42.

Bairagi, Radheshyam. 2001. Effects of Sex Preference on Contraceptive Use, Abortion and Fertility in Matlab, Bangladesh. *International Family Planning Perspectives* 27(3): 137–43.

——. 1987. A Comment on Fred Arnold's Measuring the Effect of Sex Preference on Fertility. *Demography* 24(1): 137–8.

Clark, S. 2000. Son Preference and Sex Composition of Children: Evidence from India. *Demography* 37(1): 95–108.

Chowdhury, M.K. and R. Bairagi. 1990. Son Preference and Fertility in Bangladesh. *Population and Development Review* 16(4): 749–57.

McClelland, G.H. 1979. Determining the Impact of Sex Preference on Fertility: A Consideration of Parity Progression Ratio, Dominance and Stopping Rule Measures. *Demography* 16(3): 377–88.

Ministry of Health and Medical Education. 2003. Population and Health in the Islamic Republic of Iran – DHS, 2000. Tehran: Ministry of Health and Medical Education (MOHME) and the United Nations Children's Fund (UNICEF).

Pebley, A.R., H. Delgado and E. Brineman. 1980. Family Sex Composition Preference among Guatemalan Men and Women. *Journal of Marriage and the Family* 42(2): 437–47.

Preston, S.H., P. Heuveline and M. Guillot. 2001. *Demography: Measuring and Modeling Population Processes*. Blackwell Publishing Ltd., United Kingdom.

CHAPTER 2

The Working Hours and Division of Labour with Gender Perspective in Different Family Systems

Amita Pradhan

Women are always central to population and development. Women's work is key to the population and development issues as they form half of the world's population.

Women usually work longer than men. With their domestic hours on top, women work twice as many hours as men. Women continue to perform majority of household and childcare work even when they hold full-time labour market jobs. Women's performance of the majority of domestic work is justified as a 'natural extension of their biological capacity to bear children' (Abel, 1994; Nieka, 1998; Reskin and Pedavic, 1994). Housework is not considered as work, however even though it provides goods and services that add greatly to the comforts of life and often are crucial to its maintenance (Francine and Marine, 1992). Undervaluation of women's work either in the household or in the workplace leads to women being expected to work for longer hours than men (Asian and Pacific Development Centre, 1990).

Women in South Asia and Pacific, as in other developing regions, spend most of their time working. For poor rural women, who make up the majority of women in the region, this means a daily working day of 8 to 13 hours on average. The day is divided into reproductive work of housework and childcare in the household and productive work of

---

Working hours in this study were defined as total hours the respondents devoted for reproductive and productive work per day. The respondents with paid job were recorded as 7 hours per day. The persons sitting idle doing nothing were recorded as 0 working hours per day.

bringing in income for the family (Asian and Pacific Development Centre, 1990).

In a national level study, it was found that Nepalese women spend 10.8 hours in working per day on an average whereas this is only 7.5 hours per day for men (Acharya and Bennet, 1981). Similarly, another national level study found women's working hours to be 10.8 hours as against 7.8 hours for men (Shtrii Shakti, 1995). In one village study, it was found that women work for 11.8 hours per day as against 8.6 hours by men. In this study, it was assumed that women's working day could be much more than 12 hours per day (Bhadra, 1997).

This study tried to find out whether the work burden and roles of men and women are changing in the changing context of family systems.

Objective

To determine the gender disaggregated working hour and working pattern in different family systems.

Materials and Method

The study area was Panga of Kirtipur municipality in Kathmandu. The study design was descriptive cross-sectional. In all, 64 households were selected at random. Out of these households, 34 were joint families and 30 were nuclear families. Out of 34 joint families, 17 women and 17 men were randomly selected. Similarly, from 30 nuclear families, 15 women and 15 men were selected at random. The respondents were between 15 to 49 years age group.

Semi-structured questionnaires were used to conduct an interview with the respondents. Additional information was gathered through observation and informal chat.

The collected data were analysed and interpreted through necessary tables and different statistical methods such as independent two-sample t-test and z test for proportion in proper context by using the SPSS and PHSTAT2 software package.

Results

Around 35 per cent of women were housewives and 35 per cent male were without job in joint families. Around 18 per cent of the females were without job. Around 47 per cent women from nuclear families were housewives. Higher per cent of men were in service in both nuclear and joint families. Around 29 per cent women and 23 per cent men in joint and around 47 per cent women and 53 per cent men in nuclear families were skilled labour. Women generally were involved in carpet weaving and sweater weaving. Men were more involved in carpentry.

Table 1

Per cent Distribution of Occupation of both Sexes in Joint and Nuclear Families

Occupation	*Joint family*		*Nuclear family*	
	Female, N=17	*Male, N=17*	*Female, N=15*	*Male, N=15*
No job	17.6	35.3	6.7	6.7
Skilled labour	29.4	23.5	46.7	53.3
Service	5.9	29.4	—	40
Student	11.8	11.8	—	—
Housewife	35.3	—	46.7	—

Table 2

Background Characteristics of both Sexes in Joint and Nuclear Families

Background characteristics	*Joint family*			*Nuclear family*		
(Mean ± S.D.)	*Female, N=17*	*Male, N=17*	*p value*	*Female, N=15*	*Male, N=15*	*p value*
Wake up time (a.m.)	5.24 ± 0.42	6.17 ± 0.59	.005	5.00 ± 1.32	6.09 ± 0.51	.004
Time of going to bed (p.m.)	9.58 ± 0.30	10:01± 0.41	0.78	9.54 ± 0.49	9.48 ± 0.45	0.73
Working hours per day	13.43± 3.59	5.14± 4.30	<. 001	13.48± 4.07	7.32 ± 4.37	.001

Among the main work the respondents followed in the afternoon, one was the agricultural work. Though men also followed agricultural work in the field during the season, women had to follow it throughout the year including field as well as home based agricultural work. On asking about the pattern of work in agriculture, they usually did not give concrete answers. But after some probing in both male and female group and the focussed group discussion among women, the general working areas for female in agriculture were found to be seedling, storing of the seeds, cleaning of the seeds, weeding, sowing, planting, mill processing and storing of the yields. Some of the main areas of agriculture where both male and female contributed, were levelling of

Table 3

Working Pattern of both Sexes in Joint and Nuclear Families

Activities	*Joint family*			*Nuclear family*		
	Female N=17	*Male N=17*	*p value*	*Female N=15*	*Male N=15*	*p value*
Presence in agricultural work	88.2%	52.9%	0.02	86.7%	73.3%	0.36
Washing clothes						
No wash	—	94.1%			93.3%	
Once a week	5.9%	—		6.7%	—	
Twice a week	29%	—		20.0%	—	
Thrice a week	17.6%	—		46.7%	—	
Daily wash	35.3%	—		13.3%	—	
Help	11.8% *	5.9%**		13.3% *	6.7% **	
Water fetching						
Yes	94.1%	—		93.3%	—	
No	—	82.4%		—	66.7%	
Help	5.9% *	17.6% **		6.7%	33.3%**	
Kitchen work						
Yes	70.6%			86.7%	6.7% ***	p=0.0002
No	—	100%			80%	
Help	29.4%			13.3%	13.3%	

Notes: *Females, who answered for helping out for fetching water and washing clothes, were unmarried.

**Males helped to carry the water upstairs and washed clothes on the terrace so that the female can spread the clothes to dry.

*** The male performed household chores because his wife went out for carpet weaving early in the morning.

the field, cutting of the yields, harvesting, using fertilizers and protection of the field. Digging was found to be only one male-dominated domain. On focussed group discussion, women told that though the agricultural yields were not sufficient for whole year, they had to perform the agricultural work throughout the year either in the field or at home. Additionally, during the season of agriculture, they had to work in the field as well as finish all their domestic chores.

Washing clothes was the domain, which was completely performed by the females. This was the chief activity they generally followed in the afternoon. But the above table shows overall washing activity whether performed in the afternoon or in the morning and evening simultaneously managed with other work by employed women.

Kitchen work was also completely seemed to be women's. Even though they went outside was for work, they had to perform the household duties. Around 7 per cent of males were found to be cooking meals in absence of their wife and 13.3 per cent of males helped in cooking in nuclear families. However sweeping, cleaning the house and utensils was completely females' work in both types of families.

Around 60 per cent of males having small children in both types of families (out of 10 in joint and out of 12 in nuclear) helped their wives to look after their children when they were busy.

Around 76 per cent women and 41.2 per cent men in joint families felt tired after whole day's work and the difference was significant ($p=0.03$). However, all the women and 80 per cent of men in nuclear families felt tired and the difference was not statistically significant ($p=0.06$).

Among women having home-based paid jobs and housewives, out of 14, only 21.4 per cent in joint families and out of 11, 54.5 per cent women in nuclear families took a short nap during afternoon. On probing, the women said that they did not have time for rest.

Similarly, 50 per cent men (out of 6 in joint and out of 2 in nuclear) staying at home took rest in both types of families. For men taking rest depend on their choice.

Discussion

Women work longer hours than men and have less time for sleep and leisure. Research into time-use in Third World countries including Nepal, Bangladesh and Indonesia has shown that the average woman's working day all seven days a week is between 8 to 13 hours (Asian and Pacific Development Centre, 1990). A woman has to play home production role and market production role. In developing countries, women spend from 10 to 16 hours a day doing house work, caring for children, preparing food and raising food for the family (Recphec, 1994).

According to Dhakal and Sheikh, 1997 (cited in Acharya and Bennet, 1981), in rural areas, particularly, Nepali girls and women work far more than boys and men, spending 25 to 50 per cent more time on household tasks and economic and agricultural activities.

This study result showed that in joint families, the mean ± s.d. of wake up time in the morning for female was 5.24 ± 0.42 a.m. and for male was 6.17 ± 0.59 a.m. ($p=0.005$). Similarly, the time of going to bed mean ± s.d. for female was 9.58 ± 0.30 p.m. and for male was 10.01± 0.41 p.m. In nuclear families, the mean ± s.d. of wake up time in the morning for female was 5.00 ± 1.32 a.m. and for male was 6:09 ± 0:51 a. m ($p=0.004$).

Similarly, the time of going to bed mean ± s.d. for female was 9.54 ± 0.49 p.m. and for male was 9.48 ± 0.45 p.m. Women woke up early in the morning as compared to men in both nuclear and joint families and the difference was significant. However, the time of going to bed for both sexes for both of the family systems was not found to be significantly different.

Almost 60 per cent women in nuclear and 70.6 per cent women in joint families woke up at 5.00 a.m. as compared to 13.3 per cent and 11.8 per cent men respectively. Around 41 per cent men in both families types woke up at 7.00 a.m. Significantly higher proportion of females in joint ($p=0.0004$) and in nuclear families ($p=0.008$) woke up at 5.00 a.m. as compared to males. Similarly, 60 per cent women in nuclear and 70.6 per cent in joint families went to bed at 10.00 p.m. around 47 per cent men in nuclear and 41.2 per cent in joint families went to bed at 10.00 p.m. However, the difference was not statistically significant for men and women in joint ($p=0.08$) and nuclear ($p=0.46$) families.

In joint families, the mean ± s.d. working hour for female was 13.43 ± 3.59 hours per day and for male, it was 5.14± 4.30 hours per day ($p< 0.001$). In nuclear families, the mean ± s.d. working hour for female was 13.48 ± 4.07 hours per day and for male it was 7.32 ± 4.37 hours per day ($p=0.001$).

In poorer countries of the Asia Pacific region such as Nepal, the Philippines and India, agricultural work is the largest work occupation of women, engaging more than half of women workers. Yet national statistics of these countries for the economically active population usually omits women's work done in the subsistence sector (Asian and Pacific Development Centre, 1990). This study revealed that in joint families women contributed significantly to agricultural work with 88.2 per cent of females and 52.9 per cent of males involved in it ($p=0.02$). In nuclear families, 86.7 per cent women and 73.3 per cent men were involved in agricultural work; however the difference was not statistically significant ($p=0.36$).

According to Cowan (1987), Miles (1988) (cited in Abel, 1994), housework consists of a large variety of tasks and responsibilities that have been women's work in most societies as far as history exists. According to Devault, 1987 (Abel, 1994), women's chores include cleaning, laundry, ironing and overall responsibility for family members' schedule.

This study revealed similar facts. Around 60 per cent of males with small children in both types of families (out of ten in joint and out of 12 in nuclear) helped their wives to look after their children when they were busy. Generally fathers helped children to do homework, dropped them to school and take them out roaming while the mothers worked in the house. Otherwise all other child-rearing activities were female's responsibility. None of the female respondents with children could escape this task. In both of the family systems, water fetching, kitchen work, washing clothes and child-rearing were completely found to be women's work. Around 20 per cent men in nuclear families were found involved in the kitchen work but 86.7 per cent women worked in kitchen ($p=0.0002$) and 13.3 per cent of women were found helping their mothers or sister-in-laws in the kitchen. For males who helped to fetch water (17.6% in joint and 33.3% in nuclear, $p=0.30$), usually helped to carry the water upstairs inside the home and help in washing clothes (5.9% in joint and 6.7% in nuclear, $p=0.90$) included the activity of bringing the washed clothes to the terrace so that the female can spread the clothes to dry. In both activities, men's contribution was not significantly different in joint as compared to nuclear families. The help in these activities was confined within the house so that nobody could see them doing so, otherwise washing clothes and fetching water was completely female's responsibility. The male performed household chores only in absence of his wife. Unmarried males could escape the task completely while unmarried females had to help their mothers or sister-in-laws. According to Berk and Berk, (1979) (cited in Nieka, 1998), the extensive study of organization of the household day among a cross-section of urban families showed that when the wife is present, she tends to handle the childcare and household chores; husband does household work only when the wife is unavailable.

Employed women could not escape household work in joint as well as nuclear families, however 21.4 per cent of men were found to be helping in kitchen chores in nuclear families. The difference was highly significant ($p=0.0006$). Employed women on an average devoted 5.03 ± 3.58 hours per day in joint and 7.51 ± 3.54 hours per day in nuclear families (p=0.19) for household work whereas employed men did not perform any household work in joint and minimal performance was seen in nuclear families (p=0.56). Hence, there was no significant difference in employed women's household working hours per day in joint and nuclear families. The details of who perform what specific tasks in domestic labour also shows that women do majority of this work, even when they are in the labour force. Though they gain power and contribute to family status, working women do not obtain significantly more help in household work from their husbands than do non-working women. Women continue to perform majority of household and childcare work even when they hold full-time labour market jobs. Any change in the distribution of the household work is very slight. Employed women still do twice as much housework as their unemployed husbands (Nieka, 1998).

Around 59 per cent of women and men in joint and 86.7 per cent of women and men in nuclear families were married. Working hours mean ± s.d., for females who were unmarried was 11.00 ± 4.14 and for those married was 14.53 ± 3.22 (p=0.01) and for unmarried male was 3.33 ± 3.02 and for married males was 7.23 ± 4.45 (p=0.033), showed significant increase in work after marriage. However, even the unmarried females worked for longer hours than married males (p=0.03).

Conclusion

The gender division of labour prevails. However, due to the changing family context, development pattern and employment situation, there have been seen some differences in some cases. In both of the family systems, women work significantly more than male. Married women and men both worked longer in comparison to the unmarried group. Domestic chores were still women's responsibility. However, in nuclear families, slight involvement of men was seen in kitchen work. But the noticeable fact was that the men did these chores only in absence of females. In joint families, men did not do household work, probably because of the presence of more number of females in the household.

It appears that basic attitudes about gender roles and especially about the roles of men and women in the family are deep-seated and difficult to change.

References

Abel, K.A. 1994. *Women's Work: Degraded and Devalued.* Prentice Hall, Englewood Cliffs, New Jersey.

Acharya, M. and L. Bennet. 1981. The Rural Women of Nepal: An Aggregate Analysis of Eight Village Studies on the Status of Women. Report submitted to Centre for Economic Development and Administration, Kathmandu.

Asian and Pacific Development Centre. 1990. Asian and Pacific Women's Action Series Health. Asian and Pacific Development Centre, Kuala Lumpur, Malaysia.

Bhadra, C. 1997. Intra-household Gender Analysis of Work Roles and Distribution of Resources: A Pilot Study in a Nepalese Village. Unpublished Ph. D. dissertation. Oregon State University, USA.

Francine, D.B. and A.F. Mariane. 1992. *A Comparative Economic Perspective: Women's Work and Women's Lives.* Westview Press Inc., Central Avenue, Boulder, Colorado.

Nieka, F.V. 1998. *Work and Family Linkages: Women and Work.* Vol. 1, Sage Publications Inc., California.

Recphec. 1994. *Report of Workshop on Gender and Women's Health.* Recphec, Kathmandu.

Reskin, F.B. and I. Pedavic. 1994. *Women and Men at Work.* Pine Forge Press, Thousand Oaks, London.

Shtrii Shakti. 1995. Women, Development and Democracy: A Study of the Socioeconomic Changes in the Status of Women in Nepal (1981–1993). Shtrii Shakti, Kathmandu.

CHAPTER 3

Increasing Gender Gap and Socio-economic Status of Women in North-East India

Susmita Das

Story of women in India in the past few decades is a mixed bag of hope and despair. Women have made tremendous progress and have attained success in almost all spheres of life, thanks to the increasing access to educational opportunities and employment possibilities, guaranteed for achieving an egalitarian society. In fact it was the constitution of India, which laid a framework for providing an equal status to both men and women by granting them equal political, economic and social rights without any discrimination. Also at the same time, it was realized that women are in a disadvantageous situation as they remain largely confined to domestic chores of life bearing the responsibility of looking after and caring for the members of the household. Even Gandhiji, who did much for the liberation of women during India's struggle for freedom, believed that the care of children and the household was enough to keep women fully occupied. Such a situation prevailed for centuries together, which made her suffer silently an oppressed and inferior life of no rights. The patriarchal joint family system, custom of polygamy, sati, child marriage—all hampered the freedom and liberty of Indian women. Such a situation deprived her from all kinds of resources, which remained exclusively with men, pushing her down the social and economic ladder even further. This state of women continued for a substantially long period of time. Subsequently, with India's struggle for independence and Gandhiji's calling upon women to take active part in the movement, women started believing in their ability and achieved a sense of dignity, self-confidence that helped in liberating their minds. Women also became receptive about their own problems and with independence and constitution in place women were granted equal opportunities. Eventually, a lot many laws came into existence, the movement for which was fought in the pre-independent period along with our political freedom. In fact it was during 1950s that a number of Hindu laws were enacted to liberate women from age-old bondage of social customs and practices and granting them certain rights and opportunities. The impact of some of these could be comprehended from the growing participation of women in education and employment. In 1962, when the United Nations requested the member states to prepare report on women's status in their respective countries, India came up with its own report (though it took 13 long years) entitled "Towards Equality" in 1975 (declared as the first international year of women). The report of the committee exploded many myths and marked a turning point in the history of women's movement. Although progress made in education and employment got appreciated, it was found that women's participation from organized industrial sector was fast declining. Even the poor rural women were losing the traditional economic opportunities and were becoming increasingly marginalized. The report also found a large concentration of women in the unorganized sector—on farms and homes not recognized as economic pursuit. The report also drew attention on declining sex-ratio—a clear indication of discrimination on women, from childhood onwards in every sphere of life. The fact that women's education was lagging far behind men's was also reported in the report. The revelation of the report also highlighted the fact that although today's women have been able to break the shackles of strict prescribed roles and allowed themselves to lead a life of choice, the traditional system of family norms continues to remain in place wherein a women is required to respect and follow it. On the other side, she has been able to acquire education and has contributed to the economy by being a part of the workforce. This has forced women to shuttle between various roles—often leading to a state of confusion. Thus, the dominance and guardianship of father/brother/husband continue, to influence and shape their lives in the name of care, protection and family values, and at the same time, allowed to work in order to contribute into the family (household) income. The absence of any meaningful political rights (in spite of 33 per cent seats in panchayats reserved for women), therefore, have made very little impact on their overall role in the society and to a very large extent have failed to empower and enlighten them as a 'Woman'.

Also, at the same time, another glaring and worrying aspect came to light, that is, women in India continue to suffer from an adverse sex ratio (the proportion of females to males). In fact, it has become an inevitable fact that the sex ratio is increasingly favouring men and if one examines the past hundred years' (Table 1) record, it becomes doubly clear that the proportion of females to males is falling substantially (972 in 1901 to 933 in 2001). Furthermore, the fall has been widespread across areas and communities. What is astonishing is that areas that had favourable sex ratio, are increasingly registering a fall, thus raising a lot of questions. The continuous increase in gender gap evident in every successive census enumeration on one side and gradual betterment in the rate of literacy and work participation makes women's status in the society an interesting study of contrast. Here in the present paper an attempt has been made to highlight the sex disparity and increasing gender gap and the so-called socio-economic status of women in the north-east states of India. The weakening sex ratio in the north-east India is especially surprising, as this region contains sizeable tribal population, who live in an egalitarian set-up. Also an improved state of women's educational attainment coupled with employment power, it is highly paradoxical to answer how and why the region experiences shortages of female population. The question that arises is how an improved socio-economic status of women can bring down her number resulting in an increased gender gap? And, if that is the case, why the same does not happen for 'Man'?

Table 1

Number of Females to Males in India and North-East (1901–2001)

	Females per '000 males		
Census year	*India*	*North-east*	*Differentials (NE to India)*
1901	972	938	–34
1911	964	934	–30
1921	955	917	–38
1931	950	917	–33
1941	945	898	–47
1951	946	889	57
1961	941	884	–57
1971	930	904	–26
1981	934	900	–34
1991	927	925	–02
2001	933	937	+04

Source: Census of India 2001, Series 1 Provisional Population Totals, Paper 1 of 2001.

Trend and Pattern of Sex Ratio in North-East

Sex ratio or the number of female to males has never been equal in any society. This theoretical possibility had never been achieved in any society for reasons impossible to comprehend. What is known, however, is an imbalanced ratio that had existed always in different population across the world. This imbalanced ratio depicts two possibilities, first where the females' number is less than that of males and second, vice versa. Most of the Third World countries including India belong to the first category where deficiency of women remained a rule all along. The developed nations of the world, on the other hand, had rarely experienced male favoured sex ratio.

Similar to country's situation, the north-eastern part of the country too noticed a declining sex ratio, which continued upto 1961. The noticeable difference though is that whereas in India the decline was by few points, in north-east the decline between decades went up to 19 points between 1931–1941. The decades between 1961–71 though saw sex ratio go up by 20 points and thereafter kept improving till the recent decade, with the only exception being the decade between 1971–1981, when it fell by 4 points.

A cursory look at Table 1 reveals yet another glaring truth of sex ratio that had existed in India and the north-east. In the last one hundred years, north-east India had never recorded a sex ratio that is better than that of India. The only exception is the recent decade of 2001. The difference in point-term between the country and the region was also quite substantial. The difference reached its maximum between 1941–1961 and then the gap reduced slightly to record a difference of only 2 in 1991.

Again, if one looks at how many women are less to every thousand men in India, it comes with yet another discloser that the gap has been widening as the country approached close to the twenty first century. Today, the gap stands at 67 females, which was only 28 at the beginning of the earlier century. In the north-east, the period of largest gap was between 1941–1981 when the gap was as large as hundred or more. Prior and later to this period, the gap remained within hundred. The first decade of the present century finds again the shortfall by almost the same number as was the case hundred years earlier (62 in 1901 and 61 in 2001). Thus, in the north-east in hundred years' time the imbalanced sex ratio continued uninterrupted with a well-marked period of deterioration. In absolute terms today, in India the gender gap is over by 35.7 million females. In north-east, it is about 1.2 million in a population of 38.3 million.

This pattern of sex ratio in the hilly and tribal dominated areas is a big surprise considering that the tribal societies are free from any known discrimination against women, a factor that is absolutely rigid in the non-tribal society where discrimination is so very obvious. In spite of this, the region does not display a balanced sex ratio. A period of gradual decline and increasing gender gap has almost become a rule rather than an exception, both in India and in the north-east. How long will this trend continue, only time can say?

Across the states of north-east, a varying pattern of ratio could be observed (Table 2). No more does any state of the region record a female favoured sex ratio, which had been the case in the early part of the century in at least three states (and continued to be the case in Manipur and Mizoram till 1961). Today, out of the seven states in two states (Arunachal and Nagaland) the sex ratio is lower than the country as well as the region's average (933 and 937 respectively). In two states, it is reaching close to a balanced ratio (over 970)—Manipur and Meghalaya fall in this category, while in the remaining three states—Assam, Tripura and Mizoram, it is only near the country average.

Table 2

Number of Females to Males in States of North-East India (1901–2001)

	Females per '000 males						
Census	*Arunachal**	*Assam*	*Manipur*	*Meghalaya*	*Mizoram*	*Nagaland*	*Tripura*
Year							
1901		919	1,037	1,036	1,113	973	874
1911		915	1,029	1,013	1,120	993	885
1921		896	1,041	1,000	1,109	992	885
1931		874	1,065	971	1,102	997	885
1941		875	1,055	966	1,069	1,021	886
1951		868	1,036	949	1,041	999	904
1961	894	869	1,015	937	1,009	933	932
1971	861	896	980	942	946	871	943
1981	862	910**	971	954	919	863	946
1991	859	923	958	955	921	886	945
2001	893	935	978	972	935	900	948

Source: Census of India 2001, Series 1, Provisional Population Totals, Paper 1 of 2001.

Notes: *sex ratio for Arunachal Pradesh is not available for the years 1901–1951.

** interpolated figures for Assam have been used as census could not be held.

The female-male gap is, therefore, the widest in Arunachal Pradesh and Nagaland (107 and 100 less females respectively) and the least in Manipur and Meghalaya (22 and 28 less females respectively). The trend of sex ratio emerging out from the analysis when done for a period of hundred years highlights the following broad features:

- Excepting Tripura, all other states of the region had experienced downward trend in sex ratio at some point in time. The fall is sharpest in Nagaland, which now records a sex ratio of 900, a gap of 100 females. Manipur and Mizoram too experienced a fall in sex ratio since 1901, Which is however, different from Nagaland's case, as in these two states, the sex ratio was in favour of females upto 1961 and thereafter started experiencing a fall. Assam and Meghalaya though followed the same pattern are slightly different as both these states since 1961 registered a gradual improvement.
- Tripura is the only state in the region where sex ratio with every succeeding decade has improved, perhaps also the only state in the country to have such a rare distinction.
- Arunachal Pradesh had always recorded a very high female deficiency.
- The states of the region have shown a marginal increase in the number of females to males in the last census enumeration of 2001. But the gap in male-female number still remains large and wide.

What emerges out is that the states of the region are experiencing a state of gender gap and very well identifiable areas of female paucity have now emerged out very distinctly. This aspect gets clearer when one analyses the pattern of sex ratio at the district level (Figure 1), in order to identify areas of deficiency and vice versa. It is important to mention here that there are more areas of wider gender gap and few areas of low gap. The sex ratio in the region varies between 1004 (Imphal west) and 754 (West Kameng). As many as eleven districts of the region experience a female-male gap of hundred and more and only one has more females than males. In fact in two districts the difference is as large as 246 (West Kameng) and 220 (Tawang). In all thirty-one districts of the region returned with a sex ratio less than that of the country average and in only nine districts the gap is less than 20 females (>980). The pattern of sex ratio emerging out when analysed at the district level reflects the following:

Figure 1

Sex Ratio of Population 2001 : North East India

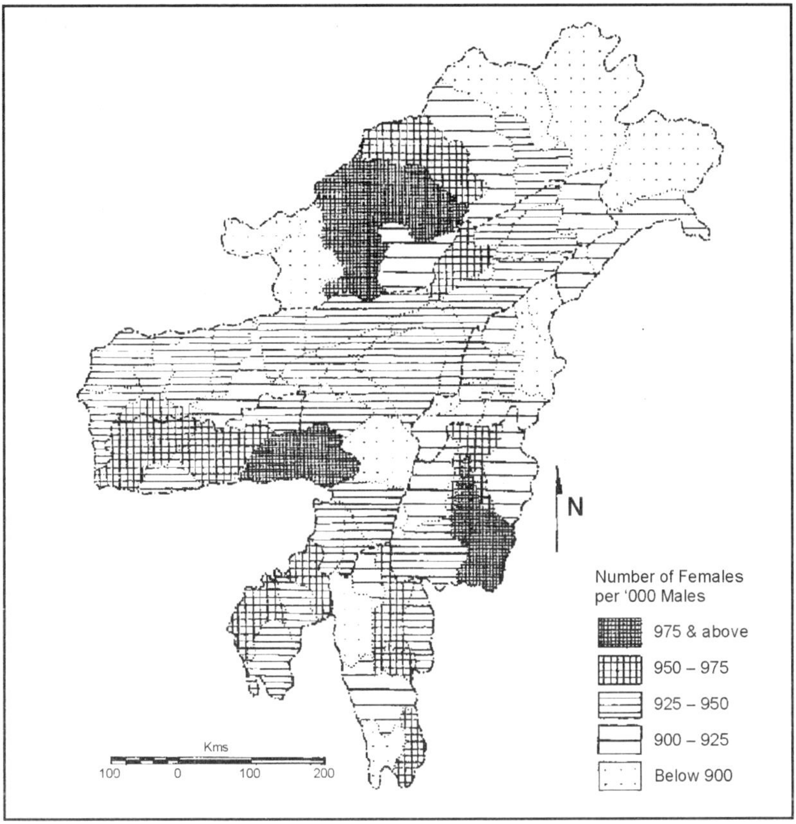

- the areas of very low (< 900) and low sex ratio (less than country average) fall in the region characterized by rugged, mountainous topography coupled with thick forest cover and heavy rainfall. Such an area comprises the states of Arunachal Pradesh, Nagaland, Manipur and Mizoram almost as a contiguous belt. Also the belt includes a few adjoining plain districts of upper Assam and the two hilly districts in the state. This belt of low to very low sex ratio is almost an uninterrupted one.
- the areas of high sex ratio (>960), on the other hand, occur in fourteen districts and in three scattered pockets. The first pocket comprises of three districts of Arunachal Pradesh characterized by

its mountainous topography, the second being in the upland part also known as Meghalaya plateau, and the third includes the Imphal valley located in the central part of the Manipur state.

The most noticeable aspect of the above pattern is that the areas of low gender gap and the areas of high gender gap coexist side by side. Moreover, leaving the plain districts of Assam and the Imphal valley, the areas of both the high and low sex ratio are occupied by the tribal communities, with no known knowledge of discrimination against women population.

- areas with sex ratio ranging between 933 and 960 occur in three contiguous belt and in a few scattered pockets. The first belt includes a number of districts of lower Assam, the second includes all the districts of Tripura, the adjoining districts of Barak valley and the eastern districts of Mizoram state. The third belt is a small one comprising a few districts of upper Assam on the northern side of Brahmaputra. Excepting the Barak valley and the region of northern Brahmaputra with majority non-tribal population, and the eastern Mizoram with majority tribal population, the rest of the areas falling in this category represent a mixed population composition.
- what, therefore, emerges out is that in general the hills and mountains depict areas of low sex ratio and thus high gender gap, plains and valleys moderate sex ratio with a deficiency of fifty females approximately and the areas of high sex ratio and low gender gap from all the three—mountains, valleys, plateaus.

An examination of child sex ratio (0–6 age group) provides us with a clear and distinct idea as to whether any discrimination and preference of male child over female exists in the region of study or not. The existing data pertaining to the north-east India do not, however, depict any evidence of such preferences and as a result the child sex ratio presents a more or less balanced picture though a few districts do record a not-so-desired ratio (Figure 2). The number of districts with a ratio of 925 and 950 is few, while majority falls in the range of 950 plus category. In three districts, females outnumber males and all these are in the state of Arunachal. Only in nine districts, the child sex ratio is less than these districts; overall sex ratio, the gap being less than ten in four (3 districts of Meghalaya and 1 from Nagaland) and in the other 5 (all from Manipur) the gap is of twenty points only. It may be mentioned

Figure 2

Child Sex Ratio 2001 : North East India

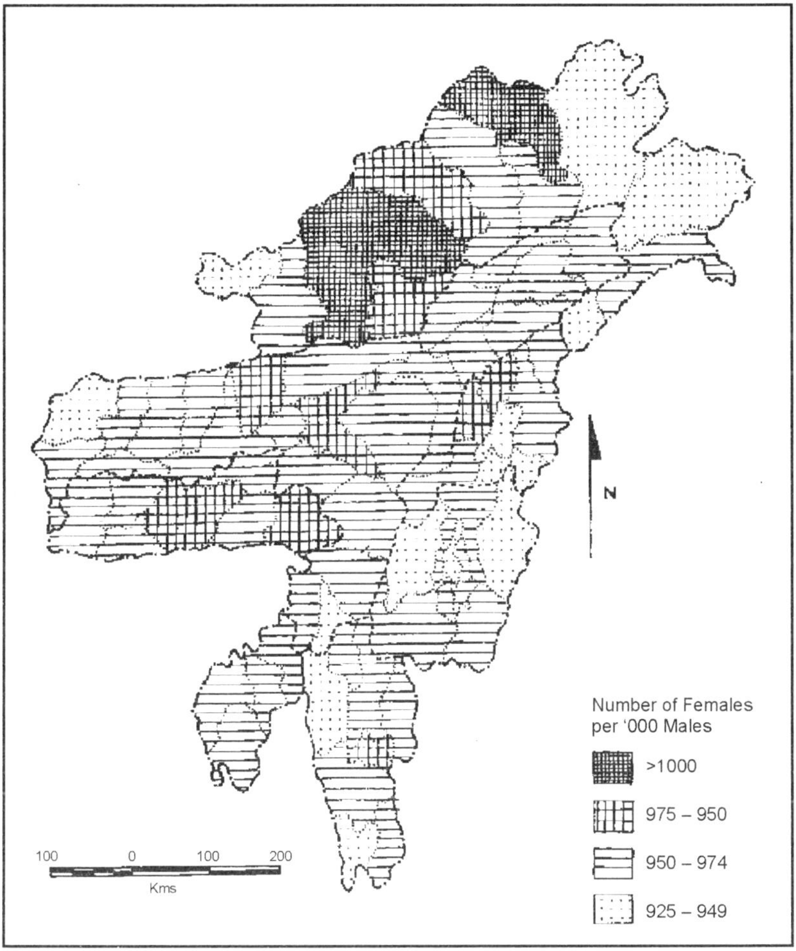

that all these districts happen to record some of the highest overall sex ratio in the region and their child ratio too is not less than 950. Some of the worst sex ratio districts of the region (mainly from Arunachal) have, however, recorded a very high child sex ratio and thus in both the cases there is very little evidence to suggest that their exists any discrimination or male preference. It is important to note that the gender bias at birth is almost non-existent as far as this region of the country is concern.

Socio-Economic Status of Women

The determination of the status of women through education and employment is perhaps the best possible indicator to do so. It must be mentioned here that in the past forty/forty-five years there has been a lot of heat generated on the issue of 'status of women' both in the west as well as in the east. In India, the debate on the issue started around 1960s when the United Nation asked all its member countries to submit a report on the status of women. Now the question is what actually constitutes female status. What is that criteria that determine her status in the society and what is that critical criteria that do not accord the same? In fact, the word status is an elusive one and carries diverse and opposite views. Though it is often felt that the opportunities of social participation, nature of work, legal status and, more importantly, the actual treatment meted out to women make her position in the society higher and otherwise. It is also a fact that women ought to achieve these by remaining and honouring those many norms that the society had identified for her. It, therefore, makes her effort towards gaining a better status of living within the patriarchal norm that much more difficult. However, it must be admitted that women in India have come a long way and access to education has definitely played an important role in their efforts to improve their lives. Also an increased access to education provided her with opportunities for employment. Thus, education coupled with employment has made them more conscious of their rights and helped in making them assert in the society. Here an attempt has been made to see the changes in order to evaluate the position of women in the north-east with particular reference to education and employment.

Educational attainment of communities is generally viewed and examined from the rate of literacy they had attained. Female literacy in India was at a dismal 0.6 per cent in 1901, and hundred years later in 2001 it stands at a modest 53.67 per cent, indicating a long journey that women in India had undertaken for improving their status in the society by being able to read and write. Though it is in no way near what men have attained in the same period, the fact that women had come this far is in itself a commendable achievement. Emphasis on female literacy and education progressed at snail pace at the beginning of the century and for about fifty years the increase in literacy rate was less than 8 per cent point (0.6% in1901 and 7.9% in 1951). With independence came a growing concern for an overall improvement of women's condition in India, which got a further boost with the provision of the constitution that guaranteed free and compulsory education upto the age of fourteen years. Such a decision immediately brought in an improvement in female literacy and in the following decades a noticeable difference could be viewed in the field of women's education. It is, however, the last thirty years that witnessed a remarkable progress in female education in India.

Table 3

Trend of Female Literacy in North-East India (1971–2001)

	Female literacy rate (in %)			
State	*1971*	*1981*	*1991*	*2001*
Arunachal	4.39	14.01	29.37	43.53
Assam	22.76	—	43.70	54.61
Manipur	22.43	34.61	48.64	60.53
Meghalaya	28.29	37.15	44.78	59.61
Mizoram	54.88	68.60	78.09	86.75
Nagaland	21.33	40.28	55.72	61.46
Tripura	24.02	38.01	50.01	64.91

Source: Census of India 1971, 1981, 1991, 2001.

Note: Percentage of literacy computed on the number of population aged 5 and above for 1971 and 7 and above for 1981, 1991, 2001. No census in Assam in 1981.

The state of north-east too made an improvement in the female literacy rate particularly between 1971–2001. In fact, it needs to be mentioned here that barring Arunachal Pradesh and Nagaland in 1971, in all the other states the rate of female literacy was always higher than the country average, indicating the fewer restrictions imposed on women's access to education. Education was never viewed as gender biased, rather availability of an educational institution always made a difference in acquiring and being deprived of it. Also the constructive role played by the Christian missionaries in improving overall education and with particular reference to female education in inaccessible areas need acknowledgement. If north-east represents today some of the better female literate states, the role of these missionaries cannot be denied. Table 3 provides the trend of female literacy in the states of the region from 1971 to 2001 and a deeper look at the table indicates a gradual and upward movement in female literacy rate in all the states. Some of the noteworthy features of female literacy in north-east are highlighted below:

- In thirty years' time, all the states of the region made significant progress, although a substantial proportion still remains illiterate.

- Mizoram in all the decades had been far ahead of all the other states. Contrary to it, Arunachal Pradesh had never been above any states.
- Arunachal's rate of female literacy had always remained below the national average. However, progress made by the state is commendable as it moved from 4.39 per cent in 1971 to 43.53 per cent in 2001, in thirty years a jump of about forty per cent.
- Progress made by Meghalaya is the least in thirty years' time. The state ranked second in 1971 and in 2001 it stands fifth above Assam and Arunachal.

Status of female literacy when examined at the district level brings out the level of regional variation clearly (Figure 3). This variation is of

Figure 3

Female Literates 2001 : North East India

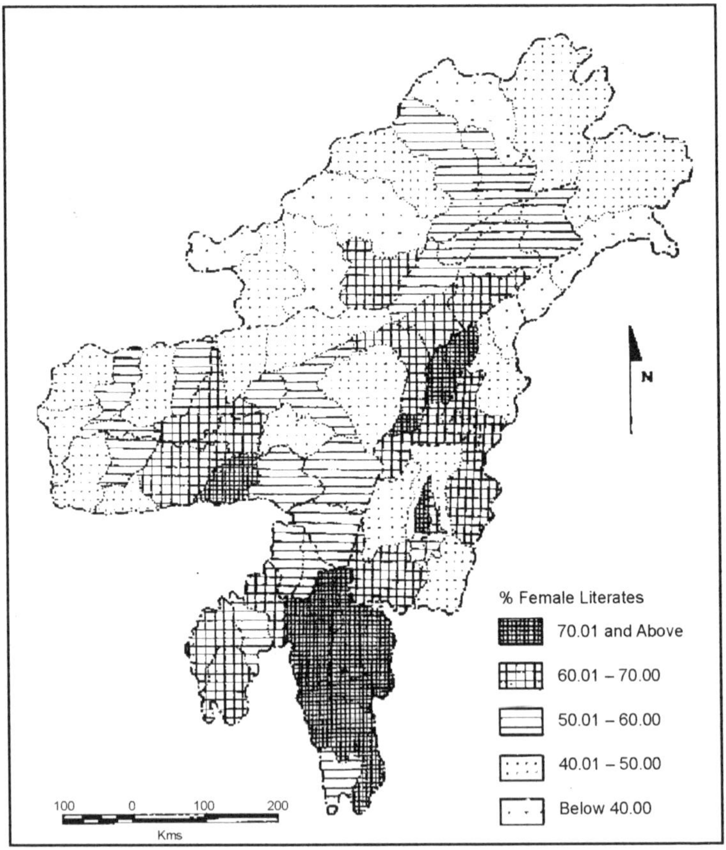

a range of 28.59 per cent in East Kameng to 96.26 per cent in Aizawl district (the most literate district of the country). A careful observation of data pertaining to the literacy rate of females reveals the following broad points:

- There is a huge variation in the rate of female literacy in north-east India. Aizawal along with Serchip and Kolasib are the most literate districts in the region with a literacy rate of over 90 per cent. All other districts of Mizoram (except Lawngtlai) record over 80 per cent literacy rate. On the other side of the pole lies the districts of Arunachal recording some of the lowest rate (28.59% in E. Kameng, 28.84% in Tirap). In fact, out of the state's thirteen districts ten have recorded a rate less than 50 per cent.
- All the districts of Assam record a literacy rate ranging between 40 and 70 per cent. Similar is the case with Manipur, Meghalaya and Nagaland (except Imphal West, East Khasi Hills and Mon district).
- It is also evident that districts falling in the high mountainous region tend to depict areas of low female literacy, while in similar areas with high Christian population gives a different result—examples are Mizoram and Nagaland.
- The plain areas with majority non-tribal population though have witnessed a remarkable improvement in female literacy but have a long way to go to come anywhere near Mizoram. A less rigid gender biased non-tribal society is perhaps the only reason why literacy rate in these areas got improved, what has not happened in the mainland India.

Economic activity in any society is generally characterized by gender biased division of labour. Indian societies are no exception to this rule. Though women perform a host of roles accorded to them to make the family run, often their work goes unnoticed and unrecognized. Their work in many cases is classified as supplementing the work carried out by men and therefore remains as unpaid labour, and they are not counted as the earning member of the family vis-à-vis society. In view of their low participation in economic activities, women are often subjected and treated as the subordinate half of the family having to live with low status. In fact, it was Karl Marx who believed that participation in economic activities is the main criteria for deciding status—a view supported by many women activists. It is, therefore, necessary to evaluate the female work participation rate in this region of the country where a substantial size of tribal and non-tribal population lives. The state of women in tribal communities is closely linked to the mode of production and the participation by both genders without any rigid bias, something which continues to remain illusive from the non-tribal society where absence of women from gainful economic employment continues to measure her and family's status.

Table 4

Trend of Female Work Participation in North-East India (1971–2001)

	Female work participation rate (in %)			
States	*1971*	*1981*	*1991*	*2001*
Arunachal	51.28	45.67	37.49	36.54
Assam	5.45	—	21.61	20.71
Manipur	23.62	39.48	38.96	39.02
Meghalaya	34.57	37.49	34.93	35.15
Mizoram	39.46	37.72	43.52	47.54
Nagaland	45.23	43.20	37.96	38.06
Tripura	4.83	12.78	13.76	21.08

Source: Census of India 1971, 1981, 1991, 2001.

Note: Percentage of female work participation calculated on the total female population. No census in Assam in 1981.

The rate of female work participation in the region had remained high all along. A cursory look at Table 4 shows the trend of female work participation rate between 1971 and 2001 clearly highlights the following:

- a high proportion of females is involved in gainful economic activities. Here, two broad patterns emerge out—one that stands for the hilly, tribal dominated areas with high proportion of females involved in economic activities and the other for the non-tribal dominated areas where female share is more or less at par with the country's average. Assam and Tripura fall in the second category while the rest of the states fall in the first.
- the pattern emerging out can be substantiated in three sentences—a gradual fall in women's participation rate has been noticed in Arunachal Pradesh and Nagaland, an upward looking trend in four states (Assam, Tripura, Manipur, Mizoram) and a stagnant trend has been noticed in Meghalaya.

- beside Assam and Tripura, in all the other states female participation rate is higher than the country average. This has been the trend all along in the region.
- women's participation in economic activities did not increase by much during this period. For instance, the increase has been only by 15 per cent point in Assam, Manipur and Tripura; around 8 per cent point in Mizoram and by a very negligible point in Meghalaya. But the most marked change occurred in Arunachal and Nagaland where a negative trend took place.

Status of female work participation when examined at the district level (2001) brings out a few interesting points (Figure 4). The female work participation in the region varied from 73.35 per cent in Champai to 10.28 per cent in Dhubri district. The interesting aspect of this study

Figure 4

Female Workers 2001 : North East India

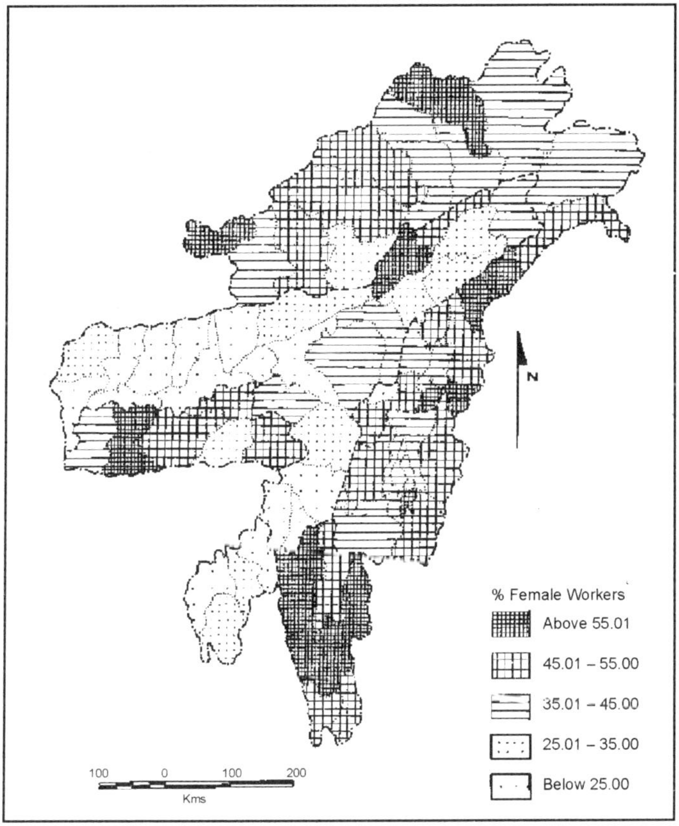

is that it provides a clear and distinct pattern, that is, tribal dominating areas representing high participation rate and non-tribal dominated areas with low participation rate. A few broad aspects arising out of the analysis reveals the following:

- a clear-cut distinction in the rate of participation has been a case in point wherein the tribal and non-tribal areas represent two different nature of work participation rate.
- plains and valleys where settled form of cultivation exists with rice as dominant crop seem to employ less females (contrary to the popular belief that rice cultivation requires more female hands) and the hills and mountains where the age-old practice of shifting cultivation is carried by female along with males who take active part in the agricultural pursuit.
- the twenty-five districts with less than 35 per cent female participation rate includes mostly the areas from the plains and valleys (except Imphal valley) beside three scattered hill districts of Papum Para, East Khasi Hills and Dimapur. Eighteen districts of Assam fall in this group, all in the Brahmaputra and Barak valley. The district of Tripura too is in this group. Thus, all the rice growing areas of the region represent areas of low female work participation region.
- participation rate of more than 55 per cent includes fourteen districts—all predominantly tribal, in scattered pockets with the exception of Lakhimpur district of Assam. District coming with 45 to 55 per cent participation rate forms a clear and distinct belt stretching across the mountain region and also the plateau of Meghalaya.

Conclusion

The status of women—social, economic and political—can be defined as the degree of equality and freedom enjoyed by them. Women's participation on equal terms with men in domestic decision-making, expression of their views freely and participation in community life allows them being recognized in the society. This, in turn, distinguishes the high and low status that the society vis-à-vis family allocates to her. Women's power of expression, capacity to reach out through their views and ideas generally comes with education and make themselves heard by their own folks as well as by the opposite sex. It is this capability of women that often spearheads the overall voice of women in the society. The educational attainment and participation in gainful economic pursuit make her strong and determined. The financial freedom that comes with employment opportunities cannot be denied and it is these two aspects that generally make a woman capable of asserting her voice both in the family as well as in the society. Once she is able to achieve this, it automatically provides her an important position in the society and she is made to feel equal if not above others within the family circle. It is this recognition of her that makes and determines what her actual 'status' is. But what happens if their very strength in number gets reduced, whereby their physical presence in itself becomes threatening. Is she be still able to exert the role allocated to her by the society and play with ease? Or she becomes increasingly vulnerable? It is this concern of an improved state of women with respect to education and employment on the one hand and gradual fall or no betterment of her physical number on the other that the present study tried to focus on. The interplay of three aspects of sex ratio, educational attainment and economic participation of women provides an understanding of her current status and represents a very complicated scenario towards an explanation of gender gap. Some of the interesting aspects arising out of the analysis made so far can be narrated below:

- sex ratio in the region as a whole and in a few states did decline in the past one hundred years. Females no longer outnumber males in any state, but now are outnumbered by males in all states. Today, there are states where the deficiency is as large as hundred females. This is one statistics that is of huge concern to all—as the region is almost free from any known knowledge of discrimination against women. It is, therefore, of tremendous surprise as how can there exist such a wide male-female gap, worse than some of the rigid son-preferring states of mainland India. Also the region is home to many tribal communities among whom the birth of a male or a female child is greeted with equal joy. Some of this poor sex ratio states happen to be overwhelmingly tribal-dominated. What does it reflect then? Fewer females on the one side and discrimination-free society with no preference for son over daughter on the other side. There is also no known evidence of female infanticide or foeticide, gender equated tribal social ethos, no evidence of strong male selective migrants to disturb the balance. Also the child sex ratio does not provide any reflective evidence of discrimination against female child. In spite of all these—sex ratio in the region remains a concern.
- women's status with regards to literacy and education had shown an improvement in the region. Today, a very high proportion of women of the region are literate something of which they were

deprived a few decades ago, not because of any taboo against females going to school but largely due to non-existence of educational institutions. The effort of the government agencies and of missionaries brought a huge change in this regard and in the absence of any taboo, the opportunities as and when they came were grabbed immediately. The result of that is what we see today. However, there is very little correlation between the level of literacy attained and the existing nature of sex ratio. Areas of low literacy have both high and low sex ratio and vice versa.

- female work has never been viewed as against the norms of family or society among the tribal communities. The reflection of which is clearly evident in the high participation rate of women in economic activities among the tribes and tribal areas. Contrary to it in the non-tribal dominated plain and valley areas women have always worked as a free service provider at home and her in-farm activities had often gone unreported—reflecting a low participation rate of females as workers in those areas. These two contrasting areas of social fabric with contrasting work participation rate depict two different sex ratio patterns. In the earlier case, a low to very low sex ratio and in the latter a moderate to moderately high ratio.

The interplay of literacy and work participation had positive impact on improving the sex ratio and on reducing gender gap in two non-tribals dominated plain areas of the region (Assam and Tripura). In the other states though literacy rate improved all along but it did not culminate into bringing more women to work. Rather opposite had happened in most states—Nagaland and Arunachal are best examples here. In the rest of the states a very fluctuating pattern emerged out indicating no immediate relation between the variables.

A few critical questions that arise at this stage include the following:

- Does high female literacy and employment rate lead to a greater risk of gender disparity?
- Is strong son preference leading to an increased manifestation of gender biasness characterizing societies?
- Does the desire for a small family result in the rise of female child deaths?
- Does sex-selective technology made it easy for couples to go for sex-selective abortion and infanticide as opposed to discrimination against living daughter leading to an imbalanced sex ratio?

Taking these important questions an attempt is made here to answer each one of them. As has been already mentioned, there is neither a positive or a negative relation existing between the variables and as such gender disparity prevalent in the region cannot be attributed to these important indicators of development. Also efforts need to be made to bring women more actively into organized sector of economy and in non-farm activities thereby releasing them from doing masculine work particularly during pre-and post-childbirth period. The absence of primary data though restricts answer to the second question, but there is no denying to the fact that the huge non-tribal population and strong tribal patriarchy feel that a son completes the family. However, birth of a son is never at the cost of death of a female foetus. As a large family in otherwise numerically small tribal communities is highly appreciated it, therefore, does not lead to any gender biasness. Moreover, the child sex ratio does not corroborate gender biased society at least in the region. One will have to wait to seek an answer as to whether desire for small family has resulted in female loss. As the phenomenon is highly urban biased and north-east continue to live in rural areas—the answer may take sometime to come. Sex-selective technology that made sex determination easy leading to an imbalanced sex ratio in many parts of the country, has made little inroads in this part due to the absence of any precise preference.

Thus, in all probability, it appears that gender discriminations happens not at birth but gradually with age and both tribal and non-tribal communities are infected by it. In most likely case the reasons for low sex ratio and wide gender gap could be happening due to high infant and child mortality rate. But does not it affect both the sexes equally? In fact, it is biologically proved that girls are stronger than boys and therefore, their chances of survival are more. It is, in all probability, the high rate of maternal death that is the most likely cause for female deficiency in the region. Most of the cases of reproductive death occur among young underaged women into childbearing situation. As in the region co-habitation leading to childbirth is not a taboo, and with high fertility rate, young age of mothers and no concept of family planning – women are put into childbearing condition frequently, often leading to the deterioration of their health and eventual death. There are also very few health centres available in rural areas to cater to the needs of pregnant mothers. Thus pre-and post-natal care is almost non-existent in the region. Also most birth related performances are carried out by untrained persons, causing occasional death. As in the tribal societies bearing and rearing of children is the sole responsibility of the mother, they often neglect their own health and start working almost immediately after the birth of the child. With most of them being in agriculture in difficult hilly terrains, the chances of their survival also drop leading to their death at times.

It is, therefore, necessary to give proper attention to manage its huge human resource by evaluating the state of health care situation prevalent in the region. Health and health care related activities need to be injected on a priority basis and to reduce the chances of high reproductive death. Also, the people in general need to be educated about health care so that the cases of preventable death can be checked. It is only then the tribal societies of the region and tribesman influenced non-tribal society can say that they are just not living in the myth of equality but in an equal society.

References

Baruah, Arunima. 2003. *Women in India: An Exhaustive Study.* Anmol Publication Pvt. Ltd., New Delhi.

Das Gupta, M. and P.N. Mari Bhat. 1997. Intensified Gender Bias in India: A Consequence of Fertility Decline. *Gender, Population and Development,* 73–93.

Das, Susmita. 2006. "Women and Agriculture: Their Overall Role" in B.J. Deb et al. (eds.), *Changing Agricultural Scenario in North-East India.* Concept Publishing Co., New Delhi.

Dash Sharma, P. 1999. "Changing Role and Status of Women among the Parhaiyas of Chotanagpur" in R. Indira et al. (eds.), *Gender and Society in India: Rural and Tribal Societies,* Vol. II. Manak Publications Pvt. Ltd., New Delhi.

Hasan, Sakina A. 1997. "Status of Women in India: Retrospect and Prospect". *Man and Development,* Vol. XIX, No. 3, Centre for Research in Rural and Industrial Development, Chandigarh.

Heer, David M. 1987. *Society and Population.* Prentice-Hall of India Pvt. Ltd., New Delhi.

Passah, P. 2000. "Population Growth and Female Literacy in India with special reference to North-East India" in B. Dutta Ray et al. (eds.), *Population, Poverty and Environment in North-East India.* Concept Publishing Co., New Delhi.

Patel, Vibhuti. 1988. "Sex Determination and Sex Preselection Tests: Abuse of Advanced Technologies" in R. Ghadiaily (ed.), *Women in Indian Society.* Sage Publication, New Delhi.

Shanthi, 1999. "Women in Tribal Societies: An Overview" in R. Indira et al. (eds.), *Gender and Society in India: Rural and Tribal Societies,* Vol. II. Manak Publications Pvt. Ltd., New Delhi.

CHAPTER 4

Status of Women Empowerment at Household Level in Eastern India

A Rural-Urban Comparative Study

Chaiti Sharma Biswas

With the advancement of the human civilization, male dominance over the society began to increase, which pushed back women in every sphere of life and they became the neglected section of the society. But women's role in the development process cannot be denied, as they were also part of the society. However, the pervasiveness of gender inequality came into focus as a major issue after the publication of the report of the 'Committee on the Status of Women in India' in 1974 (Sadhna Arya, *Alternative Economic Survey*). Since then a series of studies have been carried out on gender inequality. Even the national policy makers began to formulate many policies in favour of welfare of this weaker section of the society. Despite efforts from the government and non-governmental organizations, status of women remains to be low. Many researchers tried to focus on lack of financial power and access to property rights of the female members as the root causes behind this. After the initiation of the economic reform, a major change has begun to occur in economic sphere that affects participation of women in the workforce thus indicating changes in the empowerment of women (as per Census of India, the percentage of women workers increased from 22.73% in 1991 to 25.68% in 2001). As a result, it becomes imperative to study women's empowerment in the light of new changed situation. Accepting the existence of gender inequalities and strains, it is crucial that the upliftment of the women in a society may accelerate the developmental process. And this can be achieved by empowering them more and more. Empowerment is a package of both the financial and decision-making power. Alternatively, women's empowerment depends upon the interaction between the social and economic aspects of life (IFAD, 2000). Now empowerment is the process of increasing the assets and capabilities of individuals or groups to make purposive choices and to transform those choices into desired actions and outcomes. Empowered people have freedom of choice and action. This in turn enables them to better influence the course of their lives and the decisions which affect them. Therefore, it is important to know to what extent Indian women can exert their own decisions both at home and outside. In these circumstances, the present study explores only the status of women in decision-making at grass roots level (i.e., households or families) where decision-making refers to the process of selecting one course of action from a number of possible alternatives in solving a problem or meeting a situation (Mukherjee, 1975). Moreover, the sectoral difference of the status of women will be examined.

A study in rural Morocco shows that the women have more control on decision-making in the poorer families than the affluent families as every household decision is more crucial there (Bourqia, 1998). IFAD (International Fund for Agricultural Development) project in Tamil Nadu proves that changes in women's mobility, social interaction, labour pattern and access to control over resources help them to have more control over decision-making. GOLDA project of south Bangladesh mainly carried production related decisions of women and survival (Saha, 2001). A study on rural Bangladesh, shows that women in those areas faced social oppression and economic inequality due to low social status (Shahnaj and Leonhäuser, 2004). Gender inequality is a constraint to maternal health in Nepal, (Furuta and Salway, 2006). Women's control over household decisions may influence their health care decisions. Decision-making authority of women improves nutritional level and reduces child mortality, even after controlling for education and wealth (Desai and Johnson, 2005). In a study Helen C. Vidler shows that women's depression is related with lack of confidence, financial power, powerlessness etc. A study by A. Pandey et al., revealed the prevailing discriminatory practices against female children in seeking health care in rural West Bengal.

Present study is based on the National Family Health Survey, Phase 2 (NFHS-2) data for the year 1998–99 and concentrates on the eastern zone of India. This study will examine the role of women in taking various household level decisions such as: (i) girls' education, (ii) boys' education, (iii) desire to have second child and its sex preference, (iv) cooking, (v) staying with the family, (vi) purchasing jewellery, (vii) going to market, friends' and relatives' houses and (viii) monetary transaction. A logistic regression analysis was carried out to find out the effects of the explanatory variables namely caste, religion, age group, acquaintance with media, education, and occupational status of the female and her husband on the above-mentioned decision-making variables.

Eastern Zone Profile

The eastern region of India comprises of West Bengal, Bihar and Orissa. Populations of these states in 2001 were 80 million, 82 million and 36 million respectively. Of which West Bengal has 58 million rural and 22 million urban population, Bihar has 74 million rural and 8 million urban population and Orissa has 31 million rural and 5 million urban population respectively. Among these three states, sex ratio was highest in Orissa (972 female) whereas West Bengal and Bihar have 934 and 919 females respectively per thousand males (National Human Development Report, 2001). Total rural and urban literacy rates of Bihar were 48 per cent, 44 per cent and 72.71 per cent respectively; for West Bengal these rates were 69 per cent, 64 per cent and 82 per cent respectively; for Orissa, total rural and urban literacy rates were 63.61 per cent, 60 per cent and 81 per cent respectively (Census of India, 2001). In terms of per capita net state domestic product at 1993–94 prices, position of West Bengal (Rs 9,796) was far better than that of Bihar (Rs 3,879) and Orissa (Rs 5,663); in fact the position of Bihar was worst among these three states (Economic Survey, 2004–05).

Data and Methodology

The data extracted from National Family Health Survey (NFHS-2, 1998–99) were used in this study. The respondents were females aged between 15 to 49 years. Some household characteristics were assumed as dependent variables that lead us to capture the role of decision-making power for women on the home front. These were: (i) deciding menu for cooking in every day life (ii) decisions about purchasing jewellery, (iii) freedom of going outside the house for shopping or visit to relatives, (iv)taking decisions about staying with kins. Some factors like educational qualification, occupational standard (both for the respondent and her partner), caste, religion, mass media exposure, age group variation may have influence upon decision-making factors. Multinomial logistic regression analysis has been done to find out the likelihood of the dependent variables for each of the explanatory variables. All dependent and independent variables were recoded from the given standard codes of NFHS. These codes were as follows:

(a) *Boy's and Girl's future educational attainment*: (1) Low education (2) Medium education (3) Higher education
(b) *Religion:* (1) Hindu (2) Muslim (3) Others
(c) *Caste*: (1) Scheduled Caste (2) Scheduled Tribe (3) OBC (4) General
(d) *Education of respondent and her partner*: (1) Low—Complete primary (2) Medium—Incomplete and complete secondary (3) High—Higher education
(e) *Media*: (1) No exposure (2) Have exposure.
(f) Decisions about cooking, health care, purchase of jewellery and money transactions:
(1) respondent (2) husband (3) others
(g) Allowing shopping, visit to relatives and keeping money: (1) No (2) Yes.
(h) Occupation of the respondent and her partner: (1) Low occupation (2) Medium occupation (3) High occupation.
(i) *Age groups*: (1) 15 to 25 (2) 26 to 40 (3) 41 to 49 years.

Findings

Total number of female respondents in east India was 15,857 out of which 4,408 were in West Bengal, 7,024 were in Bihar and 4,425 were in Orissa (Table 1). Of these, 4,408 women in West Bengal, 2,461 were rural and 1,947 were urban; of 7,024 women in Bihar, 6,337 were in rural and 687 were in urban areas; and of 4,425 women in Orissa, 3,557 were in rural and 868 were in urban areas. All these women were ever married and belonged to the age group of 15–49. Most of the respondents in these states were Hindus followed by Muslims and the number of respondents belonging to other religions were very insignificant. Distribution of Hindus and Muslims in West Bengal was 79.95 per cent and 19.12 per cent; in Bihar it is 83.6 per cent and 14.6 per cent and in Orissa it is 96.2 per cent and 2.1 per cent respectively. In West Bengal, distribution of respondents by castes was 68.68 per cent general, 21.64 per cent SC, 5.46 per cent ST and 4.23 per cent OBC. But both in Bihar and Orissa, most of the respondents belonged to OBC (52.3% and 31.1% respectively). Among other castes 20.6 per cent SC, 7.9 per cent ST, and 19.2 per cent belonged to general caste in Bihar whereas in Orissa 20.7 per cent SC, 18.5 per cent ST and 29.6 per cent general castes. In the following, we will try to depict the picture of women's role in making decisions about household matters and the factors influencing their decisions.

Table 1

Demographic Profile of Eastern India and the Percentage of Women having Media Exposure, 1998–99

	West Bengal			*Orissa*			*Bihar*		
	Rural	*Urban*	*Total*	*Rural*	*Urban*	*Total*	*Rural*	*Urban*	*Total*
Population	2,461	1,947	4,408	3,557	868	4,425	6,337	687	7,024
Religion(%)									
Hindu	69.0	25.9	79.95	96.7	91.6	96.2	84.3	77.0	83.6
Muslim	27.9	2.2	19.12	1.5	5.8	2.1	14.3	20.4	14.6
Castes (%)									
SC	25.2	4.8	21.64	21.1	16.6	20.7	21.0	16.3	20.6
ST	9.3	0.1	5.46	21.3	8.6	18.5	8.5	2.0	7.9
OBC	3.9	1.3	4.23	31.7	32.5	31.1	52.6	49.5	52.3
General	61.6	22.2	68.68	25.9	42.3	29.6	17.8	32.2	19.2
Women having media exposure	95.95	98.51	97.08	40.12	76.27	47.21	22.39	66.52	26.71

Source: NFHS-2 extracted data.

It is assumed that access to information helps to increase the awareness and empowerment among the women. About 97 per cent of women in West Bengal are acquainted with media (Table 1) which is more for urban women (98.51%) than that of their rural counterparts (95.95%). Similar picture is observed both in Bihar (22.39% rural, 66.52% urban and 26.71% overall) and Orissa (4.12% rural, 76.27% urban and 47.21% overall) but the difference is that Bihar and Orissa women have less media acquaintance relative to Bengali women. The impact of media exposure is directly reflected in the opinion of the females about their wards' education. In West Bengal, irrespective of rural and urban not a single mother voted for "No education" about their offsprings. In contrast, 4.14 per cent women in Bihar think that there is no need of education for girls and 1.45 per cent women think in the same way for the boys. Like Bihar, women of Orissa (7.53% and 6.26%) also think in the same way but here the percentage was more than that of Bihar. Still most of the female respondents of these three eastern states admit that education should be given as much as a boy or girl desires to have (Table 2). Rural mothers also think in the same way

(34.32% in West Bengal, 30.00% in Bihar and 33.06% in Orissa for girls and 30.89% in West Bengal and 22.31% in Bihar for boys) while in West Bengal the urban mothers' opinion is that both girls and boys must have minimum graduate degree but both in Bihar (16.16%) and Orissa (29.84%) they believed that only boys must complete the graduate degree.

Table 2

Sectoral Distribution of Females taking Decisions about Children's Education in East Region1998–99

Level of education	R/U/T	West Bengal		Bihar		Orissa	
		Girls	Boy	Girls	Boy	Girls	Boy
No education	Rural	0.00	0.00	4.37	1.50	8.41	7.06
	Urban	0.00	0.00	2.04	1.02	3.92	3.00
	Total	0.00	0.00	4.14	1.45	7.53	6.26
Primary & Middle	Rural	30.28	18.67	25.26	4.09	11.75	2.50
	Urban	7.74	4.32	5.68	1.31	5.65	0.81
	Total	20.24	12.29	23.35	3.82	10.55	2.17
Higher Secondary	Rural	34.32	30.89	30.00	22.31	33.06	18.78
	Urban	23.08	17.21	23.73	9.32	23.73	11.06
	Total	29.32	24.80	29.38	21.04	31.23	17.27
Graduate & Professional Degree	Rural	6.00	13.13	4.51	10.95	10.85	23.05
	Urban	23.49	25.53	12.66	16.16	22.00	29.84
	Total	13.79	18.65	5.31	11.46	13.04	24.38
As much as desired	Rural	29.40	37.31	35.85	61.15	35.93	48.61
	Urban	45.69	52.94	55.90	72.20	44.70	55.30
	Total	36.65	44.26	37.81	62.23	37.65	49.92

Source: NFHS extracted data.

As the literacy rate of West Bengal is relatively higher among the three eastern states, so it is expected that at least women should have moderate degrees of freedom at household level. But in reality the picture is not so encouraging. Only 64.79 per cent (Table 3) of respondents in West Bengal can express their desire for having another child whereas 47.08 per cent women in Bihar and 48.57 per cent women in Orissa can express their desire for future child. Among the three eastern states, 28.62 per cent of urban women of West Bengal have least power to take decision about having another child. This picture becomes reverse for rural women of West Bengal (41.12%). Now we will try to find out the picture of gender preference of the future child. An unambiguous common tendency of preference for male child emerged very positively among the respondents as a whole. Surprisingly, male preference is stronger in West Bengal (38.36%) than that of Bihar (22.59%) and Orissa (15.07%) (Table 3). As usual 39.53 per cent of rural women in West Bengal desire male children whereas only 16.25 per cent women cast their vote in favour of girl child, this percentage becomes 23.28 and 2.89 per cent in Bihar and 16.14 and 3.26 per cent in Orissa respectively. Surprisingly, urban women (36.36%) of West Bengal also express their choice for male child. Both in rural and urban sector preference for girl child (rural 2.89 and urban 3.49%) is very low. Very few rural (3.35%) and urban (2.47%) women of Bihar said that they do not bother for the gender of their child.

Table 3

Distribution of Females by Desire to have a Future Child and their Sex Preferences by Sector in Eastern Region, 1998–99

States	*R/U/T*	*Desire to have future child*	*Sex preference of child*			
			Boy	*Girl*	*Does not matter*	*Upto god*
West Bengal	Rural	58.88	39.53	16.25	29.31	14.91
	Urban	71.38	36.36	16.19	35.23	12.22
	Total	64.79	38.36	16.23	31.51	13.91
Bihar	Rural	46.60	23.28	2.89	3.35	9.03
	Urban	52.29	16.30	3.49	2.47	6.70
	Total	47.08	22.59	2.95	3.26	8.80
Orissa	Rural	45.99	16.14	3.26	10.12	2.45
	Urban	58.78	10.71	3.80	8.41	1.38
	Total	48.57	15.07	3.37	9.79	2.24

Source: NFHS extracted data.

Now the focus will be on the status and autonomy of women about health care decisions in a household. It is revealed from the study that mainly husbands take the health care decisions in maximum households. Regarding health care decisions the position of women is best in Bihar (19.13%) and worst in Orissa (12%), among three eastern states; only 17.71 per cent female respondents have the autonomy to decide about health care in West Bengal (Table 4). A similar trend is observed in both rural and urban households; the only difference is that the percentage of urban respondents have little more autonomy than their rural counterparts in taking health care decisions. In West Bengal, 28 per cent urban women can take health care decisions jointly with their husbands which is higher than the state level (22%) and much higher than their rural counterparts (17%). In Bihar, 24 per cent urban women have the right to take health care decisions jointly with their husbands, which is higher than both the state level (19.59%) and rural (19.14%) level.

Generally in a household, cooking department is managed by the female members. Among the three eastern states, women in Orissa (71.59%) have the most and those in Bihar (64.64%) have the least freedom to take cooking decisions. In West Bengal, only 69 per cent women can decide the daily menu on her own (Table 4). Similar picture is revealed in both rural and urban sectors. But a remarkable feature is that in urban West Bengal (3.14%) and Bihar (6.70%) husbands impose their cooking decisions on their wives.

A very small per cent of respondents can decide on their own that whether she will stay in a nuclear family or a joint family (Table 4). Among the three eastern states, West Bengal women (15.13%) had most and Orissa women (9.08%) had the least autonomy to decide about staying in joint or nuclear family. This trend of opinion prevails in both rural and urban areas. Rural women (19.87%) in West Bengal have more autonomy to take decisions about their staying with kins than that of their urban counterparts (11.37%). In Bihar and Orissa, urban women (11.79% and 12.56%) have more freedom than their rural counterparts (9.48 and 8.24%) to decide about staying in nuclear or joint family. In West Bengal, only 25 per cent of respondents can take this staying decision jointly with their husbands which is more than urban females (20.25%) and less than rural females (31.55%). In Bihar, 23.32 per cent and in Orissa 26.96 per cent of respondents can decide jointly with their husbands about staying in nuclear or joint family, which is more than rural respondents in Bihar (22.77%) and Orissa (26.85%) but less than urban women of Bihar (28.38%) and Orissa (27.42%).

It is observed that in financial matters, women get very little opportunity to apply their choices. Same gloomy picture is revealed when we consider the case of autonomy enjoyed by the women in purchasing jewellery of their own choice. Only 17.84 per cent women in West Bengal, 9.25 per cent women in Bihar and 8.56 per cent women in Orissa can apply their choice about purchasing jewellery (Table 4). Lack of freedom is maximum for the rural women of West Bengal (48.59%), Bihar (46.50%) and Orissa (35.82%) but it is relatively less

Table 4

Pattern of Household Decisions about Health Care, Cooking and Staying with Other Family Members by Sector in Eastern Region, 1998-99

Household members	R/U/T	Percentage distribution of decisions in a household about								
		Health care			Cooking			Staying with the family		
		West Bengal	Bihar	Orissa	West Bengal	Bihar	Orissa	WB	Bihar	Orissa
Respondent	Rural	16.04	18.76	10.96	70.72	64.54	71.58	19.87	9.48	8.24
	Urban	19.81	22.56	16.24	67.88	65.60	71.66	11.37	11.79	12.56
	Total	17.71	19.13	12.00	69.46	64.64	71.59	15.13	9.71	9.08
Husband	Rural	53.60	42.15	54.51	2.74	6.97	4.81	32.27	44.88	41.72
	Urban	37.73	37.12	53.34	3.14	6.70	4.38	50.14	37.85	41.71
	Total	46.57	41.66	54.28	2.92	6.95	4.72	42.23	44.19	41.72
Jointly with husband	Rural	16.69	19.14	19.65	3.64	8.08	2.67	31.55	22.77	26.85
	Urban	27.90	23.73	18.55	3.81	8.01	3.69	20.25	28.38	27.42
	Total	21.65	19.59	19.44	3.71	8.07	2.87	25.25	23.32	26.96
Others in household	Rural	5.48	11.39	7.06	10.18	10.62	8.83	5.87	12.43	9.87
	Urban	4.01	9.17	7.37	8.75	10.33	9.56	8.18	11.21	9.79
	Total	4.83	11.18	7.12	9.55	10.59	8.97	7.16	12.31	9.85
Jointly with others	Rural	8.18	8.55	7.82	12.72	9.78	12.12	10.45	10.43	13.33
	Urban	10.55	7.42	4.49	16.42	9.46	10.71	10.06	10.77	8.53
	Total	9.23	8.44	7.16	14.36	9.75	11.84	10.23	10.46	12.38

Cont'd...

Cont'd…

		Jewellery			*Spending money*		
Respondent	Rural	14.44	8.85	7.82	12.92	9.67	7.34
	Urban	22.13	12.95	11.64	4.37	7.13	9.22
	Total	17.84	9.25	8.56	6.63	8.87	7.71
Husband	Rural	48.59	46.50	35.82	9.87	5.11	8.63
	Urban	32.37	36.54	34.22	0.45	1.46	4.15
	Total	41.41	45.53	35.50	2.95	4.84	7.75
Jointly with husband	Rural	20.00	22.83	34.27	3.74	3.76	8.80
	Urban	30.37	28.53	36.41	0.41	2.33	6.91
	Total	24.59	23.39	34.69	1.29	3.42	8.43
Others in household	Rural	7.65	12.14	9.67	0.28	0.08	0.65
	Urban	5.15	11.94	8.76	0.06	0.29	0.12
	Total	6.54	12.12	9.49	0.12	0.09	0.54
Jointly with others	Rural	9.33	9.67	12.43	1.02	0.49	1.07
	Urban	9.98	10.04	8.99	0.13	0.15	0.35
	Total	9.62	9.71	11.75	0.37	9.11	0.93

Source: NFHS extracted data.

for the urban women of West Bengal (32.37%), Bihar (36.34%) and Orissa (34.22%). The percentage of women having right to take decision jointly with their husband regarding purchasing jewellery is also not very satisfactory. Only 24.59 per cent women in West Bengal, 23.39 per cent in Bihar and 34.69 per cent in Orissa take this purchasing decision jointly with their husbands, which is more than their rural percentage and is less than their urban counterpart.

In all the three states most of the respondents have little freedom of movement. Only a few women can take decisions about visiting market (20.64% in West Bengal, 21.39% in Bihar and 19.20% in Orissa), about visiting friends' and relatives' house (15.70% in West Bengal, 20.23% in Bihar and 16.10% in Orissa) (Table 5). Though there is very little difference on this issue between rural and urban women but urban women have little more freedom of mobility than their rural counterparts. A mixed result was obtained in case of money transaction. It is notable that among the three eastern state women from Bihar (67.11%) have most freedom in dealing with money transactions whereas this percentage in West Bengal is about 56.78 per cent and in Orissa it is 48.27 per cent. In all the three states, urban women have more autonomy to handle money transactions than their rural counterpart. Women from urban Bihar have maximum (77.15%) and Orissa (66.24%) had least freedom. Percentage of this freedom in West Bengal (69.51%) lies in between. The percentage of rural women from Bihar is 66.02, West Bengal is 46.62 and Orissa is 43.89.

Table 5

Percentage Distribution of Females about Visiting Market, Friends and Relatives and Keeping Money in Eastern Region, 1998–99

Types of option	*R/U/T*	*Percentage of females taking decisions in the household about*								
		Visiting market			*Visiting friends and relatives*			*Money*		
		West Bengal	*Bihar*	*Orissa*	*West Bengal*	*Bihar*	*Orissa*	*West Bengal*	*Bihar*	*Orissa*
Yes	Rural	15.43	20.43	16.9	12.84	19.39	14.6	46.16	66.01	43.89
	Urban	27.34	30.28	28.3	19.30	27.95	22.5	69.18	77.15	66.24
	Total	20.64	21.39	19.2	15.70	20.23	16.1	56.33	67.10	48.27
No	Rural	84.60	79.90	83.1	87.16	80.60	85.4	53.84	33.99	56.11
	Urban	72.7	69.72	71.7	80.70	72.05	77.5	30.82	22.85	33.76
	Total	78.35	78.60	80.8	84.30	79.77	83.9	43.67	32.90	51.73

Source: NFHS extracted data.

In the above-said paragraphs, we review the status and rate of participation of women in households with rural-urban divide in the eastern states. From the above analysis, it is clear that women have very little control over household decisions. What were the reasons behind this? In order to find out the causes of the women's vulnerable position we take the help of multivariate analysis. For logistic regression, we accept some of the variables as dependent variables and some as explanatory variables which may influence the dependent variables. These explanatory variables were: (1) community, (2) caste, (3) media exposure, (4) age group of the respondent, (5) educational qualification of both the respondent and her partner, and (6) occupational status of both the respondent and her husband.

We will now examine the factors influencing household decision-making. In rural West Bengal, respondents' decision regarding jewellery purchase depends on their age and occupation (Table 6). Generally, respondents of age group 26–40 compared to 15–25 have more freedom to take jewellery purchasing decisions alone. Women having low occupations take their own decisions about purchasing jewellery which means women of upper class cannot exert their decisions in this regard. On the other hand, most of the rural women have the freedom to take this decision jointly with their husbands in West Bengal. But urban women of West Bengal have less freedom than their rural counterparts in taking jewellery purchasing decisions. In urban West Bengal, about 66 per cent women of 15–25 age group and 45 per cent women with low occupations can exert the jewellery purchase decision jointly with their husbands or others. Still, West Bengal women irrespective of rural or urban have more autonomy in jewellery purchasing compared to Orissa and Bihar. Both in rural and urban Orissa, respondents of 15–40 age group with low occupations have some independence to decide about purchasing jewellery. But caste plays a significant role in rural Orissa in taking joint decisions regarding jewellery purchasing. The jewellery purchasing decisions of women from rural Bihar were influenced by caste, media exposure, respondent's age, their occupation and their husband. But most of the women from Bihar have the independence of taking the purchasing decisions jointly with their husband or others. Rather, in urban Bihar respondents have very little autonomy in purchasing jewellery and it is influenced only by their age.

Table 6

Logistic Regression Showing the Odds of Preference for Jewellery Purchase in Eastern States, 1998–89

Preference for jewellery purchase	Variables influencing jewellery purchase	West Bengal		Orissa		Bihar	
		Rural	Urban	Rural	Urban	Rural	Urban
Respondent	age between 41–49 @	—	—	—	—	—	—
	age between 15–25	0.151	0.254	0.186	0.235	0.295	0.346
	age between 26–40	0.605	—	0.655	—	0.675	—
	Higher occu. of resp. @	—	—	—	—	—	—
	Low occu. of resp.	0.211	0.212	0.224	0.129	0.215	—
	Higher occu. of husband @	—	—	—	—	—	—
	Medium occu. of husband	—	—	—	—	0.582	—
Jointly	Castes						
	General @	—	—	—	—	—	—
	SC	—	—	0.672	—	—	—
	ST	—	—	0.474	—	2.724	—
	OBC	—	—	0.608	—	1.250	—
	Having media exposure @	—	—	—	—	—	—
	No media exposure	—	—	—	—	0.778	—
	Resp. age between 41–49 @	—	—	—	—	—	—
	Resp. age between 15–25	0.613	0.657	—	—	1.644	—
	Resp. age between 26–40	0.672	—	—	—	1.272	—
	Higher education of res. @	—	—	—	—	—	—
	Low education of res.	—	—	—	—	2.09	—
	Higher occu. of resp. @	—	—	—	—	—	—
	Low occu. of resp.	—	0.449	—	—	0.424	—
	Medium occu. of resp.	—	—	—	—	0.485	—

Source: NFHS extracted data.

@: reference category

Now we will look into some regular activities of the households to find out who takes decisions on these issues. First, we take into account the cooking decisions. It is revealed from Table 7 that in rural West Bengal respondents' cooking decisions were influenced by their age and husbands' occupation. In urban West Bengal, respondents' age has a significant impact on cooking decisions taken by her. In rural Orissa, the factors affecting the respondents cooking decisions were their media exposure, age and their education but urban women's cooking decisions depended on occupation of husband and respondents' age. In rural Orissa, cooking decisions taken by self were influenced by media exposure, age and education. In urban Orissa, age and occupation of husband directs towards respondents' own decision and women of 26–40 age group jointly take cooking decisions. The cooking decisions of women in rural Bihar were regulated by their age and education but women of 15–25 age group had to take this decision jointly with their husband or others. Urban women's cooking decisions were influenced only by their age.

Table 7

Logistic Regression Showing the Odds of Preference for Decisions in Eastern States, 1998–99

Cooking decisions	*Variables influencing cooking decisions*	*West Bengal*		*Orissa*		*Bihar*	
		Rural	*Urban*	*Rural*	*Urban*	*Rural*	*Urban*
Respondent	Having media exposure @	—	—	—	—	—	—
	No media exposure	—	—	1.431	—	—	—
	age between 41–49 @	—	—	—	—	—	—
	age between 15–25 yrs	0.159	0.127	0.343	0.319	0.347	0.180
	age between 26–40		0.384	—	—	—	—
	Higher education of resp. @	—	—	—	—	—	—
	Low education of resp.	—	—	—	—	2.715	—
	Medium education of resp.	—	—	2.351	—	2.259	—
	Higher occu. of husband @	—	—	—	—	—	—
	Low occu. of husband	—	—	—	0.200	—	—
Jointly	Resp. age between 41–49 @	—	—	—	—	—	—
	Resp. age between 15–25 yrs.	0.431	—	—	—	1.680	—
	Resp. age between 26–40	—	—	—	3.808	—	—
	Husband's occupation @	—	—	—	—	—	—
	Medium occupation	1.843	—	0.628	—	—	—

@: reference category

In rural West Bengal, health related decisions of the respondents were affected by respondents' age only (Table 8). Women of 26–40 age groups get the advantage of taking health decisions compared to younger and older women. But in urban West Bengal, respondents' health related decisions were influenced by their age and occupation but majority of working women had to take health decisions jointly. In rural Orissa, health decisions of the respondents were affected by their caste, age, and occupation and media exposure. Caste, occupation and media exposure of women influence them to take health decisions jointly. In urban Orissa, health decisions of respondents were related with their age. In rural Bihar, women from scheduled tribes with no media exposure and belonging to the age group 15–25 years with some occupation take health related decisions on their own. Health decisions taken jointly by women were dictated by caste, age group (15–40) and low occupation. In urban Bihar, health decisions taken by women on their own were affected by the age group (15–25).

Table 8

Logistic Regression Showing the Odds of Health Decisions in Eastern States, 1998–99

Health decisions	*Variables influencing health decisions*	*West Bengal*		*Orissa*		*Bihar*	
		Rural	*Urban*	*Rural*	*Urban*	*Rural*	*Urban*
Respondent	Castes						
	General @	—	—	—	—	—	
	SC	—	—	0.586	—	—	
	ST	—	—	—	—	4.412	
	OBC	—	—	0.558	—	—	
	Having media exposure @	—	—	—	—	—	
	No media exposure	—	—	—	—	1.389	
	age between 41–49 @	—	—	—	—	—	—
	age between 15–25 yrs.	0.223	0.193	0.305	0.194	0.406	0.406
	age between 26–40	0.668	—	0.659	0.503	0.789	—
	Higher occu. of resp. @	—	—	—	—	—	—
	Low occu. of resp.	—	0.139	0.220	0.119	—	—
	Medium occu. of resp.	—	—	0.482	—	0.701	—
Jointly	Castes						
	General @	—	—	—	—	—	—
	SC	—	—	0.530	—	—	—
	ST	—	—	0.353	—	3.036	—
	OBC	—	—	0.595	—	—	—
	Having media exposure @	—	—	—	—	—	—
	No media exposure	—	—	1.302	—	—	—
	Resp. age between 41–49 @	—	—	—	—	—	—
	Resp. age between 15–25 yrs.	—	—	—	—	1.574	—
	Resp. age between 26–40	—	—	—	—	1.284	—
	Higher occu. of resp. @	—	—	—	—	—	—
	Low occu. of resp.	—	0.502	—	—	0.477	—

Source: NFHS extracted data.

@: reference category

In rural West Bengal, decisions of women to stay with relatives depended on their age, their occupation and their husbands (Table 9) but most of these decisions were taken jointly which were dictated by their age and occupation. In urban West Bengal, the decision of staying with relatives taken by respondents was influenced by age and occupation of both respondent and her partner. In rural Orissa,

Table 9

Logistic Regression Showing the Odds of Decisions Relating to Staying with Relatives in Eastern States, 1998–99

Decisions of staying with relatives	*Variables influencing the staying with relatives*	*West Bengal*		*Orissa*		*Bihar*	
		Rural	*Urban*	*Rural*	*Urban*	*Rural*	*Urban*
Respondent	Castes						
	General @	—	—	—	—	—	—
	OBC	—	—	0.579	—	—	—
	age between 41–49 @	—	—	—	—	—	—
	age between 15–25 yrs.	0.119	0.217	0.172	0.353	0.293	0.284
	age between 26–40	0.531	0.641	0.556	—	0.700	
	Higher occu. of resp. @	—	—	—	—	—	—
	Low occu. of resp.	0.33	0.50	0.223	0.142	0.221	—
	Medium occu. of resp.	—	—	0.496	—	—	—
	Higher occu. of husband @	—	—	—	—	—	—
	Low occupation	0.147	0.232	—	—	0.598	—
	Medium occu. of husband	—	—	—	—	—	—
Jointly	Castes						
	General @	—	—	—	—	—	—
	SC	—	—	0.629	0.374	—	—
	ST	—	—	0.313	—	2.742	—
	OBC	—	—	0.519	—	—	1.027
	Having media exposure @	—	—	—	—	—	—
	No media exposure	—	—	—	—	1.37	—
	Resp. age between 41–49 @	—	—	—	—	—	—
	Resp. age between 15–25 yrs.	—	0.650	—	—	1.676	—
	Resp. age between 26–40	0.679	—	—	—	1.261	—
	Higher occu. of resp. @	—	—	—	—	—	—
	Low occu. of resp.	0.358	0.466	—	—	0.441	—
	Medium occu. of resp.	—	—	—	—	0.532	—
	Higher occu. of husband @	—	—	—	—	—	—
	Low occu. of husband	—	—	1.984	—	—	—

Source: NFHS extracted data.

@: reference category

respondents' caste, age, and occupation of both respondent and her husband have impact on the decisions related to staying with relatives. In urban Orissa, age, occupation and caste play a significant role. In rural Bihar also respondents' age, low occupation, husbands' medium occupation and caste had impact on the decisions relating to staying with relatives. In urban Bihar, this decision depends on age and caste.

Majority of women in all the three eastern states cannot take mobility decisions. In rural West Bengal, mobility of women to both market and friends or relatives was restricted by religion, age and occupation (Table 10). In urban West Bengal also the freedom of mobility to market and friends or relatives depended on age and occupation of the respondent. In rural Bihar, mobility to market and friends or relatives was guided by caste, respondents' age, husbands' education and occupation. In urban Bihar, women's freedom of mobility to the market and friends or relative was guided only by their age. In urban Orissa, this mobility to market and friends or relatives depends on caste, age and occupation of the respondents and in urban Orissa this mobility freedom depends on caste, age, and occupation of both respondents and their husbands.

Concluding Remarks

From the above study, it is clear that though West Bengal is supposed to be socially and culturally rich but this aspect has very little impact on the status of women. It cannot be claimed that in this state the status of women is much better than those of their counterparts in Bihar and Orissa. Rather in some spheres of women autonomy Orissa and Bihar beats West Bengal. But overall the status of women is not very impressive in the eastern region, in fact, except some of the households they have almost no power to carry out any decision on their own. Whenever money matters are involved, the male members of the household take the final decisions, like purchasing jewellery, taking health care decisions etc. Otherwise, those activities which do not require involvement of money were, to some extent, carried out by the females of the household. Though the status of urban women is better than their rural counterparts as a whole but there were some spheres where the rural women's household decision-making autonomy supercedes the urban women's autonomy. On the one hand, rural women can take decisions about cooking and staying with kins or other members in a household more independently than their urban counterparts; on the other hand, they have more freedom of movement like

Table 10

Logistic Regression Showing the Odds of Mobility Decisions in Eastern States, 1998–99

Preference	*Variables influencing the decisions*	*W B*		*Orissa*		*Bihar*	
		Rural	*Urban*	*Rural*	*Urban*	*Rural*	*Urban*
	Visit market						
Cannot take decisions	Religion						
	Others @	—	—	—	—	—	—
	Hindu	0.187	—	—	—	—	—
	Muslim	0.136	—	—	—	—	—
	Castes						
	General @	—	—	—	—	—	—
	ST	—	—	1.521	—	4.210	—
	Resp. age between 41–49 @	—	—	—	—	—	—
	Resp. age between 15–25 yrs.	0.243	0.329	0.363	3.998	0.280	0.423
	Resp. age between 26–40	0.662	0.609	0.672	—	0.602	—
	Husband's higher edu. @	—	—	—	—	—	—
	Husband's low education	—	—	—	—	1.516	—
	Higher occu. of resp. @	—	—	—	—	—	—
	Low occu. of resp.	0.415	0.498	0.195	5.473	—	—
	Medium occu. of resp.	—	—	0.416	—	—	—
	Higher occu. of husband @	—	—	—	—	—	—
	Medium occu. of husband	—	—	—	—	0.702	—
	Visit relatives/friends						
Cannot take decisions	Religion						
	Others @	—	—	—	—	—	—
	Hindu	7.686	—	—	—	—	—
	Muslim	9.575	—	—	—	—	—
	Castes						
	General @	—	—	—	—	—	—
	ST	—	—	—	2.991	2.988	—
	Resp. age between 41–49 @	—	—	—	—	—	—
	Resp. age between 15–25 yrs.	4.596	3.465	0.343	3.395	0.312	0.473
	Resp. age between 26–40	1.640	1.793	0.629	—	0.629	—
	Higher edu. of husband @	—	—	—	—	—	—
	Low edu. of husband	—	—	—	—	1.464	—
	Higher occu. of resp. @	—	—	—	—	—	—
	Low occu. of resp.	3.276	2.415	0.209	4.886	0.526	—
	Medium occu. of resp.	—	—	0.455	—	—	—
	Higher occu. of husband @	—	—	—	—	—	—
	Medium occu. of husband	—	—	—	1.853	0.715	—

Source: NFHS extracted data.

@: reference category

visiting market, friends and relatives than the urban women. The reasons behind low status of women in eastern region can be found in the education of the parents, awareness, age, caste and community. With age women appear to have more autonomy. Also autonomy increases with education particularly with mother's education. Hindu women and women of other religions have more autonomy than Muslim women. Higher caste women enjoyed more autonomy than that of the lower castes. So it can be suggested that special attention towards increase in female education can help much. Also developmental policies should pay more attention towards the upliftment of the Muslim community and the lower caste Hindus, which ultimately increases awareness and self-assessment about them. With increase in the level of education, there will be corresponding increase in becoming more informative that will help women of these categories to enjoy more respectable status in a household.

References

Arya, Sadhna. 1999. *Women: Alternative Economic Survey 1991–1988: Seven Years of Structural Adjustment*, Lokayan, Delhi.

Bourqia, Rahma. 1998. Survival, Change and Decision-making in Rural Households: Three Village Case Studies from Eastern Morocco. IFAD, Rome.

Desai, Sonalde and Kiersten Johnson. 2005. "Women's Decision-making and Child Health: Familial and Social Hierarchies" in Sunita Kishor (Edited), *A Focus on Gender.* Calverton, Maryland, ORC Macro.

Economic Survey. 2004–05. Ministry of Finance, Government of India.

Furuta, Marie and Sarah Salway. 2006. Women's Position within the Household as a Determinant of Maternal Health Care Use in Nepal. *International Family Planning Perspectives*, 32 (1): 17–27.

IFAD. 2000. Tamil Nadu Women's Development Project Completion Evaluation. The Republic of India, Report No. 340-IN, IFAD/OE, Rome.

Mukherjee, Biswanath. 1975. Marital Decision-making and Family Planning. *The Journal of Family Welfare* XXI(3): 77–101.

Pandey, A. et al. 2002. Gender Difference in Health Care-seeking during Common Illnesses in a Rural Community of West Bengal, India. *Journal of Health, Population and Nutrition*, 20(4): 306–11.

Planning Commission. 2002. National Human Development Report 2001, Government of India.

Registrar General of India. 1981, 1991 and 2001. General Economic Tables Census of India.

Saha, Rama. 2001. Women's Role in Decision-Making in Gher Farming-GOLDA Project, *http://www.cwereinternational.org.uk/resource_centre/agriculture/golda/*Social/Women's%20Role%20in%20Economic%20Decision%20Making %20in%20Gher%20Farming.PDF.

Shahnaj, Parveen and Ingrid-Ute Leonhäuser. 2004. Empowerment of Rural Women in Bangladesh: A Household Level Analysis. Conference on Rural Poverty Reduction through Research for Development and Transformation.

Vidler, Helen C. 2005. Women Making Decisions about Self-Care and Recovering from Depression. *Women Studies International Forum* 28, Elsevier, 289–303.

CHAPTER 5

Declining Sex Ratio in a Prosperous Region

Economic Perspectives from Northern States of Haryana, Delhi, Punjab and Chandigarh

Sunil Kumar Gulati and Aswini Kumar Nanda

One of the most important outcomes of Census 2001 was the observation that the Child Sex Ratio (CSR) has declined significantly in the country. It shows the worst states to be Haryana, Punjab, Delhi and Chandigarh, whereas the best are Kerala, Tamil Nadu, Chhattisgarh, and Andhra Pradesh. The above data sets the thought rolling: does sex ratio have anything to do with development? Analysis of child sex ratio (0–6 age group) across India as per 2001 census shows that while the country figure declined significantly (a decline of 18 points for 945 in 1991 to 927 in 2001) it fell most alarmingly during 1991–2001 in the northern belt of India. For instance, it fell in Punjab from 875 to 793 (a decrease of 82 points), in Haryana from 879 to 819 (a decrease of 60 points), in Chandigarh from 899 to 845 (a decrease of 54 points) and in Delhi from 915–865 (a decrease of 50 points). There is a decline in sex ratio in each and every district in these states.[3]

These are all relatively prosperous regions of India but are by no means following the world trend. It is also clear that sex selective migration cannot be blamed for this phenomenon. So perhaps apart from the socio-cultural factors some micro-economic parameters may also be involved. The imbalance that has set in 0–6 age group will be difficult to remove in near future. Districtwise figures are more alarming. For example, during 1991–2001 child sex ratio (0–6 age group) declined from 874 to 754 (by 120 points) in Fatehgarh Sahib in Punjab and by 104 points (from 888 to 784) in Ambala district of Haryana. The sinful association between 'desire for a son' and technology (ultrasound, and possibly female infanticide and foeticide) is perhaps playing havoc with our society. This paper looks at various socio-economic parameters as given based on data of household amenities from census and to examine whether we can infer some influencing relationship to changing sex ratios.

Setting the Context: Haryana as a Typical Case

The fertility behaviour in India can be said to be a function of social, religious, cultural and economic factors. It has been observed that "Not only is the fertility decision of couples influenced by a wide range of factors such as education, the position of women and their participation in the workforce, economic condition, urbanization, social security systems and so on, but it differs between husband and wife, and between urban and rural areas" (Thiruvenkitasamy, 1992).

It would be useful to set the context by considering the case of a typical low sex ratio in the north Indian state of Haryana which at 861 is the worst amongst Indian states and perhaps the civilized world as against 933 females per 1000 males for India as per final results of the Census of India, 2001. The total sex ratio in Haryana was 865 in 1991. It is not surprising that sex ratio in all the districts of Haryana is below the national average (933). The drastic fall in sex ratio in the rural areas is shown in Table 1 with villages with more than 25 per cent deficit increasing by 14 per cent to become 27.4 per cent (almost one in every four villages has a one in four deficit of girls). Comparing this with the urban areas and we can see that the fall in rural sex ratio is worse.

Table 1

Changing Sex Ratio Pattern in Rural Haryana

Sex ratio	*Number of villages*		*Difference*	*Percentage*	
	2001	*1991*		*2001*	*1991*
>1.334 (<750)	1,852	977	875	27.38	13.71
1.33–1.11 (751<CSR<900)	3,359	3,142	217	49.66	44.1
1.11–1	1,057	1,818	–761	15.63	25.52
1–0.83	367	949	–582	5.43	13.32
>0.83	129	239	–110	1.91	3.35

Source: Census of India : Haryana 2001.

The sex ratio of the region known as Haryana (since its formation in 1966) was 867 in 1901, 835 in 1911, 844 in 1921, again 844 in 1931, 869 in 1941, 871 in 1951, 868 in 1961, 867 in 1971, 870 in 1981 and 865 in 1991. It is notable that sex ratio of Haryana region has been consistently low since recorded (1901) and is now at its lowest since independence. This historical reality again indicates that there are some micro-economic factors at play which needs attention.

The abysmally low sex ratio in the 0–6 age group shows that while perhaps the son preference has remained as before or perhaps gone down in the society, the availability of sex selective technology has led to elimination of the female child. It is also vital that the sex ratio at birth at the various hospitals and institutions has been checked up and found to be grossly adverse (CRS Data). The shocking thing is that percentage of institutional deliveries as per NFHS-II (1998–99) are 22.3 per cent in Haryana, these are 28.9 per cent in Himachal Pradesh, 35.6 per cent in Jammu & Kashmir and 37.5 per cent in Punjab. Despite having created health infrastructure for over 50 years and connecting each village with road, the percentage of non-institutional deliveries being so high shows that the low sex ratio is not a matter of accident, it's a matter of choice. With 78 per cent of the deliveries being non-institutional, it is quite likely that male deliveries are being ensured at hospitals/nursing homes and other deliveries are taking place at home. There are unconfirmed reports that in case of birth of female foetus the birth attendant/*dai* simply puts a lump of salt in the mouth of the foetus and pronounces a still born delivery within minutes.

What could be the factors behind this kind of hard decision which obviously has tacit/direct participation of the mother? A study in Haryana/Punjab area states the main causes of female foeticide to be: (i) the extremely high dowry and wedding expenses (ii) poor law and order situation where parents feel unsafe about girl children (iii) likelihood of daughter being killed or maltreated for dowry and (iv) generally low respect for women persuade them not to have daughters (Nayar, 1995). In this context, the economic aspects of sex ratio have been examined.

Some Theoretical Considerations

Demand and Supply of Girl Child

Previous research on sex preferences for children reveals that couples who have more sons among their surviving children are more likely not to desire additional children. When couples have had one or more son/s they are more likely to accept contraception. Having sons not only motivates parents to accept contraception but also sterilization (Malhi and Singh, 1995, others in www.gendwaar.gen.in[4]). Moreover, couples with sons have longer birth intervals and fewer subsequent births. Son

Figure 1

Symbolic Relationship of Elimination of Girl Child as Fertility Declines Much Faster than Son Preference

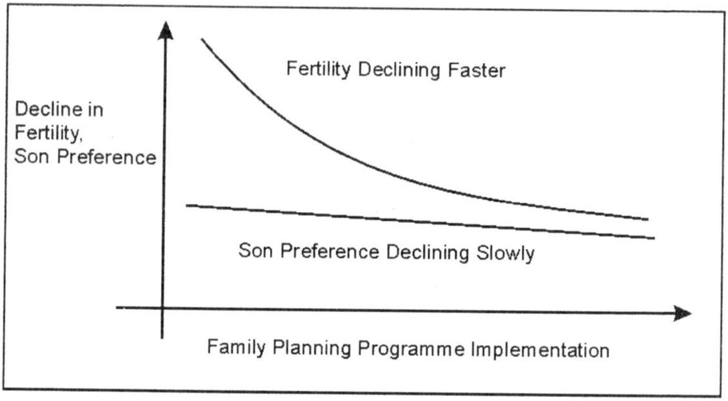

preference has also been reported to be an important reason for use of prenatal sex identification tests and sex-specific abortions (Pandhya, 1988; Yi et al., 1993 in www.gendwaar.gen.in[5] and Sarma, 1988).

One thing is very clear from above references that given the national reality that the families want to have smaller family size, either voluntarily, due to economic reasons such as desire for a better standard of living, due to incentives provided by the local government or out of compulsion such as abiding by the two child norm (Panchayat Act of Rajasthan Govt. etc.) which way will the decision go? Obviously, son preference remaining the same or declining slowly, the girl child is being sacrificed. Recent interviews conducted by the author showed that parents in Mewat area of Haryana used the term *Bachcha* which literally means 'children' only for male children as if the female children were not children at all. Also in 90 per cent instances, yearning for three children meant two boys and a girl and a single child family meant one that stopped at just one son. This is pictographically depicted in Figure 1.

Demand and Supply of Male Child: Son Preference

Table 2 explores as to how son preference in a typical affected state (Haryana) is influenced by various socio-economic factors.[6] This shows significant son preference as seen from the number of boys as against girls given a total fertility rate (TFR) (number of children born live to ever married couple). This applies amongst all communities and groups(SC/others). However, with respect to economic categories based on income groups we find that it is the low income group who has more TFR and son preference, obviously for supplementing family income.

Table 2

Preferred Sex of Child in various Socio-Economic Groups: Haryana

Group	*TFR*	*Boys*	*Girls*	*Either sex*
Category		**Religionwise**		
Hindu	2.5	1.3	0.9	0.3
Muslim	3.7	2.2	1.2	0.3
Sikh	2.3	1.3	0.8	0.2
Group		**SC/Others**		
SC	2.7	1.5	0.9	0.3
Others	2.4	1.3	0.8	0.2
Group		**Standard of Living**		
Low	3.1	1.8	1	0.3
Med	2.7	1.5	0.9	0.2
High	2.3	1.4	0.9	0.2

Source: NFHS, 1998–99: Haryana.

Study shows that fertility reduction in Haryana and Punjab was principally achieved through the implementation of a strong family planning programme without a commensurate decline in sex preference (Nanda, 2005).

The Idea of Market for Male Child

The proponents of free market argue that market throws up a P-signal (price). The sex ratio indicates that presently the signal is a siren in favour of males. Currently, the dowry of All India Service officers quoted in crores, ostentatious marriage industry, the numerous marriage palaces, depiction of big marriages in Indian cinema, industrialists spending crores on marriages of their daughters etc., throws up a price signal which none can afford to miss. People have the choice to invest on the winning formula (i.e., boys!) or avoid the girl child. It needs to be explored whether this market for male child satisfies all the four criteria of efficiency of a free market or not?

Consumer sovereignty: Nature on its own does not give parents the choice of sex of child to be born, though son preference was always there. Earlier the parents did not have a choice on the sex of the child to be born. Infanticide was looked down upon as sinful. The problem has started since the time when the technology came in and gave humans the choice to determine the sex before the child was born. Also the materialism has put people in a race 'to get rich fast'. The Pre-natal Diagnostic Techniques (Regulation and Prevention of Misuse) Act (PNDT Act) tries to stop the tests but there is little it can do about this. What has indeed happened that the rates and the associated "rent seeking behaviour" of the doctors and the "regulators of the doctors" have gone up. Else, in a country of 20 crore households do we believe that only about 50–80 cases have been registered under PNDT Act (Haryana leads with 22 cases). People vote with their currency and display their wealth and the census result shows that as of now the vote as well as the display is for the "male child".

Relationship with cost: The perceived costs of bringing up a girl child are much higher than the boy. Repeated studies have shown that parents consider the daughter as a lifetime expense account "a *dendari*, perpetual debt" and the male as a "profitable proposition" (encashable investment). So what they spend on education etc., of the male child they treat it as an investment recoverable many times over when dowry will come. On the other hand, the monies spent on girl child are treated as repaying debt of the past birth. So the focus is on avoiding the girl if you can as long as the marginal cost of ultrasound, abortion etc., is less than the cost of bringing up a female.

Decision regarding the *exact number of children* to produce. The number of children the family can afford depends on the budget line of the family. It can be said that the family sees the 'Marginal Benefit' of having a child vis-à-vis the 'Marginal Cost' (MC, which is perceived to be much more for a female) and decide. Usually, the decision is as per the occupation as well. There is more demand for male child in land or such labour-oriented occupational households where wage earner is an asset. Further, the idea of prevention of fragmentation of already small holdings acts as a deterrent to having many more children. But in vocations that are not inheritable e.g., teachers, or public companies, we find the sex ratio will be better. Given the cost consideration, the second child being a girl becomes an expensive proposition with no return in sight. The cost of providing protection and security to the girl child and risk of loss of prestige if something happens is phenomenal.

The curves drawn in Figure 2(a) and (b) are intended to show that for male child the initial marginal benefit (MB) is perceived by families to be high and remains so till at least the second male issue, whereas the cost is perceived to go up slowly. On the other hand, the marginal benefit of a girl child is perceived to be negative and goes on like that. The cost curve for girl child is perceived to be very steep. These drawings are hypothetical/figurative models and any misrepresentation is unintentional and only the essence should be seen.

Figure 2

Perceived Marginal Cost/Benefit

(a) Male Child *(b) Female Child*

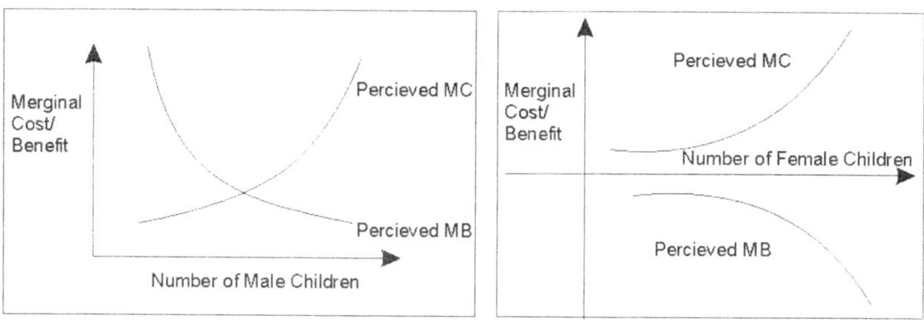

Here the male child not only serves the present but also the future. A male child would help a "future income stream" (including prestige, old-age security, liberation in next birth if cremated by male etc.,) while a female child would go to some other household. The male will even bring an additional working hand in due course (the daughter-in-law) and will further consolidate the wealth (property) or at least it will remain within the family are all the cost criteria which weigh heavily in favour of the 'male' child.

Market Failure

There appears to be hardly a *'free market'* for first girl child except amongst the salaried urban middle classes with non-inheritable kind of vocations. Other cases are the 'misses' amongst people who were trying for a male (hits) or who believe it to be a *fait accompli*. Even when there are two or more girls in the household, the reason invariably is that there was no male issue earlier. So if we remove these "unfortunate (as they call themselves) families", the sex ratio of rest of the families may turnout to be a horror story in north India especially.

Market Failure Framework depicted in Figure 3 says that markets fail when the 'costs of completing a transaction' become unbearable due to a combination of human and environmental factors. The human factors involved are bounded rationality and opportunism and the environmental factors are uncertainty/complexity and the small numbers. Let us see if the market for a girl child is failing due to a combination of the above factors as depicted in the Figure 3 below.

Figure 3

Market Failures Framework

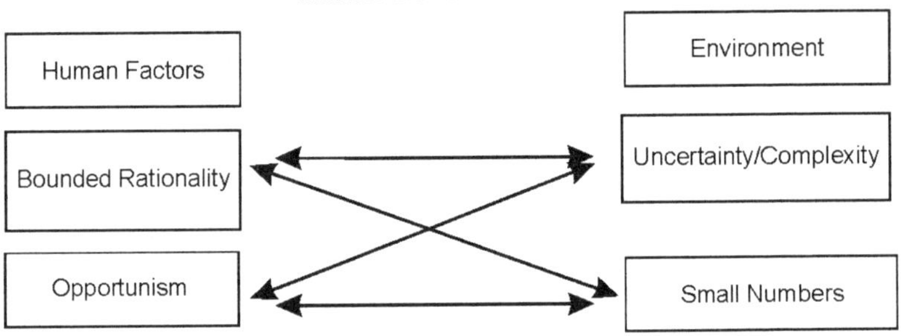

Bounded Rationality is seen in the following:

- The belief that only a male child gets you deliverance (*Moksha*) from birth and death or heaven etc.
- The belief that only a male will look after us when we grow old. Who knows?
- The belief that 'marrying off' a daughter will involve huge costs!
- The post-Mandal Commission era has brought back the "caste system". Caste has increasingly become the medium of exhibiting socio-political power. Marrying as per the caste system forces the marriage market to become an "inefficient" market.

Opportunism is depicted by:

- Being sold out to the concept of male dominance or superiority.
- The desire of male children not to share ancestral property with female sibling.
- The tendency to use the female as unpaid labourer by exploiting her higher emotional content and frailness (biological weakness).
- Pressures of consumerism after liberalization have made the pressure for higher incomes high. And males being wage earners traditionally have gained more economic power.

- Women's earning is seen as supplemental to the male's earnings whereas female savings are counted as the family's savings rather than 'her' saving. The same rule rarely applies to disposable savings from male's income.

Complexity

- Brought about by taboos on inter-caste marriage.
- Customs such as "arranged marriage", marriage for honour of family etc.
- Limited geographical sphere of awareness of parents. Marriage websites, newspaper matrimonial etc., are still preserves of the upper and middle class only.
- Liberalization has forced a lot of migration and nuclear families are coming up out of economic necessity. Marriages of daughters in these nuclear families to "clan man" are seen as more difficult since culture and customs 'lag' far behind the reforms.

Small Numbers

- The break-up of joint family and the strong 'clan' concepts of the past have made people feel vulnerable. Lack of sound public social security system leads to 'old-age risk' avoidance behaviour by going in for the male child.
- Socio-economic conditions have led to the emergence of nuclear families and falling apart of joint family system wherein the brother's son is not good enough and each nuclear family must have its own heir for carrying out of business, lineage and old-age security. The link between nuclear family and sex ratio can be a worthwhile study.

Objectives and Scope of this Analysis

Several theoretical formulations are available in the literature to account for the relatively stronger desire for sons in the northern states of the country (e.g., Dyson and Moore, 1983; Das Gupta, 1987; Basu, 1992). In the most significant conceptualization, Dyson and Moore (1983) related stronger son preference in the north to relatively "lower social status" and limited autonomy of women in the northern part of the country. According to the authors, north and south India differ in kinship and cultural practices. Under the north Indian kinship system, the preferred pattern of marriage is exogamous and post-marital residence is typically patrilocal. The practice of marrying into an extended kin household of strangers physically as well as psychologically isolates the women from her natal kin and hence makes them powerless in their husband's home. The only source of power for the young brides in the north is their ability to produce children, especially sons. In contrast, under the south Indian kinship system, marriages are endogamous and this accords women greater autonomy. Women may inherit property and bride wealth practice is common. Daughters, like sons, can and do render old age support to their parents. Although sons are still favoured in the south, a woman's position in the family is not determined by her ability to bear sons (Malhi and Jerath, 1997). This explains the vast differences in status of women in north and south India.

The Determinants of Status of Woman

An eminent study says "it seems that women's future decisions to accept contraception are clearly linked to the number of living sons among their surviving children. In a society experiencing fertility transition, the preference for at least two surviving sons is going to emerge as a major constraint for the family planning programme, especially in the north. Thus, it is important that the Indian government instead of propagating the two-child family norm across the board, emphasize those policies that actively enhance women's status and change attitudes towards female children" (Malhi and Jerath, 1997).

According to the United Nations, the status of woman in society can be determined by her composite status which can be ascertained by the extent of control that she has over her own life derived from access to knowledge, economic resources and the degree of autonomy enjoyed in the process of decision-making and choices at crucial points in her life cycle. Social status can be assessed by such data as access to food, education, age at marriage, ownership of land, employment and work participation, and the existence of enabling enactments relating to public welfare. As per Census 2001, a significant set of house-listing data that may have an impact on the status of women is the availability of amenities necessary for decent standard of living for the family. Here we can note that in the absence of these amenities it is the female members of the house (including often the young daughters) who have to suffer and be the beasts of burden. Some of these amenities are availability of a good house, having at least two rooms in the house, latrine, bathroom, drainage, kitchen, fuel used for cooking, source of clean drinking water, access to TV, telephone, bank account. These have been treated as our proxy variables for determining the status of women.

Scope of the Study

This study is restricted to the economic aspects (including literacy). It is based on Census 2001 house-listing data which is empirical data. Sex ratio is treated as a dependant variable and status of women as affected by amenities available to women. The economic strength of women based on purchasing power etc., are not available in the census and so have not been considered as only empirical data available for the universal population was sought to be used to establish whether correlation existed or not between the chosen variables and sex ratio. The district level total, rural and urban data has been used to establish outcomes that exist across the chosen northern states (46 districts) vis-à-vis what position exists at an all India basis (593 districts). Of course, the rural and urban number is not always same as total number of districts as some districts at all India/northern states level do not have any rural areas whereas some at urban level have no rural areas.

This is a limited study intended more as a demonstrator that a lot of detailed studies into amenities which affect the status of women and their impact on sex ratio are possible using the empirical data on amenities available even upto household, *tehsil* (sub-district) and district level. It can be attempted at disaggregated levels too.

Methods

The Hypothesis

In this instance, the district level data of northern states of Punjab, Haryana, Chandigarh and Delhi, the worst four states in sex ratio in India (called northern states) have been taken up for comparing with all India district figures of the total 593 districts in India data on the variables affecting the status of women. The basic hypothesis in this paper is that since it is the woman who gives birth to the prospective child obviously she would like to make a choice that enhances her status. The search boils down to what ultimately determines the status of women in real life. Are there any concrete measurable indicators of status of women and if so how do they influence the sex ratio?

The Variables

Data on the amenities available to the households have been collected in the Census of India 2001 during the house-listing operations. The data collected for house is the condition being good or liveable or dilapidated, the number of rooms, and availability in terms of 'yes' or 'no' for latrine, bathroom, kitchen, TV, telephone, bank account, etc. Regarding drainage, the type of drainage was asked as *pukka, kutcha* or no drain at all. Regarding fuel used for cooking all the fuels were enumerated. The sources of clean drinking water and its distance from place of residence were enumerated.

For the purpose of this study some other variables have also been introduced data on which is available in the Census of India 2001. These are female and male literacy, male workers in non-agricultural occupations (important because it is also a proxy used in working out whether an area is urbanized or not), female workers in non-agricultural occupations and child sex ratio. Some of the variables used were derived from the existing ones. For instance, the variable 'Smoke Fuel' was derived based on fuel used for cooking which was reclassified as non-smoky being kerosene oil, LPG and electricity, while all others are treated as smoky fuels. 'No Room' was a variable derived by clubbing all cases where the number of rooms in the house was reported to be one or none. 'No Tap' was a variable derived based on source of drinking water being not a tap but something else. Non-availability of electricity to the household was indicated as 'No-Elec'. Non-availability of latrine as 'No Lat', no drainage at all as 'No Drain', no bathroom as 'No Bath', non-availability of access to TV and telephone or bank account as 'No TV', 'No Tel' and 'No Bank'. Non-availability of any specified asset such as radio, TV, telephone, bicycle, scooter, car, jeep etc., is reflected by the variable 'No Asset' The variable names are given in brackets. Variables used were: (i) Female Literacy (FEMLIT); (ii) Male Literacy (MLIT); (iii) Male Workers in Non-Agricultural Occupations (MaleW); (iv) Female Workers in Non-Agricultural Occupations (FemW); (v) Good House (as perceived by respondent) (GH); (vi) No Room or one-room House (NR); (vii) Tap Water as Source of Water (No Tap); (viii) No Drainage from House (No Drain); (ix) Electricity as Source of Illumination (No Elec); (x) Latrine in House (No Lat); (xi) Bathroom in House (No Bath); (xii) Access to Telephone in House (No Tel); (xiii) Television in House (No TV); (xiv) No Bank Account in Household (No Bank); (xv) Asset in House (No Asset); (xvi) Smoky Fuel (Smoke Fuel); (xvii) Child Sex Ratio.

Source of Data

Primary census data from office of Registrar General of India was collected in respect of 593 districts on household amenities on 32 parameters. This is available on Total, Rural and Urban (T/R/U) basis (Gulati, 2004).

Techniques

The districtwise data of the 46 districts of north Indian states and all India data (593 districts) of the selected variable and sex ratio were subjected to corelational and regression analysis using SPSS for rural, urban and total. Initially, analysis was done for sex ratio and again with child sex ratio as dependent variable. It was found that the sex ratio being the parent gave more satisfactory explanations to the national reality than Child Sex Ratio (CSR). Whereas the total sex ratio gave values of R^2 ranging from 0.775 to 0.934 on various parameters, child sex ratio gave R^2 ranging from 0.305 to 0.615. So while both ratios are relevant, the child sex ratio accounts for only 15 per cent of population whereas the total sex ratio accounts for full population. Hence, total sex ratio (referred to as sex ratio) and not child sex ratio was chosen for carrying out the corelational analysis. Regression analysis was also carried out similarly on sex ratio. The detailed outcomes of both co-relational and regression analysis are discussed separately below.

Analysis of the Findings

The detailed correlation of the variables mentioned earlier with total sex ratio which is a gross picture of the historically achieved status of sex ratio by the society and the policy implications thereof has been next attempted in relation to each variable and is given below. The consolidated picture is given in Annexure I for northern states as well as all India as a whole.

Female Literacy (FEMLIT)

It can be generally argued that if the women are educated the chances of female foeticide should be low and the sex ratio should have positive correlation with female illiteracy. Table 2, which correlates sex ratio with female literacy shows that while the correlation at all India level is indeed slightly positive for T, R and U, but the outcome of our study for these north Indian states shows otherwise. It is moderately negatively correlated for rural as well as urban areas of north Indian states (significance levels are reasonably good except rural north India). It could be concluded that the literate women of north India, given the higher aspirations prevalent in the society and having become more capable of locating and using the sex-selection technology, are perhaps using the same resulting in lower sex ratio in favour of male child over time.

Table 2

Correlation of Sex Ratio (All India and Northern Belt) with Female Literacy

Correlation of with	*All India sex ratio*			*Northern states sex ratio*		
	Total	*Rural*	*Urban*	*Total*	*Rural*	*Urban*
Female Literacy	0.125	0.172	0.123	–0.424	–0.241	–0.242
Significance	0.002	0.000	0.003	0.003	0.115	0.105

The 'Census Paper Two' on Haryana strongly confirms this and says that "When, we see our districts compared with total 593 in India, we find that none of Haryana districts fares in the top 300 districts of India in terms of sex ratio or child sex ratio. Panchkula (579) is the last and Mahendargarh the most backward is best and ranked 374. For child sex ratio all Haryana districts are in the last 100 zone. Range is from Kurukshetra (590) to Gurgaon our best but ranking 527 in India. In literacy, Haryana ranks better with ranks between 106 for Panchkula to Fatehabad (416). Eight districts have figured above 100 but below 200 and 6 between 201–300. In female literacy, the ranks are between 91 (Panchkula) and 391 Fatehabad. This also establishes that sex ratio has nothing to do with being educated. Rather the educated are perhaps more prone to attempting manipulating the sex of the child to be as having a male child brings her social status" (Gulati, 2002).

Perhaps the women are unable to find education as an enabler. The quality of education being rendered to the 'girl child' itself needs to be gone into. This definitely needs further study as the investment in human capital formation would be rendered futile if the females are not equipped to earn, if necessary, through reservation in their favour, a decent standard of living. Perhaps then they will be able to resist the tendency of sex-selective birth in favour of males. It can be hoped that once they are enabled to earn they may be able to break the concept that only males can provide security at old-age as south India is already showing. There are vast north-south differences in trends in this respect which are worth going into. This also points out to the need of urgency in passing the reservation bill for women.

Male Literacy (MLIT)

The trend in male literacy is exactly same as explained for the female literacy given above. The significance levels are very good (low) for all India but are 5–6 per cent for north as can be seen from Table 3. There is problem perhaps with the content of education and perhaps the values it is generating that enables crass consumerism leading to female foeticide. The males are largely the perpetrators of injustice in the north. Not only they indulge in frequent alcoholism, domestic violence, but also they burden the females heavily while themselves smoking *Hookah* and playing cards. It is said in Haryana that if a farmer's buffalo is ill he will rush to the veterinary doctor even at 2 a.m. in the night. But if his wife is ill she will be told to wait and see the doctor herself the next day after finishing all the work.

Table 3

Correlation of Sex Ratio (All India and Northern Belt) with Male Literacy

	All India sex ratio			*Northern states sex ratio*		
	Total	*Rural*	*Urban*	*Total*	*Rural*	*Urban*
Male Literacy	0.140	0.155	0.135	–0.407	–0.282	–0.301
Significance	0.001	0.000	0.001	0.005	0.064	0.042

Haryana, for instance, has a scheme to take women in labour by ambulance to the hospital for delivery. The ambulances are there, the power to reimburse is of the Gram Panchayats, but in the whole year in 6374 villages only about 30/40 bills were reimbursed all over the state in 2003. The outcome was that 85 per cent of the deliveries were indoors (non-institutional deliveries). This for a state that surrounds the capital on three sides. Obviously, there are other reasons for home delivery like perhaps it makes it easier to dispose off the foetus (if female) if at home. The sex ratio at birth for hospitals in Haryana is in the range of 500–600 indicating that usually if people know that the foetus is a male, the delivery is done in a hospital to save the same. The solution could be visible economic empowerment of women, especially through their self-help groups. The involvement of women in their welfare can be increased by reimbursing ambulance expenses through the Mahila Swasthya Sanghas.

Male Workers in Non-Agricultural Vocations

The agricultural vocations are generally employing a lot of marginal and household workers so the male workers in non-agricultural vocations as a share of the main plus marginal workers (i.e., excluding non-workers) gives a more fair estimate of the economic activity (as a proxy to earning capacity) of the population of the district in question. This is a standard practice in Census of India.

Table 4

Correlation of Sex Ratio (All India and Northern Belt) with Male Workers

	All India sex ratio			*Northern states sex ratio*		
	Total	*Rural*	*Urban*	*Total*	*Rural*	*Urban*
Male Workers	–0.129	–0.022	–0.206	–0.687	–0.645	–0.645
Significance	0.002	0.600	0.000	0.000	0.000	0.000

Table 4 shows that the results for all India as well as northern states have high confidence level (low significance) except all India rural data where indeed this was a difficult question to canvass. The data shows that economic prosperity at the all India level of male workers (indicating income to the family) as well as in north is perhaps leading to "Opportunism" resulting possibly from the ability to practice sex selection (except that we are not at all confident to say such a thing about the rural male worker).

The force of the correlation is quite severe resulting in great loss of sex ratio in the north. There is not much rural and urban differential indicating that the attitudes are more related to economic aspirations of the households irrespective of location. The cost of ultrasound of Rs 400–500 is easily affordable being equivalent to about 3–4 days' wages and accessibility in terms of roads etc., is excellent in the north so it is quite apparent that sex selection is being practised.

Female Workers

The correlation of sex ratio with female workers in Table 5 shows that results for all India as well as northern states' economic prosperity of the women (who suffer as the beasts of burden) perhaps does not dent the practice of sex selection. Though the significance levels are reasonable, but the force of the negative correlation is much more severe in the north resulting in greater loss of sex ratio. The all India rural correlation is slightly more significantly explained than in the urban areas. In both the regions, the negative push to sex ratio is more by the well-heeled urban female worker which confirms our view on economic aspirations (in fact urbanization itself is a reflection of aspirations of the society). The data indicates that 'social status' is perhaps more important than even economic status and by avoiding having a girl child in some way the mother (woman) tries to avoid the suffering for the next generation girl like herself. So perhaps the recent 'Domestic Violence Act' or giving rights to women in parental property may have more impact on status of women if handled sensitively.

Table 5

Correlation of Sex Ratio (All India and Northern Belt) with Female Workers

	All India sex ratio			*Northern states sex ratio*		
	Total	*Rural*	*Urban*	*Total*	*Rural*	*Urban*
Female Workers	–0.207	–0.178	–0.156	–0.455	–0.332	–0.393
Significance	0.000	0.000	0.000	0.002	0.028	0.007

One obvious conclusion about sex ratio of main workers is the predominance of males amongst main workers. In fact in urban areas of Haryana this ratio is as low as 136 against 320 for rural areas and 264 overall, at the same time for marginal workers the sex ratio is as high as 1952 for rural areas and 665 for urban areas. This again reflects the marginalizing and resultant lower status of women.

Housing Condition

The house census takes as 'Good' if the respondent calls it good. In some sense, this is more of a subjective assessment of the house-owners' attitude. This again is a sign of prosperity. The all India correlation worked out in Table 6 is small but positive and more in rural than in urban areas while in north India urban is more and rural is less but both are positive. This perhaps shows that if the family "feels" prosperity it may think more in terms of gender equity. The negative in respect of total shows that since the significance is also very high there could be some problem with data and we can safely ignore it. This characteristic is primarily subjective but rural-urban should go with total and this aspect needs further study.

Table 6

Correlation of Sex Ratio (All India and Northern Belt) with Good House

	All India sex ratio			*Northern states sex ratio*		
	Total	*Rural*	*Urban*	*Total*	*Rural*	*Urban*
Good House	0.195	0.205	0.110	–0.113	0.171	0.266
Significance	0.000	0.000	0.008	0.453	0.268	0.074

This refers to a situation where the household has just one room or no exclusive room to stay i.e., it is living on sharing basis. This indicator has been selected precisely because it is a non-subjective indicator of prosperity (one can actually see the house where the household is dwelling). Table 7 shows the correlation of households having no exclusive room or single room with sex ratio.

Table 7

Correlation of Sex Ratio (All India and Northern Belt) with No Room in the Household

	All India sex ratio			*Northern states sex ratio*		
	Total	*Rural*	*Urban*	*Total*	*Rural*	*Urban*
No Room	–0.029	–0.015	–0.071	–0.707	–0.802	–0.722
Significance	0.487	0.714	0.085	0.000	0.000	0.000

While at all India level, the relation is insignificant (significance level is very high and can be safely ignored) at the northern states level it is very strongly negative, more so in rural areas. It is also an indicator of relatively nuclear households and the question of security during old age may be getting important. Both these factors perhaps add up to show that as the families may be driven by relative deprivation and enhancing family earning is a prime concern which could be leading to a tendency to go in for sex selection so as to add male wage earners into the household. It is vital to note that in this segment the daughter-in-law would be looked upon to be an additional wage earner so son preference would be more. This gives us a strong indication of giving more emphasis of selecting such areas for setting up more girls' schools and providing more family welfare counselling and monitoring outcomes of pregnancies through Integrated Child Development Scheme (ICDS) more closely if the female foetuses are to be saved.

Water Supply and Drainage

This variable depicts the situation that the drinking water to the family is not available from tapped water supply for the household. This indicates in some sense the backwardness of the area. Table 8 indicates that though at all India level the correlation is not driving the sex ratio, it is very much there for northern states where the correlation is significant. Due to backwardness, lack of awareness even about sexuality in general and early marriage, especially in rural areas, the sex-selective child birth is generally not implemented at the first birth. It is treated more as an act of God. Hence, the positive correlation with sex ratio indicates that the non-development has to some extent come to the rescue of girl child.

Table 8

Correlation of Sex Ratio (All India and Northern Belt) with No Tap and No Drain

	All India sex ratio			*Northern states sex ratio*		
	Total	*Rural*	*Urban*	*Total*	*Rural*	*Urban*
No Tap	0.081	–0.067	0.130	0.630	0.506	0.285
Significance	0.049	0.105	0.002	0.000	0.000	0.055
No Drain	0.468	0.450	0.307	0.503	0.135	0.094
Significance	0.000	0.000	0.000	0.000	0.384	0.533

The lack of drainage ('No Drain') to households has similar importance (as lack of tapped water) i.e., indicating backwardness. That it has a very significant correlation even at the all India level (low α and for the northern states 'total' but there being (high α) for rural and urban (R/U) individually is worth investigating further. It is generally found that while the public health department has its own agenda to ensure that water reaches to the village, no provision for draining out of the waste water, leading to spread of diseases. The outcome is that many residents of the north confirm that "villages were much cleaner when there was no water supply". And this affects the whole community so may be as a policy to conserve ground water and to prevent accumulation of water it can be made a policy directive that "No source of water will be left unconnected to a drain/soakpit anywhere be it a rural area or urban". In fact any plan for supplying water should not be approved unless drainage of run-off and used water is studied and provided for at the initial stage itself. This will reduce the workload as also disease burden especially for women who are more exposed to home environment and definitely raise the status of women. People prefer marrying their daughter into a village that has 'covered and *pucca*' drains.

Electricity and Sanitation

Table 9 reveals that correlation has turned out to be insignificant and at the northern states level too only the overall figure is marginally significant and needs further study.

Table 9

Correlation of Sex Ratio (All India and Northern Belt) with No Electricity

	All India sex ratio			*Northern states sex ratio*		
	Total	*Rural*	*Urban*	*Total*	*Rural*	*Urban*
No Electricity	0.052	–0.012	0.082	0.302	0.060	–0.026
Significance	0.207	0.779	0.047	0.041	0.698	0.864

Latrine is a basic necessity. Yet 63 per cent households in India didn't have toilets as of 2001. The impact that this has on the desperation, health and self-respect of women can be significant. Here it is treated as an indicator of backwardness of the district. Analysis of Table 10 shows that at all India level, the correlation is not very powerful but is nevertheless significant. Presently, therefore, these regions seem to have a significant positive correlation as was explained for No Tap item above. In urban areas, it indicates the presence of slum-like situation and has a negative impact on sex ratio but needs further study. Total slum population of Haryana comes to 14.22 lakhs i.e., 23.25 per cent of total urban population lives in slums. Sex ratio in slums is generally expected to be poor indicating male selective migration. Overall sex ratio in slums of Haryana has turned out to be 824.

Table 10

Correlation of Sex Ratio (All India and Northern Belt) with No Latrine and No Bath

	All India sex ratio			*Northern states sex ratio*		
	Total	*Rural*	*Urban*	*Total*	*Rural*	*Urban*
No Latrine	0.173	0.088	0.210	0.538	0.419	–0.068
Significance	0.000	0.033	0.000	0.000	0.005	0.654
No Bath	0.151	0.115	0.040	0.192	0.027	–0.291
Significance	0.000	0.006	0.335	0.200	0.862	0.049

The bathroom correlation is weaker than latrine possibly because this question is again private and answer may not be easily forthcoming and usually people do have a makeshift arrangement which some enumerators capture while others perhaps don't. The position's ambiguity is revealed by the both all India urban as also north (rural) and needs to be examined further.

Telephone and Television Facilities

Table 11 reflects the correlation of sex ratio with 'No Tel' and 'No TV'. Firstly, it is to be noted that at the time of census the income tax department had just started its campaign of people having "any one of the six things (including telephone)" to file return compulsorily. So often people thought census department will leak this information to the income tax department and even though households had a telephone they would not say so. This perhaps has got reflected in the high α.

Telephone and TV represent connectivity of the society. What these positive correlations show is that the chances are much higher of sex ratio being better in households not connected or hooked on to the modern civilizations so to say.

Table 11

Correlation of Sex Ratio (All India and Northern Belt) with No Telephone and No TV

	All India sex ratio			*Northern states sex ratio*		
	Total	*Rural*	*Urban*	*Total*	*Rural*	*Urban*
No Tel	0.172	0.009	0.107	0.603	0.192	0.117
Significance	0.000	0.837	0.009	0.000	0.211	0.437
No TV	0.240	0.189	0.174	0.310	0.083	–0.253
Significance	0.000	0.000	0.000	0.036	0.591	0.090

The question is whether it can be inferred that the modern facilities not having reached certain backward areas are a kind of blessing for the girl child. Modernization brings "Complexity" in the age-old social systems leading to sowing the seeds of market failure. These both items have aspirational value and we can safely confer the negative effect of connectivity to the world on sex ratio in particular and aspirations in general. The correlations of 'No TV' are stronger and significant as well α except for rural north. If we reverse it we can infer that areas with high TV have low sex ratio. With the kind of reach TV is providing to homes it is a major input into sowing seeds of economic aspirations.

Economic Mobility

By 'No Asset' we refer to households which do not have any significant assets like even a bicycle, TV, scooter, etc. Similarly, having a bank account in the household is taken as a proxy for economic mobility of the family. This parameter of the population is difficult to capture as people are hesitant to reveal about their bank account and also asking about poverty becomes slightly tricky and so many high α in Table 12 are not very surprising in this item.

Nevertheless, it is an indicator of relative backwardness of the area and on all India basis as well as for the northern states the findings confirm that backwardness is indeed linked to a higher sex ratio but that it only makes them more vulnerable to the forces of change in times to come.

Table 12

Correlation of Sex Ratio (All India and Northern Belt) with No Asset and No Bank Account

	All India sex ratio			*Northern states sex ratio*		
	Total	*Rural*	*Urban*	*Total*	*Rural*	*Urban*
No Asset	0.202	0.169	0.173	0.151	0.102	–0.177
Significance	0.000	0.000	0.000	0.318	0.509	0.240
No Bank account	0.094	–0.001	0.377	0.101	–0.126	0.046
Significance	0.022	0.988	0.000	0.506	0.414	0.761

Fuel for Cooking

Surprisingly, the fuel used for cooking can be a very powerful indicator of the upward socio-economic mobility of the households. To calculate the percentage of households using 'Smoky Fuel' we have added use of all non-clean fuels like coal, firewood, cow dung cakes, crop residue etc. In some sense, this is the residual of "clean fuels" like LPG, kerosene oil and electricity for cooking. This directly impinges upon the health of the females in the house and exposes them to a very significant health hazard.

Table 13

Correlation of Sex Ratio (All India and Northern Belt) with Fuel for Cooking

	All India sex ratio			*Northern states sex ratio*		
	Total	*Rural*	*Urban*	*Total*	*Rural*	*Urban*
Smoky Fuel	0.286	0.225	0.327	0.721	0.685	0.581
Significance	0.000	0.000	0.000	0.000	0.000	0.000

Table 13 reveals correlation of smoky fuels with sex ratio with very strong significance levels which again is an indicator of choiceless backwardness of households. In fact in many northern states people have started refusing giving their daughters in marriage to households not having a clean, so to say, modern cooking media. From the girls' point of view, this becomes a major requirement.

In male dominated societies of the north India especially, the women keep suffering while the males use the surplus money for liquor in a rampant manner. What inhibits the usage of LPG is its huge replacement cost. From a policy perspective the need is to empower the woman to switch to cleaner fuel to save her health. What can perhaps be done is that cylinders can be redesigned with a money box on top in which the lady of the house can drop in her daily savings, change etc., and at the end of month it can pay for the cost of full gas cylinder itself. Of course, to prevent the male from robbing/forcefully taking away the savings, a standard key should be designed to be available only to oil agency workers. This correlation being strongly positive indicates that as of date backwardness has contributed to the safety of the girl child.

Child Sex Ratio

Table 14 shows that the significance levels are low, and the problem is real and cannot be wished away. The more alarming thing is that regions which always have had a high sex ratio in north India have almost come back with a vengeance in reporting low sex ratios. This explains the high negative correlation child sex ratio has with sex ratio in the northern states. Otherwise one would naturally expect the child sex ratio to have a good positive correlation with the sex ratio. One obviously expects traditionally high sex ratio districts to have high child sex ratio as well. But up in the north it's not peacetime. It is war against the girl child so to say.

Table 14

Correlation of Sex Ratio (All India and Northern Belt) with Child Sex Ratio (CSR)

	All India sex ratio			*Northern states sex ratio*		
	Total	*Rural*	*Urban*	*Total*	*Rural*	*Urban*
Child Sex Ratio	0.455	0.454	0.421	–0.503	–0.409	–0.564
Significance	0.000	0.000	0.000	0.000	0.006	0.000

The child sex ratio is obviously an outcome of what has been happening in the relatively recent pregnancies as it covers children less than 7 years of age as on 1st March 2001. So this is in some sense reflective of the post-reforms era and the start of the ultrasound era. And the way child sex ratio has dropped is alarming. May be the minds need to be reformed first, else the mindless forces of greed will make everyone a loser. At a policy level, the implication is clear, that not only north India but anywhere in India where the drop in sex ratio has been significant over the decade, special action plan must be made and strong positive incentives be provided to save the girl child before it is too late. The unthinkable level of crimes and violence involving young males is a pointer to the need to take urgent action. There are villages in Haryana who have scores of male youth already history sheeters and people refuse to marry their daughters in such villages. Recently in Gurgaon, nine youths 18–25 years killed 28 men in eleven months just to make easy money. In Ghaziabad in the first week of November 2006, 17,000 young police recruit aspirants went on rampage on GT Road for eight hours. There are scores of such cases of sheer male power going berserk.

Regression Analysis

It was important to understand the fit between total sex ratio and other variables and it is found that there does seem to be a logical fit as indicated above. However, post-regression intentionally attempt has been made not to change the comments given earlier only to preserve original thinking.

Regression on Total Sex Ratio, All India

Model Summary

This model shows that sex ratio indeed is dependent on many factors but the level of impact and significance of various factors differs as is captured by the Table 15. The R square value is a significant 0.526 and cannot be ignored. This shows that sex ratio is more affected by child sex ratio (0.635), Female Literacy (1.179 and positive), Good House (0.836), No Room (0.309), No Electricity (0.475), No Latrine (0.770), No Drain (+0.867), No Bath (–0.697), No TV (–1.614), No Bank(–0.405), No Asset (0.454) and Smoky Fuel (1.629). One can only regret leaving out the others whose significance level exceeded 5 per cent despite the hunches. Thus, if the explanations given above were too strong on certain points that have missed the bus, it is felt that the times are changing fast and may be the left outs like 'Tap water', 'Telephone' etc., will become vital in another decade or so. Mobile telephones in fact are already changing lifestyles and may be safe water at premises may become more important than tap water. In fact 'Source of Water' away from home may be a better indicator of backwardness in a future study. Not surprisingly though, 'Male Literacy' loses out to 'Female Literacy' as a determinant as if to justify the saying that 'when you teach a girl you teach three generations'.

Table 15

Regression on Total Sex Ratio

Model	*R*	*R square*	*Adjusted R square*	*Std. error of the estimate*	*Durbin-Watson*
1	0.725	0.526	0.512	44.05	1.043

a. Predictors: (Constant), Smoky Fuel, NR, GH, CHSEXR, NO LAT, MLIT, NO ASSET, NO DRAIN, NO BANK, NO TAP, FEMW, NO BATH, NO ELEC, NO TEL, MALEW, FEMLIT, NO TV.

b. Dependent Variable: Sex Ratio.

Table 16

Regression on Total Sex Ratio

Variable	*Unstandardized coeff*		*Standardized coeff*	*t*	*Sig.*
Model1	*B*	*Std. error*	*Beta*		
(Constant)	133.508	72.285		1.847	0.065
CHSEXR	0.635	0.059	0.478	10.793	0
MLIT	0.353	0.48	0.063	0.736	0.462
FEMLIT	1.179	0.391	0.289	3.017	0.003
MALEW	0.15	0.274	0.047	0.547	0.585
FEMW	6.99E–03	0.174	0.003	0.04	0.968
GH	0.836	0.148	0.205	5.65	0
NR	–0.309	0.138	–0.078	–2.237	0.026
NO TAP	1.15E–02	0.125	0.005	0.092	0.927
NO ELEC	0.475	0.166	0.21	2.869	0.004
NO LAT	0.77	0.135	0.284	5.721	0
NO DRAIN	0.867	0.119	0.325	7.276	0
NO BATH	–0.697	0.177	–0.241	–3.947	0
NO TEL	0.156	0.643	0.018	0.242	0.809
NO TV	–1.614	0.396	–0.466	–4.079	0
NO BANK	–0.405	0.189	–0.096	–2.141	0.033
NO ASSET	0.454	0.202	0.111	2.247	0.025
Smoke Fuel	1.629	0.225	0.516	7.25	0

a. Dependent Variable: sex ratio.

Relating the Findings to Other Empirical Evidence

The discussion of the data shows that the 'backwardness' as we understand it and high sex ratio are generally positively correlated. But do we presume that the backward areas are safe heavens for the girl child? Urbanization is an inevitable phenomenon and these backward areas are largely rural presently. With the increasing migration from rural areas to cities the slums will grow. And they already are pockets of low sex ratios. What then is the solution?

Some studies give evidence showing high sex ratio among women enjoying a high status in the family, (as evidenced by the west), thereby emphasizing the need to raise female status. This is possible through their greater involvement of women in more modern occupations, which would provide them with greater economic freedom. This could be achieved by promoting higher levels of formal education and vocational education such as teacher training, nursing, etc. The provision and effective implementation of reservations in educational institutions and work places for females as also giving them an equal right over property would raise their status and help in curtailing high fertility. Income generating schemes such as tailoring, carpet making, embroidery, poultry and dairy farming etc., should be promoted through vocational training and subsidized loans which would help women to earn money and to free them from economic dependence on male members, thereby enabling them to gain a higher status in the family and society (Hari, 1991).

Conclusion

The seeds sown by the society will come back to the society and the sharp fall in child sex ratio is a symptom of the disease which any sane society should not ignore. Already there are villages with 20–25 per cent female deficit and this is making living difficult for the rest of the society with raging crime and squabbles amongst the frustrated youth. Marriage is a stabilizing phenomenon in the society. It is the origin of household economic demand for the market economy. If the institution of marriage will become deficient then it will impinge upon all the demand variables and multipliers of the economy. So as much as the sociologists do, the economists too should be concerned about the falling sex ratio. It will also in the long-run change consumption pattern in female deficient areas to more masculine things (like male parlours, dance and liquor bars, narcotics, cigarette, pan shops etc.). The market for sexual services for the males, legal or illegal, will also go up (along with complementaries like AIDS kits, STD medicines etc.). So the administrative departments like police, health, excise and taxation, vocational and other education etc should give special attention to and not neglect the "female-deficient regions" in the states.

This study concludes that indeed a market failure condition can be located in the marriage market based on the conditions of bounded rationality, complexity, opportunism and small numbers. It appears that the forces of economic reforms coupled with rising aspirations of people could be the reason behind failure of the market for girl child while the male issue market is yet going strong till time will impinge upon it too.

The study of Census 2001 data, especially of amenities covered in the house-listing establishes that there is a noticeable negative correlation between sex ratio and two progressive indicator variables the male and female workers whereas positive correlations are revealed with Child Sex Ratio, Male female Literacy, No Room, No Drain, No Bath, No Latrine, No Tel, No TV, No Asset and Smoky Fuel variables. This shows that the lack of amenities indicates backwardness and though currently the sex ratio is being affected positively, in the long run it will hurt the very existence of women. Imagine the daily drudgery[7] of women on account of lack of basic amenities in the country with there being no taps in 75.7 per cent of the rural households, no toilets in 78 per cent rural households and no bathrooms in 64 per cent houses. Nearly 40 per cent houses do not have any worthwhile asset, even a bicycle, and most women (rural 90%) sacrifice their health sitting before smoky stoves cooking food (using crop residue, cow dung, wood instead of LPG or kerosene oil). Further, there is significant positive correlation at northern states level (Punjab, Haryana, Chandigarh and Delhi, the worst four have been chosen for study) between sex ratio and of many backwardness drivers listed above like non-availability of electricity, non-availability of latrine, to non-availability of bathroom, drainage, no tap water, smoky fuel and some correlation to television, bank account, non-availability of any asset etc. Here again the progressive indicator variables like the 'Male and Female Literacy and Workers' have powerful adverse impact on sex ratio as also 'No room' has. All this shows that opportunism and market forces are dominating the decision to avoid female issue (or even eliminate it) in preference to male foetus.

On the other hand, regressional analysis shows that total sex ratio is positively affected by child sex ratio (0.635), Female Literacy (1.179 and +ve), Good House (0.836), No Room (0.309), No Electricity (0.475), No Latrine (0.770), No Drain (+0.867), No Asset (0.454) and Smoky Fuel (1.629). Male Worker, Female Worker, Male Literacy and No Tap seem to be not having predictable impact on the sex ratio.

And negative determinants being No Bath (–0.697), No TV (–1.614), No Bank (–0.405). This analysis also shows that the variables that could not make significant impact on urban sex ratio are No Tap, No Tel, Male Literacy and No Asset. Similarly to rural sex ratio insignificant contributors are Male Literacy, Male Workers, Female Workers, and No Bathroom. Rest all variables namely Female Literacy, Good House, No Electricity, No Laterine, No Asset and Smoky Fuels are positively affecting rural sex ratio while No Tap, No Room, No TV, No Bathroom are significantly having negative impact on rural sex ratio. Urban sex ratio is being positively affected by child sex ratio, Female Literacy, Fem Workforce, Good Houses, No Lat and No Drain. It is negatively impacted by No TV, No Bath Room and Male Workers.

There are significant differences noticed in respect of correlation with rural and urban sex ratios noticed for No Tap, No Lat, No Bathroom and tangibles like No TV, No Bank, No Assets. At the all India level, the differences are significant in correlation with respect to female workers (urban more negative), lack of latrines and bank accounts (urban more positive), No Drainage and No TV (rural more positive).

This analysis is intended to set the ball rolling amongst thinkers and researchers and a lot more can be done by state level analysis to reach policy decisions. The solution lies in raising status of women, making the presence of women felt, and actively contributing to raising their status in decision-making at community and family level. Youth, who are more open to such progressive ideas can be motivated and moulded to contribute to raising the status of women. Right from a very early age the boys should be made to do all the things the girls are “expected’ to do so that this fixed role images can be eliminated. Labelling of works as feminine and masculine should be biological, if at all. Society can also give more sanction to old parents living with daughters and daughters doing the last rites. This will restore the balance for the females and once they are as much welcome as men, then socially the sex ratio will come up on its own. So the NGOs and state should invest on girls’ education and provide amenities which will help raising their status like free bus passes for girl students, easy LPG connections, etc.

Epilogue

The central and state government as also the NGOs in particular and public in general have taken note of these developments seriously.

Campaigns have been started by centre as well as state to implement the Pre-Natal Diagnostics Act seriously. The religious and community leaders have been involved in a big way.

Over 250 religious leaders met then Human Resources Development Minister, Mr Murli Manohar Joshi, the then Health and Family Welfare Minister, Mr C.P. Thakur, then Minister of State for HRD, Sumitra Mahajan, Delhi Chief Minister, Mrs Shiela Dixit and Health Minister, Mr A.K. Walia on 26th June, 2001 in New Delhi and discussed ways of ending the practices of female foeticide. Akal Takhat has issued a Hukamnama that "any one indulging in the unhealthy practice of female foeticide would be excommunicated from Sikh religion." This clearly shows how serious our political as well as religious leaders are about this unhealthy practice of the society. The time has come to act before it is too late. On the other hand, there is the news that henceforth merely blood test of pregnant mother will be able to tell the sex of the forthcoming baby. This is a very serious threat to the female foetuses and should not be taken lightly.

Annexure I

Correlation Sex Ratio for Select North Indian States

Variable name	*Variable description*	*Corr. with*	*Total sex ratio*	*Rural Sex ratio*	*Urban sex ratio*
CHSEXR	Child Sex Ratio 0–6	Pearson Corr	–0.503	–0.409	–0.564
		Sig. (2–tailed)	0.000	0.006	0.000
FEMLIT	Female Literacy	Pearson Corr	–0.424	–0.241	–0.242
		Sig. (2–tailed)	0.003	0.115	0.105
MLIT	Male Literacy	Pearson Corr.	–0.407	–0.282	–0.301
		Sig. (2–tailed)	0.005	0.064	0.042
MALEW	Male Workers	Pearson Corr.	–0.687	–0.645	–0.645
		Sig. (2–tailed)	0.000	0.000	0.000
FEMW	Female Workers	Pearson Corr.	–0.455	0.332	0.393
		Sig. (2–tailed)	0.002	0.028	0.007
GH	Good Houses	Pearson Corr.	–0.113	0.171	0.266
		Sig. (2–tailed)	0.453	0.268	0.074
NR	No Room	Pearson Correl	–0.707	–0.802	–0.722
		Sig. (2–tailed)	0.000	0.000	0.000

Cont'd...

Cont'd...

NO TAP	No Tap	Pearson Corre	0.630	0.506	0.285
		Sig. (2–tailed)	0.000	0.000	0.055
NO ELEC	No Electricity	Pearson Corre	0.302	0.060	–0.026
		Sig. (2–tailed)	0.041	0.698	0.864
NO LAT	No Latrine	Pearson Corr	0.538	0.419	–0.068
		Sig. (2–tailed)	0.000	0.005	0.654
NO DRAIN	No Drain	Pearson Corr	0.503	0.135	0.094
		Sig. (2–tailed)	0.000	0.384	0.533
NO BATH	No Bath	Pearson Corr	0.192	0.027	–0.291
		Sig. (2–tailed)	0.200	0.862	0.049
NO TEL	No Tel	Pearson Cor	0.603	0.192	0.117
		Sig. (2–tailed)	0.000	0.211	0.437
NO TV	No TV	Pearson	0.310	0.083	–0.253
		Sig. (2–tailed)	0.036	0.591	0.090
NO BANK	No Bank	Pearson	0.101	–0.126	0.046
		Sig. (2–tailed)	0.506	0.414	0.761
NO ASSET	No Asset	Pearson Corr	0.151	0.102	–0.177
		Sig. (2–tailed)	0.318	0.509	0.240
Smoky Fuel	Smoky Fuel	Pearson Corr	0.721	0.685	0.581
		Sig. (2–tailed)	0.000	0.000	0.000

Notes

1. Census of India 2001.
2. Based on NFHS 1998–99, Haryana.
3. Census of India 2001, Amenities data: House-listing.

References

Dyson, Tim and Mick Moore. 1983. On Kinship Structure, Female Autonomy and Demographic Behaviour in India. *Population and Development Review*, 9(1): 35–60.

Gulati, S.K. 2002. Population Paper Two, Haryana: Rural and Urban, March, DCO Haryana, Sec 19 Chandigarh. www.gendwaar.gen.in/sex selection/sstm.htm

Gulati, S.K. 2003. Population Paper Three, Workers and Non-Workers of Haryana, May 2003 DCO Haryana, Sec 19 Chandigarh.

——. 2004. Analysis of Amenities of Haryana, August 2004 DCO Haryana, Sec 19 Chandigarh: 141.

Hari, M. 1991. Modernization, Status of Women and Fertility. *The Journal of Family Welfare*, 37(2), June, 62–7.

Malhi, Prahbhjot and Jagat Jerath. 1997. Is Son Preference Constraining Contraceptive Use in India? *Guru Nanak Journal of Sociology*, 18(2), October, 77–92.

Nanda, A.K. and Jacques Veron. 2005. "Child Sex Ratio Imbalance, Fertility Behaviour and Development in India: Recent Evidence from Haryana and Punjab" in Isabelle Attane and Jacques Veron (eds.), *Gender Discrimination among Young Children in Asia*. French Institute of Pondicherry, Centre for Population and Development.

Nayar, Usha. 1995. A Study into Causes of Son Preference. NCERT published, New Delhi.

Sharma, B.B.L. 1988. Value of Children Concept: A Framework. *Rural Health and Family Welfare Trust Bulletin*. Gandhigram Institute, Vol. 23, Nos. 1, 2 and 3.

Thiruvenkitasamy, S. 1992. Economic Motivation and Fertility Behaviour: A Comparison of Rural and Urban Areas in Tamil Nadu. *The Journal of Family Welfare*, 38(1), March, 68–79.

CHAPTER 6

Victims of Violence Against Women in Bangladesh

Some Consequences

A.K.M. Ahsan Ullah

The level of dehumanization against women has not declined in the contemporary so-called civil societies, even long after slavery was abolished in most of the world (ACD, 1999; Bradley, 1990; ALRC, 2004). Women's shackles are poor education, economic dependence, limited political participation and power, and limited or no access to fertility control, unfair social conventions and inequality in the eyes of law. Violence is a key instrument often used to keep these shackles on (Archavanitkul, 1990). There is abundance of literature generated on violence against women (VAW), however, literature on its health consequences still remains an undocumented issue.

Each year over 1.6 million people lose their lives to violence which is among the leading causes of death for people aged 15–44 years worldwide, accounting for 14 per cent of death among males and 7 per cent of deaths among females for every person who dies as a result of violence (Day, 1995; WHO, 2002) which encompasses, inter alia, psychological violence occurring in the family and in the general community, including battering, sexual abuse of women and children, dowry-related[1] violence, rape, female genital mutilation and other traditional practices, non-spousal violence and violence related to exploitation, sexual harassment and intimidation at work, in educational institutions and elsewhere, trafficking in women, and forced prostitution. Media often reveals (see Annex 4) how brutally the women folk fall victims to violence (Ellsberg, 1996; Islam, 2004: 119) that affect their autonomy, productivity, and capacity to care for themselves and children and subsequently their overall health status and quality of life. Female genital mutilation and other traditional practices detrimental to humanity have become another form brutal violence against women, mostly in African nations.

Over the past decade, the growing body of research on violence against women has brought the issue from a position of near invisibility to prominence on the social scene (Klein and Chao, 1995). Contemporary researchers in Bangladesh have studied the prevalence of physical, sexual and mental abuse, associations between violence and physical and mental health, characteristics associated with the risk of experiencing violence, particularly spousal violence, and women's attitudes towards spousal violence and coping strategies (Rahman, 2002; Rahman, 2004: Rashid, 2003).

This research however tries to explore the health consequences of violence perpetrated upon three categories of victims namely: rape victims; assault and acid victims. 33 rape victims; 21 assaulted (physically) and 23 acid victims were studied during their treatment in different hospitals across Bangladesh. Doctors treating those victims were interviewed to know the aftermath health result of the violence they were sustaining. The hospitals the study covered include: Barisal Sher-e-Bangla Medical College; Dhaka Medical College and Hospital, Acid Survivors Foundation, Bangladesh; Mymensingh Medical College; Rajshahi Medical College; and Ad Deen Hospital, Dhaka. The research team rushed to those hospitals once media reported of such violence.

Forms of Violence in Bangladesh

Behaviour against women may take a number of forms such as physical violence which includes all aggressive behaviour inflicted on the body of victim by an aggressor such as pushing, pinching, grabbing and pulling by the hair, chucking, burning, stabbing, throwing acid or boiling water, and shooting (Walker, 1993; Watts, 1995). Sexual violence includes physical attacks on victim's erogenous organs, e.g. breast and genitals of forced sexual activity accompanied by physical violence (Parker, McFarlen and Soeken, 1994). Psychological violence is committed by using verbal threats of violence against the victim or a person dear to her, forcing the victim to degrade herself: excessive controlling, curtailing and/or disruption of routine activities such as pattern of sleeping or eating, social relationship, access to money and verbal insult (Plichta and Abraham, 2004; Parker, McFarlen and Soeken, 1994).

Some other forms of violence include: self-directed violence that refers to violence in which the perpetrator and the victim are the same individual. Interpersonal violence refers to violence between individuals.

The former category includes child maltreatment; intimate partner violence; and elder abuse, while the latter is broken down into acquaintance and stranger violence and includes youth violence; assault by strangers; violence related to property disputes; and violence in workplaces and other institutions. Collective violence refers to violence committed by larger groups of individuals. Violence committed by family members within the family is the most serious and repugnant of all types of violence. Their mother-in-law, father, physically or mentally tortures them in law and sister-in-law or brother-in-law for dowry (*Daily Star*, 2004). The homicide rate has peaked in the early 1930s, 1980, and 1991 worldwide. The lowest rates of homicide were observed in the late 1950s. At present, the homicide rate in the US is in a period of decline (Fingerhurt, 1998).

In addition to the above, trafficking in human has become another form of violence, primary victims of which are women and children. Women are abducted and lured by traffickers through threats, physical force, illegal confinement and debt bondage. Over the past decade, more than 500,000 Bangladeshi women and children have been trafficked into prostitution across country borders. The huge profit reaped by the perpetrators, increasingly linked to organized crimes has turned this trade into a rapidly growing menace in the South and Southeast Asian region. It is extremely difficult to assess the actual number of humans trafficked in from Bangladesh.

Voilence Against Women arises from a combination of individual, biological and psychological characteristics as well as social, economic and political factors (Rodgers, 1994; Schei, 1989). More than 70 per cent of women in some regions of Bangladesh suffer from domestic abuse. One study shows that in 750 cases of family violence in Bangladesh, male relatives account for all but 29 cases of violence. Nearly 50 per cent of all murders of females in Bangladesh can be attributed to domestic violence. There were 239 reports of dowry-related violence in 1998, an increase of 25 per cent from the year before. Because of the vast number of under/unreported incidents, this number is significantly higher. Physical and verbal abuse of wives due to non-fulfillment of dowry occurs in at least 50 per cent of recent marriages (*Daily Star*, 2004). In the year 2000, the total number of rape was 571 as reported in the daily news. Of these, 302 cases involved the rape of minor girls and 276 cases involved women above 18 years of age. In several incidents of rape there was more than one woman who was assaulted, thus for 1,519 incidents the number of people assaulted were 1,543 (Naripokkho and Bangladesh Mahila Parishad, 2005).

Table 1

Different Forms of Violence by Year

Types of violence	*Year*										
	1990	*1991*	*1992*	*1993*	*1994*	*1995*	*1996*	*1997*	*1998*	*1999*	*2000*
Dowry Induced	82	79	101	134	122	267	594	747	832	1119	8585
Physical Torture	258	300	217	350	469	808	1664	2029	1431	1654	—
Acid Attack	21	20	29	39	19	51	83	117	120	117	327
Rape	407	982	749	526	285	651	1415	2224	3011	3382	8527
Murder	1904	1500	1879	2269	806	1787	1839	2426	3290	2385	6288

Source: DWA, 1997, 1998, 1999, 2000, 2001.

Consequences of VAW

Gender violence represents traditional attitudes by which women are regarded as subordinate to men or as having stereotyped roles perpetuate widespread practices involving violence or coercion. Level of consequence depends on the form of violence. Physical injury, pregnancy, disability and death are most common health consequences. Trauma, depression, anxiety, isolation and disturbed conjugal life are the most common psychological effects of all kinds of violence.

Table 2

Acid Attack Statistics (January–September 2007)

Months	*Number of accidents*	*Number of survivors*
January	8	11
February	10	10
March	15	16
April	14	14
May	18	22
June	15	17
July	12	17
August	5	8
September	17	19
Total	114	134

Source: ASF, 2007.

Acid Violence

Acid throwing, one of the deadliest and heinous violence is rocking the conscience of the civil society. It has today emerged as a vicious and damaging form of violence in Bangladesh where acid is thrown in people's faces. The overwhelming majority of the victims are women, and many of them are below 18 years of age. Acid violence is used as measure of personal vengeance, family feud and between couples and feuds between two families and kinship (ASF, 2001). The young and teenaged girls fall victim of acid burn because of refusal to marriage and rejection of love proposal given by a young man.

> ... Just after midnight on April 16, 2000, 13-year-old Jannatul Ferdous awoke from her sleep with the sensation that an extra linen sheet was being pulled over her body. Seconds later, excruciating pain enveloped her chest and face. A sudden pain jolted the back of her brother, who was sleeping beside her in the small bed. A cup of battery acid thrown through the window engulfed the young girl and her brother as they lay sleeping. The perpetrator was a young man in his twenties, angry that Jannatul had refused his wedding proposal. Jannatul's family had heard about acid attacks on women, but it was not until after daybreak that her parents realized the severity of the situation and took her to a nearby medical clinic in the rural Lakshmipur region of Bangladesh, several hundred kilometres north of downtown Dhaka. The next day she was treated at the Dhaka Medical College Hospital, having spent hours in the waiting room despite her third-degree burns.... (Swanson, 2002)

Sulfuric acid, cheap and easily accessible has emerged as a weapon used to disfigure and sometimes kill women and girls. Taking revenge on the opponent using acid does no longer spare the children. Therefore, number of child victims of acid violence is on an increase. With the most common reasons for attack being the refusal of marriage, the denial of sex, and the rejection of romance (Swanson, 2002). Documentation from Acid Survivors Foundation (ASF) reveals that young women are more commonly the targets of acid attacks. Out of total 252 women assaulted with acid, from 1995 to 1998, 134 (53%) were below 20 years of age, 8 (3%) were minor girls below 10 years of age. In comparison to other forms of violence against women (such as murders) more of such cases, 52 per cent incidents were filed, another study revealed (Naripokkho and Bangladesh Mahila Parishad, 2005).

Table 3

Acid Attack Statistics (1999–2006)

Period	*Number of accidents*	*Number of survivors*
1999	115	138
2000	172	232
2001	250	347
2002	366	489
2003	335	411
2004	266	325
2005	214	270
2006	180	221
Total	1898	2434

Source: ASF, 2007.

Male ego and problems in dealing with rejection is another important cause of acid throwing. In some cases, it is because a young girl or women has spurned the sexual advances of a male or either she or her parents have rejected a proposal of marriage. Recently, however, there have been acid attacks on children, older women and also men.

Acid attacks leave victims horribly disfigured. There were over 200 reports of acid mutilations in Bangladesh in 1998 alone; however, the actual number of cases is much higher. The consequence of acid attacks on survivors brings dramatic changes in their lifestyles. Most of them have to give up their education or work. Social isolation, fear of further attacks, and insecurity damage their self-esteem and confidence (ASF, 2001; 2007). After marriage when dowry demands are not met, brides may become victims of acid throwing. Other causes of acid throwing include family dispute, protest of husband's second marriage, failure to misappropriate wife's wealth, sterility, and getting divorce from wife, refusal of sexual relationship, failure to kidnap, the woman not being agreeable to prostitution and the woman's refusal to agree with husband's second marriage.

Table 4

The Aftermath of Acid Violence on the Victim

Consequences	*f*	%
Face disfigured	23	100
Eyesight lost/blinded	11	48
Serious and permanent scar on other parts of the body	23	100

Source: Survey data, 2004.

Although laws have been made against such cruelty, in most instances, the offenders go unpunished. According to the report of Ain O Salish Kendra,[2] 262 incidents of acid-throwing have been recorded between January and December 2002 of whom only 63 have been litigated (Rashid, 2003; Ullah, 2004).

Figure 1

Showing the Number of Perpetrators Convicted

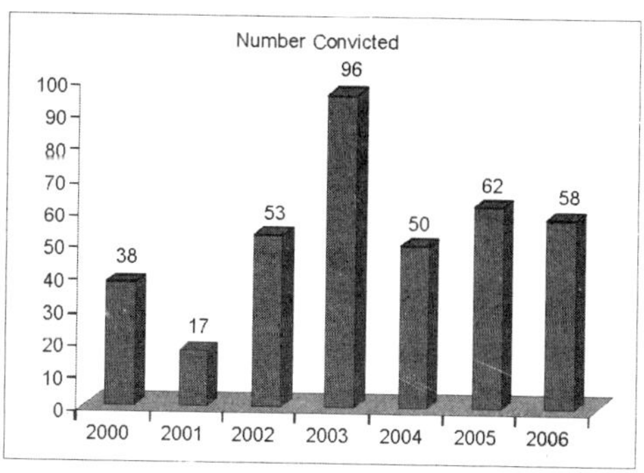

The *Daily Star*[3] reported that participants at an opinion exchange programme on 'social initiatives to prevent this violence' hold the view that crime like acid violence continued to take place regardless of enactment of a new Women Repression Prevention Law. The participants identified lack of proper implementation of the law and negligence by the law-enforcing agencies as the main cause of such crime. Nevertheless, some triumphs have occurred in the past several years. Since 1998, 25 perpetrators of acid violence have been offered punishment among 750 reported assault cases (ASF, 2007). A verdict was given based on the extent of burning that is caused by the assault which is usually a life sentence or death penalty. In another case, nine among 25 attackers found guilty were awarded death penalty. In each case, the victim was either partially or fully blinded. The verdict on acid violence to population at large has been a good signal though it sounds cruel (Swanson, 2002).

Physical Assault

Researches confirm that most women who die of homicide are killed by their partner or ex-partner. In a conservative and predominantly poverty-prone society like Bangladesh, dowry might breed more violence when parents fail to fulfill dowry demands. Violence that begins with threats may end in forced "suicide", death from injuries, or homicide. Many assault incidents result in injuries, ranging from bruises and fractures to chronic disabilities.

Studies further showed that violence during pregnancy as a risk to the health of both mothers and their unborn foetuses. Research in this area has shown increased levels of a variety of conditions (Parker et al, 1994). Intimate partners, employers, mother-in-laws and sister-in-laws are the primary perpetrators. Violence knows no boundaries. For example, in Papua New Guinea, 18 per cent of all urban married women sought hospital treatment following domestic violence (Bradley, 1990). Another study found that 50 per cent of all women in Cambodia reporting abuse had sustained injuries (Nelson, 1996). Canada's national survey on violence against women revealed that 45 per cent of wife assault incidents resulted in injuries, and of the injured women, 40 per cent subsequently visited a doctor or a nurse (Rodgers, 1994). Data show that majority of the assault victims are in the age group of 20–30 years (Table 5).

Table 5

The Aftermath of Assault Violence on the Women

Consequences	*f*	%
Abortion	2	24
Permanent injury	19	90
Lost eyesight/blinded	12	57
Other complications/crippled	15	71

Source: Survey data, 2004.

Rape Violence

Although most institutional records show that younger women are more susceptible to rape, a detailed look at institutional case records reveal that the age of women is not recorded in most court dockets. Different studies have explained consequences of rape in various ways. Akanda and Shamim (1985) have classified the consequences of rape into three categories: Murder, severe injuries and long-term mental trauma (Islam, 2004). Rape impacts also on victim's health such as pelvic inflammatory disease, chronic pelvic pain, asthma, irritable bowel syndrome, partial or permanent disability, delayed physical effects like arthritis, hypertension and heart disease, unwanted pregnancy, pregnancy complications, or premature labour, miscarriage, maternal mortality from excessive bleeding, and HIV infections are vital (BPFA, 2002; Islam, 2004: 129).

In 2002, 1412 women in Bangladesh have been victimized of whom 149 have been killed after rape (Rashid, 2003). These deaths are dramatic testimony to the paucity of options for women to escape from violent relationships (Stark, 1991; CDC, 1997; Ullah, 2004). In 2001, according to BNWLA[4] and Naripokkho[5] as many as 605 rape incidents were documented (Islam, 2004). Even many known cases are not reported in the press or cases are not filed in police station because of the social stigma attached to it. Misery of the victims does not end here as it extends to social condemnation and isolation.

Suicide because of occurrence of rape among young girls is very common. Apart from suicide, other serious health consequences in case of rape victims are the following: being affected by STDs, pregnancy, abortion, permanent damage to the reproductive tracts and other organs, child birth and forced motherhood. An overwhelming majority of the rape victims were in the age group between 5 and 15 years.

Fifteen of them were gang raped. During the interview, doctors were not sure yet about the consequence of the seven victims.

> ... Rahela, a working class teenage girl who was gang raped led by a former colleague. Her throat was slit and her body was mutilated. Before her painful death she could name the devils to her mother. A case is on trial in court and the first hearing was on October 29, 2007. A leading human rights organization "Ain O Salish Kendra" is fighting for justice for Rahela and is leading the court battle. The accused are hiding from the law...

Table 6

The Aftermath of Rape Violence on the Women

Consequence	*f*	%
Gang raped	5	15
Genitals injury	17	51
Genitals infections	9	27
Mental disorder	14	42
Lost fertility and reproductive capacity	26	79
Survived with serious mental disorder	7	21
Doctors were not yet sure about the consequence	7	21

Source: Survey data, 2004.

The level of brutality against women within this sub-continent is almost identical. In India, 20 per cent of all pregnancies of adolescent abortion-seekers occurred because of forced sex, 10 per cent from rape by a male domestic servant, 6 per cent from incest, and 4 per cent from other rapes (Divekar, 1979). Violent sexual assault may also increase their risks because resulting tears to delicate vaginal tissue allow the virus easier entry into the bloodstream (Koss, 1991). For women who are beaten or sexually assaulted, the emotional and physical strain might lead to depression (Stark, 1991; CDC, 1997; Marocco et al, 2000). As with unwanted pregnancy, women are vulnerable to contracting sexually transmitted diseases (STDs) because they are unable to negotiate protection (Archavanitkul, 1990). Women with STDs have a higher risk of complications during pregnancy, including sepsis, spontaneous abortion and premature birth.

Constitutional Protections of Gender Violence

The constitution of Bangladesh contains the provision of gender equality, prohibition of gender-based discrimination and extension of opportunity of women in all spheres of civic life. The preamble of the constitution clearly states that a society in which the rule of law, fundamental human rights and freedom, equality and justice, political, economic and social will be secured for all citizens. It further states that the local government institutions be composed of representatives of peasants, workers and women (Article 9); steps will be taken to ensure participation of women in all spheres of national life (Article 10); ... all citizens shall be paid for their work on the basis of principle "from each according to his abilities to each according to his work" [20(1)].

Rights of women are included in "Fundamental Principles of State Policy" which guide the legislators while making laws. Further, in the "Fundamental Rights" of the constitution the article 27 provides that all citizens are equal before law and are entitled to equal protection and article 29 clause (1) provides equality of opportunity for all citizens in respect of employment or office in the service of the republic, the clause (2) of the same article states no discrimination will be done on grounds of religion race, caste, sex or place of birth for any employment in the republic. The Government of Bangladesh has made strides in harmonizing national legislation with international commitments to protecting women's rights and eliminating violence against women. For example, articles 27 and 28 of the constitution specifically guarantee women's equal rights before the law. Other acts to protect women's rights include: The Dowry Prohibition Act (1980; 1986), The Prevention of Women and Child Repression Act (2000), The Cruelty to Women Ordinance (1983). Furthermore, Bangladesh has ratified the Convention on the Elimination of All Forms of Discrimination against Women (1979), which calls for the protection of women from gender-based abuse. The government is committed to eliminating violence against women by 2015 in Bangladesh, as stated by the Minister of Health and Family Welfare and as detailed in target 6 of Millennium Development Goal to improve maternal health (Bangladesh Constitution, 2001).

Discussions and Conclusions

The Government of Bangladesh along with some NGOs have launched a number of initiatives for the advancement of women following the declaration[6] of UN Decade of Women (1976–1985). Over the last two decades, women in Bangladesh have gradually become more visible in the labour force, in development programmes and local institutions such as local government bodies. The Bangladesh Constitution and the general laws of the country entitle women to equal rights and status equal to those of men in public life, however, non-discrimination in the private sphere is not guaranteed. Limited access to economic opportunities, education, health services and in decision-making perpetuate women's subordination to men and susceptibility to violence.

Since the Beijing Platform for Action (1995), the Government of Bangladesh has also identified violence against women as a priority issue. Given this recognition, incidences of violence against women today receive greater attention than they did a decade ago. There are different socio-economic, political, cultural and religious components which have contributed to the increased vulnerability of women to violence. In Bangladesh, an important mechanism of male dominance is the propagation of gender ideology through sanctions of religious texts and their gender-selective interpretation by the community leaders.

A common myth both within Bangladesh and beyond holds acid violence to be permanently and historically ingrained in Bangladeshi society. Such a perspective is clearly inconsistent with historical evidence. Acid violence was first identified as a problem in the region of Bangladesh in the 1960s. Although acid attacks may have occurred prior to this time, political turnover and a lack of documentation preclude conclusive evidence. However, often rape and assault violence is evidence in the history clearly dates back in Mughal and British period during the fifteenth century.

Some argue that there is a rising trend of all forms of violence but until more reliable longitudinal data is available, one cannot confidently conclude that, in general, violence against women is increasing. In the backdrop of psychological and emotional maladjustment, the victim can be habituated in smoking, drug, unprotected sex with multiple patterns, prostitution and alcohol or drug abuse, humiliation, guilt, shame, embarrassment, self-blame, anger and helplessness. Sometime, these situations push the victim towards depression. The repercussions of violence against women reverberate throughout the family and community. Theoretically, the state treats man and women equally. Bangladeshi legal system has done little to diminish women's vulnerability to violence. However, the state's concern to preserve the existing patriarchal social order is clear from the ways law operate in respect to violence against women.

Notes

1. Dowry is the payment of a settlement for the family of the bride to the groom. This practice has grown in recent past despite the fact that it is not part of the Muslim marriage contract. Traditionally, Muslims voluntarily give gifts to their daughters during her wedding and there is also scope for their daughters inheriting property, albeit less than what their brothers can inherit. These days, it has become an economic compulsion to give dowry to the prospective groom, otherwise it is difficult for parents to get their daughters married. Normally, the groom's family or the groom himself asks for prior commitments before marriage.
2. Ain O Salish Kendra (ASK) is a legal aid and human rights resource centre. It provides free legal aid to the poor women, workers and child workers. ASK's legal activism has led to public campaigns and advocacy in defense of individual and group rights within a framework of democracy. Besides providing free legal aid, ASK seeks to create awareness of legal and human rights so as to empower citizens to negotiate their rights.
3. Dhaka based English Daily, 14 January 2001.
4. BNWLA (Bangladesh National Women Lawyers Association): This organization has a resource centre enriched with information on trafficking in persons, violence against women and children and many other issues.
5. A Dhaka-based women's right organization. Their area of work is trafficking in persons, violence against women and children.
6. The declaration on the elimination of violence against women, adopted by the United Nations General Assembly in 1993 defines violence against women as "Any act of gender based violence that result in or is likely to result in physical, sexual or psychological harm or suffering to women, inclouding threat of such acts, coercion or arbitrary deprivation of liberty, whether occurring in public or private life. Article-2 of the declaration states violence against women shall be understood to encompass, but not be limited to the following: (i) Physical, sexual and psychological violence occurring in the family, including battering, sexual abuse of female children in the household, dowry-related violence, marital rape, female genital mutilation and other traditional practices harmful to women, non-spousal violence and violence related to exploitation; (ii) Physical, sexual and psychological violence occurring within the general community, including rape, sexual harassment and intimidation at work, in educational institutions and elsewhere, trafficking in women and forced prostitution and (iii) Physical, sexual and psychological violence perpetrated or condoned by the state, wherever it occurs.

References

ACD (Association for Community Development). 2002. A Research on Rape and Burden of Proof. Bangladesh National Women Lawyers Association (BNWLA), Dhaka.

Akanda, Latifa and Israt Shamim. 1985. Women and Violence: A Comparative Study of Rural and Urban Violence against Women in Bangladesh. Women for Women, Dhaka.

ALRC. 2004. Statement on 'Violence against Dalit Women in India and Nepal', received by Commission on Human Rights. Retrieved from Asian Legal Resource Centre (ALRC), Hong Kong website http://www.alrc.net/mainfile.php/60written/

Archavanitkul, K. and A. Pramualratana. 1990. "Factors affecting Women's Health in Thailand". Paper presented at the Workshop on Women's Health in Southeast Asia, Population Council, Jakarta, 29–31October.

ASF (Acid Survivors Foundation). 2001. Acid Throwing Fact Sheet. Dhaka, Bangladesh.

——. 2007. Acid Throwing Fact Sheet. Dhaka, Bangladesh.

Bangladesh Constitution. 2001. Government of the Peoples' Republic of Bangladesh. Bangladesh.

Bradley, C. 1990. Why male violence against women is a development issue? Reflections from Papua New Guinea. Occasional Paper, United Nations Fund for Women (UNIFEM), New York.

Carillo, R. 1992. Battered Dreams: Violence against Women as an Obstacle to Development. United Nations Fund for Women (UNIFEM), New York.

CDC (Centres for Disease Control). 1997. Rates of Homicide, Suicide and Firearm-related Death among Children. MMWR 46(5): 101–5.

Daily Star The. (11 November 2004). Elimination of Violence against Women.

——. (14 January 2001). Gender Gap Cause of Acid Throwing. Electronic Source. http://www.dailystarnews.com/200101/14/n1011410.htm. Accessed 13 December 2001.

Day, T. 1995. The Health Related Costs of Violence against Women in Canada: The Tip of the Iceberg. Centre of Research on Violence against Women and Children, London, Ontario.

Divekar, S.A. et al. 1979. Abortion in Unmarried Girls. *Health and Population Perspectives and Issues*, 2(4): 308–21.

DWA (Department of Women's Affairs). 1990–2001. Dhaka Government of Bangladesh.

Ellsberg, M. et al. 1996. Domestic Violence and Emotional Distress among Nicaraguan Women: Results from a Population-based study. *American Psychologist*.

Fingerhut, L.A., C.S. Cox and M. Warner. 1998. International Comparative Analysis of Injury Mortality. *Advance Data from Vital and Health Statistics*, No. 303. Hyattsville, MD, NCHS. http://www.who.int/media centre/factsheets/fs239/en/, http://www.who.int/violenceprevention/approach/definition/en/index.html

Huq, Nasreen. 2004. Naripokkho: With Victims and Other Leadership Personnel of Naripokkho. *Personal Interview*, 14 June, 2001, Dhaka, Bangladesh.

IRIN.2004.retrievedfrom: http://www.irinnews.org/report.asp?ReportID=45340&SelectRegion=Central_Asi

Islam, Md. Rabiul. 2004. Recent Trends and Consequences of Rape in Bangladesh: A Study on Violence against Women, Girls and Adolescent. Rajshahi University, *Social Science Journal*, Vol. 9, 119–34.

Klein, H. and B. Chao. 1995. Sexual Abuse during Childhood and Adolescence as Predictors of HIV-related Sexual Risk during Adulthood among Female Sexual Partners of Injection Drug Users. *Violence against Women*, 1(1): 55–76.

Koss, M., P. Koss and J. Woodruff. 1991. Deleterious Effects of Criminal Victimization on Women's Health and Medical Utilization. *Archives of Internal Medicine*, 151: 342–7.

Moracco, K.E., Runyan, C.W. et al. 2000. Killed on the Clock: A Population-based Study of Workplace Homicide, 1977–1991. *American Journal of Industrial Medicine*, 37: 629–36.

Naripokkho and Bangladesh Mahila Parishad. 2005. Facilitating the Fulfillment of State Obligations towards Women's Equality. Baseline Report Violence against Women in Bangladesh. International Women's Rights Action Watch Asia Pacific (IWRAW Asia Pacific) Kuala Lumpur, Malaysia.

Nelson, E. and C. Zimmerman. 1996. Household Survey on Domestic Violence in Cambodia. Ministry of Women's Affairs, Project against Domestic Violence. Cambodia.

Parker, B., J. McFarlane and K. Soeken. 1994. Abuse during Pregnancy: Effects on Maternal Complications and Birth Weight in Adult and Teenage Women. *Obstetrics and Gynecology*, 84(3): 323–38.

Plichta, S.B. and C. Abraham. 1996. Violence and Gynaecological Health in Women <50 Years Old. *American Journal of Obstetrics and Gynaecology*, 174: 903-7.

Rahman, A.B.M. Bazlur. 2004. Violence against Women. *The Daily Prothom Alo*, January, 10: 13.

Rahman, Saheen. 2002. Women Violence: Concept, Types and Protection (in Bangla) Unnayan Padakkhep. Vol. 25, January-March.

Rahman, Saira. 2004. Reflections on Women and Violence in Bangladesh. Internet: www.hurights. or Jp/asia-pacific/no_24/05 saira.htm-13k–6 Nov.

Rashid, Harun et al. (eds.). 2003. Violence against Women in Bangladesh: Causes and Remedies. Professor's BCS General English, Professor Prokashon, Dhaka, 314–8.

Rodgers, K. 1994. Wife Assault: The Findings of a National Survey. *Juristat Service Bulletin*, Statistics Canada, 14(9).

Schei, B. and L. Bakketeig. 1989. Gynecological Impact of Sexual and Physical Abuse by Spouse: Study of a Random Sample of Norwegian Women. *British Journal of Obstetrics and Gynaecology,* 96: 1379–83.

Stark, E. and A. Flitcraft. 1991. "Spouse Abuse" in M. Rosenburg and M. Fenley (eds.), *Violence in America: A Public Health Approach*. Oxford University Press, New York.

Swanson, Jordan. 2002. Acid Attacks: Bangladesh's Efforts to Stop the Violence. *Harvard Health Policy Review Archives*, Spring, Vol. 3, No. 1.

Ullah, A.K.M. Ahsan. 2004. Empowerment of Women in Bangladesh: Does it Help Make Reproductive Decision. *Asia-Pacific Journal of Rural Development (APJORD)*, Vol. XIV(1), July, Singapore/Dhaka.

Walker, E.A. et al. 1993. Histories of Sexual Victimization in Patients with Irritable Bowel Syndrome or Inflammatory Bowel Disease. *American Journal of Psychiatry,* 150: 1502–6.

Watts, C., S. Osam and E. Win. 1995. The Private is Public: A Study of Violence against Women in Southern Africa. Women in Law and Development in Africa, Zimbabwe.

WHO (The World Health Organization). 2004. *World Report on Violence and Health*. 3 October.

Zierler, S. et al. 1991. Adult Survivors of Childhood Sexual Abuse and Subsequent Risk of HIV Infection. *American Journal of Public Health*, 81(5): 572–5.

Appendix

Annexure 1

Trend in Acid Attack in Bangladesh

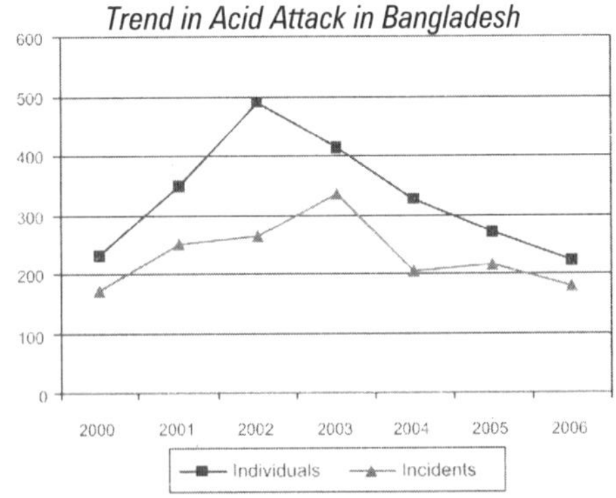

Section II

Fertility and Family Planning

CHAPTER 7

Salafism and Overpopulation

A Challenge for Indonesia[1]

Burhan Ali

Following World War II and continuing today, countries with a majority of Muslim citizens are, generally speaking, characterized by high birth rates (*The Oxford Encyclopaedia of the Modern Islamic World*, 1995). There are reliable data that "the population growth rate in Muslim countries is among the highest in the world. The crude birth rate of the forty-six Muslims countries is 1 per cent higher than that of the developing world as a whole. In the mid-1980s even countries that adopted family planning programmes in the early 1960s had very high natural increase rates of the population. For example, Pakistan's rate of increase was 2.8 per cent, Egypt's rate was 2.6 per cent, while the rate of increase in non-Muslim countries such as India and Colombia was 2.3 per cent and 2.1 per cent" (Ammar, 2000).

Some countries like Indonesia and Iran, however, show the decreasing phenomena. Indonesia, a country with the largest Muslim population in the world, is approaching replacement level (Jones, 2005). This is because of the success of government's family planning programme by New Order regime, supported primarily by two agencies, BKKBN (The National Board on Family Planning Coordination) and religious leaders. The successful story of New Order's family planning programme, we can say, remains influential in practice until today. In general, Indonesian population has been growing relatively slow for decades (BPS, 2003).

But the wind perhaps will change together with some reports showing that there is a decreasing trend of participation in family planning programmes (*Kompas*, 21 May 2006), the change of policy structure of the BKKBN from central government to local autonomy, reduced number of family planning officials (*Kompas*, 01 July 2006), and an increase of Islamist movements within various levels of

Indonesian society after the fall of Soeharto in 1998. The conservative characteristics of those Islamic groups raise worries of a future return to high levels of fertility in Indonesia, perceived as a universal trait of Muslim countries, as shown in the first paragraph. Some provinces (Yogyakarta, Riau, and South Sulawesi) with high prevalence of Islamist Muslims are reported to increase their rate of population growth although the change is relatively small (Ananta, 2003). Even though there are many causes of a population growth rate, migration for example, the fact that the regions in question have many Islamists who generally support large families must be examined carefully.

Considering this phenomena, this research tries to explore population issues within a particularly small (but growing) group in Yogyakarta called Jamaah Salafi. As declared by its followers, the group is not an organization but only a "*jamaah*", a group of people who share the same concern regarding religion (Islam). It has approximately three hundred followers in Yogyakarta.

The data collection was conducted through interviews with teachers and followers of the Jamaah and participatory observation in some *pengajians* (religious learning sessions), mosques, *pesantrens* (Islamic boarding schools),[2] and their neighbourhood. In addition, a literature study on Salafi books, magazines, and websites was done to complete data collection and analysis. While I am aware of the objection of Chamie (1981) to the error of generalizing from the official doctrines and theology of a religion to the fertility behaviour of its members (Jones and Karim, 2005) and recognize that some scholars (Omran, 1992; Jones, 2005; Karim, 1997) have challenged the idea of a monolithic, unchanged (perhaps 'immutable') Muslim fertility (Jones and Karim, 2005), this study finds, on the contrary, the fact that some Islamic teachings, at least as interpreted and practised at the behavioural level of the Jamaah, do support large families and continue to be influential in producing the larger family and *ummah* (Islamic community).

The paper is divided into five parts: introduction (including methodology), the profile of the Jamaah, the teaching and behaviour of the Jamaah, analysis and implications, and finally I try to draw three challenges related to the position of Salafis in terms of population issues that are faced by Indonesian government in the future. Therefore, in many parts this study tries to compare and tie Jamaah Salafi with other Salafi groups, which I think are very diverse in means (*uslub*) but have a commonality on reproductive ethics, which is pro-natalist. I had planned to interview female members of Jamaah but unfortunately, the strict rules of Jamaah regulating relations between men and women (the concept of *muhrim* and dignity) forced me to limit my interviews to male members of the Jamaah.

The Profile of Jamaah Salafi

General Characteristics of Salafism

Salafism is a term used to describe an international movement that seeks to return to what is understood by its adherents as the purest form of Islam, that practiced by the Prophet Muhammad and *Salafus Shalih* (the pious classical people).[3] To support the view that the further away from the time of the Prophet, the more impure Islam became, they cite *hadith* (tradition of the Prophet): "the best of you are those with me, and the group that comes after, and the group that comes after them"; and "there is not a year or a day when the one that follows is not worse than the one before it" (ICG, 2004: 1). They also consider themselves as *Ahl-al Sunnah Wa al-Jamaah* or group that is mentioned in one of the traditions of the Prophet Muhammad that Muslims in the future will split into 73 groups, all of them go to hell, except one, *ahl al-sunnah wa al-jamaah* (people who follow Muhammad and his teachings). In practical terms, this means rejection of unwarranted innovations (*bid'ah*) of doctrine and practice that Muslims brought to the religion in later years.

Salafi ideas can be traced back historically to the teachings of Ibn Taymiyah (14th CE) and the movement of Muhammad Bin Abdul Wahhab (18th CE) in Saudi Arabia. Though Salafism is actually a broader term than Wahhabism (Fadl, 2003: 197) and tries to reject the four traditional Sunni schools (Syafi'i, Hanafi, Maliki, Hanbali), Salafi is very close to Wahhabi—a term used by outsiders to call Muhammad Bin Abdul Wahhab followers—which refer to Hanbali in terms of law (*hukm*). Hanbali is the strictest among the four Sunni schools, and adhered strictly to the Qur'an and Sunnah/*Hadith* (tradition of the Prophet Muhammad).[4] Imam Ahmad bin Hanbal al-Syaibani (786–855 CE), the founder of Hanbali, was one of the compilers of *hadith* and allowed only limited usage of *ijma* (consensus of juristic opinion) and *qiyas* (analogy). He preferred a weak *hadith* to a strong *qiyas* (Jones and Karim, 2005: 43). Recent Salafis, however, reject the adherence towards the four schools and prefer to refer directly to the Qur'an,

Tradition, or through *Ahl al-Hadith* (People of the Tradition). Among Salafis, referring to books written by Islamic scholars from other schools is only allowed after the books have been purified (*tashhih*) by Salafi scholars.

On another level, being Salafi means following a rigid dress code, with short pantaloons for men and long veil (*jilbab*) covering the whole body for women. Men need to let their beards grow long and cut their mustache like the Prophet did. Salafi rejects theology, philosophy, sufism, and some inventions and developments that strict Qur'anic interpretation seems to ban, such as photography, most forms of music, conventional banking, and elections. Certain technologies, like television, radio, and the internet, are considered acceptable by some Salafi scholars if they are used to propagate Salafi teachings. Salafis are not tied with any formal organization, because they view that to some extent organization can become a violation of *tauhid* (oneness) of Allah. Salafis have organizational management but prefer to call themselves only a *jamaah* (group) bound by similarity of intention and actions, i.e., to worship God and to find religious knowledge. Salafis do not recognize any form of leadership or hierarchy other than the commander of the faithful (*amir ul-mukminin*). They reject democracy, including elections, and consider nationalism as a *thaghut* (idol) (ICG, 2004).

The main sites for spreading Salafi teachings are *pesantren*, mosques, and university campuses (ICG, 2004: 10). Salafi teachings have also been disseminated through magazines and books published by the salafi community, including translations of the writings of the great Saudi salafi scholars. But the focus on publishing is also indicative of the highly literate community that forms the basis of the Salafi constituency in Indonesia: these magazines are not produced for visual appeal or designed for the rural poor. The target audience appears to be very much an educated middle class (ICG, 2004:12).

Indonesian Salafis tend to desire to study at one of four major universities: the Islamic University of Imam Muhammad Ibn Saud in Riyadh; the Islamic University of Medina; the Ummul Qura University in Mecca; and Punjab University in Lahore (ICG, 2004: 3). The names of seven or eight salafi scholars in Saudi Arabia are particularly golden in salafi circles. They include, among others, the late Abdullah Bin Baz, Muhammad Nashiruddin Al-Albani, and Muhammad Bin Shalih al-Utsaimin, as well as several men who are still actively teaching: Rabi' Bin Hadi al-Mudkhali, Muhammad Bin Hadi, Shalih Bin Fauzan al-Fauzan, and one scholar based in Yemen, Muqbil Bin Hadi Al-Wad'i (Usamah, 2005).

There is diversity in Salafi groups, however, in today's movement. According to Tariq Ramadhan, there are at least three major distinct flavours: Salafi Literalism, Salafi Reformism and Political Literalist (Ramadan, 2005). Salafism. *Literalist Salafi* rejects any mediation to the text of Qur'an and Sunnah. They ban interpretation and permissive usage of text. They refuse any kind of involvement in a space that is considered non-Islamic, and this includes, perforce, Muslims whom they put into a list of deviants. *Salafi Reformists* claim theological lineage with the salaf and tend to bypass the traditional schools. Different from literalists, these Salafis employ reasoning (*'aql*) to deal with social issues. They refer mostly to Hasan Al-Banna and Muhammad Abduh. In Indonesia, PKS (Justice and Prosperous Party) is the best example of a Salafi reformist organization. Political literalist Salafists, finally, share many characteristics with the other salafi flavours and gel a literal reading of the texts with political mechanisms usually concerning management of power, law, authority and caliphate. Groups like Hizbut Tahrir, Majelis Mujahidin Indonesa (MMI), Salafi Jihadi are part of this Salafi flavour. The broader influences of Salafism in Indonesia, indeed, exist and continue to penetrate to Muhammadiyah and Nahdlatul Ulama, two biggest Muslim organizations, and also many different layers of institutions (educational and governmental) in contemporary Indonesian society. The efforts of applying *Perda Syariah* or Syariah-like local laws by some Muslims in many districts are part of these influences (see Challenges section).

Jamaah Salafi Yogyakarta

Indonesian Salafi *da'wa* (mission) is prevalent after the coming of Abu Nida (Chamsaha Sofwan) to Yogyakarta. He first taught at *Pesantren* Al-Mukmin Ngruki, Solo in 1985 and then in *Pesantren* Ibnul Qoyyim, run by DDII (*Dewan Dakwah Islamiyah Indonesia*/The Islamic Propagation Council of Indonesia) in Yogyakarta. He started an Islamic student organization, *Jamaah Shalahuddin*, at Gadjah Mada University (UGM) and developed *dauroh* and *halaqah*[5] among the students with some teachers from *Pesantren* Al-Irsyad, Tengaran Salatiga. After a dispute with Ikhwan al-Muslimin's activists in the university in 1990s, he became closer to Al-Irsyad. The Salafi movement grew significantly when Ja'far Umar Thalib came to Yogyakarta and established *Pesantren* Ihyaus Sunnah in Degolan Kaliurang in 1993, after studying at LIPIA

(*Lembaga Ilmu Pengetahuan Islam dan Arab*/The Institute for the Study of Islam and Arabic) and Maududi Institute Pakistan, joining the Afghan war, studying with the most prominent Salafi teacher now, Muqbil bin Hadi al-Wad'i, in Dar al-Hadith, Dammaj Yaman. A historical study by International Crisis Group (2004), however, shows that Salafism in Indonesia can be traced from the so-called Padri Wars in Sumatra from 1803 to about 1832.[6] Salafi influences then came into Persis (*Persatuan Islam*/Islamic Union), DDII, Al-Irsyad, LIPIA, the conservative wing of Muhammadiyah (ICG, 2004: 6).

For years after that Indonesian Salafis disputed with each other for various reasons and split into many groups, including Ja'far Umar Thalib's group which is marginalized from the mainstream Salafi. The recent Salafi movement can be divided into two groups: non-FKASWJ (Forum Komunikasi Ahlussunnah Wal Jamaah)[7] and "The Purists". The purists, this research is mainly about, reject any association with groups or individuals willing to compromise religious purity for political goals and reject more tolerant and inclusive groups willing to acknowledge some good even in deviant teachings. They also reject funding from any source that has deviant organizations among its grantees (ICG, 2004: ii).

The "purists" are led by Umar Sewed, Lukman Ba'abduh, Dzulqarnain Abdul Ghafur al-Malanji and other former members of the forum; and the non-forum Salafis. The Sewed group is probably the most exclusivist and quickest to brand fellow Salafis as *bid'ah* (ICG, 2004: 19). The group runs a website (www.salafy.or.id) and publishes the magazine, *Asy-Syariah* (www.asysyariah.com). In Yogyakarta, where this research is mainly focused, the purists run a *pesantren,* Al-Anshar, in the northern part of Yogyakarta, and it has approximately 300 hundreds followers, some of them concentrated at Perum Veteran neighbourhood, Cangkringan, Sleman, Yogyakarta. They also held regular religious teachings in the mosques surrounding universities, like Pogung mosque (MPR) and Al-Marhamah mosque around the corner of Gadjah Mada University.

Salafi Teachings and Behaviour on Family Planning Issues

There are many issues related to the pro-natalist stand of the Jamaah, gender role of women, and their implication to the education of the children. The Salafi teachings on family planning are prevalent in Salafi books, magazines and the explanation of the *ustadz*s (teachers) in the *pengajians*. Freedom of expression, beginning in the reformation era

(1998) especially enables the publications of the teachings of Jamaah to grow fast among their followers and in Indonesian society in general.

Contraception

The official Jamaah Salafi magazine, *Asy-Syari'ah*, recently raised an issue regarding contraception. Quoting Syaikh 'Utsaimin, one prominent Salafi scholar, in his book *Risalah fi al-Dima' Al-Thabi'iyyah li al-Nisa*, a Salafi woman, Ummu Abdirrahman, wrote that "there are two ways of contraception: permanently and temporally. Permanent prevention of pregnancy is not allowed because it ends reproduction, thereby lessening offspring, and in this way opposes the objective of *syari'ah* (Islamic law) to produce a large number of *ummah*. So, if the woman has frequent pregnancies that will make her weak, she is allowed, with the consent of her husband, to regulate the pregnancy every two years and so on" (Abdirrahman, 2006).

Ummu Abdirrahman added that preventing pregnancy with pill, removing uterus (hysterectomy-trans) or the others, are not allowed. She warned that enemies of Islam decorate things that violate religion. They campaign to Muslims to limit births whereas they themselves continue to multiply their number (ibid.). She continued, "I ask you my brothers and sisters. If this time, in this era, people have ten children, do you see does Allah *Subhanahu wa Ta'ala* ignore them? Or instead you see Allah has opened the *rizq* (livelihood) from the way you never predicted? If someone limits the fertility because of a worldly fear (of the less *rizq* for example, trans.), verily he is wrong. Because God of Greatness has said in His Holy Book, "And there is none that walks upon the earth whose sustenance does not depend on the mercy of Allah - He knows where it shall stay and where it shall be deposited; everything is in a clearly explained book (Hud, 11:6). And also his words, "And many creatures walk upon the earth that do not carry their own sustenance; Allah provides the sustenance to them and to you; and only He is the All Hearing, the All Knowing" (Ankabut, 29: 60).

In another article, under the column of "*Keluarga Sakinah* (Harmonious Family),"[8] Ummu Abdirrahman also wrote that Muqbil bin Hadi Al-Wad'i, one well-known Salafi *ulama*[9] from Yemen, once was asked about a husband who agrees for his wife to be sterilized by the hospital. He then issued his *fatwa* (legal opinion): "A husband could not allow it", while the Prophet said, "Marry so that your number will be great because indeed I will be proud of your number in the presence of other *ummahs* on Judgment Day." The Prophet also once prayed to

Allah for the wealth and children of Anas bin Malik to be multiplied. In addition, we will never know God's fate, such as the death of our children in the future" (Abdirrahman, 9 April 2006).

Salafis thus reject all family planning services, including pills, spirals and also condoms. The only contraception allowed by the Prophet is *'azl* (withdrawal or coitus interuptus). A book written by one of the most prominent Salafi *ulamas*, Syaikh Nasiruddin Al-Albani, *Adab al-Zifaf,* (Albani, 2004: 117–119) mentioned that there are three *hadith*s on '*'azl*:

1. Jabir said, "we used to practice *'azl* during the time of the Prophet while the Qur'an was being revealed." In another form it is reported, "We used to practice *'azl* during the time of the Prophet. The Prophet came to know about it, but did not forbid us (doing it)."[10]
2. Abu Sa'id Al-Khudry he said, "Once a man came to the Prophet and said, "I have a woman slave and I want to do *'azl* when I do something that man usually does, while Jews said that *'azl* is a small infanticide (*al-mau'udah al-sughra*). The Prophet then replied, "The Jews lied! Because when Allah will to make it (the sperm that poured) into a child, then you have no power to reject it."[11]
3. Jabir said, "Once a man came to the Prophet and said, "I have a slave woman ..., I want to have sex with her but I don't want her to be pregnant." The Prophet said, "Do *'azl* if you want, though indeed what has been decided will happen." The man then returned to his home (After a few days) he came again and said to the Prophet, "Really my slave is pregnant!" He answered, "Indeed, I have told that what was determined will happen."[12]

Albani then concluded his opinion on this issue by establishing one more chapter, "It's Better Not To Do *'Azl*" (Albani, 2004: 120). In one *hadith* the Prophet called *'azl* as "a hidden infanticide (*al-wa'dul khafiy*)"[13] when his companions asked him about it. Regarding this *hadith*, Albani continued, Ibnul Qayyim in the book of *at-Tahdzib* (III/85) said that the Prophet's analogy of *'azl* to the hidden infanticide shows that the status of the *'azl* is *makruh* (hated). To Albani, it is implied by the *hadith* that it is better for us to avoid practicing *'azl* (Albani, 2004: 122), and it is insisted in a *hadith* transmitted by Abu Sai'd Al-Khudry, "The problem of *'azl* had been discussed (by his companions) in front of the Prophet. He said, "Why did one of you do that? The Prophet did not say, "Do not do that!"—Indeed, none of the living soul but Allah creates."[14]

In this chapter also, Albani stated that the law of *'azl* is *makruh* (hated) and insisted that it is better for a husband not to do *'azl* because of two reasons. First, *'azl* will disadvantage the wife because it can interfere with her pleasure. Even if the wife consents to *'azl*, it is not good because it is inconsistent with one of the goals of marriage, that of increasing the *ummah* of the Prophet as it is stated in a *hadith*. Albani understood that the usage of modern and sophisticated contraceptive tools like condoms and IUD cannot be judged as hidden infanticide (*al-wa'd al-khafiy*) and small infanticide (*al-mau'udah al-shughra*) as the *hadith* addressed. These tools have to be rejected, he said, only by those two reasons above, especially the second reason.

> There should be no objective like infidels have of doing *'azl* for fear of poverty because of a lot of children and being burdened by feeding and educating them. If these things exist the *hukm* (the legal status) becomes *haram* (forbidden), because of the similarity of intention with the objective of infidels where they kill their children because of the fear of feeding them and poverty. If the woman is sick, then she is allowed to use contraception temporarily. If her sickness is really dangerous and endangers her life, then, it is a must for her to do tubectomy (*rabthul mawasir*) to preserve her life. (Albani, 2004: 136–137; Ishaq Zulfa, 29 June 2003)

From the interviews I have conducted, Jamaah Salafi members have never used contraception except *'azl*. Abdul Mu'thi (30), an *ustadz* who leads the Salafi *pesantren Al-Anshar* in Cangkringan Sleman Yogyakarta, explains, "The Prophet said: *Tazawwadul wadudul walud*. Marry an honest, fertile woman because I will be proud of your big number at the Final Day.[15] So this *hadith* encourages us to have as many children as possible. Allah does not limit the Muslim people in having children, instead it is encouraged. In a society that is densely populated, violence cannot be blamed on the number of children, but first because of the lack of understanding of religious teachings, and second, because of not using religious teachings. So to overcome this problem we must learn and use our religion. And because of this we need Allah's laws so this issue can be dealt with fairly and not by blaming the population density." And when Mu'thi was asked, does it mean that he does not agree with family planning carried out during the New Order? Abdul Mu'thi said, "Yes, I very much disagree."

Through observation of their housing complex in Perum Veteran which consists of one hundred households, of which 80 per cent are Salafis, I saw many children playing in a relatively small neighbourhood and Osama, who lives there, said that there are approximately 4–5 children in each house, ranging from 1–9. It is common to see Salafis whose age is below thirty living with their four children. The Veteran complex has the same size houses and each house has an area of 9×9 metres divided into four parts, bedroom, dining room, kitchen, and porch in the front. Salafis usually put a curtain to divide the dining room, creating a parlour in order to protect their wives from being seen by their guests.

Abu Mujahid who always brings his three children aged four months, two years, and three years to the religious sessions (*pengajian*), said family planning is basically forbidden by *syar'i* (Islamic law). Islam only allows '*'azl* (withdrawal). "We only use family planning if there is a problem like exhaustion, to control births (read: make births less frequent). But we will not use permanent birth control. There are no members of the Jamaah who follow the government's family planning. They have about five or six children and there's no problem. I see them, they are smart. Blessings are decided by Allah. We don't know about verses of the Qur'an or *hadith*. But *insya'allah* (If God is willing) everything we do has a foundation. Best to ask the *ustadz* about that."[16]

When I asked about the difficulties of having many children, Mujahid replied, "*Al-ilmu wal iman wal amal* (Knowledge is with faith and deed). The important thing is our good deeds are accompanied by faith. *Insyaallah* there will be no problem. If there is knowledge but no action, then it's worthless, this is true also action without knowledge and faith is not good. Faith is also *bikhoirihi wa sarrihi* (with all of its risks, good and bad). My friend, Abdul Basith, has five children. Two are at a *pesantren*. His livelihood (*rizq*) is fine. ...If Allah gives me another child, yeah I will accept it." The similar tone was expressed by Yuli by quoting a verse from Qur'an, "*Man yattaqillaha yaj'allahu makhrajan* (Whoever submits to God, He will serve him/her a solution). A *hadith* narrated by Ibn Mas'ud also said that Allah created humanity each with his/her own blessings (*biqadri rizqihi*)," he added.[17]

Even though they find it difficult to say, however, some members admit that it is hard to have many children. "I think that six is enough; if I have another it is okay, but if I calculate, it's heavy. ... It is pretty heavy. For example, their education is expensive and because of that we limit it with the way that God blessed. ...Nevertheless, this (family

sakan when she understands the right and position of her husband, and, at the same time, fulfils that right in accordance with her obedience to God with all joy and submission. The conditions of *sakan* include:

1. Absolute obedience to her husband as the leader in circumstances that are not against God's law. The Prophet said, "Suppose that I can order someone to worship except God verily I will order to worship (*sujud*) to the husband." Obedience to the husband is prioritized to the recommended religious services (*ibadah sunnah*) as he has the right of intimacy and this must be fulfilled by the wife anytime he wants (Albani, 2004: 250n–251).
2. Doing household work such as cooking, cleaning, and so on.
3. Keeping secrets and guarding the honour of the husband so that he will have complete trust in her.
4. Keeping the property of the husband, including taking care of the children, giving them education and settings example, and also managing the household.
5. Having a good manner to her husband, such as forgiving his faults, calming him when he gets angry, showing love and honour, saying good words and giving him a cheerful face and serving him in eating and dressing.
6. Arranging that all works are done on time, keeping the house clean and tidy which makes the husband and kids comfortable.
7. Being honest to the husband in everything.

Third, to educate the children (*tarbiyatul aulad*). This duty, together with the husband, becomes the most important responsibility in the home because it means preparing a good and blessed generation by God. Both of them will be asked for this responsibility on the Judgment Day (Tahrim 66: 6).[34]

Fourth, to do other jobs if there is an opportunity to help the husband feed the family, such as sewing and so on.

Family, in this group, is interpreted for the women as the balance between household life and the life for the Day After. They have duties to serve the husband, treat and educate children and at the same time educate themselves by attending *pengajian*s, which ironically teach in support to the superiority of the husband. By quoting Qur'anic verses and *hadith*s, the male *ustadz*s emphasize the importance of the women to stay at home and obey their husbands. The *pengajian* is employed, in some way, to spread the hegemony of the masculinity and establishing the low status of women in Salafi families.

Education

Regarding the issue of education, Jamaah Salafi considers the knowledge of the Day After (*ilmu akhirat*) as more valuable than worldly knowledge (*ilmu al-dunya*). What people should find is useful knowledge (*ilmu manfaat*), that is *ilmu akhirat* as primary knowledge over the worldly as it leads to salvation in the Day After. Thereby worldly knowledge is considered useful when it leads people to the possibility of salvation. People will be regarded as losing out when they do not have *akhirat*/religious knowledge. Salafi madrasahs then become the primary place for them to send their children for education.

Osama admits that he prefers to send his children to Salafi *madrasahs* than to general schools. "In early years, around 3–6, they will go to *Tarbiyatul Aulad* (TA) to start reading and memorizing Qur'an. Usually it includes class A, B, C, and then *Tahfidul Qur'an* (*Tahfid*), 6–13 years, in *halaqah*s in the presence of the teachers. Basic mathematics is taught here. When they are 13–17 years, I will send them to *Tadribud Du'at* (TD) directly under the guidance of *masayikh*s (grand teachers). The curriculum here is perhaps higher than in IAIN (State Institute of Islamic Studies).[35] In second year class will be taught in Arabic and they are encouraged to communicate in Arabic.[36] After that, if there is a chance they can go to *mulazamah*,[37] but if there isn't they can do *mulazamah* here in front of the *masayikhs'* students, before they finally independence (*mandiri*)." Tajuddin, who has 4 children, said that actually parents have the responsibility of educating their own children until they are *baligh*.[38]

Salafis prefer to send their children to *madrasahs* as the place of study and this preference is based on their thinking on the prevalence of *bid'ah* (innovation) in the present era. "The basic *hukm* (law) of studying at university is allowed but there is a fear of mixing between men and women so that it is not absolutely required. ...The source of destruction is theology and philosophy because it makes people confused. The scholars that are cited are even *kafir*/infidels. It is not based on the Qur'an and *hadith*."[39] Osama convinced, "...I will not send my children to study at university, but I will equip them with knowledge of computers and machines/machinery. Actually I can teach my children about pistons, burning, how gasoline becomes fuel for machinery, in a week. It doesn't require years. That is knowledge that can be learned by themselves." His opinion is relatively the same as Yuli, who is registered as a second year student at UGM. He admitted, "...that actually we don't need to go to the university because we can find knowledge by ourselves. We can learn management, economics, by ourselves. There are so many ways to get it today, books are everywhere and you can find anything in the Internet, even how to make a bomb. Now students are smarter than their teachers. So I prefer the valuable (*manfaat*) knowledge."[40]

Analysis: Findings and Implications

The interviews show that none of the jamaah members uses contraception, except natural contraception, i.e., *'azl* and calendar family planning. No abortion cases were reported. This behaviour is mainly undergirded by their strong belief in their religious teachings based on the Qur'an and *hadith*. As a result, Salafis have approximately 4–5 children (range from 1–9 children) and with such large family size, the Jamaah has proved to be an anomaly within the success story of the "Two Is Enough" campaign by the Indonesian New Order regime. From the young age of the second generation of Salafis in Yogyakarta, it can also be induced that since the beginning of its prevalence (1990s) the members of the group remain untouchable by the government family planning programme.

Large family size causes economic problems for the members. Food, clothes, and education are basic needs to be fulfilled. Some Salafi families live at the level of subsistence, with *tempe*[41] as their daily side dish. This situation sometimes creates a dilemma within their heart, between their faith that God gives them an order to produce a big community and the factual condition that too many children will make their life in difficulties. Salafis eventually subdue this "inappropriate" personal feeling to God's will and accept it as part of their fate (*takdir*). In this way of thinking, it is reasonable that though they are familiar with poverty and simplicity is a main value in their life, this economic hardship is considered as a small problem compared to the difficulty of fulfilling the true teachings of Islam. One of the biggest problems for them is educating children, especially in the present environment where *bid'ah* (innovations) are prevalent. Principally, this is based on their belief that they will be asked by God about this responsibility in the Day of Judgment.

The importance of (religious) education for bringing their children to the *pengajians*, usually wearing long *jilbab* and cap like their parents, is to be familiar with *majlis al-ilmu* (learning sessions) from the early childhood. The primary emphasis in Salafi *pesantrens*, therefore, is on the remembrance of Qur'anic verses and *hadiths* so that they can tightly hold on these bases.[42]

The adherence towards the same Islamic virtues makes Salafi members want to marry other Salafis. If someone desires to get married, he/she asks the *ustadz* and *ustadz* will find for him/her someone who is interested and shows a picture of the candidate. If it is a deal then they marry. The age of marriage is quite diverse. Women are highly appreciated in the Jamaah as they are considered as "the guard of the *ummah*" who holds a significant role in keeping the family institution established. Her rights, however, are considered secondary under the superiority of the husband as the leader (*qawwam*), even closer to God.[43] A woman should stay at home and do household work, such as cooking and cleaning. The patriarchal relationship between man and women remains tenacious.

This dependent economic, cultural and doctrinal position of a woman places her in a very fragile and defenseless condition, likely to be punished or hurt by the husband. Despite this, some Salafi families, like Osama's, have a relatively "equal" relation between husband and wife in terms of communication. Observation showed that Osama frequently asked his wife about things. This was partly because of, in my view, the education of the wife who holds a bachelor degree in chemistry from a very prestigious university. Osama himself never finished his studies in agricultural technology in one private university in Yogyakarta, which is less prestigious than her wife's. Education here seems to be influential in constructing the relationship within the family, and in particular, the status of women.

Some families restrict expenditure of money to the husband. The husband often goes to the market to shop daily for food for fear that the wife will mix (*ikhtilath*) with men. Women live in the private room and they do not pray in the mosque. They go outside only if she is accompanied by the husband or the *mahram*. When they attend the *pengajian*s in the mosque, they will be located at the back or at a certain area covered by curtain (*hijab*). In their houses, the dining room is separated from the sitting room with a long big curtain. Drinks for the guests are placed by the wife behind the curtain and the husband will take them and serve the guests. The whole process is done in silence without any voice from the wife. A wife will not receive a guest without the presence of the husband and in an emergency they will talk to the guest from behind the wall or curtain.

Salafi members live differently from the rest of society. People usually regard them as strange because they wear different dress, speak a different language and behave differently. In Yogyakarta, as in many places, Salafis wear short pantaloon combined with long *jubah* (Arabic dress) for men and long big veil, covering their faces, for women. They also use Arabic terms often in conversation and prefer to live concentratedly with other Salafi members in daily activities. Salafis, with the puritanical characteristics of their understanding, considers outside society as *ahl al-bid'ah* (people who conduct *bid'ah*) or *kafir* (infidels). When the earthquake shook Yogyakarta in May 2006, Jamaah Salafi formed an Earthquake Concern Team to help Salafi members. Despite helping in the name of humanity, in the report they made divisive categorization between *ahlussunnah* (read, Salafi Muslim), Muslims in common, *bid'ah* doers, *fasik* (people who conduct big sin), and *kafir* (infidel) (*Salafy*, 19 July 2006). They look suspicious towards others. However, Salafis are not polemicists like activists from Hizbut Tahrir. They are just Muslims who want to do their religious teachings in the purest form referring to a model of Muhammad and *Salafus Shalih*.

The political stance of the Jamaah is being apolitical. This is driven by the fear that any link to an organization will lead to the violation of the single *ummah*. The group's policy on family planning, however, is directly in opposition to the official family planning policy of the government. On this point, since the religious authority is in the hands of grand *shaikhs* in Middle East countries, the government will face difficulty in dealing with the Jamaah.

The reproductive behaviour of the Jamaah basically has its foundation in their ethics and worldview. Their religious ethics are based in Qur'an and Sunnah, referring to the life of Muhammad, and *Salafus Shalih*. This ideological root, therefore, will battle with other ideological roots, i.e., Western ideology, since the West is considered as enemy and less moral, non-Muslims, and the rest of Muslims who are considered to be deviant. The historical shadows of Muslim and non-Muslim wars in the past have also contributed to the phenomena. The West is imagined as people who relentlessly want to destroy Islamic society (www.asysyariah.com). Programmes like family planning and gender equality are seen as part of the propaganda and conspiracy from the West. Abdul Aziz bin Abdullah bin Baz, the most referred-to Salafi ulama, when he was the Grand Mufti of Saudi Arabia, was the person, allegedly with the Vatican, who strongly called other Muslim countries to boycott the Action Plan on Reproductive Health in The International Conference on Population and Development in Cairo 1994. He attacked the Action Plan as an agenda of immorality and permissiveness (MacFarquhar, 1994). So big the image of Western's hostility to Islam in the Jamaah that it covers the fact that most Western countries now have succeeded in decreasing their fertility growth rate to a very low level.

The literal characteristic of Salafi religious understanding assures that their reproductive behaviour is mainly driven by their religious piety, i.e., to practice what they consider as the true Islam. Anthropological studies, however, have insisted that what people called religion is actually part of the culture (Geertz, 1973). Religion is constructed in a specific time and place and is bound to the socio-cultural conditions at the time. As a German philosopher, Martin Heidegger, stated that human, as the creator of culture, is trapped into history. He/she is a captive in this world...and it influences how he/she interprets the world (Heidegger, 1996). Moreover, this historical consciousness is very important to understand the true spirit of a religion. Islamic academia recognizes disciplines which study historical matters of verses and *hadith*s/traditions, i.e., *Asbab an-Nuzul* (the cause of the revelation of Qur'anic verses) and *Asbab al-Wurud* (the cause of the emergence of *hadith*). The Jamaah, however, shows that the Salafis do not develop these two socio-historical disciplines into their madrasahs (Hasan, 2006). Salafis instead, as their Sheikhs who are primarily *ahlul hadith*s, people who inherit and remember thousands of *hadith*s with all of their transmissions, highlight the remembrance of *hadith*s, in addition to Qur'anic verses, as the foundation of their Islamic education. This create such a low historical consciousness among Salafis, and consequently, Salafis less consider a historical fact that high mother-child birth mortality is the (underlying) reason for pro-natalist behaviour (United Nations, 1973: 58–60, 142–158)—things that might happen in Islam during the era of the Prophet as well.

The lack of socio-cultural understanding of the Jamaah is partly because of their cultural and educational background. Noorhaidi Hasan records that most Salafis are "*abangan* converts" (2006).[44] My observations also found that most Salafi followers in Yogyakarta originate not from *santri* (more pious Muslim) families. They easily change their Javanese names into Arabic names, such as Ngadiran into Abu Muammar or Sutinah into Ummu Farihah. They first study at general high school, not *pesantren*s, and entered the universities mostly in scientific faculties like engineering, chemistry, physics, mathematics, architecture, economics, and agriculture. Almost none of the Salafis come from social sciences and humanities. "The idea of certainty and objectivity" pursued in sciences fixes with the Salafi promise of true, simple, teachings and the reward of *Akhirat* (Day After).

The characteristic of the group to tend to label other people or groups *bid'ah* indicates the "enclave culture" of the Jamaah. This is due to "the primary impulse that lies behind the rise of the tradition so as to forestall the danger of being sucked into the vortex of modernity" (Sivan, 2003: 30). In this enclave culture they usually construct a "wall of virtue" based on moral values. This wall separates the saved, free, and morally superior enclave from the hitherto tempting outside community. The enclave places the oppressive and morally defiled outside society in sharp contrast to the community of virtuous insiders. In contrast to the inside, anything outside is black. It is conceived as a polluted, contagious, and dangerous area (Sivan, ibid.: 30). The idea of an enclave is related to the question of space in its symbolic and social meanings. It is a separate space in which behaviour, language and dress code are strictly regulated. The significance of strictness is to dictate a strict order because of the gravity posed by the outside danger (Hasan, 2006). The reproductive ethics and behaviour of the Jamaah, therefore, in this view can be seen partly as related to their enclave identity: to define themselves as the part of the one *ummah*, the one and only among the 73 broken Islamic groups, who are saved, blessed by the Prophet, and enter the heaven of God.[45]

The spirit of these Salafis in practicing their religion is so high that it is difficult for the government to penetrate. The approach used by the former New Order in cooperation with religious leaders (Subahar, 2005: 157–173; The State Ministry for Population/BKKBN, 1998; Niehof, 2003) will absolutely fail. Contraception can be easily regarded as *bid'ah* if they think it threatens their faith and sustenance, which they get from dependence on God. This is why the appropriate approach is needed in order for government efforts at family planning to succeed. An approach has to be built on the characteristics of the Jamaah: first, the strict literal understanding and belief in the "true" Islam, second, the wall of virtue from behind which they launch the idea of *bid'ah* to other kinds of Islamic practices and by which they differentiate themselves from other members of society, and third, the most the important one, the transnational network between senior teachers and *shaikhs* in Saudi, Yemen and Pakistan from where they receive *fatwa*s. These transnational *fatwas*, together with the Jamaah rejection of other Islamic practices and doctrines, will block the influences of local religious leaders, such as Nahdlatul Ulama and Muhammadiyyah, two groups that contributed a lot to the success of family planning programmes in the New Order era, if not render them impotent. The authority of the Indonesian Council of Ulama (MUI, a semi-governmental body) is not influential either, because of Salafi rejection of nationalism as *thaghut* (an idolatry).

Despite some oppositional stand of the Jamaah Salafi towards family planning and modernity, an identification of being different from rest of society makes followers of the Jamaah stay tied to each other strongly manifested in economic cooperation, financial help, and religious guidance. Solidarity is high among them and sincerity between them becomes the basis of life and relationships.

Challenges

Here I want to extend Jamaah Salafi's teachings towards a greater challenge posed by Salafism in general in Indonesia in terms of population issues and, therefore, three inter-related points must be mentioned: Decentralized policy of BKKBN, Syariahization of Indonesia through Syariah-like local laws, and transnational Salafi Ulamas. These three developments ironically contradict the efforts of the government to refresh family planning programme in the country.

In his visit to New York, US, September 2005, to attend a meeting with UNFPA, President Susilo Bambang Yudhoyono insisted on his commitment to the implementation of the Action Plan of ICPD Cairo 1994. Together with the meeting, the government also launched a proposal entitled "*Revitalisasi Dukungan Tokoh Agama untuk Kependudukan, Kesehatan Reproduksi dan Keluarga Berencana*" (The Revitalization of the Support of Religious Leaders for Population, Reproductive Health and Family Planning). The president has also publicly expressed his strong commitment to the family planning programme on several national occasions (BKKBN, 30 June 2006). As part of this agenda, BKKBN, with the support from the vice president, has further set a regional target for the family planning programme. Even though these can be seen as a good sign of the commitment of the government, there are three actual challenges that the government must pay attention to:

Decentralized Policy of BKKBN

The falling of Soeharto and the beginning of reformation era (1998) created a big change in family planning policy. Under Law No. 22/1999 on decentralization, the management of BKKBN has been given over to local governments, districts or municipalities, while the provincial level is still under the central structure of BKKBN. The districts/municipalities responded to this law by placing BKKBN offices into existing government departments (*dinas*), such as the department of population. Only a few districts established an independent *dinas* for family planning. The previous officials of BKKBN, who spearheaded the New

Order's success, have now become officials within the departments. Instead of going to the field, explaining family planning programmes, now they stay in the office fulfilling administrative duties. At the same time, the number of family planning officials has decreased from 40,000 to 22,000 (*Kompas*, 1 July 2006). It also means that family planning management is now in the hands of echelon III officials. With only this level of authority, suggestions from family planning officials are frequently not heard by the heads of districts/municipalities, and family planning officials are not involved in important meetings regarding district/municipal management.

This phenomenon is accompanied by a lack of political commitment from the local government and lack of awareness among grass roots leaders. It is reported by the head of BKKBN, Dr Sumarjati Arjoso SKM, that in 2004, 279 districts/municipal (from 410 throughout Indonesia, therefore slightly over 50%) left under BKKBN's coordination (BKKBN, 14 December 2004). This has created a shrinking enthusiasm in society for family planning services. The Coordinator of the Ministry of Welfare, Aburizal Bakrie, conveyed that since the reformation era there has been a reversal of the trend of family planning participation (BKKBN, 1 February 2006). Visits to local areas recorded that the participation of society in family planning services were not very lively (BKKBN, 23 September 2005). The most recent news said that because of the decentralization policy, in Ende, Nusa Tenggara Timor, the number of family planning acceptors has been dropping uncontrollably. At the same time, fertility, maternal mortality, and infant mortality rates have increased (*Kompas*, 24 July 2006).

Syariah-ization of Indonesia[46] through Syariah-like Local Laws

Another trend in Indonesia is the growing Islamism in the public arena, which I think will go hand in hand with decentralization policy in creating new challenges for family planning services in the country. After the fall of Soeharto in 1998, the wind of freedom is blowing. The failure to put the seven words of The Jakarta Charter[47] into the Preamble of Indonesian Laws 1945 (UUD 1945) and the eradication of Muslim activists in Tanjung Priok in 1984 cannot make Islamists cease their effort to insert Syari'ah (Islamic law) as part of Indonesian political life. In the annual session of the Representative Council (MPR) in 2002, Islamists in the Council tried again (though they failed) to make an amendment to the Preamble by putting the seven words of the Jakarta Charter. Islamism is prevalent in mosques, schools, and governmental institutions.

There is also an increasing awareness of Islam in society and tendency towards showing Islamic symbols in public. The *fatwa* of Majelis Ulama Indonesia (MUI) on liberalism, secularism, and pluralism; and the people's support on Anti-Pornography law draft, shows the prevalence of the fear of public immorality in Indonesia. The rejection of some ulamas and religious organizations of condom vending machines launched by BKKBN to prevent pregnancy and the spread of HIV/AIDS is part of this fear (*Pikiran Rakyat*, 26 December 2005). The fear of public immorality, on the one hand, and the failure of the Islamist movement on the national level, on the other, have revealed a new strategy to Islamists, that of approaching local governmental leaders. The decentralization policy gives local leaders more influence over their own district/municipal to apply Syari'ah or syari'ah-like laws (Suhadi, 16 June 2006). A local leader who has been pioneering the creation of syari'ah-like rules in one district in West Java is known as an important figure in the Kongres Penegakan Syariat (Congress of Syari'ah Establishment) held by Majelis Mujahidin Indonesia in 2000 in Yogyakarta. The laws themselves can be categorized into three groups: first, related to Muslim dress code, like the wearing of *jilbab* in schools. Second, related to moral development (*akhlaqul karimah*) or anti-*maksiyat* (immorality), like issues of prostitution and alcohol. Third, related to the internal development of Islamic faith, like the obligation of Qur'anic literacy and group prayers (Suhadi, 25 June 2006).

Fifty-six members of MPR have rejected these regulations, but Hidayat Nur Wahid, Head of MPR from PKS (Justice Welfare Party), criticizes these 56 people by saying that they don't understand the prevalence of prostitution, gambling, immorality and so on, among the society in the areas where the rule would be applied (Hidayat, 16 July 2006). One hundred and thirty-four members of DPR then signed a counter-memorandum in support of the application of the regulations (*Gatra*, 04 July 2006). Regardless of all the debates, 30 districts have now applied syari'ah-like regulations, including Aceh, Pamekasan in Madura, Tangerang in West Java, Riau in Sumatra, and Maros, Takalar, Enrekang, Gowa, Sinjai, Bulukumba, all in South Sulawesi (*The New York Times*, 27 June 2006).

If the two phenomena, local autonomy and local Syariah regulations, meet, cooperate and embrace a more conservative stand towards family planning issues it will be a great danger for the future of population issues in Indonesia. The annual population growth rate of South Sulawesi increased from 1.42 per cent in 1980–1990 to 1.49 per cent in 1990–2000; for Riau it is 4.22 per cent in 1980–1990 to 4.35 per cent in 1990–2000 and Yogyakarta increased from 0.57 per cent in 1980–1990 to 0.72 per cent in 1990–2000 (BPS, 2001). There are many causes of this population growth, like internal migration. The fact that these areas are the bases of Islamists, especially Yogyakarta and South Sulawesi, strongholds of Syari'ah regulations, and also have prevalent populations of Salafis, especially in Yogyakarta and South Sulawesi, can be a hint for the influence of Islamism on population growth and fertility. Future research will be needed to explore the connections more fully.

Transnational Salafi Ulamas: The Impotency of Local Ulamas

Salafis in Indonesia are in constant communication with scholars (*mostly ahl al-hadith* or people of the traditions) based primarily in Saudi Arabia. The supremacy of these scholars is primarily because of the doctrinal consideration of Salafis that people who hold valid *hadith*s with valid transmissions are entitled to be honored and justified to spread the true teachings of Islam from the Prophet Muhammad. If Salafis in Indonesia face problems, they will call their teachers on the telephone to ask for their *fatwas* (legal opinions), including the question of Laskar Jihad, which sent hundreds of Salafis to fight against Christians in Moluccas in 2000. This preference for Saudi scholars will eventually lead to invalidity of local sources of knowledge and lack of recognition of local ulamas. Local ulamas, from Nahdlatul Ulama and Muhammadiyah used to be the key agents of the great success of family planning programme during New Order's era are now impotent and their *fatwa*s are useless for these Salafis.

Conclusion

This study concludes that Jamaah Salafi does support large families as indicated by the high fertility rate among their followers in Yogyakarta. The reproductive behaviour of the Jamaah is driven by their literal understanding of Islamic teachings based on the model of Muhammad and Salafus Shalih, using Qur'an and *Hadith* as their primary source of religiosity. Mosques, *pesantren*s and universities are the main sites of dissemination of Salafi ideas, in addition to the abundance of publications through books, magazines, and websites. The strong transnational network between Jamaah members and their grand Salafi *sheikhs* in Saudi Arabia and Yemen also supports dissemination of Salafi ideas. The right, status and public participation of women are low, but they regard domestic work as a noble duty to guard the *ummah*. Regardless of all the problems caused by large number of children, the Jamaah followers show a strong acceptance of fate, lead a simple life, and have a high level of solidarity among themselves.

Politically, Jamaah Salafi is not dangerous; however, it poses a real challenge to the government because of their oppositional stance in population issues, like family planning, gender equality, and education. The puritanical characteristics of Jamaah—the rejection of nationalism, democracy, and any kind of authority besides their transnational (Middle Eastern) Salafi *ustadz*s and their disciples in the country—will make any effort of cooperation regarding family planning services difficult. Furthermore, those *ustadz*s, with their primary source of authority in Islamic teachings, will make the teachings of local ulamas on reproduction and family planning impotent. With such teachings in family planning, Jamaah Salafi, together with other Salafi groups such as Jamaah Tabligh, MMI/Majelis Mujahidin Indonesia, DDII/The Islamic Propagation Council of Indonesia, Persis, Hizbut Tahrir, PKS/Welfare and Justice Party, conservative wings of Muhammadiyah and Nahdlatul Ulama, blending with the growing Islamists in general, will make a danger in population issues in the future of Indonesia. It is not impossible that this Salafism will create really challenging problems in social and political arena. We have seen one of these problems in Bali bombing done by Indonesian Jihadi Salafists.

Based on these findings, I urge the government to give a special treatment for Jamaah Salafi, and also Salafism in general, related to population issues by considering their special ethics, worldview, and the culture of the group. The understanding of their ethics, worldview and specific culture is essential for the government if they want the family planning programme to succeed in the future in the country.

Notes

1. I specially thank my mentor, Prof. Gavin Jones, for his critical comments on this writing and Asia Research Institute (ARI), National University of Singapore, for generously supporting this research.
2. More widely known as *madrasah*.
3. *Salafus Shalih* are believed by Salafis as the three generations that lived after the Prophet: those are *sahabat* (the companions of the Prophet), *tabi'in* (the followers of the teachings and behaviour of the companions) and *tabi'it tabi'in* (the second generation of followers, who follow the *tabi'in*).

4. Sunnah or *Hadith*, or as widely known as tradition, is the saying and behaviour of the Prophet Muhammad, and also things agreed by the Prophet. Islam recognizes six major books (*kutub al-sittah*) of these *hadith*s written by six early Muslim experts: Muslim, Bukhari, Abu Dawud, Nasai, Ahmad and Ibnu Majah.
5. *Dauroh,* literally means going around, is a religious session/*pengajian* held from town to town; *halaqah* means small group guidance.
6. The war between the purists, led by Imam Bonjol who is a disciple of Muhammad bin Abdul Wahhab, and the *adat*s, traditionalists.
7. FKASWJ was founded by Ja'far Umar Thalib and was the nurture of Laskar Jihad, a Muslim paramilitary group which sent Muslims to fight against Christians in Moluccas in 2000. FKASWJ consists of 16 Salafi *pesantren*s. See further in ICG, 2004.
8. Surprisingly that the column is supervised by female teachers. Two names often appeared as writers are Ummu Ishaq Zulfa Husein Al-Atsariyyah and Ummu 'Abdirrahman Anisah Bintu' Imran.
9. *Ulama* are religious leaders.
10. Authenticated by Bukhari in his book, *Sahih*.
11. This *hadith* is transmitted by Nasai with a valid transmission (*sanad*).
12. Authenticated by Muslim, Abu Dawud, Baihaqi and Ahmad.
13. Albani emphasizes that this *hadith* is undoubtedly valid as authenticated by many Muslim scholars like Muslim, Ath-Thahawi, Ahmad and Baihaqi. See Albani, 2004: 120.
14. Authenticated by Muslim, Bukhari and Nasai.
15. Mu'thi said that this *hadith* is authenticated by Nasai. Ustadz Abdul Mu'thi, interview 27 February 2006.
16. Abu Mujahid (35), a trader, married in 1999. Interview 28 May 2005.
17. Yuli, interview 20 July 2006.
18. Osama, interview 12 April 2006.
19. "And how will you take it back whereas you have become unveiled before each other, and they have taken a strong pledge from you?"
20. "They are coverings for you and you are coverings for them."
21. "And among His signs is that He created spouses for you from yourselves for you gain rest from them, and kept love and mercy between yourselves; indeed in this are signs for the people who ponder."
22. "Men are in charge of women, as Allah has made one of them superior to the other, and because men spend their wealth for the women."
23. "And We did not send *(Prophets)* before you except men, to whom We sent divine revelations – therefore, O people, ask the people of knowledge if you do not know."

24. "Husbands have one level higher than the wives."
25. "And do not long for things by which Allah has given superiority to some of you over others; for men is the share of what they earn; and for women the share from what they earn; and seek from Allah His munificence; indeed Allah knows everything."
26. Salafis tightly tied with specific way of behaviour, dress and language that they believe as representing the true Islam. These are what they rigidly called ethics. See further in Sivan, 2003.
27. *Mahram* or *muhrim* are people who are prohibited to be married because of their close blood relation. Including to *mahram* are father, brother and sister, uncle, etc. For more conservative Muslims, it is only their *mahram* who are allowed to guard a girl/woman.
28. "And remain in your houses." The objects of this verse are the wives of Muhammad but in term of meaning, according to Al-Atsariyah, it can be inferred all women in general.
29. "Do not expel them from their houses during the appointed period nor should they leave on their own." Syaikh Shalih bin Abdillah Alu Fauzan in his book *Daurul Mar'ah fi Tarbiyatul Usrah*, said that even though this verse is intended to the divorced women, it is also applicable to all women. See in www.alfauzan.net.
30. The wife said that she liked to pray together with him and the Prophet said, "...your praying in a special room in your home is better than in your room, your praying in your room is better than in your home, your praying in your home is better than in the mosque of your community and your praying in the mosque of your community is better than praying in my mosque."
31. "And I created the jinns and men, only for them to worship Me."
32. "And remain in your houses and do not unveil yourselves like the unveiling prevalent in the times of ignorance, and keep the prayer established, and pay the charity, and obey Allah and His Noble Messenger; Allah only wills to remove all impurity from you, O the People of the Household, and by cleansing you make you utterly pure."
33. "And among His signs is that He created spouses for you from yourselves for you gain rest from them, and kept love and mercy between yourselves; indeed in this are signs for the people who ponder."
34. "O People who Believe! Save yourselves and your families from the fire, the fuel of which is men and stones—appointed over it are the extremely strict angels, who do not refuse the command of Allah and carry out whatever they are commanded."
35. IAINs has been recognized as important agent in modernizing Islam in Indonesia. Today, some IAINs like Jakarta and Yogyakarta, have further developed and elaborated their departments into various disciplines in

sciences (mathematics, chemistry, engineering, etc.) and change their names into State Islamic Universities (UINs) to accommodate new development of the society. Conservative Muslims, however, see this modernization in those institutions as part of secularizing Indonesian Muslims. Hartono Ahmad Jaiz, one salafi Muslim from DDII, recently launched a book entitled *Ada Pemurtadan di IAIN* (*Conversion in IAIN*) in which he severely accused IAINs as the agents of conversing Muslims into non-Muslims' way of life because of Western style of thinking, references and methods IAINs adopted in their curriculum. See Jaiz, 2005.

36. Arabic became a very familiar language among this Jamaah. Often, they attach some Arabic expressions in the middle of the daily conversation. Arabic, to Jamaah, is considered the best language, because it is the language of Qur'an (God).
37. The true *mulazamah* (literally it means continuing) for them is going to the syaikhs in Saudi Arabia, Yemen, and Pakistan to learn Islam.
38. Tadjuddin, interview 13 April 2006. *Baligh* age in Islam is signified by a boys' first wet dream. In a deeper meaning, *baligh* means kids at the age that they can start to consider what is right and what is bad.
39. Osama, interview 20 July 2006
40. Yuli, interview 20 April 2006
41. Indonesian traditional cheap meal made from sprouted soybean patty.
42. This mastering of Qur'anic verses and *hadiths*, with its explanations of Salafi syaikhs, or in another word, their high concern on knowledge becomes "the selling point" of Jamaah Salafi among other Salafi groups. Jamaah Salafi believes that *ibadah* (rituals of submission) without '*ilm* (knowledge) is nothing.
43. A *hadith* by Ahmad, "Supposed that I can order someone to worship except God verily I will order to worship (*sujud*) to the husband."
44. The term *abangan-santri-priyayi* is originally introduced by Clifford Geertz as a typology of Javanese religions. In opposition to the Santri group, who practice puritanical Islam committed to a normative profession of the faith, Islamic Abangan is compatible with local customs influenced by Animism, Hinduism and Buddhism. See further in Geertz, 1960.
45. *Saved*, to some extent, is relatively similar as interpreted in Christianity. People join into the Jamaah (*Ahl al-Sunnah wa al-Jamaah*), then he/she will be saved, and enter the Heaven of God.
46. A term used by Syafii Anwar, a liberal Indonesian Muslim scholar. See Vatikiotis, 2005.
47. The Jakarta Charter is the origin of Pancasila (five tenets), the ideological basis of Indonesia. When the Preamble of UUD 1945 was announced on 18 August 1945, as the official manuscript of Pancasila, seven words "*dengan*

kewajiban menjalankan syariat Islam bagi pemeluk-pemeluknya (with the obligation to do Islamic Syariah for its adherents)" previously existed in the charter were omitted from the first point and left it with only "*dengan berdasarkan pada ketuhanan Yang Maha Esa* (based on the Oneness of God)."

References

Abdirrahman Anisah, Ummu. (accessed on 9 April 2006). "Hukum Alat Kontrasepsi Untuk Mencegah Kehamilan" in www.asysyariah.com

Albani, M. Nashiruddi. 2004. *Adab az-Zifaf: Panduan Pernikahan Nabi*. Indonesian edition, Yogyakarta: Media Hidayah.

Ammar, Nawal. 2000. "An Islamic Response toward Manifest Ecological Crises" in Harold Coward and Daniel C. Maguire (eds.), *Visions of a New Earth: Religious Perspectives on Population, Consumption and Ecology*. State University of New York Press, New York.

Ananta, Aris, L. Suryadinata and E.N. Arifin. 2003. *Indonesia's Population: Ethnicity and Religion in a Changing Political Landscape*. Institute of Southeast Asian Studies, Singapore.

Hanifah, Roni (ed.). *Fatwa-fatwa Kontemporer Ulama Ahlus Sunnah*, Purwokerto: Qaulan Karima.

BKKBN. 1 February 2006, in www.bkkbn.go.id

——. 14 December 2004. "Desentralisasi Genap Satu Tahun" in www.bkkbn.go.id

——. 23 September 2005, in www.bkkbn.go.id

——. 30 June 2006. "President Meminta Program KB Nasional Digalakkan Kembali" in www.bkkbn.go.id

BPS, BKKBN. Dept. of Health and Macro Inc. 2003. *Survai Demografi dan Kesehatan Indonesia*. Jakarta.

Chamie, Joseph. 1981. *Religion and Fertility: Arab Muslim-Christian Differentials*. Cambridge University Press, Cambridge.

East-West Centre. 2002. *The Future of Population in Asia*. East-West Centre, Hawaii.

Fadl, Khaled Abou El. 2003. *The Authoritative and the Authoritarian in Islamic Discourse*. Arizona State University, Arizona, Indonesian edition, *Yang Berwenang dan Yang Sewenang-wenang dalam Islam*. Serambi, Jakarta.

Findlay, Allen and Allan. 1987. *Population and Development in the Third World*. Methuen, London and New York.

Gatra. 04 July 2006. "Risau Beleid Bilah Bambu" in http://www.gatra.com

Geertz, Clifford. 1960. *Religion of Java*. Free Press, Glencoe.

——. 1973. *The Interpretation of Culture.* Basic Books, New York.

Hasan, Noorhaidi. 2006. "Salafi *Madrasas* and Islamic Radicalism in Post-New Order

Hassan, Riaz. 1986. *Islam: Dari Konservatisme Sampai Fundamentalisme,* CV Rajawali Press, Jakarta.

Hasyim, Syafiq (ed.). 1999. *Menakar Harga Perempuan: Eksplorasi Lanjut Atas Hak-Hak Reproduksi Perempuan Dalam Islam.* Mizan, Bandung.

Heidegger, M. 1996. *Being and Time.* Trans. Joan Stambaugh, State University of New York Press, Albany.

Hooker, V. and G. Fealy (eds.). 2006. *Voices of Islam in Southeast Asia: A Contemporary Sourcebook.* ISEAS, Singapore.

ICG (International Crisis Group). 2004. *Indonesia Backgrounder: Why Salafism and Terrorism Mostly Don't Mix.* ICG Asia Report No. 83, September 13.

Indonesia. Paper presented at the International Workshop: Voices of Islam in Europe and Southeast Asia, 20–22 January, Nakhon Si Thammarat, Thailand.

Ishaq Zulfa, Ummu. 29 June 2003. "Penggunaan Obat Untuk Mencegah Haid" in www.asysyariah.com

——. 14 December 2004. "Jangan Terlalu Membenci Istri" in www.asysyariah.com

——. 17 October 2004. "Sedekah yang Paling Utama" in www.asysyariah.com

——. 29 June 2003. "Nahkoda Dalam Bahteraku" in www.asysyariah.com

——. 5 July 2003. "Haruskah Kebersamaan Kita Berakhir Di sini...?" in www.asysyariah.com

——. 9 April 2006. "Permisalan Wanita yang Baik Bagi Insan Beriman" in www.asysyariah.com

Jaiz, Hartono Ahmad. 2005. *Ada Pemurtadan di IAIN.* Pustaka Al-Kautsar, Solo.

Jones, Gavin. 2005. *A Demographic Perspective on the Muslim World.* Asia Research Institute, Working Paper Series No. 42.

—— and Mehtab S. Karim (eds.). 2005. *Islam, the State and Population.* Hurst & Company, London.

Karim, Mehtab S. 1997. *Reproductive Behaviour in Muslim Countries,* DHS Working Papers, No. 23, Macro International Inc., Calverton and United Nation Population Fund, New York.

Kasun, Jacqueline R. 1999. *The War against Population: The Economics and Ideology of World Population Control.* Ignatius, San Francisco, 2nd edition.

Kompas, 21 May 2006.

Kompas, 01 July 2006.

Kompas, 24 July 2006.

Lubis, F. and A. Niehof (eds.). 2003. *Two is Enough: Family Planning in Indonesia Under the New Order, 1968–1998*. KITLV Press, Leiden.

MacFarquhar, Emily. 12 September 1994. "Population Wars" in http://www.keepmedia.com/pubs/USNewsWorldReport/1994/09/12/

Musallam, Basim. 1983. *Sex and Society in Islam: Birth Control before the Nineteenth Century*. Cambridge University Press, Cambridge.

Omran, Abdul-Rahim. 1992. *Family Planning in the Legacy of Islam*. Routledge, London; UNFPA, United Kingdom.

Oxford Encyclopaedia of the Modern Islamic World. 1995. Oxford University Press, Oxford.

Pikiran Rakyat, 26 December 2005.

Ramadan, Tariq. 2005. "Three Flavors of Salafism" in http://higher-criticism.blogspot.com/2005/10/three-flavors-of-salafism.html

Rifa'i, Akhmad. 1997. "Muslim Fertility in Indonesia: A Feature of Proximate Determinants of Java-Bali" *Al-Jami'ah*, Sunan Kalijaga State Institute of Islamic Studies, Yogyakarta, No. 60, 224–43.

Salafy, 19 July 2006. "Laporan Tim Peduli Musibah" in www.salafy.or.id

Salleh, Maarof. 2005. "Labelling Terrorism: Where do we place Salafi and Wahabi?" *The Muslim Reader*, Vol. 23, No. 1 (January–April), Dar al-Arqam, Singapore.

Searle, Rick. 1995. *Population Growth, Resource Consumption and the Environment: Seeking a Common Vision for a Troubled World*. Centre for Studies in Religion and Society, University of Victoria, Canada.

Sihbudi, R. and E. Turmudi (eds.). 2005. *Islam dan Radikalisme di Indonesia*. LIPI Press, Jakarta.

Sivan, E., G.A. Almond and R.S. Appleby. 2003. *Strong Religion, the Rise of Fundamentalism around the World*. The University of Chicago Press, Chicago and London.

State Ministry for Population/National Family Planning Coordinating Board (BKKBN), 1998. "The Role of Muslims Leaders and Organizations in Indonesian National Family Planning/Reproductive Health Program". Paper presented to the Fourth Annual Board Meeting of the Partners in Population and Development, 07–12 November, Cairo, Egypt. Suadi, Al-*Ustadz* Qomar, 7 August 2004. "Syubhat-Syubhat Seputar Takfir" in www.asysyariah.com

Subahar, A.H. and Faturochman, 2005. "Islamic Teachers and Reproductive Health Issues in Madura, Indonesia" in Gavin Jones and Karim S. Mehtab (eds.), *Islam, the State and Population*. Hurst & Company, London.

Suhadi, 16 June 2006. "Perda Syariat Di Negeri Pancasila" in www.parasindonesia.com

——. 25 June 2006. "Politics of a Language Game: Adakah Perda Syariat Itu?" in www.parasindonesia.com

Sulaimi, Al-*Ustadz* Ruwaifi' Bin, 24 March, 2006. "Siapakah Wahhabi?" in www.asysyariah.com

The New York Times. 27 June 2006.

United Nations. 1995. *Women's Education and Fertility Behaviour: Recent Evidence from the Demographic and Health Survey*, New York.

——. 1973. *The Determinants and Consequences of Population Trends*. New York.

Usamah Bin Rawiyah, Abu. 5 February 2005. "Ciri-ciri Ulama" in www.asysyariah.com

Utsaimin, Syaikh Muhammad Bin Shalih. *Risalah fid Dima' al-Thabi'iyyah li al-Nisa'* (A Treatise on Natural Blood for Women), 57–63.

Vatikiotis, Michael. 3 September 2005. "Islamizing Indonesia" in *International Herald Tribune*.

Wahid, Hidayat Nur. 16 July 2006. in http://hnw.or.id/id/www.alfauzan.net.

CHAPTER 8

A Quantitative and Qualitative Investigation of Role of Gender-Power Relations on Women's Contraceptive Choices in Nepal

Bina Gubhaju

Worldwide, fertility has declined and a significant change in contraceptive behaviour in the developing world has occurred in the last four decades. Whereas in the 1960s, relatively few couples practiced contraception, now more than half are current users (Bongaarts and Johansson, 2002). Much of the demographic and sociological literature on fertility behaviour has focused on explaining the causes of the transition that has now occurred in incredibly diverse settings. Moreover, increases in population due to slow reductions in fertility following the mortality decline in developing countries sparked numerous studies on the obstacles to fertility decline. As one of the proximate determinants of fertility, contraceptive behaviour has been studied extensively in the literature in an effort to increase contraceptive use.

With such rapid increases in contraceptive prevalence, accumulated experience with using various methods of birth control has also increased and thus emerging research and policy questions have now progressively tended to focus more on contraceptive method-mix, how couples choose between contraceptive options that are offered in the family planning programme, and ensuring contraceptive satisfaction and continuation. The contraceptive choice literature underscores the importance of demographic, socio-economic, access, and policy-level determinants on the choices that couples make in choosing an appropriate method. In particular, Bulatao's (1989) framework considers a set of social and economic factors that he labels as contraceptive competence, goals, access, and evaluation related dimensions. Research that has followed gives considerable attention to many of the factors emphasized by Bulatao, yet what has been less investigated are the gender-based constraints to women's contraceptive choices, which is of particular relevance in patriarchal settings where women's status is low. Ringheim (1996) argues that in developing country contexts, the burden of contraception has fallen mostly on women who are the ones to bear the personal, social, physiological and psychological costs of contraception. This pattern suggests that broader gender imbalances may have considerable influence on the types of methods that are more frequently used by couples. Consequently, aspects of gender-power relations, as defined in the women's status and empowerment literature, that have in fact been given a great deal of attention in the study of fertility and contraceptive use, (Presser and Sen, 2000; Mason, 2001) may also be crucial in limiting or enabling the use of certain methods.

Thus, the question as to how such gender-power relations, as defined in the women's status literature, would influence the type of method a couple chooses to adopt remains relatively unexplored. The main objective of this paper is to link the women's empowerment and contraceptive choice literature to examine how women's status and gender dimensions in a patriarchal society such as Nepal influences women's contraceptive choices. Information as such would aid in better understanding of gender-based constraints to the choices that are accessible and available to couples. The level of autonomy and decision-making that women have may have implications for whether they are able to negotiate male-controlled methods with their husbands, particularly the use of condoms, or if they are able to use temporary spacing methods that require repeated visits to health facilities. The 2001 Nepal Demographic and Health Survey and qualitative data collected from focus group discussions in Kathmandu valley has been used to explore this link.

Literature Review

The importance of studying contraceptive choice emerged in the literature in the mid-1980s when it became evident that contraceptive prevalence was increasing and a majority of couples around the world were practising some form of birth control. Previous goals of increasing contraceptive uptake had been realized in several contexts, and thus the policy and research focus shifted to ensuring contraceptive continuation and exploring method choice among users (United Nations, 1984 {cited in Palmore and Bulatao, 1989}). While research was being carried out in a number of different contexts and settings, Bulatao attempted to synthesize the fragmented literature and devised a framework that posits that method choice is affected by factors within four broad dimensions: (i) contraceptive competence, (ii) contraceptive goals, (iii) contraceptive access and (iv) contraceptive evaluation. Contraceptive competence is the ability to use a particular method effectively. Various factors such as individual and class differences in access to information are expected to influence this ability. *Contraceptive goals* are the specific fertility effects a woman or couple seeks to achieve. Whether to space or limit child bearing is an important distinction in this dimension. *Contraceptive access* affects choice in that the method must first be available and accessible for an individual to use it. And lastly, *contraceptive evaluation* refers to the practical and moral implications of using a specific method and judgments that people may have of family planning in general (Bulatao, 1989).

Since then studies have examined method choice from a comparative country-level policy perspective to analyses of individual-level determinants in a single country as well as specific regions of a country (Bhende et al., 1991; Entwisle et al., 1996; Potter, 1999; Khan and Rahman, 1997; Mannan, 2002; Ergocmen et al., 2004; Kulczycki, 2004). Potter (1999) compares different histories and population policies of Mexico and Brazil and how they have contributed to the predominance of a limited number of methods—sterilization and IUDs in Mexico and sterilizations followed by a caesarian section birth in Brazil. He argues that government policies implemented during the early phase of the fertility transition, through the process of "path dependency", continues to influence present circumstances even though current needs and conditions differ. Turkey has been a focus of several studies on contraceptive method choice because of high rates of withdrawal (Koc, 2000; Ergocmen et al., 2004; Kulczcki, 2004). While studies have found that the use of withdrawal mainly reflects husband's preferences, women prefer the method because of the absences of side-effects (Ergocmen et al., 2004; Kulczycki, 2004).

In Asia, recent work in Bangladesh by Mannan (2002), where pills are the predominant method used, extends Bulatao's framework by including several direct indicators of access that measure availability and affordability of current method. The study also considers two programmatic factors, visit by a fieldworker and visit to a satellite clinic. Results indicate that side-effects of other methods, convenience or ease of current method, and the availability and accessibility of a method are important predictors of method-choice. Moreover, results show that use of pills and condoms increases significantly with higher levels of husbands' education. Sterilization use compared to other modern methods is less common among better educated couples. A previous study done by Khan and Rahman (1997) also finds that in Bangladesh temporary methods such as pills, IUD, condoms, and traditional methods are preferred by educated women, while injections and permanent methods are more common among lesser educated women. More recently, Basu (2005) highlights an interesting paradox in India where 'traditional' women—which she defines as rural, uneducated, and poor—are the women who tend to choose modern methods and that 'modern' women—educated and urban—are relying more on traditional methods.

Prior studies of contraceptive choice have paid very little attention to the role of gender-power dynamics in the decision that couples make in choosing a method. While education levels of husbands and wives have had particularly strong and varying effects on method choice, this relationship has not been investigated in relation to broader gender and power structures. Next, I review the theoretical propositions of the women's status and fertility literature to situate the contraceptive choice literature within the framework of gender-power dynamics.

Women's Status, Fertility and Contraceptive Behaviour

In the past several decades there has been a rising interest in the relationship between women's status and fertility outcomes. The concept of female autonomy was first introduced by Dyson and Moore (1983) as an explanation for the north-south dichotomy in demographic behaviour in India. Since then a vast literature has emerged that emphasizes the reality that women's desire and ability to manage their fertility are in part affected by their status, self-image, and sense of empowerment (Mason, 1987; Sathar et al., 1988; Gage, 1995; Martin, 1995; Govindasamy and Malhotra, 1996; Hogan et al., 1999; Presser and Sen, 2001; Kishor, 2005).

Despite the volume of work that has been done to date on women's status and fertility outcomes, the empirical evidence on this relationship has been mixed, partly because of the lack of theoretical and conceptual clarity concerning the definition of women's status (Mason, 1987; Presser and Sen, 2001). In the early empirical literature, the most commonly used proxy indicators were women's education and employment status (Cochrane, 1979; Jejeebhoy, 1995; Martin, 1995). Other indicators of women's status that have also been explored are age at marriage, age difference between husbands and wives, and spousal communication (Gage, 1995; Sathar et al., 1988; Hogan et al., 1999).

In response to the need for better measures of women's status, attempts have been made to develop direct indicators of the multiple dimensions of women's lives in relation to gender-power relations. Various studies explicitly examining women's status at a smaller scale using quasi-anthropological, qualitative and survey methods have included measures of women's mobility, participation in domestic decision-making, control over household resources, and ability to communicate fertility desires and family planning needs (Morgan and Niraula, 1995; Niraula and Morgan, 1996; Balk, 1994; Mason and Smith, 2000). At a national scale, the demographic and health surveys (DHS) have been one of the frequently used data sources to examine gender effects on reproductive outcomes. Beginning with the Egypt DHS in 1988, the survey added a women's status module that included several direct measures of women's participation in household decision-making in relation to financial control, household purchases, and health care. Women were also asked questions on their freedom of movement and their opinions on specific issues of gender inequality such as domestic violence and sexual rights. Currently, the women's status module has been implemented in several countries.

The inclusion of these measures has been pioneer in making a nationally representative survey such as the DHS more conducive to research on gender issues (Govindasamy and Malhotra, 1996; Hogan et al., 1999; Moursund and Kravdal, 2003). While measures available in the DHS have been used extensively, researchers continue to grapple with how best to conceptualize concepts of women's empowerment and ongoing efforts still need to detangle its effects on different outcomes in various contexts (Kishor, 2005). Nonetheless, literature on women's status, fertility and family planning provides some, but not conclusive, evidence that when women's position is low—whether through education, employment status, decision-making, or various aspects of autonomy—they are likely to face greater costs of contraception due to their lack of access and familial and social opposition to family planning. However, the focus of past research has been on the relationship between women's status and contraceptive use, regardless of the types of methods chosen. At best, studies have distinguished between traditional and modern methods of contraception (Gage, 1995). While the notion that broader gender imbalances could have a substantial impact on the type of methods more frequently adopted has been around (Ringheim, 1996; 1999), only recently have studies begun to empirically test this idea. A small scale study done by Chapagain (2005), in an attempt to explore reasons for the high prevalence of female contraceptive methods in rural Nepal, acknowledges that stereotypical gender roles are influential in contraceptive choice. He concludes that unequal husband-wife power relationships leads to husband's domination in contraceptive decision-making that tends to favour use of female methods. Results of Mumtaz et al.'s (2005) study on condom use in Uganda and Zimbabwe in the context of HIV/AIDS further provides evidence that gendered couple-dynamics and communication about sexual issues play a substantial role in determining use of condoms.

Moreover, in the context of Nepal, similar to other countries in South Asia, permanent methods of male and female sterilization have been the main emphasis of the government's family planning programmes, particularly targeted at the illiterate and rural population. Prior studies in South Asia have shown that permanent methods of male and female sterilization are used more commonly by lesser educated couples. Bulatao (1989) also argues that sterilization may have been more frequently used by lesser educated couples due to their perception of being less competent in use of other temporary hormonal methods. In Nepal, temporary methods of family planning have only been recently emphasized in the family planning programme. These methods require repeat visits to health service outlets rather than a one-time visit for sterilization operations. Temporary methods have been less popular and hence the use of temporary methods can be considered "innovative" behaviour, against a history of a predominance of permanent methods. Thus, it may be a behaviour that is more likely to be adopted by better educated women.

Once the decision to adopt a method of contraception has been made, it is likely that a multitude of gender-power related factors further limit women's choices and preferences, in addition to the socio-economic factors addressed by Bulatao and the literature on contraceptive method choice. In this paper, I apply the framework proposed by Bulatao and re-conceptualize his *contraceptive competence* dimension to incorporate several aspects of gender-power dynamics to explore what role, if any, gender-power relations have on women's choice of contraception, beyond dimensions of *goals*, *access*, and *evaluation*. It is expected that greater competence as indicated by increases in women's power in spousal relations would lead not only to a higher likelihood of using contraception, but also greater use of male methods and/or temporary spacing methods: That is, greater use of methods other than female sterilization, particularly user-dependent methods such as condoms and pills.

Data and Methods

Data for the analysis presented in this paper comes from both quantitative and qualitative sources. The 2001 Nepal Demographic and Health Survey (NDHS) is used for the quantitative analysis. Qualitative data from focus group discussions with married women and men will be used to elaborate further on the link between gender and power dynamics on contraceptive choices.

Quantitative Component

The NDHS, which is part of the worldwide demographic and health Surveys, is a nationally representative cross-sectional survey of ever-married women 15 to 49 years of age. Data were collected from 8,726 women to provide detailed information on fertility, family planning, and reproductive health. Two-stage estimation models are chosen for the analysis. This is considered an appropriate method to model contraceptive choice with the assumption that contraceptive decision-making is a two-stage process in which the decision to use is the first stage followed by the selection of a specific method (see Mannan, 2002 for a similar estimation procedure). Hence, in the first stage of the analysis, the sample consists of all currently married women. After excluding women who are currently pregnant and cases with missing values on the dependent and independent variables, the final sample consists of 7,504 women. In the second stage of the analysis, only women that are currently using a method of contraception are selected, resulting in a sample of 3,296 women.

Dependent Variable

Table 1 provides descriptive statistics for the dependent variables in the model.

The dependent variable used for the first stage of the analysis is women's current contraceptive use. This is a dichotomous variable coded as 1 if the woman is currently using a method and 0 if not using any method. Slightly over 40 per cent of women in the sample are currently using a method of contraception.

Two dependent variables are created for the second stage of analysis. All women were asked questions about the method of family

Table 1

Per cent Distribution of Dependent Variables, NDHS 2001

Stage 1		
All Women		7504
Contraceptive Behaviour		
% using either a temporary or permanent method	43.4	3320
Stage 2		
Contraceptive Users		3296[1]
Male methods[2]	32.8	1090
Type of Method		
Female sterilization	38.1	1208
Male sterilization	16.2	531
Injections	21.7	739
Pills	4.1	144
Condoms	7.1	252
Traditional (periodic abstinence, withdrawal)	9.5	307
IUD/Norplant/other	3.4	115

[1]An additional 24 women are excluded from the contraceptive users sample because of missing values on the independent variable: decision to use contraception (asked only of users).

[2]Male methods includes male sterilization, condoms, and traditional method

Note: Percentages are based on weighted data. Frequencies reported are unweighted.

planning they are currently using. The first dependent variable is a dichotomous measure of women's use of a male-controlled method versus use of a female-controlled method. Woman are coded as 1 if using a male-controlled method, which includes male sterilization, condoms, and traditional methods (withdrawal and periodic abstinence), and 0 if using a female-controlled method (female sterilization, injections, pills, IUD, Norplant, foams and jelly). While the separation of male versus female-controlled is not as clear-cut as this categorization suggests and "control" does not necessarily imply dominance, in general methods classified as male-controlled require active involvement and co-operation from the husband while female-controlled methods are ones that women could potentially use without co-operation and consent from their spouses [although in some contexts women rely on their husbands for a continuous supply of pills and knowledge on how to use the method correctly (Khan, 2001)]. Method-use in Nepal is heavily dominated by female-controlled methods with two-thirds of women using some kind of female contraceptive method.

The second dependent variable is a seven-category response variable indicating the specific type of contraceptive method used. The responses have been categorized as follows: (i) female sterilization, (ii) male sterilization, (iii) injections, (iv) pills, (v) condoms, (vi) traditional methods (withdrawal and periodic abstinence) and (vii) IUD/Norplant. The IUD/Norplant category also includes a very small per cent, less than 1 per cent, of women using foams and jelly. While grouping together all male-controlled methods in one category can identify certain trends in contraceptive method-mix associated with explanatory variables of interest, separation of type of methods further identifies differences in the specific choice of method. Among users, female sterilization is the predominant method with about 40 per cent of women currently using the method, 15 per cent are using male sterilization, slightly above 20 per cent are using injections and less than 10 per cent are using pills, condoms, traditional methods and IUD/Norplant.

Independent Variables

The main independent variables in the model are dimensions of gender-power relations that are presumed to capture the multidimensional nature of the broader concept of women's status. Table 2 shows the frequency distributions of the variables as entered in the analytical models.

Table 2

Per cent Distribution of Independent Variables, NDHS 2001

	All women *N=7504*	*Current users* *N=3296*
A. Gender-power relations (contraceptive competence)		
Women's education		
No education	72.0	66.5
Incomplete primary education	11.6	12.6
Complete primary/incomplete secondary	12.5	15.1
Complete secondary and higher	3.9	5.8
Husband's education		
No education	34.5	29.3
Incomplete primary education	25.1	25.2
Complete primary/incomplete secondary	31.3	33.2
Complete secondary and higher	6.7	10.4
Don't know husband's education	2.4	1.9

Cont'd...

Cont'd...

Women's occupation		
Not working	16.2	14.9
Working in agriculture	76.2	73.3
Working in non-agriculture	7.5	11.8
Women's decision-making		
No decision—health	71.7	67.4
No decision—large household purchases	66.5	59.5
No decision—visit to family/friends	59.9	53.4
No decision—contraception	N/A	9.5
Gender role norms		
Wife beating is justified—yes	28.8	27.7
Right to refuse sex—yes	90.0	89.3
Barriers in seeking medical care for self		
Problems getting permission to go	16.7	12.1
Problems getting money	65.5	58.6
Problems of health facility being too far	49.7	41.9
Problem of no female health provider	48.9	44.5
Discussion of family planning		
Discussed family planning with husband	41.2	52.4
Discussed family planning with other family members/friends	31.2	42.0
B. Contraceptive Goals		
Age		
15–24	81.1	15.1
25–34	36.2	42.3
35–49	35.7	42.7
Has one or more sons	76.2	91.1
Has one or more daughter	71.5	77.7
Desire more children		
Want no more	70.4	N/A
Want within two years	12.4	N/A
Want after two years/unsure	17.2	N/A
Wanted last child		
Wanted then	N/A	23.5
Wanted later	N/A	6.6
Wanted no more	N/A	16.1
No births in past 5 years	N/A	53.9

Cont'd...

Cont'd...

Currently breastfeeding	46.3	N/A
Husband lives in house	78.5	88.7
Experience of child death	31.0	30.0
C. Contraceptive Access		
Urban residence	9.7	15.1
Lives in Kathmandu valley	3.2	5.4
Region of residence		
Central	32.4	32.9
Eastern	23.9	27.9
Western	20.5	19.0
Mid-western	13.7	12.6
Far-western	9.5	7.6
Visited by family planning worker in last 12 months	11.1	14.0
No media exposure to family planning messages	40.1	30.1
D. Contraceptive Evaluation		
Couple's approval of family planning		
Wife approves/husband disapproves	15.2	N/A
Husband approves/wife disapproves	1.2	N/A
Both approve	78.2	N/A
Neither approve	5.4	N/A
Husband approves of family planning	N/A	94.3

Bulatao's *contraceptive competence* dimension is re-conceptualized to incorporate aspects of gender status, decision-making, attitudes towards traditional gender-roles, and autonomy. Measures of gender status include women's education and employment status. In addition, husband's education is considered as its value relative to wife's education can be a useful proxy measure of status. Several other indicators that portray women's decision-making in the household, attitudes towards traditional gender-roles, and autonomy—as measured through women's perceptions of barriers in accessing medical care, and communication of family planning with spouse and other household members are entered in the analytical models. Following is a detailed discussion of each one of these variables:

Women's participation in decision-making: The variables considered gauge women's decision-making in three areas: (i) their own health care (health), (ii) major household purchases (economic), and (iii) visits to family and friends (social). A fourth decision-making variable—decisions about contraceptive use—was asked only from women currently using a method of contraception, therefore this variable is included only in the second stage of analysis of contraceptive users. All women were asked who in their family has final say on the specified decisions. Responses are coded as "respondent only", "husband/partner only", "respondent and husband/partner jointly", "respondent and someone else jointly", "someone else" and "decision not made/not applicable." For this analysis, "husband/partner only" and "someone else" are coded as the respondent having no say in the decision-making v/s all other possible categories as this captures the extent to which women are completely absent from the particular decision that is under consideration. Some prior studies have created a scale from the decision-making items. However, in this analysis I keep each decision related measure as a separate variable to examine the effects of decision-making in each area on contraceptive behaviour.

Gender-role norms: Women's attitudes towards traditional gender-role norms and expectations are measured by two attitudinal variables that explore women's acceptance of their subordinate role. The first variable indicates whether the woman agrees that wife-beating is justified under *any one* of the following four circumstances: if she burns food, if she argues with him, if she goes out without telling him, if she neglects the children, and if she refuses to have sex with him. It is assumed that women who justify wife-beating on any one of the circumstances hold traditional gender-role norms. The second variable indicates whether the woman agrees that she has the right to refuse sex with her husband under *all* four of the following circumstances: if she knows the husband has a sexually transmitted disease, if she knows the husband has had sex with other women, if she has recently given birth, and if she is tired or not in the mood. It is assumed here that women who do *not* hold traditional gender role norms would agree that a wife should have the right to decide when and whether she wants to have sexual relations with her husband, thus agreeing under all circumstances.

Barriers in accessing health care: The extent to which gender-related constraints inhibit women from accessing medical care for themselves are measured by a series of questions that assess problems women perceive in (i) getting permission to go, (ii) money needed for treatment, (iii) distance to health facility and (iv) not having a female provider at the clinic. Responses are coded as "a big problem" v/s "not a big problem". Each one of the barriers is also assessed independently. Barriers associated with problems of getting "money needed for treatment" and "distance to health facility", while a measure of gender-power constraints, could also reflect economic and access-related constraints. It is assumed that women that perceive big problems in accessing health care are less autonomous than women that do not perceive big problems.

Discussion of family planning: Discussion of family planning with husband and discussion with other members of the family and friends are also included in this dimension, as it depicts women's greater autonomy and negotiating power in their relationships. Discussion with husband is treated as a separate variable from discussion with other members of the family and friends. While it is assumed in some of the literature that women with increased status have greater ability to communicate matters of family planning, the literature also acknowledges the fact that women using contraceptive methods have a greater need to discuss such issues compared to women that are not currently using contraceptive methods.

Control Variables

Necessary controls that have been shown in previous studies to be determinants of contraceptive behaviour are also incorporated in the models. These have been grouped into Bulatao's dimensions of goals, access and evaluation. Variables considered under goals are age, has one or more sons, has one or more daughters, desire for more children, whether the last child was wanted, whether the woman is currently breastfeeding, whether the husband lives in the house, and whether the woman had experienced a child death. Contraceptive access-related measures are urban residence, residence in Kathmandu Valley, region of residence, whether the respondent has been visited by a family planning worker and has media exposure to family planning messages. Finally, contraceptive evaluation is assessed through a measure of couple's approval of family planning, constructed from responses to questions asked whether the woman herself approves of family planning and whether she thinks that her husband also approves of family planning. The two variables are combined to create a new variable coded as "wife only approves", "husband only approves", "both approve" and "neither approve" of family planning. However, since 99 per cent of women currently using contraception approve of family planning, in the second stage of analysis only husband's approval of family planning is entered in the models. All of these variables are entered as controls and their effects after controlling for gender-power-related measures will be discussed only briefly.

Analytical Strategy

Logistic regression models are used to examine effects of the independent variables on two dichotomous outcomes: (i) use versus non-use of contraception, (ii) male-controlled versus female-controlled method-use. A seven-category multinomial logistic regression model is used to predict the likelihood of using a specific contraceptive method, in reference to female sterilization. The results of the analysis are presented as odds ratios to facilitate interpretation of findings.

Qualitative Component

Qualitative data were collected during a four-month project in Kathmandu valley from September to December 2004. The location of the field research was in urban areas of the three districts (cities) of Kathmandu valley: Kathmandu, Bhaktapur, and Lalitpur. Kathmandu Valley was chosen as the field site for collection of qualitative data since it is an area that is well-served with health facilities and family planning clinics so that actual distance and availability of services and contraceptive methods will not be a major barrier to contraceptive use. The three districts of the valley have the highest per cent of contraceptive use in Nepal which makes it an ideal place to study variations in method choice and women's experiences with using various methods.

Sample

The main source of information gathered was focus group discussions with nine groups of married women and two groups of men (two men in the groups were unmarried), resulting in a total of 80 informants. The focus group is considered an appropriate method for investigating the topic under study as it is expected that the group interactions will elicit participants' understanding of the cultural context of contraceptive decision-making. It is also possible to observe agreements and disagreements about health concerns, family/spousal oppositions, and opinions of contraception via discussions elicited in a group (Hay, 2000; Morgan, 1993). Educational composition of the groups ranged from women with no education to women with master's degree. An important aspect of the study was to hold discussions with educated women since this has often been neglected in studies of family planning. The age of

Table 3

Determinants of Women's Contraceptive Behaviour: Logistic Regression Odds Ratios (Binomial and Multinomial), NDHS 2001

	Current use	Male method	Ref: F. sterilization					
			M. Sterilz	Inject	Pills	Condom	Trad	IUD/Norp
Gender-Power Relations (Contraceptive Competence)								
Women's Education								
No education	ref	ref	ref	ref	ref	ref	ref	ref
Incomplete primary	1.06	1.26+	1.34	1.29	1.31	1.84*	1.38	1.56
Incomplete secondary	1.31*	1.84***	2.26***	1.52*	1.48	2.72***	2.23**	1.13
Complete secondary and higher	1.89***	1.95**	1.22	2.27*	3.58*	5.91***	5.17***	5.88***
Husbands' Education								
No education	ref	ref	ref	ref	ref	ref	ref	ref
Incomplete primary	1.28***	1.23+	1.85***	1.17	1.77*	1.47	0.76	0.90
Incomplete secondary	1.23*	1.42**	1.74**	0.98	1.61	1.92*	0.96	0.98
Complete secondary and higher	1.77***	2.86***	3.48***	1.16	0.88	5.24***	1.57	1.17
Don't know husband's education	0.80	1.38	1.77	0.48+	1.71	0.49	0.65	0.32
Women's Occupation								
Working in agriculture	ref	ref	ref	ref	ref	ref	ref	ref
Not working	0.76**	0.63***	0.38***	0.74+	0.54+	0.72	0.57*	0.35**

Cont'd...

Cont'd...

Working in non-agriculture	1.44**	0.66**	0.88	1.33	0.70	1.01	0.52**	0.84
Women's Decision-making								
No decision—health	0.94	1.07	0.99	0.66**	0.77	0.69+	0.89	0.92
No decision—large purchases	0.89	1.00	1.20	1.50**	0.58*	1.53*	0.82	0.80
No decision—visit to family/friends	0.93	0.89	0.77+	0.83	1.39	0.81	1.05	1.35
No decision—contraception	n/a	6.33***	5.97***	0.95	0.61	6.37***	5.53***	0.47
Gender Role Norms								
Wife beating is justified—yes	0.93	0.93	0.94	1.17	1.03	0.98	1.06	1.04
Right to refuse sex—yes	0.68***	1.53**	2.37***	1.53*	1.84+	1.28	1.88*	1.22
Barriers in Seeking Medical Care								
Problems getting permission to go	0.99	0.73*	0.87	1.42*	1.99*	0.78	0.96	0.93
Problems getting money	0.97	0.97	0.90	0.99	1.51+	1.04	1.19	1.11
Problems health facility too far	0.76***	1.26*	1.46**	1.33*	0.77	1.23	1.19	0.76
Problem no female health provider	0.85**	1.26*	1.53***	1.33*	0.99	1.55*	1.18	1.21
Discussion of Family Planning								
Discussed FP with husband	1.64***	1.10	0.73*	4.94***	7.15***	8.73***	6.24***	3.02***
Discussed FP with other family/friends	1.32***	0.62***	0.70**	1.00	0.79	0.45***	0.66**	1.42

Cont'd...

Cont'd...

Contraceptive Goals								
Age								
15–24	0.73***	1.22	1.21	2.33***	2.30**	3.63***	1.80*	2.43**
25–34 (ref)	ref	ref	ref	ref	ref	ref	ref	ref
35–49	0.71***	1.08	1.12	1.18	0.82	0.92	1.20	0.67
Has one or more sons	2.67***	0.56***	0.52+	0.21***	0.10***	0.09***	0.13***	0.33*
Has one or more daughters	1.04	0.88	1.18	1.57**	0.92	0.84	1.01	1.76*
Desire More Children								
Want no more (ref)	ref	n/a	n/a	n/a	n/a	n/a	n/a	n/a
Want within two years	0.07***	n/a	n/a	n/a	n/a	n/a	n/a	n/a
Want after two years/unsure	0.42***	n/a	n/a	n/a	n/a	n/a	n/a	n/a
Wanted Last Child								
Wanted then (ref)	n/a	ref	ref	ref	ref	ref	ref	ref
Wanted later	n/a	0.78	0.54	1.01	1.01	0.72	0.94	0.73
Wanted no more	n/a	1.30+	1.74*	0.71*	1.28	0.96	0.86	0.95
No births in past 5 years	n/a	1.07	1.08	0.19***	0.39***	0.34***	0.28***	0.44**
Currently breastfeeding	0.30***	n/a	n/a	n/a	n/a	n/a	n/a	n/a
Husband lives in house	3.44***	1.18	1.23	2.48***	4.00**	2.18**	3.33***	2.87*
Experience of child death	0.78***	0.89	0.98	1.39**	1.30	1.16	1.03	1.19

Cont'd...

method-specific use by occupation are significant between women working in the agricultural sector and women not employed. Women not employed are more likely to be using female sterilization compared to IUD/Norplant, male sterilization, and traditional methods and it is also partially ($p<0.10$) significant for greater use of female sterilization vs injection and pill use. The notion of female sterilization weakening the body could be a factor explaining lesser reliance on female sterilization by women working in the agricultural sector since it would interfere with hard labour required of agricultural work.

Gender-Power Relations: Measures of Decision-Making, Gender Roles and Autonomy

While indicators of women's decision-making do not provide any consistent evidence, one notable result is with regards to decision-making on the use of contraception.[1] The effect of this variable is rather interesting in that women who say they had no say in their contraceptive decisions are in fact more likely to be using male-controlled methods and in particular male sterilization, condoms and traditional methods in reference to female sterilization. Since all of these methods are male-controlled and require a degree of cooperation from their husbands, it is possible that despite their involvement in the decision-making process women perceive that the final say rests with their husbands. Similar to findings in Turkey (Kulczycki, 2004), the use of male-controlled methods may reflect decision-making by the husband but within woman's preferences and desires to avoid side-effects of other hormonal methods, thus in fact indicating sharing of contraceptive responsibility.

Gender-role norms as measured through women's opinions on their right to refuse sex also show an interesting relationship. Counter to expectations women expressing liberal attitudes on the right to refuse sexual advances by the husband are less likely to use contraception. It is plausible though that women holding such views have reduced coital frequency within marriage or are relying on traditional methods that are often underreported in surveys. Among current users, these women are opting for male-controlled methods, and in particular male sterilization and traditional methods in reference to female sterilization. The use of male sterilization and traditional methods compared to female sterilization is expected of women with liberal views on gender role norms, as it indicates a greater sense of control that women may feel over their own reproductive lives, since these methods require cooperation from the husband and less reliance on solely female-controlled methods.

With regard to barriers in seeking medical care for self, women who perceive distance to the health facility and not having a female health provider at a health facility as a big problem in accessing health care are less likely to use contraception. Perceived barriers related to distance to health facility may also reflect actual accessibility to health facilities and remoteness of place of residence, thus having an effect on lower likelihood of women using any method. However, the results are also consistent with the women's empowerment explanation. Distance and the absence of female health provider may not be perceived as hindrances by women that are more likely to be willing to engage in innovative behaviour, such as contraceptive adoption (Caldwell, 1986; Mumtaz and Salway, 2005). On the other hand, women that perceive distance and absence of a female health provider at health facility as big problems are more likely to be using male-controlled methods. These variables may be capturing actual problems of accessibility of methods and reluctance to undergo sterilization operations with male providers, which may necessitate the use of male methods. Women who perceive problems of getting permission to go are significantly less likely to be using male-controlled methods. Problems in seeking permission in accessing health care for self demonstrates women's dependence on other household members and this finding supports the assertion that greater use of female-controlled methods may be indicative of broader societal imbalances (Ringheim, 1999).

The effects of discussion of family planning either with the husband or other members of family and friends on women's contraceptive choices points heavily to the arguments of reverse causality rather than the notion of discussion as a source of autonomy for women. Women who have initiated contraceptive use are the ones that have a greater need to discuss method-related issues; therefore women who report that they discuss family planning have a higher likelihood of adopting contraception. It is interesting that discussion of family planning with the husband does not exhibit a significant relationship with the use of male versus female-controlled methods but discussion of family planning with other members of the family and friends decreases the likelihood of women using male-controlled methods. Method-specific multinomial regression shows that types of methods more likely to be used when it involves discussion with the husband are IUD/Norplant, injections, pills, condoms and traditional methods compared to female sterilization. These are all the methods that require consent and cooperation from the husband and may thus suggest that women who are able to discuss family planning with their husbands are less likely to rely on female sterilization.

In method-specific regressions, women who have discussed family planning with other members of the family are less likely to be using male sterilization, condoms and traditional methods in reference to female sterilization. This might be because women feel obliged to do what everybody else in their social networks does and since these are less popular methods, discussion with friends and family has a negative social influence on the likelihood of women using such methods. However, the results are also consistent with the reverse causality argument that women discuss experiences of side-effects and seek advice on female contraceptive methods with other members of the family and friends, and hence resulting in the higher likelihood of use of female-controlled methods. While these issues are very difficult to solve with cross-sectional data, not being able to discuss issues of family planning has been found to be a hindrance to women's family planning initiation in a study using longitudinal data (Ayaga, 2002).

Overall, quantitative results support the assertion that beyond Bulatao's framework of *goals, access,* and *evaluation* related dimensions, aspects of gender-power relations also play a crucial role in limiting choices that are available to women. In general, women's greater power in spousal relations led to greater use of male-controlled methods, and use of methods other than female sterilization, in particular condoms and traditional methods. Several factors considered as controls in the study (see Table 3)—variables under the dimensions of *goals*, *access* and *evaluation*—continue to exhibit significant effects on women's contraceptive behaviour, suggesting their prominence in method choice. We now turn to results from the qualitative analysis to further explore the intricacies involved in the decision-making process in choosing a specific method.

Qualitative Results

The Role of Education

While quantitative results of women's education have shown that as women's education increases the method-mix becomes more varied, focus group discussions also attest to these differences in women's experiences of using specific methods by educational attainment. What was particularly striking was the difference in the way women talked about condom use and relying on traditional methods. Indeed, the use of condoms and traditional methods came up often in discussions with educated women, though this had to do mostly with their fear of side effects of other methods. A 28-year old woman with a bachelor's degree comments:

> *If one can stay on the safe side naturally then why resort to such methods. If your husband has that much power, then why use things that have such side-effects. It's not your husband that has to suffer, it's you.*

Similarly, a condom user says:

> *... it's only the condom that doesn't have any of these side-effects but the only fear is that it might break. That's the only fear so I think the best method is the condom.*

However, there was a very different reaction to condoms in discussions with women with lower levels of education. Issues of power in the relationship, trust in their partners, and trust in the method itself were some underlying concerns expressed by women. For some, they are not able to negotiate condom use with their husbands, while for others husbands are unwilling to use condoms even if the wife feels that it is an appropriate method. In some instances though the way women themselves view condoms is quite different from the way educated women view the method. This woman says:

> *It would be easy. It doesn't have any side-effects on you or your husband...but then you have to be afraid that these men will carry it with them wherever they go.*

> *I think the injection is fine with me. That thing you have to carry around with you. Now you can't trust men...that's what I think.*

Both of these women associate condom use with extra-marital affairs and their distrust in men prompts them to use a hormonal method despite side-effects. For some other women there is a lack of proper knowledge of the method and distrust of condoms being a secure method of contraception. A woman whose husband is willing to use the condom, but she herself does not want to use narrates:

> *My husband sometimes does say that he'll use condoms. He says it's quite difficult for me, my head hurts, my stomach hurts. He says he will use a condom but I don't let him. I'm afraid that something might happen and I'll get pregnant so I feel safer using Depo. Some say that if you use a condom, it can break and you can get pregnant. Some say that it can go inside the womb and get stuck there and could even kill you. My friends have told me this, so I'm afraid to use condoms.*

There seems to be a great sense of fear of having an unwanted pregnancy among women with lower levels of education. They prefer a more secure method, despite the side-effects, and hence the preference for methods such as injections and sterilization. This might also be because of less access to abortion, while educated women may have the option of an abortion if faced with an unwanted pregnancy. During the discussions, a few educated women openly talked about either having had previous abortions themselves or that they had friends who had abortions. Focus group discussions, hence, point to various structural and gender-based constraints facing women of lower levels of education—unfamiliarity and lesser emphasis on condoms, less negotiating power in sexual relationships for the use of male methods, dependence on their husbands, as reasons for choosing female sterilization and other female methods. Educated women, on the other hand, have an even more heightened sense of awareness and fear of side-effects and because of their status have greater ability to choose among non-hormonal methods. The choice is also greatly facilitated by husband's co-operation.

The greater tendency among the highly educated women using traditional methods of contraception conforms to Basu's (2005) study that similarly finds that in the context of India, it is in fact the most highly educated and urban women that are most likely to use traditional methods of family planning. This paradoxical trend has been found in some other less developed countries and this study finds further support for this trend in Nepal as well. It is interesting that with the greater choices of methods of birth control that are now available educated women are relying more on natural methods. Though the use of traditional methods reflects educated women's greater power in their sexual relationships, there does seem to be a naivete of other methods among educated women. An educated women responds (when asked about her knowledge of other methods), "I can't actually say I have much knowledge about these methods. It may be because I am using the condom and really haven't paid much attention to the other methods. So I'm not very familiar with how the other methods are used." A newly married educated woman similarly comments, "I guess it is better for one to be on the safe side. I have no idea of other things..." Thus, while educated women do seem to have a greater control over their reproductive lives, there is an unmet need for more effective methods and women do not seem to be getting accurate information on other methods to make an informed choice.

Women's Dependency and Choice of Methods

Another aspect of gender-power dynamics, revealed in the focus group discussions, that bears on choice of method is women's sense of dependency on their husband's earnings. Women's use of female-controlled methods was a way of not placing the burden of family planning on their husbands. Discussions show that women that are dependent on their husband's earnings felt a greater sense of responsibility in using a method themselves, consistent with results from the quantitative analysis that women currently not employed have a higher probability of using female-controlled methods (especially female sterilization) and least empowered concerning aspects of contraceptive behaviour. Their economic dependency makes them reluctant to have their husbands undergo male sterilization, as the following participant remarks, "What to do…we have to live off their earnings. They go out to earn money. We stay at home, that's why I use a method myself." Similarly, another participant says, "After the operation one has to rest for 2–3 months. We can't eat if the husband doesn't work so that's why we get sterilized ourselves."

Also, women's acceptance of taking up the burden of family planning onto themselves when they are the ones staying at home is reflected in the following quotes:

> *I will* [when asked who plans on getting sterilized]. *He has to go out a lot so it will be hard for him. My friends say that it's a bit difficult. We stay at home. We don't have to go anywhere so it's better for us to do it. But then some people say that it is easier for the man to do it. I don't know who I should listen to…*

> *Husbands have to work. They have to do some hard work. We can't really tell them to get an operation. We just stay at home and get fed easily. He has to do a lot of work. That's why I've told him not to get sterilized.*

There is an attitude among women that men need to be protected from the harmful operation of sterilization while it is okay for women to suffer the side-effects.

Spousal Opposition/Attitudes of Men

The extent to which men play a role in women's contraceptive decision-making was also evident in the discussions. There were many cases in the discussions where women talked about their husband's opposition to the use of family planning. However, some women came to the clinics despite such objections from the husband and other family members. The use of injections, in fact, facilitates such secret use because it is a method that can be used discreetly. In other cases, women stopped using and some women had never used because they thought their husband would not approve of and did not bring up the discussion. Therefore, focus group discussions do reveal that not being able to discuss issues of family planning is a hindrance to women's family planning initiation.

Two focus group discussions were conducted with men of varying educational levels. While one must be very cautious in making any claims with only one focus group with educated men and one focus group with lesser educated men, there was a sense from the discussions that lesser educated men were less concerned and interested in issues of family planning. One participant answered, *"I don't know. I have never paid attention to these things"*, when asked about what they know of family planning. Similarly, another participant in the same group says, *"I also don't know much about these things. I do see it on television but I don't pay attention to it much."* The following are further quotes from men of lesser education. They both hint at men's irresponsibility in the arena of family planning:

> *"What I know is that a lot of people don't do anything because it makes them weak. In fact they don't use any method at all. Some men are like this that they don't even use the condom because it doesn't give them satisfaction. They don't care about other consequences. I have learned these things from other men."*

> *"What I think is that rather than the male, it is more of a woman's responsibility. The reason I am saying this is that some men drink a lot of alcohol. They sometimes only have one thing in mind..."*

A male with an above high-school education, however, has a contrasting attitude:

> *"If you look at all of Nepal, it is usually the male who plays the main role......And women are also a bit superstitious and they listen to other people saying that they have to have many children. So, then I think men have to be in control over these matters."*

While the dichotomy is not so stark there does seem to be a division between ambivalence and irresponsibility regarding family planning among the lesser educated to control and dominance among educated men, which is consistent with findings from quantitative analysis that husband's education increases the likelihood of use of male methods and also that women who say they have no say in their contraceptive decision are the ones more likely to be using male methods. This, however, raises further questions as on whose decision the use of male methods actually rests upon, and to what extent men agree to use a male method because of side-effects experienced by their wives. Yet a range of responses did come from men in the discussions. While some opposed to certain methods, some were ambivalent to the choices available, and many were in fact supportive with concerns mainly for their wife's health. Further information from the perspective of men will indeed be helpful in the study of gender and contraceptive choice.

Conclusion

While the contraceptive choice literature has given much attention to various socio-economic correlates of method choice, the women's empowerment and fertility literature stresses the importance of gender-related dimensions on various reproductive health outcomes, particularly differentials in women's contraceptive uptake. In this paper, using both quantitative and qualitative sources of data, the two theoretical perspectives were linked to examine what role, if any, gender-power relations have, not only in determining women's contraceptive use, but also on choice of a particular method of contraception. By re-conceptualizing Bulatao's contraceptive choice framework to incorporate dimensions of gender-power dynamics, this paper sought to examine whether contraceptive competence captured through measures of gender status, decision-making, attitudes towards gender-roles and autonomy would lead to women's higher odds of using contraceptive methods as well as higher likelihood of using other methods besides sterilization, and particularly male-controlled methods.

Results support the assertion that beyond Bulatao's framework of goals, access, and evaluation related dimensions, aspects of gender-power relations also play a crucial role in limiting (or enabling) choices that are available to women. In general women's greater power in spousal relations leads to greater use of male-controlled methods, a wider range of temporary spacing methods, and use of methods other than female sterilization, in particular user-dependent methods of condoms and traditional methods. Education, both of the wife and husband, results in greater variation in contraceptive method-mix and increased use of male-controlled methods. While the quantitative analysis does not provide explanations for the compelling role of education, results from focus group discussions offer some insights about why education strongly influences method choice. Various structural and gender-based constraints facing women of lower levels of education—unfamiliarity and lesser emphasis on condoms, less negotiating power in sexual relationships for the use of male-controlled methods, less access to abortion if faced with an unwanted pregnancy—are among the reasons for choosing female sterilization and other female-controlled methods. On the other hand, educated women have an even more heightened sense of awareness and fear of side-effects, and, further, because of their status are more able to choose among non-hormonal methods such as condoms and traditional methods that do not have undesirable side-effects on their bodies. This is greatly facilitated through co-operation from the husband as well.

While this research has shown that the role of the husband is pervasive in women's decisions, more needs to be understood from the perspective of men. It has been argued in previous studies that because of Nepal's inherent patriarchal family structure, husbands' domination in contraceptive decision-making obliges women to use female contraceptive methods despite their reluctance. Chapagain's (2005) study in rural Nepal implies that women's contraceptive decisions are within the framework of husbands' choices and usually that choice centres on female contraceptive methods. The results of this study illustrate that with higher levels of husbands' education, contraceptive choice may however shift to male methods, and increasing men and women's education in Nepal may be a crucial factor in changing the high prevalence of female contraceptive methods in the country.

Other quantitative indicators of women's decision-making, attitudes towards gender-roles, and autonomy show relationships in the expected direction, but the results are mixed. While there is some evidence that women's increased autonomy and decision-making enables use of male-controlled methods and other temporary methods, the pattern is not consistent and systematic. The measures of women's status in the Demographic and Health Surveys, as useful as they have been in studying certain aspects of gender and power relations, may not adequately capture nuances of women's power in spousal and household relations (may confound with actual problem of access). Moreover, decision surrounding use of a specific method is multifaceted and the influences of gender-power relations may interact with numerous other factors—such as government policy, personal preferences, limited access and knowledge of methods, and life stage—in determining choices that are available to couples.

In conclusion, results thus far have provided evidence on the complexity surrounding women's decision to use a specific method of contraception. Even once the decision has been made to adopt a method, the choice as to which one is the most appropriate method is likely to be determined not only by contraceptive goals, access, and evaluation, but also by a myriad of gender-power relationship structures. Emphasis should be given on providing women with appropriate information on choices that are available, taking into consideration constraints posed by Nepal's patriarchal family structure that limits women's power in spousal relations and negotiating power in sexual relations. In particular, appropriate information on condoms and traditional methods should be given to women of lower levels of education that express a desire to use non-hormonal methods. Moreover, educated women should be adequately informed of available hormonal methods. Family planning programmes should also make an effort to increase involvement of husbands and other family members that often play a crucial role in women's decisions to adopt and continue methods. Further research in other contexts should be conducted to assess if similar gender-based constraints apply in other settings as well. Given that the type of method that predominates and the reasons for the predominance differ greatly from one context to another (Potter, 1999; Sullivan et al., 2005), it would be interesting to investigate the effects of gender-power relations on contraceptive choice in different contexts.

Note

1. A fourth aspect of women's decision-making was included for the contraceptive users only as this question was asked only to women currently using a method of contraception.

References

Ayaga, B. 2002. Spousal Communication and Family Planning Behaviour in Navrongo: A Longitudinal Assessment. *Studies in Family Planning*, 33(2): 185–94.

Balk, D. 1994. Individual and Community Aspects of Women's Status and Fertility in Rural Bangladesh. *Population Studies*, 48: 21–45.

Basu, A.M. 2005. Ultramodern Contraception: Social Class and Family Planning in India. *Asian Population Studies*, 1(3): 303–23.

Bhende, A.A., M.K. Choe, J.R. Rele and J.A. Palmore. 1991. Determinants of Contraceptive Method Choice in an Industrial City of India. *Asia-Pacific Population Journal*, 6(3): 41–66.

Bulatao, R.A. 1989. "Toward a Framework for Understanding Contraceptive Method Choice" in R. Bulatao, J.A. Palmore and S.E. Ward (eds.), *Choosing a Contraceptive: Method Choice in Asia and the United States*. Westview Press, Boulder, 277–304.

Chapagain, M. 2005. Masculine Interest behind High Prevalence of Female Contraceptive Methods in Rural Nepal. *Australian Journal of Rural Health*, 13: 35–42.

Cochrane, S.H. 1979. *Fertility and Education: What Do We Really Know?* Johns Hopkins University Press, Baltimore.

Dixon-Mueller, R. 1993. *Population Policy and Women's Rights: Transforming Reproductive Choice*. Westport, Connecticut.

Dyson, T. and M. Moore. 1983. On Kinship Structure, Female Autonomy and Demographic Behaviour in India. *Population and Development Review*, 9(1): 35–60.

Entwisle, B., R.R. Rindfuss, D.K. Guilkey, A. Chamratrithirong, S.R. Curran and Y. Sawangdee. 1996. Community and Contraceptive Choice in Rural Thailand: A Case Study of Nang Rong. *Demography*, 33(1): 1–11.

Ergocmen, B.A., I. Koc, P. Senlet, E.K. Yigit and E. Roman. 2004. A Closer Look at Traditional Contraceptive Use in Turkey. *The European Journal of Contraception and Reproductive Health Care*, 9: 221–44.

Gage, A.J. 1995. Women's Socioeconomic Position and Contraceptive Behaviour in Togo. *Studies in Family Planning*, 26(5): 264–77.

Govindasamy, P. and A. Malhotra. 1996. Women's Position and Family Planning in Egypt. *Studies in Family Planning*, 27(6): 328–40.

Hay, I. 2000. *Qualitative Research Methods in Human Geography*. Oxford University Press, South Melbourne.

Hogan, D.P., B. Berhanu and A. Hailemariam. 1999. Household Organization, Women's Autonomy and Contraceptive Behaviour in Southern Ethiopia. *Studies in Family Planning*, 30(4): 302–14.

Jejeebhoy, S.J. 1995. *Women's Education, Autonomy and Reproductive Behaviour*. Clarendon Press, Oxford.

Khan, M.A. and M. Rahman. 1997. Determinants of Contraceptive Method Choice in Rural Bangladesh. *Asia-Pacific Population Journal*, 12(3): 65–82.

Kishor, S. 2005. "Introduction" in S. Kishor (ed.), *A Focus on Gender: Collected Papers on Gender Using DHS Data*. ORC Macro, Calverton, 1–13.

Koc, I. 2000. Determinants of Contraceptive Use and Method Choice in Turkey. *Journal of Biosocial Sciences*, 32: 329–42.

Kulczycki, A. 2004. The Determinants of Withdrawal Use in Turkey: A Husband's Imposition or a Woman's Choice? *Social Science and Medicine*, 59: 1019–33.

Larson, U. and M. Hollos. 2003. Women's Empowerment and Fertility Decline among the Pare of Kilimanjaro Region, Northern Tanzania. *Social Science and Medicine*, 57: 1099–115.

Mahmud, S. and A.M. Johnston. 1994. "Women's Status, Empowerment and Reproductive Outcomes" in G. Sen, A. Germaine and L.C. Chen (eds.), *Population Policies Reconsidered: Health, Empowerment and Rights*. Harvard University Press, Cambridge, MA.

Mannan, H.R. 2002. Factors in Contraceptive Method Choice in Bangladesh: Goals, Competence, Evaluation and Access. *Contraception*, 65: 357–64.

Martin, T.C. 1995. Women's Education and Fertility: Results from 26 Demographic and Health Surveys. *Studies in Family Planning*, 26(4): 187–202.

Mason, K.O. 1986. The Status of Women: Conceptual and Methodological Issues in Demographic Studies. *Sociological Forum*, 1(2): 284–300.

1987. The Impact of Women's Social Position on Fertility in Developing Countries. *Sociological Forum*, 2(4): 718–45.

— 2001. Gender and Family Systems in the Fertility Transition. *Global Fertility Transition*. (Suppl. to Vol. 27 of the *Population and Development Review*): 160–76.

Mason, K.O. and H.L. Smith. 2000. Husbands' versus Wives' Fertility Goals and Use of Contraception: The Influence of Gender Contexts in Five Asian Countries. *Demography*, 37(3): 299–311.

Morgan, D.L. (ed.). 1993. *Successful Focus Groups: Advancing the State of the Art*. Sage Publications, Newbury Park, London, New Delhi.

Morgan, P.S. and B.B. Niraula. 1995. Gender Inequality and Fertility in Two Nepali Villages. *Population and Development Review*, 21(3): 541–61.

Moursund, A. and O. Kravdal. 2003. Individual and Community Effects of Women's Education and Autonomy on Contraceptive Use in India. *Population Studies*, 57(3): 285–301.

Mumtaz, Z. and S. Salway. 2005. 'I never go anywhere': Extricating the Links between Women's Mobility and Uptake of Reproductive Health Services in Pakistan. *Social Science and Medicine*, 60: 1751–65.

Mumtaz, Z., E. Slaymaker and S. Salway. 2005. "Condom Use in Uganda and Zimbabwe: Exploring the Influence of Gendered Access to Resources and Couple-level Dynamics" in S. Kishor (ed.), *A Focus on Gender: Collected Papers on Gender Using DHS Data*. ORC Macro, Calverton, 117–45.

NDHS. 2001. *Nepal Demographic and Health Survey 2001*. Macro International Inc., Calverton.

Niraula, B.B. and M.S. Philip. 1996. Marriage Formation, Post-Marital Contact with Natal Kin and Autonomy of Women: Evidence from Two Nepali Settings. *Population Studies,* 50(1): 35–50.

Palmore, J.A. and R.A. Bulatao. 1989. "The Contraceptive Method-Mix: An Overview" in R. Bulatao, J.A. Palmore and S.E. Ward (eds.), *Choosing a Contraceptive: Method Choice in Asia and the United States*. Westview Press, Boulder, 3–36.

Potter, J. 1999. The Persistence of Outmoded Contraceptive Regimes in Mexico and Brazil. *Population and Development Review*, 25(4): 703–39.

Presser, H.B. and G. Sen. 2000. "Women's Empowerment and Demographic Processes: Laying the Groundwork" in H.B. Presser and G. Sen (eds.), *Women's Empowerment and Demographic Processes: Moving beyond Cairo*. Oxford University Press Inc., New York, 3–11.

Riley, N.E. 1997. Gender, Power and Population Change. *Population Bulletin,* 52: 1.

Ringheim, K. 1996. Whither Methods for Men? Emerging Gender Issues in Contraception. *Reproductive Health Matters*, 7: 79–89.

— 1999. Reversing the Downward Trend in Men's Share in Contraceptive Use. *Reproductive Health Matters*, 7(14): 83–96.

Saleem, S. and M. Bobak. 2005. Women's Autonomy, Education and Contraception Use in Pakistan: A National Study. *Reproductive Health* 2(8). http://www.reproductive-health-journal.com/content/2/1/8

Sathar, Z.A., N. Crook, C. Callum and S. Kazi. 1988. Women's Status and Fertility Change in Pakistan. *Population and Development Review*, 14(3): 415–32.

Sen, G. and S. Batliwala. 2000. "Empowering Women for Reproductive Rights" in H.B. Presser and G. Sen (eds.), *Women's Empowerment and Demographic Processes: Moving beyond Cairo*. Oxford University Press Inc., New York, 15–36.

Sen, G., A. Germaine and L.C. Chen (eds.). 1994. The Meaning of Women's Empowerment: New Concepts from Action. *Population Policies Reconsidered: Health, Empowerment and Rights.* Harvard University Press, Cambridge, MA.

Thapa, S. and M. Friedman. 1998. Female Sterilization in Nepal: A Comparison of Two Types of Service Delivery. *International Family Planning Perspectives*, 24(2): 78–83.

Upadhyay, U.D. 2001. Informed Choice in Family Planning: Helping People Decide. *Population Reports*, Series J, No. 50. Baltimore, Johns Hopkins University, Bloomberg School of Public Health, Population Information Program.

CHAPTER 9

Decision-Making Pattern of Family Planning Method Acceptors

H.R. Channakki and C.G. Hussain Khan

The population continues to grow at a faster rate than anticipated by India's planners and policy makers and every census sends shock waves to them. Even though India was the first country to have launched a well-defined family planning programme in 1951 but it failed to achieve its stated goals and objectives. This programme was intended to balance the population with resources available. The main objectives of the family welfare programmes are as follows—To bring down population growth, so as to ensure a better standard of living; to improve the health of the mothers and their children so that a healthier society emerges; to reduce the maternal and infant mortality rates in developing countries, about half of the estimated 4,50,000 annual maternal deaths and nearly six million infant deaths might be avoided if all pregnancies occurred to women between the ages of 18–35; if the intervals between pregnancies were at least two years and if no woman had more than four children, to reduce the number of unwanted pregnancies and illegal termination could be avoided (Park, 2001).

For the fulfilment of these aims, it becomes necessary for the programmers to understand the levels of knowledge of family planning acceptors, their attitudes and behavioural aspects with regards to family planning methods and their use. These aspects, in turn, influence the people's decision-making process in terms of the method chosen, time of acceptance; place of seeking services, and also as to who is the user-wife or the husband? Hence, there is an urgent need to understand the perspectives and processes of decision-making of family planning acceptance, which would go a long way in helping the programme mangers to design an appropriate intervention, keeping in view the people's need. Such an attempt has been made here to understand the family planning acceptors' perspectives and the process of decision-making of those who visit the Family Planning Clinic in the Post Partum Centre, Department of Obstetric and Gynecological, Karnataka Institute of Medical Sciences, Hubli in Dharwad district in Karnataka state.

The main research questions which guided this empirical investigation have been: (a) What is the decision-making process involved in accepting family planning methods, in terms of choice of methods, choice of place, person who is the acceptor and choice of timing? (b) What are the main reasons for these choices and who is/are the key person/s involved in this decision-making?

Objectives

1. To know the decision-making process while accepting a family planning method.
2. To study the factors affecting the decision-making on the choice of method, the timing, acceptor and place of accepting family planning method.

Materials and Method

Study area: The empirical investigation was conducted at the family planning clinic of the post partum centre of Department of OBG in Karnataka Institutes of Medical Sciences (KIMS), Hubli (Karnataka state). This institute is the largest hospital-cum-medical college in North Karnataka. It caters to a large population of the North Karnataka region.

Study population: The respondents selected for this study were those who were waiting for accepting a contraceptive (family planning) method at the Karnataka Institute of Medical Sciences. The total sample size is 59 out which 57 were females and 2 were males (one adopted Non-Scalpel Vasectomy and another adopted condom) respondents. They were interviewed by a pre-coded questionnaire.

Methodology

This study was done as a partial fulfilment of "The International Diploma in Reproductive Health Management" (IDIRHEM) course of Karnatak University Dharwad. The study was focussed on the decision-making process in accepting the contraceptive methods. As this is a hospital based cross-sectional study, the data collected were analysed by using STATA software package.

Conceptual Framework

The decision-making process involved in accepting a particular family planning method is depicted in the form of a conceptual framework. The decision-making process is influenced by a range of factors especially the basic background characteristics of a person, like age, sex, education, place of residence, religion and caste and place of service.

Findings and Discussion

A variety of socio-economic and demographic characteristics in terms of age, sex, education, religion and caste of the respondents, as mentioned in the conceptual framework, have been considered. The respondents in this investigation were in the age group of 19–48 years.

Figure 1

Conceptual Framework

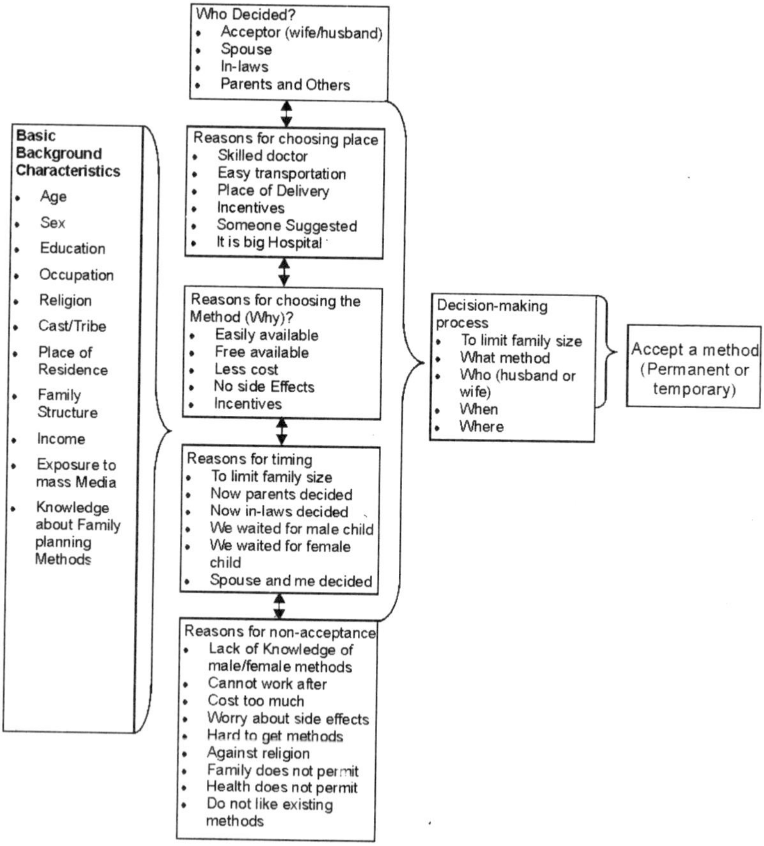

The majority of the respondents who attained their family size were under the age group of 25–48 years. Among the respondents, 72.88 per cent were Hindus, 47.46 per cent had higher education followed by 28.81 per cent illiterates. A majority of the people under study viz., 93.22 per cent were housewives. Around 64 per cent of the respondents were from the nuclear families and rest were from the extended families.

Current Use of Family Planning Methods

Table 1 provides information on per cent distribution of the respondents who are intending to use specific method at the family planning clinic of Karnataka Institute of Medical Sciences, Hubli. During the fieldwork, the question asked to each respondent was 'which method do you intend to use now? About 67.80 per cent of the respondents said that they were intending to go for female sterilization, followed by Oral Contraceptives Pills (OCP) 15.25 per cent, Intrauterine Device (IUD) 13.56 per cent, condom 1.69 per cent and male sterilization 1.69 per cent.

Table 1

Per cent Distribution of Respondents by Methods they Currently Use

FP methods	*Percentage*
OCP	15.25
IUD	13.56
Condom	01.69
Female sterilization	67.80
Male sterilization	01.69
Total	100.00

Family Planning Method Ever Used

In the present study, each respondent was asked to ascertain whether any family planning method was ever used prior to their coming to KIMS to adopt the present family planning method. To elicit this information, following question was posed 'have you ever used any contraceptive method?' Table 2 represents the pattern of ever use of family planning methods by the people who are waiting to adopt a method now at KIMS. About 36 per cent of respondents have ever used oral pill, 29 per cent have used IUD, 5 per cent have used injections, 24 per cent

Table 2

Per cent Distribution of Respondents Who have Ever Used the Methods

FP methods	*Percentage*
OCP	35.59
IUD	28.81
Injections	05.08
Condom	23.73
Rhythm	57.63
Withdrawal	11.86
Total	100.00

have used condom, 58 per cent have adopted rhythm and 12 per cent have adopted the withdrawal method. The ever use of contraception is higher in rhythm (traditional) method because it is said to be easy and convenient to use for the couple.

Knowledge of Contraceptives

In order to know the respondents' knowledge about the family planning methods, each respondent was asked about the various methods of family planning methods he or she knows. This was asked to elicit their knowledge on each of the methods. This was a very sensitive matter, especially in case of women respondents. Some women showed shyness[1] and they were reluctant to answer the question. In such cases, assistance of the staff-nurse who distributes the pills, IUD and condoms at the Post Partum Centre (PPC) ward was taken. It was found that some women at the clinic showed eagerness to know about the natural methods[2] (rhythm and withdrawal) from the staff nurse. This study attempted to assess respondents' knowledge of contraceptive methods like, IUD, injections, condom, female sterilization, male sterilization, rhythm and withdrawal. Table 3 shows the extent of knowledge the respondents have about the contraceptive methods. Almost 94.92 per cent of respondents have the knowledge of female sterilization, 79.66 per cent of IUD, and 77.97 per cent of rhythm method. The knowledge of male contraceptive methods is relatively low as compared to female methods. About 67.80 per cent of respondents know male sterilization and 52.54 per cent of respondents are aware of condom. Only 22.03 per cent of respondents have the knowledge of injection.

Table 3

Per cent Distribution of Knowledge of Contraceptives

FP methods	*Percentage*
OCP	79.66
IUD	77.97
Injections	22.03
Condom	52.54
Female sterilization	94.92
Male sterilization	67.80
Rhythm	77.97
Withdrawal	44.07

Note: Percentages may add to more than 100.00 due to multiple responses.

Key Persons Involved in the Decision-Making in Family Planning Methods

The decision-making process in family planning is influenced to a significant extent by socio-cultural and traditional practices, individual's basic background characteristics and the place of accepting the family planning methods. The family members like husband/wife, parents, in-laws and friends have been found to influence such decisions. Therefore, it is important to know the decision-making process in the acceptance the family planning methods. Table 4 shows the key persons involved in the decision-making process in terms of methods, timing, person and place while deciding for the family planning methods. The decision-making in terms of methods, for temporary methods 88.89 per cent of the respondents decided by themselves, 83.33 per cent respondents decided along with their partner, 16.67 per cent decisions were taken by the parents of the respondents and for 11.11 per cent were decided by their in-laws. In permanent methods, 51.22 per cent of respondents themselves decided, 97.56 per cent of respondent decided along with their spouses, 51.22 per cent of respondents reported that the decision was taken by their parents and 63.41 per cent of respondents said that decision was taken by their in-laws. From this it is clear that when it comes to the decision of permanent methods, acceptor had less power because permanent methods were accepted only after they reached desired family size, once the permanent method has been accepted, there is no chance of pregnancy again but in case of temporary methods there is a likelihood of pregnancy in future.

The decision-making in terms of timing (when), 57.63 per cent of respondents were decided by them, 89.83 per cent were decided with their partner, for 33.90 per cent were decided by their parents and for 42.37 per cent were decided by their in-laws. To decide about timing both husband and wife had greater say.

In deciding about the person who will accept the methods, 66.10 per cent respondents had the power, 84.75 per cent of respondent decided with their husband, for 30.51 per cent were decided by their parents and for 33.90 per cent were decided by their in-laws.

When it comes to decision about the place (KIMS) 57.63 per cent respondents decided by themselves, 83.05 per cent took the decision along with their husband, for 35.59 per cent were decided by their parents and for 32.30 per cent were decided by their in-laws.

When it comes to parent's involvement in decision-making, they have lesser role to play in deciding about the temporary methods compared to permanent methods. To decide as to who would adopt the method, it is found that the husband becomes important because he holds a greater say over the life of the child to be born. One of the respondents said during the interview that *"her husband is the main bread winner and head of the family who decides everything...."* Thus, it is evident that during the time of acceptance of the family planning method both wife and husband play greater role than the parents and in-laws because it is the couple who are going to take care of the child. Even in the case of deciding as to who is going to accept the contraceptive method, again it is both wife and husband who often make the decision compared to the acceptor himself/herself or parents or in-laws.

Table 4

Per cent Distribution of Decision-Making in Terms of Methods, Timing, Person and Place (KIMS)

Decision-making in terms of FP methods	Key persons involved in the decision-making process			
	Acceptor	Both (Husband and wife)	Parents	In-laws
Temporary	88.89	83.33	16.67	11.11
Permanent	51.22	97.56	51.22	63.41
Timing (When)	57.63	89.83	33.90	42.37
Person (Who)	66.10	84.75	30.51	33.90
Place (KIMS)	57.63	83.05	35.59	32.30

Note: Percentages may add to more than 100.00 due to multiple responses.

Reasons for Choosing a Particular Contraceptive Method

There are several reasons for choosing a particular method of contraceptive. They may have experienced illness before they came to accept new methods prior to this study. Suppose a person feels illness, pain, or any other side effects due to the use of any contraceptive methods. Cost and incentives do not form the main reasons to accept a method. To limit the family size is one of the reasons for accepting contraceptive methods. Table 5 explains the various reasons to choose the current method. For the temporary methods, 66.67 per cent accepted easily available of contraceptive methods, 88.89 per cent respondents chose because of the free availability, 61.11 per cent for no side effects, 27.78 per cent to limit their family size, and 22.22 per cent because some-ones suggested to accept a particular method. Whereas in permanent method, 56.10 per cent because of easily available, 51.22 per cent for free of cost, 2.44 per cent for less cost, 21.95 per cent for no side effects, 85.37 per cent to limit their family size and 2.44 on someone's suggestions.

Table 5

Reasons to Choose Family Planning Methods

Reasons to choose a FP methods	*Temporary methods*	*Permanent methods*
Easily available	66.67	56.10
Freely available	88.89	51.22
Less cost	00.00	02.44
No side effects	61.11	21.95
Incentives	00.00	00.00
To limit family size	27.78	85.37
Someone said	22.22	02.44

Note: Percentages may add to more than 100.00 due to multiple responses.

Reasons Why Acceptor Uses and Why not His/Her Spouse

In the decision-making process the husband has more power to decide as to who would be the acceptor as well as the place, timing and method of contraceptive. This happens even when he lacks knowledge of contraceptives. In this study, there are only two male respondents. Among whom one adopted the temporary method and the other has adopted a permanent (non-scalpel vasectomy) method. Though unaware of the male methods of contraception they have adopted these methods as per the doctor's advice. It is they who often decide that their wives should go for contraception.

Table 6 describes the reasons why acceptors use a particular method but not the spouse for temporary and permanent methods. In temporary methods, 94.44 per cent of respondents decided to accept a family planning method because of lack of knowledge about the male/female methods of contraceptives, 77.78 per cent were said that his/her spouse cannot work after accepting a method, 55.56 per cent were reported to worry about side effects, 5.56 said that it was against religion, 16.67 per cent mentioned that because of family did not agree and 27.78 were because of health doesn't permit to accept a method to his/her spouse. Whereas in permanent methods, 87.8 per cent were because of lack of knowledge of female/male contraceptives, 92.68 per cent were said that they (spouse) can't work after, 17.07 per cent reported that they worry about side effects, 2.44 per cent were because of hard to get the methods, 36.59 per cent mentioned that because they didn't agree to accept a contraceptive method to his/her spouse, 9.76 per cent were said that their spouse health doesn't permit to accept a method and 2.44 per cent were because of they do not like existing methods of contraceptives.

Many respondents reported that temporary methods are easily available in government hospital, private hospital and pharmacy shops When all the family planning methods are available free of charge, no one had said that these methods cost too much. Higher percentages of respondent who had adopted temporary methods said that "health gets, affected by its usage", but this is not the case in permanent methods as it is usually after the delivery that permanent contraceptive is adopted.

Table 6

Per cent Distribution of Respondents' Reasons to Choose Acceptor Him/Herself

Reasons to choose acceptor	*Temporary methods*	*Permanent methods*
Lack of knowledge	94.44	87.80
Cannot work after	77.78	92.68
Cost too much	00.00	00.00
Worry about side-effects	55.56	17.07
Hard to get methods	00.00	02.44
Against religion	05.56	00.00
Family did not agree	16.67	36.59
Health does not permit	27.78	09.76
Do not like existing methods	00.00	02.44

Note: Percentages may add to more than 100.00 due to multiple responses.

Reasons to Accept a Method

The reason for adopting the contraceptive method is to limit the family size, or the decision to adopt family planning method has been taken now by the spouse or parents or parents in-laws, or the doctor has advised to go for family planning method because of fragile health. The reasons for accepting a family planning method as expressed by the respondent during the time of fieldwork were many—desired family size, spouse, parents and in-laws may decide now to accept the method or during their last visits to the hospital the health does not permit to accept the method or they need one or more female children.

Table 7 shows the reasons for accepting the method. Almost 88.14 per cent of respondents have reported that they have gone for family planning methods because they have reached desired family size. Whereas 20.34 per cent of respondents reported it is now that their in-laws have permitted to go for a particular method. Nearly 28.81 per cent of respondent said that now their in-laws were decided to accept a particular contraceptive method. Only 15.25 per cent of respondents reported that they waited for a male child, and now it has been achieved so they had decided to accept a family planning method. Only 13.56 per cent reported that they waited for female child and after getting it they had decided to go for family planning method. From this finding, it is clear that the couples were not only preferring the male child but they also preferred the female child in some other cases. The remaining 47.46 per cent respondents said that they and their spouses could together decide now to go for a particular method. In the choice of method, the acceptor and his/her spouse had a greater role to play and this is after they reached their desired family size.

Table 7

Per cent Distribution of Respondents' Reasons for Timing of Acceptance of a Family Planning Method

Reasons to accept FP method (now)	*Percentage*
To limit family size	88.14
Now parents decided	20.34
Now in-laws decided	28.81
We waited for male child	15.25
We waited for female child	13.56
Spouse and me decided	47.46

Note: Percentages may add to more than 100.00 due to multiple responses

Reasons to Decide the Place

Table 8 shows the reasons to decide the place KIMS to accept a particular family planning method. Almost 96.61 per cent of respondents said that they have came to KIMS for adopting the family planning method because of skilled doctors and because KIMS is the only one institute which is catering to a large number of patients from north Karnataka region and it is the only one government hospital-cum-medical college in this region. Nearly 77.27 per cent of respondents said that because of transportation from their residence to KIMS; 38.98 per cent of respondent accepted the family planning method because they went there for delivery, only 1.69 per cent of respondents accepted because of incentives. Nearly 25.42 per cent of respondents said that because KIMS is a big hospital so they accepted the family planning method, in patient facility was also available with cost-free service.

Table 8

Per cent Distribution of Respondent Reasons' to Choose KIMS

Reasons to decide Place (KIMS) to accept a FP method	*Percentage*
Skilled Doctor	96.61
Easy Transportation	76.27
Place of Delivery	38.98
Incentives	01.69
Someone Suggested	25.42
It is big Hospital	77.97

Note: Percentages may add to more than 100 due to multiple responses.

Conclusions

This study reveals that people visiting KIMS possess the knowledge of one or the other method of contraceptives. However, the use or non-use of contraceptive method is dependent on the respondents' basic background characteristics, their family, parents' and in-laws' decisions. These decisions again are dependent on method, timing, place and acceptor. The present study shows, while making decision with regards to method, timing, person and place, the opinions of spouse, parents and in-laws constitute important factors.

It is evident from this investigation that the traditional family planning methods like, rhythm and withdrawal are perceived to be harmless as compared to modern family planning methods. Majority of people opt for these methods, however, it is seen that these methods have generated less interest among the policy makers because they are traditional methods which call for the active participation and co-operation from the males. This aspect seems to have been not addressed adequately in the reproductive health programmes. It becomes necessary to explore the possibilities of encouraging the use of traditional methods. And these possibilities need to be incorporated into the policies and programmes related to reproductive health. It is in this way that people's unmet needs could be fulfilled. Therefore, as these methods find a greater acceptance and yield the desire results. It becomes imperative that the policies and programmes on reproductive health need to incorporate the traditional contraceptive methods while designing reproductive health programmes so as to meet the unmet needs of the community. Further, fuller awareness and right information about these methods especially as to when to use, how to use and the effectiveness of its usage be disseminated among the people.

As regards reproductive health and family planning decisions are concerned, it is found in this study that it is not individuals but the important members in the family who involve collectively for making decisions. Especially, the basic background characteristics and the traditional practices that are followed by the family members of respondents.

It is these family members who influence the decision-making patterns with regards to the contraceptive acceptance, especially when to accept, who accepts and where to accept a particular method of contraceptive. While making these decisions, the acceptor and spouse of the acceptor also exhibit significant roles as they are the principal care takers of their offsprings. These dynamics of decision-making during the adoption of family planning methods are to be kept in view while designing the family planning and reproductive health programmes. In order to design appropriate and suitable reproductive health and family planning programmes that are people-specific and context-based; it becomes necessary that programme and policy makers adopt a broader holistic perspective of people's decision-making process rather than to depend only on the people's practices.

Notes

1. Shyness – when the researcher asked the question about the traditional methods like rhythm and withdrawal, they were hesitant to answer in this situation. The researcher took the help from the staff nurse to explain about the traditional methods. In that time, the respondents were shy and they were reluctant to answer.
2. There are two types of family planning methods, natural and modern methods.

References

International Institute for Population Sciences and ORC Macro. 2000. *National Family Health Survey (NFHS-II)*, Mumbai.

Park, K. 2001. *Park's Textbook of Preventive and Social Medicine*. Banarsidas Bhanot, Jabalpur, India.

CHAPTER 10

Poverty and Fertility in India

The Demographic Field Theory Viewpoint

Shekhar Mukherji

Despite a massive increase in the number of poor (430 million or 36% of population in 2005) in India (NSSO, 2006: 1–125, Dev, 2007: 509–521), combating poverty is still not considered the greatest priority by the Government of India; nor most demographers are interested in unfolding the most essential nexus between poverty and fertility. Suitable demographic theory is also lacking. Thus, for filling the lacuna, a new and novel Demographic Field Theory is presented in this chapter.

Objectives

1. To present an organized and mathematically verifiable theory, and capable of unfolding the nexus of poverty and high fertility.
2. To perform powerful canonical analyses, using NFHS-I/II data, which may generate canonical equations, *causally linking* poverty and fertility. Results would also corroborate the theory.
3. To examine Census 2001, SRS 2003 and RCH 2004 data in order to observe changes in that causal relationship, over time.
4. To highlight findings of causal relationships between poverty and fertility and recommend policies and strategies for alleviating the situations.

The discussion is presented in following seven interrelated parts:

Part I: The Demographic Field Theory—brief presentation of salient features of the theory.

Part II: Canonical Models—analytical models for linking three data matrices of the theory.

Part III: Demographic, Socio-economic and Policy Sets of 1992–93, and analysis (Table 1).

Part IV: Factor-cum-Canonical Analysis of Demographic, Socio-economic and Policy Sets of 1992–93 (Table 2).

Part V: Demographic and Socio-economic Situation, 1998–99 and canonical analysis.

Part VI: Most Recent Poverty-Fertility Situation (2001–4) (Tables 3–4).

Part VII: Required Policies.

I
The Demographic Field Theory

This new and novel theory is briefly described in the four sections.

Concept of Demographic Field

Demographic field is a system consisting of three parts:

(a) Individual family's socio-economic attributes, needs and stresses in a geographical setting;
(b) Family's population policy considerations; and
(c) Different patterns of fertility, mortality and migration behaviour of family, and complex interrelationships between them. These are interdependent parts of family's demographic field (Mukherji, 1977b: 250–266).

In Figure 1(a), specific pattern of needs, roles, poverty, and stresses of a rural family, and related to that, specific population policies followed by family, may induce a specific demographic behaviour (high IMR, high TFR and poverty-induced migration). Conversely, in Figure 1(b), different sets of needs, roles of an educated and urbanized family, and related to that, different population policies, may induce different demographic behaviour (low TFR, low IMR, and upward mobility).

General Statement of Demographic Field Theory

These are discussed at the following two levels:

(a) At *family level*, demographic behaviour of family, located in particular setting, is a linear function of both that family's socio-economic-cultural attributes, needs, and stresses, and specific policies that family considers or adopts (Mukherji, 1983: 1–65).
(b) At *aggregate level*, structure of socio-economic attributes of population, structure of population policies, and resultant demographic behaviour patterns, are interdependent parts of *demographic field*, in which any change in one generates corresponding change in other (Mukherji, 1983: 1–141). Presently, aggregate model is considered, taking Indian states as units.

Figure 1a

Demographic Field of a Rural (Semi-Literate) Peasant Family

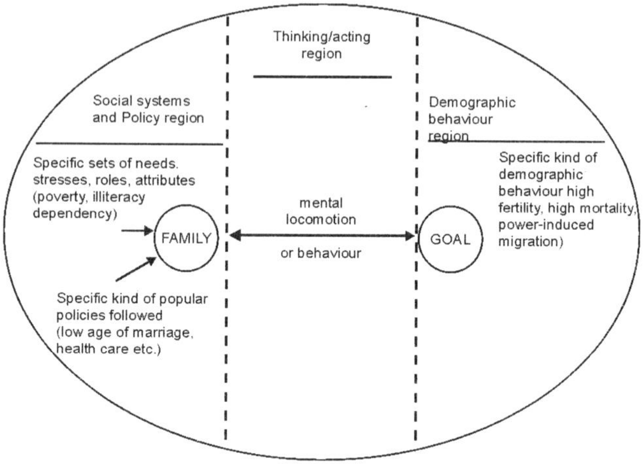

Specific patterns of social needs, aspirations, poverty and stresses of a rural peasant family and specific kinds of population policy followed by the family, may induce it to show a specific kind of demographic behaviour.

Figure 1b

Demographic Field of Another Family (Urbanized-Educated-Affluent)

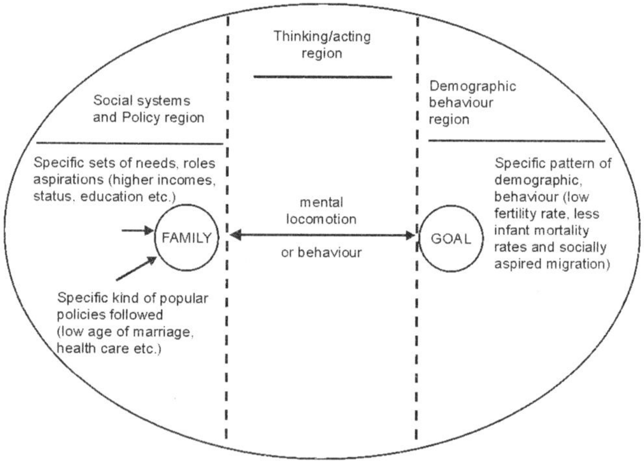

Different sets of social needs, roles, aspirations of an urbanized and educated affluent family and different sets of population policies adopted by that family, may induce to show on different kind of demographic behaviour patterns (mod./low fertility, less IMR) and upward social mobility due to migration.

Two Main Propositions

(a) Socio-economic vectors S_1, S_2, ... etc., in S-space, which describe socio-economic system of regions, and P_1, P_2, ... etc., which describe population policies operating therein, are *social field forces* that determine the location D_1, D_2, ... etc. vectors in demographic D-space according to linear function:

$$\sum \beta_m D_m = \sum \alpha_q S_q + \sum \alpha_r * P_r$$

That is, demographic behaviour of a population, located in a particular context, is a linear function of that population's or group's specific socio-economic attributes, and related to that, of specific population policies prevailing therein, in given space and time (Mukherji, 1999: 250–270).

(b) Demographic behaviour space D and combined S-P (socio-economic-cum-population policy) spaces are coincident, such that each can be predicted by the other (Mukherji, 1989: 343–373).

Links between Demographic System, Socio-economic System and Population Policy Set

And finally, the crux of theory lies in assessing degree of interdependencies between patterns of social-cum-policies and patterns of fertility and mortality, which is performed by *canonical analysis* (Mukherji, 1997a: 1–6; 2005b: 38–75). Canonically, DFT is represented as: $D \sim (S + P)$.

II
Canonical Models

Causal Relations in Canonical Models

After factor analysing, finally, canonical analysis of those three factor score matrices is performed, which answers *two* interrelated basic questions (Mukherji, 1982: 65–121; 1993: 245–275):

(a) What is overall "general statistical relationship" between socio-economic-cum-population policy matrix of a state and corresponding demographic behaviour?

(b) Given that overall relationship, what are "underlying causal relationships" between a specific combination of socio-economic system-cum-population policies and fertility and mortality behaviour of state? (see Figure 2)

Figure 2

Conceptual and Analytical Design of the Demographic Field Theory Canonical Model

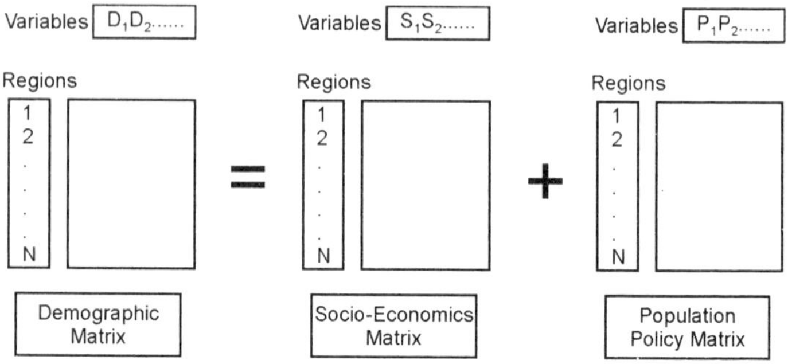

$$\Sigma\beta_m D_m = \Sigma\alpha_Q S_Q + \Sigma\alpha^*_R P_R$$

Unravels Actual Canonical Linkages between three Sets

Canonical analysis makes *a least square fit* between two sets, uncovering causal socio-economic-cum-policy and demographic linkages. The *first set of answer* is given by *trace correlation* shows statistical overlap between (2); and *second set of answers* is given by *series of canonical correlations* (show maximal correlations between matched pairs from two sets). Canonical model is much higher form of regression, but here, instead of one dependent variable, entire dependent matrix is utilized, and instead of one, many canonical linkages emerge (Mukherji, 1975: 20–65; 1979: 1–80). Model's technical details are given (see Hotelling, 1935: 321–377; Cooley and Lohnes, 1962: 45–65; Rummel, 1966: 45–65; Rummel and Mukherji, 1981: 21–81; Philips, 1972: 1–21). Utility, elegance, details and applications of Demographic and Mobility Field Theories are given elsewhere (Mukherji, 1995: 1–45; 1997b: 1–12; 1999: 250–270: 2001: 1–145; 2005b: 38–75).

III

Demographic, Socio-economic and Population Policy Sets of 1992–93

This section has five sub-sections, starting with discussion on rural poverty and ending with specific canonical linkages, and their policy significance.

Female Illiteracy or Poverty in Rural India

National Family and Health Survey (NFHS-I) data were used (NFHS, 1995). Only rural India is shown (Figure 3). Highest female illiteracy was in Rajasthan (82%), followed by a vast belt from Haryana to Bihar and Uttar Pradesh to Karnataka (60–80%). Next belt (40–60%) covered Gujarat, Maharashtra, Tamil Nadu, West Bengal, Assam, Punjab, Himachal Pradesh and Jammu & Kashmir. Goa had lower illiteracy (20–40%), Kerala lowest illiteracy (<20%). Widespread rural female illiteracy (poverty) acts as barrier to demographic transition and the solution lies in war on rural female illiteracy/poverty.

Figure 3

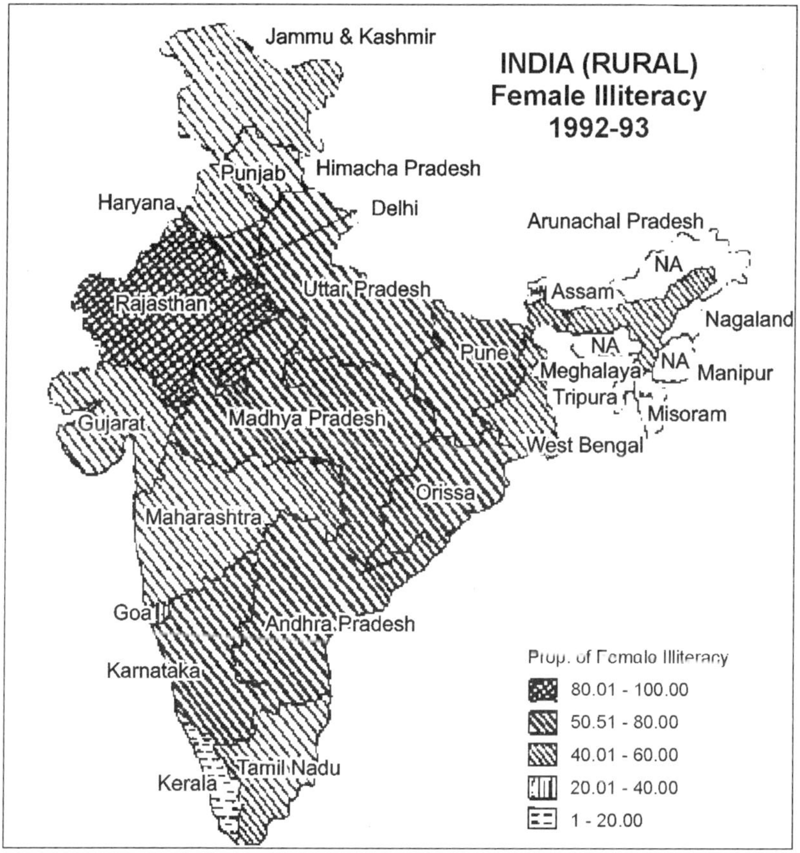

Source: NFHS-I survey.

Total Fertility Rate in Rural India

Likewise, fertility map of rural India (Figure 4) is a replica of all-India fertility map. Uttar Pradesh had highest fertility (>5 children), followed by northern heartland (except Rajasthan) (4–5 children). Deccan (3–4) and eastern states had less fertility (2–3). Kerala/Goa had < 2 children. Corollary is: we must reduce rural fertility first, before all-India fertility will decline. And, rural poverty alleviation is a must, before rural fertility, and also all-India fertility decline.

Figure 4

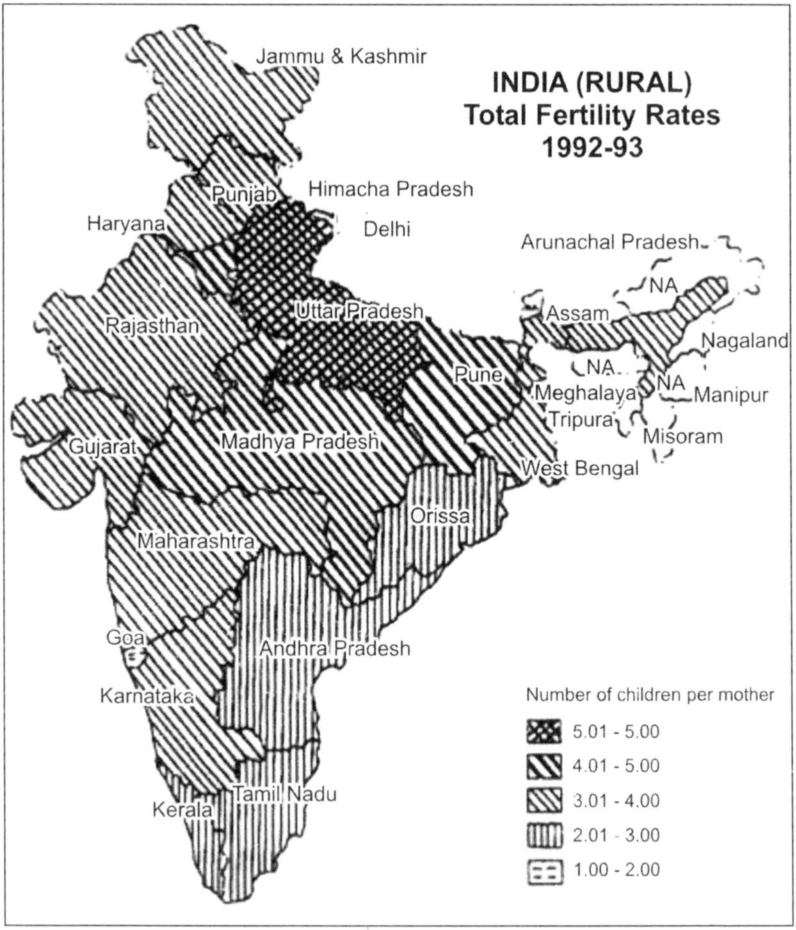

Source: NFHS-I survey.

Crucial Findings of Direct Canonical Analysis, Model I

Four canonical linkages have emerged between three matrices, linking only those from both sets that are causally linked, belonging to that particular *demographic field,* reducing others to zero. Canonical correlation between pair maximized. Important loadings are in bold. *Trace correlation* is very high, i.e., 0.90, explaining 81 per cent variance. Four very highly significant results also emerged, with canonical values 0.99, 0.96, 0.86, 0.78—all very powerful and meaningful (Mukherji, 2005a: 1–38).

Table 1

Canonical Structure Matrix, India, NFHS-I Data, 1992–93 (Model I)

		Canonical Variate			
		1	*2*	*3*	*4*
A.	**Demographic Matrix (Dependent Set)**		**Canonical Weights**		
1.	IMR (Infant Mortality Rate)	0.73	–0.38	–0.33	0.38
2.	CMR (Child Mortality Rate)	0.61	0.46	–0.27	–0.44
3.	CBR (Crude Birth Rate)	0.14	–0.55	–0.35	–0.57
4.	TFR (Total Fertility Rate)	0.25	0.56	0.82	0.56
B.	**Socio-economic-cum-Policy Matrix (Independent Set)**				
5.	Prop. adult females illiterate	0.52	0.06	0.43	0.33
6.	Per cent girls going school	37	–0.53	0.11	–0.29
7.	Prop. women married <18 yrs	0.09	0.04	–0.04	–0.24
8.	Per cent households with water	0.05	–0.05	0.16	09
9.	Per cent households without toilet	0.01	–0.21	–0.32	0.10
10.	Per cent use contraceptives	0.07	0.42	–0.09	0.27

Cont'd...

Cont'd...

11.	Prop. females sterilized	0.14	–0.25	0.34	0.11
12.	Unmet need in family planning	0.28	0.22	0.17	0.23
13.	Got ante-natal care (ANC)	0.33	0.02	–0.48	–0.53
14.	Prop. got tetanus toxoid injection	–0.01	–0.35	–0.01	0.25
15.	Delivery in PHC/CHC	0.24	–0.04	0.23	0.23
16.	Delivery assisted by professionals	–0.37	0.32	–0.18	0.13
17.	Per cent oral rehydration solution given	–0.05	–0.07	–0.01	0.00
18.	Per cent child immunized	–0.35	0.33	0.27	0.00
19.	Per cent children breastfed	–0.09	–0.06	–0.10	–0.09
20.	Children breastfed + mushy food given	0.00	0.01	0.27	0.22
21.	Per cent under weight babies	–0.09	–0.07	–0.15	–0.29
C.	**Canonical Correlation**	**0.99**	**0.97**	**0.86**	**0.79**
D.	**Meaning of Canonical Linkage Pair**	High IMR due to high female illiteracy, and also due to less child immunization and less assisted by health professional	High TFR, due to less females going to school, and also less sterilization, and less TT for mothers.	High TFR, due to female illiteracy, little ANC care, and inspite of some sterilization.	Less CMR, due to fewer underweight babies who are breastfed- and got solid, mushy food. TFR also moderately high due to less ANC care.
E.	**Trace Correlation**	=0.904 (general statistical overlap between 2 sets= 82%, trace correlation, squared times 100)			
	Chi-square	= 121.098			
	Significance	= 0.0001			

Source: See Text: Computed Canonical Equation Results, using data of NFHS-I as inputs.

Canonical Linkages

These canonical causal relationships are interpreted as follows:

(a) High IMR occurs in India due to high female illiteracy, and due to less immunization and less professional assistance in delivery (canonical correlation 0.98) (Mukherji, 2005b: 38–75).

(b) High TFR and high CMR occur, because less girls attending schools, and also less sterilization/TT given to mothers (canonical correlation 0.965).

(c) Very high TFR occurs due to high female illiteracy, and also due to little ANC given, in spite of some sterilization (canonical correlation 0.867).

(d) Less CMR occurs due to less underweight babies, who were breastfed and got solid/mushy food. TFR is also moderately high due to less ANC (canonical correlation 0.787).

Significance of Canonical Findings (Model I)

(a) Canonical correlations are consistently very high. According to Rummel (1966: 183–197), to obtain such a high value of canonical correlations in a single multivariate analysis, even in physical sciences, very rare, and to obtain them in social sciences, very remarkable!

(b) Findings show that widespread poverty is mainly responsible for high fertility and infant mortality, specially in backward UP, MP, Bihar and Rajasthan (Mukherji, 2000: 1–5).

(c) Evil syndrome between poverty and high fertility must be de-linked urgently, by providing universal education to all girls/women, if we really want TFR and IMR reduction. One single factor, universal female literacy, will greatly reduce TFR/IMR.

IV

Factor-Cum-Canonical Results of Three Systems —Demographic, Socio-economic and Policy Set 1992–93 (Model II)

In Model II, analyses are performed in two parts: (1) separately first factor analysing three matrices, and then (2) performing canonical analysis on those factor scores (Mukherji, 2007: 20–85).

Trace Correlation and Two Canonical Linkages

Trace is very high, i.e., 0.78, explaining 64 per cent of variance. Two very highly significant results also came, with values as 0.87 and 0.66. Two canonical linkages are:

(a) High TFR occurs, because of high female illiteracy and due to very little contraceptives/ANC, and high IMR occurs due to little/no immunization (canonical correlation 0.879)
(b) Less female illiteracy, so less IMR occurs. And, high TFR also occurs in spite of slight contraceptives/ANC used. This is a bipolar variate (canonical correlation 0.665).

Table 2

Canonical Structure Matrix, India, 1992–93 (Model II)

Variables/Factors		*Canonical Variate*	
		1	2
A.	**Demographic Factors (Dependent Set)**		
1.	High IMR, High CMR, much underweight babies	0.60	–0.79
2.	High TFR, and High CBR	0.79	0.60
B.	**Socio-economic-cum-Policy Factors (Independent Set)**		
1.	High female illiteracy, girls not attending school, women married young, houses without toilet, and breastfeeding not done	0.64	–0.68
2.	Breastfeeding and mushy food not given though water facility available	0.20	0.14
3.	Contraceptives not used, sterilization not done, ANC care not given, children not immunized, little health services given	0.53	–0.65
4.	ORS given, some immunization, breastfeeding not done	–0.04	0.29
C.	**Canonical Correlation**	0.87	0.66
D.	**Meaning of Canonical Linkage**	High fertility, because high female illiteracy, high IMR, and little immunization and ANC given, and very little contraceptives used.	Less female illiteracy, so less IMR. And, also high TFR, in spite of some ANC given and Some contraceptives used (as a opp. polarity)
E.	**Trace Correlation**	= 0.77 (i.e., independent set explains 0.78 squared times 100 = 64% of variance in dependent set)	
	Chi-square	= 44.5	
	Significance	= 0.0001	

Source: See Text: Computed Canonical Equation Results, using data of NFHS-I as inputs.

Table 3

Recent Data of Female Illiteracy and Total Fertility Rates, India, (Census of India, 2001 and SRS 2003) (arranged according to Female Illiteracy Levels)

State	Total			Rural			Urban	
	Female Illiteracy (Age 15–44), Census 2001	Total Fertility Rate (TFR), SRS, 2003	% below Poverty Line NSS (1999–2000)	Female Illiteracy (Age 15–44), Census, 2001	Total Fertility Rate (TFR), SRS, 2003	% below Poverty Line NSS (1999–2000)	Female Illiteracy (Age 15–44), Census, 2001	Total Fertility Rate (TFR), SRS, 2003
India	44.2	3.0	27.4	52.8	3.2	24.7	24.1	2.2
Cluster 1: High Female Illiteracy (High Poverty) and High Fertility States								
Bihar*	68.2	4.2	44.1	72.1	4.4	33.7	35.9	3.1
UP***	60.6	4.4	31.4	67.4	4.6	30.6	36.2	3.4
Rajasthan	58.4	3.8	13.4	66.3	4.0	19.5	35.0	2.7
MP**	49.3	3.8	37.5	58.7	4.1	38.6	27.1	2.4
Cluster 2: Moderately High Female Illiteracy (Moderate Poverty) and Mod. High Fertility States								
Haryana	43.0	3.0	7.4	41.8	3.1	10.2	22.9	2.4
Assam	43.2	2.9	40.4	41.7	3.0	7.6	17.3	1.8
Gujarat	40.0	2.8	12.5	51.0	3.1	14.8	22.9	2.1
Orissa	46.3	2.6	48.3	50.7	2.6	43.8	23.5	2.0
Karnataka	41.1	2.3	16.9	51.4	2.5	24.7	22.9	1.9
West Bengal	38.7	2.3	31.8	45.9	2.5	15.0	21.5	1.6
Cluster 3: Comparatively Less Female Illiteracy (Poverty) and Slightly Less Fertility States								
AP	49.3	2.2	10.9	57.8	2.3	38.6	28.9	1.9
Punjab	31.2	2.3	6.2	36.5	2.4	5.5	21.4	2.0
Maharashtra	27.9	2.3	23.6	36.2	2.4	26.9	17.7	2.1
HP	23.9	2.1	7.6	25.2	2.1	4.6	10.9	1.7
Cluster 4. Low Female Illiteracy (Less Poverty) and Low Fertility States								
Tamil Nadu	30.3	1.9	20.6	39.6	2.0	22.7	18.4	1.7
Kerala	5.3	1.8	9.6	5.9	1.8	20.0	3.6	1.7

Sources: (1) Census of India, 2001, Age and Cultural Tables, India Series 1, New Delhi (2001: 1–20), (2) Statistical Report of 2003, Report 2 of 2005, Sample Registration Survey, Census of India, New Delhi (2005: 45–135). (3) For poverty data, NSS Round 55 (1999–2000), New Delhi (2002: 5–125).

Note: *includes Jharkhand. ** includes Chhattisgarh. *** includes Uttaranchal.

Figure 6

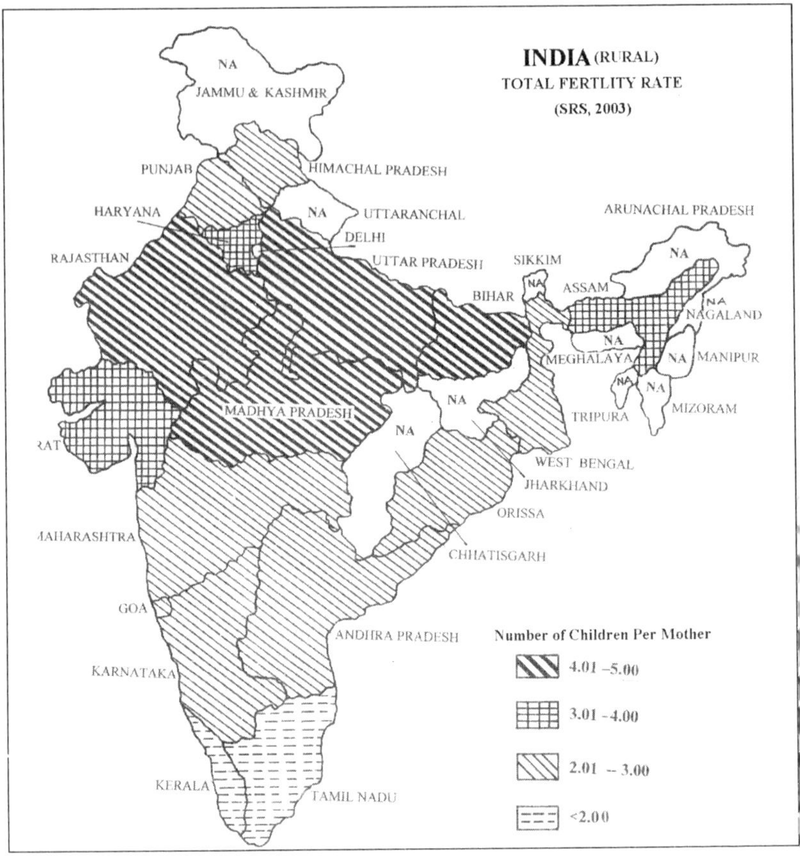

SRS 2003 Fertility Data and Clusters according to Illiterates and Literates (SRS, 2005)

Table 4 presents SRS 2003 fertility data (SRS Report, 2005), classified according to illiterates and literates. It is a great eye-opener, confirming what is stated above. According to literates-illiterates, another type of clusters can be identified. These are:

- *Cluster 1:* High female illiteracy (high poverty) and high fertility states: serious problematic states—Uttar Pradesh, Bihar, Madhya Pradesh and Rajasthan.
- *Cluster 2:* Moderately high female illiteracy (moderate poverty) and moderately high fertility states—problematic states: Haryana, Assam, Gujarat, Orissa, Karnataka and West Bengal.

- *Cluster 3:* Comparatively less female illiteracy (poverty) and slightly less fertility states: transitory states—Punjab, Himachal Pradesh, Andhra Pradesh and Maharashtra.
- Cluster 4: Low female illiteracy (less poverty) and low fertility states: Demographic transition states—Tamil Nadu and Kerala.

Findings from Reproductive and Child Health (RCH) 1998–2004 Data

Both RCH 1998–1999 survey data (RCH, 2001: 1–135) and RCH 2002–2004 survey data (RCH, 2005: 1–120) are examined, which show that due to very high female illiteracy (viz., UP/Bihar), access to health services are very low; consequently, fertility is very high, not vice versa. Conversely, where such illiteracy low (e.g., Kerala/Tamil Nadu), access to health services is easy and utilization higher; consequently, fertility has declined. Keywords are female illiteracy and poverty, which determine access and utilization of services, and, in turn, control TFR and IMR. Opposite argument is very naïve. So, given female's literacy, education, employment, empowerment, they will have much easy access to better health services, hence, these states will also achieve soon fertility decline. Policies must be implemented accordingly. Priority must be given to neglected states, districts, and remote tracts.

VII
Required Policies

Top of all, canonical linkages repeatedly show a 'one-to-one relationship' between poverty (illiteracy) and fertility. It emphasizes that in India it is basically widespread female illiteracy (or poverty), which is the fundamental "cause", and high fertility is resulting "effect", not vice versa.

- Powerful canonical findings reiterated an urgent need for universal female literacy for fertility and IMR control. Without this, specially in rural Uttar Pradesh, Bihar, Madhya Pradesh and Rajasthan (with over 70% illiterates), nothing can be achieved, no matter how we motivate 200 million poor/illiterate/hungry women to adopt small family norm! This is the greatest need now!
- Great need is also to revamp family planning, ANC and RCH. Canonical results repeatedly proved that PHCs must be re-strengthened, especially in rural, backward, neglected and remote regions. So poverty reduction and family planning programmes should go simultaneously, not in isolation!

Table 4

Recent Total Fertility Rates among Illiterates and Literates, in Rural and Urban Areas, India, Sample Registration Survey, 2003 (arranged according to TFR among the Illiterates, Total Series)

State	Total		Rural		Urban	
	Total Fertility Rate (TFR), SRS, 2003, among		Total Fertility Rate (TFR), SRS, 2003, among		Total Fertility Rate (TFR), SRS, 2003, among	
	Illiterate	Literate	Illiterate	Literate	Illiterate	Literate
India	4.0	2.4	4.1	2.6	3.1	2.0
Cluster 1: High Female Illiteracy (High Poverty) and High Fertility States: Very Seriously Problematic States						
UP	5.4	3.1	5.5	3.3	4.5	2.7
Bihar	5.0	3.0	5.0	3.2	4.6	2.4
MP	4.7	3.2	4.8	3.6	3.1	2.3
Rajasthan	4.5	2.8	4.6	2.9	3.3	2.5
Cluster 2: Moderately High Female Illiteracy (Moderate Poverty) and Moderately High Fertility States: Much Problematic States						
Haryana	4.0	2.5	4.0	2.7	4.2	2.0
Assam	3.9	2.5	4.0	2.6	2.0	1.7
Gujarat	3.8	2.4	4.0	2.7	3.0	2.0
Orissa	3.0	2.3	3.0	2.4	3.1	1.7
Karnataka	2.9	2.1	2.9	2.3	2.6	1.7
West Bengal	2.9	2.1	2.9	2.3	2.4	1.5
Cluster 3: Comparatively Less Female Illiteracy (Poverty) and Slightly Less Fertility States: Transitory States						
Punjab	3.0	2.1	3.1	2.2	2.4	1.9
HP	2.9	2.0	3.0	2.0	2.1	1.7
AP	2.7	1.9	2.8	2.0	2.5	1.7
Maharashtra	2.5	2.2	2.5	2.3	2.6	2.1
Cluster 4: Low Female Illiteracy (Less Poverty) and Low Fertility States: Demographic Transition States						
Tamil Nadu	2.5	1.9	2.7	2.0	1.8	1.8
Kerala	1.8	1.4	1.8	1.5	1.7	1.2

Source: Sample Registration Survey of 2003, SRS Report, New Delhi (2005), pp. 45–135.

- Current abysmally low health utilization rates will rise, but only after poverty reduction.
- Causal relationship between illiteracy (poverty) and very high IMR/CMR among mothers also emerged repeatedly, so also between high TFR and high female illiteracy. Such evil syndromes between poverty, IMR and TFR must be de-linked, before demographic decline could set in India. Without such fundamental transformations, very little can be expected
- Analysis of NFHS-II data yielded almost similar canonical findings, as earlier, albeit in slight modified form. Such reconfirmation tremendously verified Demographic Field Theory. Crucial policy significance is also re-emphasized. Nothing changes in India overnight. TFR and IMR declined, but not substantially in UP, Bihar, MP and Rajasthan. We must urgently eliminate massive female illiteracy and poverty, and de-link them from high TFR and IMR.
- Census (2001) and SRS (2003) data revealed that while TFR and IMR rates improved very slightly, poverty/female illiteracy not improved much, in spite of tall claims of economic growth. RCH surveys (1998–99) and (2002–04) data unraveled that improvement in most health indicators are slow, requiring much strenuous efforts, before MDGs can be realized.
- Finally, wide spatial variations emerge in all demographic, socio-economic and health indicators (RCH 2004 data). Such variations are very prominent in backward zones. Much over-time variations also arise (1992–2004). Backward areas thus require top attention (Mukherji, 1977a: 1–40; 2006: 298–325; 2007: 220–275).

Conclusion

In sum, much more emphasis needs to be given to urgent and effective socio-economic development and poverty eradication programmes for de-linking the evil syndrome of poverty and fertility, rather than only upon sterilization and family planning. Of course, family planning is very essential, and must be enhanced more rigorously, specially contraceptives must reach to the poor, who are denied access to health services. At the same time, such programmes will be much more effective, only when proper motivation, hope and aspirations are created among the poor rural masses for small family norm. Unless poverty is alleviated, such motivation is very hard to emerge and survive! A very recent World Bank report unfolds that half of the world's poor live in India, where 42 per cent of the total population or about 500 million Indians live under the poverty line of less than $1.25 per day (World Bank, 2008: 1–35). We must all combat now against abject and widespread poverty in India!

References

Census of India 2001, Social and Cultural Tables, Series I, India, Census Commissioner's Office, New Delhi, Various Data (CDs), 2003.

Cooley, W.W. and Lohnes, P.R., 1962, *Multivariate Procedure in the Behavioural Sciences*. New York, Wiley: 45–65.

Dev S. Mahendra and Ravi, C. (2007), "Poverty and Inequality: All-India and States, 1983–2005," *Economic and Political Weekly*, February 10, 509–521.

Hotelling, Harold, 1936, "Relations Between Two Sets of Variate. *Biometrika*, 28: 321–377.

Ministry of Health and Family Welfare (MOHFW), Government of India (GoI), 2001, Reproductive and Child Health Survey, Round-I (Phase I/II, 1998–99), New Delhi and IIPS, Mumbai, Tables: 1–135.

Ministry of Health and Family Welfare (MOHFW) (GoI), 2005, Reproductive and Child Health Survey, Round –II (Phase I/II,2002–4), New Delhi and IIPS, Mumbai, Tables 1–120.

Mukherji, Shekhar, 1975, Mobility Field Theory of Human Spatial Behavior: A Spatial Behavioural Approach to Study of Migration and Circulation in India. PhD thesis, Department of Geography, University of Hawaii, Honolulu and Ann Arbor: Michigan Univ. Microfilms: 20–65.

Mukherji, Shekhar, 1977a, Spatial Disorganization and Internal Migration in India: Alternative Strategies for Restructuring Space Economy and Development, Paper presented to Expert Meeting Population and Economic Development, UN-ESCAP, September, Bangkok: 1–40.

Mukherji, Shekhar, 1977b, "Assesses Interrelationships Between Population Policies, Social Systems, and Demographic Behaviour in India". *Demography India,* 6(1–2): 250–266.

Mukherji, Shekhar, 1979, The Mobility Field Theory: A Spatial Behavioural Foundation to Movement Dynamics, with Application to India. IGU Working Group on Transformation of Rural Habitat and National Geography. Society. of India, Monograph 25, Varanasi: 1–80.

Mukherji, Shekhar, 1982, *Poverty and Mobility in India: A Field Theoretic Perspective*. Kolkata, Prajna Publishers: 1–248.

Mukherji, Shekhar, 1983, *The Demographic Field Theory: Population Policies and Demographic Behaviour in India*. Allahabad, Thinkers Library: 1–141.

Mukherji, Shekhar, 1989, "Application of Demographic Field Theory to Study Demographic Behaviour, Socio-economic System and Population Policies in India. *In*: K. Srinivasan and K.B. Pathak (eds), *Dynamics of Population and Family Welfare* 1989, Himalaya Publications, Mumbai: 343–373.

Mukherji, Shekhar, 1993, "Canonical Model Linking Spatial Structure and Inter-state Migration in India". *In:* K.B. Pathak et al (eds), *Dynamics of Population and Family Welfare* 1993, Himalaya Publications, Mumbai: 245–275.

Mukherji, Shekhar, 1995, Syndrome of Poverty and High Fertility in India and Third World: Strategies for Fertility Decline. Paper presented to International Seminar on Population and Health in Developing Countries, Dept of Geography. December, Banaras Hindu Univ., Varanasi: 1–45.

Mukherji, Shekhar, 1997a, Poverty and Fertility in India: Findings of Demographic Field Theory—Linking Demographic Behaviour, Socio-economic System, and Population Policies in India. International Institute for Population Sciences (*IIPS*) *Newsletter*, January (4–6): 1–6.

Mukherji, Shekhar, 1997b, Syndrome of Poverty and Fertility in India, Paper presented to IGU Seminar on Gender, Environment, and Health, Chiang Mai Univ., Thailand, Proceedings: 1–12.

Mukherji, Shekhar, 1999, "Poverty and Fertility in India: Required Policy Changes". *In*: Jayashree De (ed), *Changing Health Problems in Developing Countries,* M.S. University of Baroda, Vadodara: 250–270.

Mukherji, Shekhar, 2000, Syndrome of Poverty and Fertility in India, *Yojana*, Ministry of Information and Broadcasting, New Delhi, May 1–5.

Mukherji, Shekhar, 2001, Application of Demographic Field Theory to India: Linkages between. Demographic Behaviour, Socio-Economic System and Population Policies. Research Monograph 25, International Institute for Population Sciences (IIPS), Mumbai: 1–115.

Mukherji, Shekhar, 2005a, "Syndrome of Poverty and High Fertility in India: Programmes for Poverty Eradication and Better Health Services". *In:* Shekhar Mukherji, *Poverty and Population in India,* Prof. R.N. Dubey Foundation, Allahabad: 1–38

Mukherji, Shekhar, 2005b, "Syndrome of Poverty and High Fertility in India". *In:* Shekhar Mukherji, *Poverty and Population in India,* R.N. Dubey Foundation, Allahabad: 38–75.

Mukherji, Shekhar, 2006, *Migration and Urban Decay: Asian Experiences*. Jaipur and New Delhi, Rawat Publications: 298–325.

Mukherji, Shekhar, 2007, *Poverty and Fertility in India: The Demographic Field Theory Perspective.* Jaipur and New Delhi, Rawat Publications: 20–285.

National Family and Health Survey (NFHS-I), 1995, National Family Health Survey-I, India (1992–93). Mumbai, International Institute for Population Sciences (IIPS).

NFHS, 2000, National Family Health Survey-II, India (1998–99). Mumbai, International Institute for Population Sciences (IIPS).

National Sample Survey Organization (NSSO), 2002, National Sample Survey, Round 55 (1999–2000). New Delhi, NSSO.

National Sample Survey Organization (NSSO) (2006) Consumer Expenditure Surveys, 2004–05 (61st round), NSSO, New Delhi, pp. 1–125. Also see 1999–2000 (55th round); 1993–94 (50th round); 1987–88 (43rd round), and NSSO, *Sarvekshana*, Vol. 13, 1989.

Phillips, Warren, 1972, *Understanding Canonical Analysis*, Department of Political Science, Ohio State University, Columbus: 1–21 (Mimeo).

Rummel, R.J., 1966, "A Field Theory of Social Action with Application to Conflict within Nations. *General Systems*, 10: 183–197.

Rummel, R.J. and Mukherji, Shekhar, 1981, *Analyzing Population Policy and Demographic Change*. Kolkata, Prajna Publishers: 1–81.

Sample Registration Survey, 2005, Statistical Report of 2003, Sample Registration Survey Unit, Registrar General and Census Commissioner of India's Office, New Delhi: 45–135.

Wood, Donald A. (1973) Toward the Interpretations of Canonical Dimensions, *Multivariate Behavioural Research,* Vol. 7, No. 4, October 1973: 477–482.

World Bank (2008), World Development Report, 2008, Washington D.C., 1–35.

Section III

Reproductive and Child Health

CHAPTER 11

Men's Awareness of Pregnancy Care in Bangladesh

A Multilevel Data Analysis

Mohammad Amirul Islam, Sabu S. Padmadas and Peter W.F. Smith

Bangladesh is one of the countries which has achieved a considerable progress towards implementation of most of the International Conference on Population and Development (ICPD) goals (Hardee et al., 1999; UN, 1995). But men's involvement in the reproductive health (RH) programme in terms of their awareness of pregnancy care has received inadequate attention among researchers and policy makers. Even though, as part of the ongoing RH programme men's involvement in this area has been emphasized, it is still at the planning stage.

Men's involvement in pregnancy care has been emphasized in different studies identifying the sectors where men can contribute for the well-being of their pregnant wives (Drennan, 1998). Men can plan their families, promote safe motherhood by arranging for skilled care during delivery, and ensuring nutritious food for their wives during pregnancy (UNICEF, 1998). Men are often the ones who decide when a women's condition is serious enough to seek medical care (Drennan, 1998). Men's decision and action during the pregnancy, delivery and after the baby is born often make the difference between illness and health, life and death (Thaddeus and Maine, 1994).

Men's involvement in safe motherhood is limited due to social system and culture in Bangladesh. Traditionally, men have been excluded from activities related to pregnancy care. The only time the father's help is required is when an emergency requires the women or child to seek treatments in hospitals, or when an external doctor is needed (Akhter et al., 1996; Population Council, 2001). Usually, men do not have enough information to make good decisions and, consequently, when an obstetric emergency arises they are unable to take quick action (Piet-Pelon, 1997).

This article investigates men's awareness of pregnancy care in Bangladesh and further explores the associated determinants using the 1999–2000 Demographic and Health Survey (DHS) data. The results of this study are expected to provide programme and policy recommendations that will help to ensure men's greater and effective participation in RH issues, especially in pregnancy care, both at the individual and community levels.

Data and Methods

The study uses the couple data set (N=2249) based on the 1999–2000 Bangladesh Demographic and Health Survey (BDHS) (National Institute of Population Research and Training (NIPORT), Mitra and Associates (MA), and ORC Macro (ORCM), 2001). The couple data set is generated by linking spouses from the male data set constituting a sample of 2,556 currently married men aged 15–59 years and that from females which has a sample of 10,544 ever married women aged 10–49 years. The BDHS data is nationally representative two-stage sample and covers all the six administrative divisions. In urban strata the primary sampling units (PSUs) are *mahallas* and in rural strata these are *mauzas*. In the forthcoming analysis PSUs will be referred as 'communities' while interpreting the regression results. Since, the objective of BDHS was to provide separate estimates for each division as well as for urban and rural areas, it was necessary to increase the sampling rate for Barisal and Sylhet divisions, so that BDHS sample is not self-weighting. For the convenience of the readership, 'husbands' will be interchangeably used as 'men' or 'respondents'.

A two-level multinomial logistic regression model was fitted to identify the significant determinants of the "Degree of husbands' awareness of pregnancy care". The response variable is coded as poor, moderate and high (reference category). Degree of awareness of pregnancy care is computed by combining the responses of the men's knowledge of pregnancy complications, attitude towards check-up during pregnancy of women if not sick and their perception regarding eating changes of women during pregnancy. If a man knows at least one serious complication regarding pregnancy, approves pregnant women of having check if not sick and believes that pregnant women should eat more than before, he is considered to be highly aware of pregnancy care. He is considered to be moderately aware, if he conforms to at least two of the above, otherwise, he is considered to be poorly aware of pregnancy care.

Table 4

Men's Degree of Awareness of Pregnancy Care by Selected Individual and Couple Characteristics, Bangladesh, 1999–2001 (%)

Characteristics	*N*	*Degree of awareness of pregnancy care*		
		Poor	*Moderate*	*High*
Individual				
Age (p=0.003)				
Less than 25	126	20.6	40.5	38.9
25–39	1120	15.2	33.4	51.4
40 and above	1003	20.2	34.2	45.6
Division (p=0.001)				
Barisal	199	18.1	27.1	54.8
Chittagong	389	18.0	38.0	44.0
Dhaka	582	14.4	31.6	54.0
Khulna	404	21.0	35.1	43.8
Rajshahi	460	15.4	35.7	48.9
Sylhet	215	24.7	35.3	40.0
Area of residence (p=0.0001)				
Urban	690	11.6	33.8	54.6
Rural	1559	20.5	34.3	45.2
Education (p=0.0001)				
No education	740	28.8	37.7	33.5
Primary	666	18.8	35.9	45.3
Secondary	529	9.1	33.3	57.7
Higher	314	4.1	23.6	72.3
Religion (p=0.409)				
Islam	1925	18.1	34.2	47.6
Other	324	15.4	33.6	50.9
No. of living children (p=0.0001)				
0	201	14.4	39.3	46.3
1–2	939	15.8	31.5	52.7
3–4	700	17.9	33.9	48.3
5 and above	109	23.7	38.1	38.1
Access to newspaper (p=0.0001)				
No	1587	22.2	36.3	41.5
Yes	662	6.9	29.2	63.9
Access to TV (p=0.0001)				
No	996	27.5	38.4	34.1
Yes	1253	10.0	30.8	59.2

Cont'd...

Cont'd...

Access to radio (p=0.0001)				
No	1080	24.0	34.0	42.0
Yes	1169	12.0	34.3	53.7
Husband's occupation (p=0.0001)				
Unemployed	77	19.5	27.3	53.2
Professional/managerial/technical	692	10.5	32.9	56.5
Agriculture self-employed	581	22.0	34.9	43.0
Agriculture employed	159	26.4	36.5	37.1
Skilled manual	283	9.9	36.0	54.1
Unskilled manual	457	24.7	34.1	41.1
Couple				
Age difference between spouses (p=0.285)				
Less than 3	144	15.3	34.7	50.0
3–7	731	16.1	33.0	50.9
8 and above	1374	18.9	34.7	46.4
Marital duration (p=0.002)				
Less than 5	391	14.6	35.8	49.6
5–10	473	12.9	34.7	52.4
11 and above	1385	20.3	33.5	46.2
Total	2249	17.7	34.1	48.2

Note 1: Row sum to 100 per cent.

Note 2: p-values are based on chi-square tests.

awareness of pregnancy care more. As the number of children increases the degree of poor awareness of pregnancy care increases among the surveyed men. Men who have access to mass media are more likely to have high degree of awareness of pregnancy care. Men engaged in professional/managerial/technical jobs are more likely to show high degree of awareness of pregnancy care, while men engaged in employed agriculture are less likely to have high degree of awareness of pregnancy care than their counterparts.

High degree of awareness of pregnancy care is observed more among men with age difference between spouses less than 7 years. Men with marital duration 5–10 years are more likely to have high degree of awareness of pregnancy care (52.4%).

Regression Analysis

A single-level multinomial logistic regression model was fitted to identify the determinants of 'Degree of husbands' awareness of pregnancy care' (using SPSS 12.0). The response variable is coded as poor, moderate and high (reference category). All the variables listed in Table 4 were considered in the analysis as independent variables. Only the significant variables, except division and place of residence (to control for over enumeration) were considered in the single-level final model. The same model was then refitted as a two-level random intercept multinomial logistic regression model in order to identify the possible community (PSU) level variation in the data (using MLwiN 2.0). As significant community (PSU) effect was found in the data the two-level multinomial logistic regression model is retained as the final model (Table 5).

Men aged less than 25 years are significantly more likely to have poor degree of awareness of pregnancy care, while men aged 25–39 years are less likely to have poor degree of awareness of pregnancy care than men aged 40 years and above when compared with high degree of awareness of pregnancy care (Table 5). Men from Barisal, Dhaka and Rajshahi divisions are significantly less likely to have poor degree of awareness of pregnancy care than men from Sylhet division. Men with education of higher than secondary level are significantly less likely to have poor degree of awareness of pregnancy care than men with education of secondary level and below. Men who do not have access to mass media (radio, TV and newspaper) are significantly more likely to have poor degree of awareness of pregnancy care. Men who are engaged in professional/managerial/technical and skilled manual type of jobs are significantly less likely to have poor degree of awareness of pregnancy care than men involved in unskilled manual type of jobs.

We have significant community effect for poor degree of awareness when compared with high degree of awareness of pregnancy care in the model. The intra-community correlation coefficient[1] indicates that 9 per cent of the variation in having poor degree of awareness of pregnancy care is due to community factors not accounted for in the model (for details about intra-community correlation coefficient see Snijders and Bosker, 1999).

Men aged less than 25 years are significantly more likely to have moderate degree of awareness of pregnancy care than men aged 40 years and above when compared with high degree of awareness of pregnancy care. Men from Barisal and Dhaka divisions are significantly less likely to have moderate degree of awareness of pregnancy care than men from Sylhet division. Men with education of less than higher secondary level are more likely to have moderate degree of awareness of

Table 5

Multinomial Logistic Regression Parameter Estimates for the Effect of Demographic and Socio-economic Characteristics on the Degree of Husbands' Awareness of Pregnancy Care, Bangladesh, 1999–2000

Independent variables	*Estimates (degree of awareness of pregnancy care)*			
	Poor		*Moderate*	
	β	*SE*	β	*SE*
Intercept	–2.777***	0.430	–1.057***	0.261
Age (r: 40 and above)				
Less than 25	0.644**	0.278	0.482**	0.225
25–39	–0.313**	0.146	–0.043	0.112
Division (r: Sylhet)				
Barisal	–0.790***	0.298	–0.630***	0.217
Chittagong	–0.149	0.255	0.124	0.181
Dhaka	–0.784***	0.243	–0.357**	0.171
Khulna	0.198	0.247	0.131	0.179
Rajshahi	–0.793***	0.249	–0.227	0.176
Place of residence (r: Urban)				
Rural	0.202	0.176	–0.122	0.111
Education (r: Higher)				
No Education	1.807***	0.364	0.983***	0.197
Primary	1.254***	0.356	0.678***	0.186
Secondary	0.634*	0.358	0.500***	0.173
Access to TV (r: Yes)				
No	1.020***	.0138	0.626***	0.102
Access to Radio (r: Yes)				
No	0.568***	0.127	0.036	0.095
Access to Newspaper (r: Yes)				
No	0.459**	0.216	0.170	0.133
Number of living children (r: 5 +)				
0	0.008	0.275	0.123	0.210
1–2	–0.165	0.189	–0.255**	0.150
3–4	–0.230	0.168	–0.191	0.136
Occupation (r: Unskilled-manual)				
Unemployed	0.233	0.341	–0.101	0.280
Professional/managerial/technical	–0.347*	0.187	0.133	0.141
Agriculture self	–0.102	0.165	0.055	0.138
Agriculture employed	–0.218	0.230	0.009	0.196
Skilled manual	–0.485**	0.246	0.115	0.168
Community level variance	0.326***	0.093	0.000	0.000

Note: Level of Significance: *$p<0.10$, ** $p<0.05$, *** $p<0.01$; SE denotes Standard Error; r denotes reference category.
† based on wife's perception of husband's approval of FP.

pregnancy care than men with education of higher secondary level. Access to TV conforms that respondents are less likely to have moderate degree of awareness of pregnancy care than those who do not have access to TV when compared to high degree of awareness of pregnancy care. If the respondents have 1–2 children they are less likely to have moderate degree of awareness of pregnancy care than the respondents who have 5 and above number of children.

Conclusion

Men's involvement in RH is a priority of the ongoing RH programme of Bangladesh. But a little has been achieved to involve men in the pregnancy care, in terms of their perception, attitude and overall awareness. The programme components are used to disseminate information regarding various aspect of pregnancy care but the effectiveness of these interventions has not been examined properly. Again, men's performance against individual programme component may not necessarily ensure their good motivation/involvement, because absent of one component may result in ineffective practice. For example, if a husband knows all the complications of pregnancy but disapproves pregnant women of having check if not sick and thinks pregnant women should eat less than before, his motivation and subsequent practice will end up with unfavourable pregnancy outcome. This paper goes beyond the traditional approach of measuring men's awareness of pregnancy care and considers combining some of the information collected by DHS to generate a composite indicator named 'Degree of awareness of pregnancy care' to better understand men's awareness of pregnancy care. Men's involvement in RH is still not satisfactory in terms of their degree of awareness of pregnancy care. Sylhet division is still lagging behind in this area. Mass media can be involved to increase men's awareness of pregnancy care. Men should be more involved in the pregnancy care component of the ongoing RH programme, which is recognized as women oriented to ensure better RH of women. The results highlight the need for appropriate community-level interventions to improve men's involvement in RH process.

Note

1. Intra-community correlation coefficient, $\rho = [\sigma_u^2/(\sigma_u^2 + \pi^2/3)]$. Where σ_u^2 is the community level variance in the model and $\pi = 3.142$.

References

Akhter, H.H., M.E.E.K. Chowdhury and A. Sen. 1996. A Cross-sectional Study on Maternal Morbidity in Bangladesh. BIRPERHT, Dhaka, Bangladesh.

Drennan, M. 1998. Reproductive Health: New Perspectives on Men's Participation. *Population Reports*. Series J, No. 46.

Hardee, K., K. Agarwal, N. Luke, E. Wilson, M. Pendzich, M. Farrell and H. Cross. 1999. Reproductive Health Policies and Programmes in Eight Countries: Progress since Cairo. *International Family Planning Perspectives* 25 (Supplement): S2–S9.

National Institute of Population Research and Training (NIPORT), Mitra and Associates (MA) and ORC Macro (ORCM). 2001. *Bangladesh Demographic and Health Survey 1999–2000*. Dhaka, Bangladesh and Calverton, Maryland, (USA).

Piet-Pelon, N.J. 1997. Male Involvement in the Bangladesh Family Planning and Reproductive Health Programme. Male Involvement in Family Planning: Experiences from Innovative Projects, Final Report. *Population Council*. Bangladesh.

Population Council. 2001. Involving Men in their Wives' Antenatal and Postpartum Care in India. Research Update, March. *Frontiers in Reproductive Health*. Population Council, India.

Snijders, T. and R. Bosker. 1999. *Multilevel Analysis: An Introduction to Basic and Advance Multilevel Modeling.* Sage Publications, Thousand Oaks.

Thaddeus, S. and D. Maine. 1994. Too Far to Walk: Maternal Mortality in Context. *Social Science and Medicine* 38(8): 1091–110.

United Nations (UN). 1995. Programme of Action of the International Conference on Population and Development (Cairo). UN, New York.

United Nations Fund for Children (UNICEF). 1998. *The State of the World's Children: Focus on Nutrition*. UNICEF, New York.

CHAPTER 12

Determinants of Male Involvement as Supportive Partners in Women's Reproductive Health

H.C. Srivastava

Reproductive health has long been viewed as solely a woman's issue; family planning and reproductive programmes have largely focussed exclusively on women. Biology, however, demands that men play a central role in reproduction and sexual health. Reproductive health services that focus only upon women have limited impact and effectiveness. The Cairo (International Conference on Population and Development, ICPD) 1994 and Beijing conferences held in 1995 have emphasized the necessity of involving men as the supportive partner in their wives reproductive health care.

"Male involvement" in reproductive health and family planning programmes is not just promoting the use of male methods of contraception, but men's supportive roles in their families, communities and workplaces to promote gender equity, girls' education, women's empowerment and sharing of child rearing. It also suggests the importance of responsible, respectful and non-coercive sexual behaviour and of shared reproductive decision-making (UNFPA,1995).

Men can play major role in promoting reproductive health of the women, and one way of making pregnancy safe is by incorporating them in all related safe motherhood. This safe motherhood information is important and touches on care before pregnancy, during pregnancy, delivery and after delivery. In brief it touches: family planning where each individual has the information and services to plan the timing, number and spacing of pregnancies, antenatal care to prevent complications and when detected treated appropriately. Clean, safe delivery handled by trained personnel. After delivery, the need to recognize any post-birth complications, promotion of breast-feeding and immunization (Ondimu, 1998).

Men have been involved in reproductive health at several levels, and must show responsibility in doing so. They are not only responsible for their own reproductive and sexual health and behaviour, they also often play an important role in the decisions regarding family size and contraceptive use within their own families and thereby in the fulfilment of their partners' reproductive health and rights. A high percentage of men in developing countries know at least one method of family planning (UNDP, 1995).

One of the major obstacles to increase male involvement and responsibility in reproductive health stems not from the men themselves but from the service delivery systems, which are almost entirely oriented to women and often provide little or no information about male contraceptive methods. Physicians often show negative attitudes toward vasectomy, and health workers are sometimes poorly trained in counselling men about safer sexual practices and male methods (UNFPA, 1995). Since gender inequalities favour men in patriarchal societies and sexual and reproductive health decisions are made by them, there is a growing realization that unless men are reached, programme efforts will have limited impact while focussing on women and addressing their reproductive health needs, special efforts should be made to encourage men to take responsibility for reproductive health as responsible sexual partners, husbands and fathers (Pachauri, 1997a).

Recently there have been calls for increased attention to the social, psychological and biological factors that determine the high risk behaviour and increase in the risk of HIV transmission, including a greater focus on men's beliefs and experiences about sexuality (Campbell, 1995).

Male dominance, physically, socially and most notably in sexual relationships can put women at risk of unwanted sexual encounters, pregnancy and infections. Better, more open and egalitarian communication between men and women and mutually supportive reproductive health behaviour are not only necessary to achieve widely held social goals but also lay a practical foundation for the improvement in women's reproductive health in all the key areas namely, sexuality, safe motherhood, fertility regulation, avoidance of sexually transmitted diseases, pregnancy and childbirth and children's health (Raju, 1999).

Besides, couples' disagreement can lead to a continuation of ongoing behaviour which may be resolved in favour of the spouse with more power in affecting his or her desires. Failure to communicate about sex and other reproductive matter may lead to act on commonly held preferences (Walle and Maiga, 1991).

Research finds (Moore, 1999) that men's knowledge of women's reproductive health was limited. Around 78 per cent men were unable to correctly identify the fertile period in the menstrual cycle. Only 33 per cent of male who had completed high school knew the correct fertile period and knowledge of symptoms of pregnancy complications were highest among men with high socio-economic status. Nearly 47 per cent were not able to correctly identify a symptom of serious pregnancy or childbirth complications. About 71 per cent did not know that symptoms were not always apparent with a sexually transmitted disease (STD). Approximately 47 per cent were not aware that STDs could be transmitted from a pregnant woman to a foetus or a newborn.

A majority of husbands did accompany their wives for the first check-up to confirm pregnancy; the wife generally went alone or with the other female members of the family for subsequent visits. Also, husband ignored wife's health care during pregnancy, except for the awareness for the need for antenatal registration and a nutritious diet. Delivery and post-delivery periods were found to be exclusively women's affairs (Barua, 1998).

To be fair, men are products of their culture and socialization. Some cultures demand proof of manhood on number of children, particularly son. Rites of passage to manhood include sexual initiations with commercial sex workers (CSWs) or older women in the community. Men were expected to be sexually experienced before marriage. They are even socialized to view women as property to be owned rather than life partners who share equally in joys and sorrows (Raju, 1999).

Study in rural Gujarat reveals that not only women were not prepared in any way for sexual intercourse but also that frequent incidence of coerciveness occurred during marriage. Husbands take as a "right" to have complete control of their wives. Any resistance on the part of women to summit to the sexual desire of their husbands could lead to violence (Khan et al., 1997b).

Need for the Study

Since more than a decade the male involvement in female's reproductive health is a major concern (ICPD, 1994) for researchers, policymakers and the government of different countries. In our country, very little effort has been given to various programmes from the point of view of male participation in the reproductive health of female so far, although the Ministry of Health and Family Planning, Government of India, is committed to implementing ICPD Programme of Action, addressing these issues. So it is high time to examine the role of men in the reproductive health of female.

Content Analysis of Various Programme Documents from the Point of View of Male Involvement

Name of document	*Year*	*Contents with respect to male involvement*
Action Plan for Revamping the Family Welfare Programme	1992	A 12-point strategy for revamping the family welfare programme. No mention of gender disparity or male involvement.
Draft National Population Policy	1994	A significant departure from demographic goal oriented population policy. Suggests holistic approach to the family welfare programme. Issues related to the elimination of gender inequality are raised prominently in many places. Need for male involvement is in a gender framework. Indicates limitations of top-down target approach and justification of its withdrawal and replacement by a need-based approach.
Manual of Target Free Approach in Family Welfare Programme.	1996	Neither gender issues nor male involvement find any reference.
Manual of Community Need Assessment Approach	1998	Some of the forms designed for monitoring purposes, collected data by sex.
Reproductive and Child Health Programme (RCH)—Schemes for implementation	1997	Outlines philosophy of RCH, stresses urgency of making the programme need-based, client-oriented and demand-driven. Quality of services, follow-up of the acceptors and client satisfaction are considered important pillars of the programme. Provision of Mother and Child Health, Reproductive Tract Infection/Sexually Transmitted Disease and family planning services is conceived of as a package of services, which cannot be separated. Interestingly, however, no allowance is made for gender issues or male involvement. Need for interpersonal communication in providing district level information to women is emphasized. Among the list of interventions, a line item includes "IEC activities and counselling on health, sexuality and gender."

Cont'd...

Cont'd...

Reproductive and Child Health Programme—Progress report up to 31 March 1998	1998	Gives progress report of RCH programme. No reference to gender or male involvement.
Population, Family Welfare and Health: Chapter in approach Paper to 9th Five-year Plan 1997–2002.	1998	Only a two-line reference is made, stating, "promoting male participation in the planned parenthood movement and increasing level of acceptance of vasectomy" (p. 85).
Survey Instruments for RCH Baseline Survey	1998	No questions on husband-wife communication, gender issues or women's autonomy in decisions about reproductive goals. In household schedule, a set of 13 questions to a male member of the household on STD and AIDS awareness and the disease.
National Population Policy	2000	Under the section "Unserved Population Group" in a paragraph on "Increased participation of men in planned parenthood" the role of men in family formation is recognized. Need for promoting non-scalpel vasectomy and focusing family planning educational campaigns on men is emphasized.

Source: Khan et al., 2001.

In the absence of clear policy directive and a monitoring system to measure achievements of the programme in enhancing male involvement in reproductive health programmes, it is difficult to understand how the family welfare programme could address this issue, which is not only new but also difficult to implement. Hence, there is the importance or need for the study from the point of view of policy implications.

Objectives

The main objective of the present paper is to study the determinants of male involvement, as supportive partner, in their wives' reproductive health, however, the specific objectives are as under:

1. To understand husband's knowledge, perception and behaviour towards reproductive and sexual health of their wives.
2. To study factors determining husbands' involvement in reproductive health care of their wives.

Sampling Techniques and Methodology

The study was carried out in three villages namely Dabok, Vishanpura and Vasnikala in Udaipur district of Rajasthan. For the purpose of required data 374 households spread in these three villages were selected. While selecting the household the criteria was that, it must have at least one eligible couple whose wives were in the reproductive age group 15–49. Both quantitative and qualitative techniques have been used for data collection. As many as 419 husbands and 417 wives were interviewed for the purpose of the study. Also, six focus group discussions (FGDs) have been conducted to accomplish the qualitative survey.

For analysing the data uni-variate and bi-variate analyses have been done. Besides, one index of involvement of the husbands regarding reproductive health issues of their wives has been constructed to capture the picture of male involvement in their wives reproductive health.

The variables considered for the construction of the Index of Husbands' Involvement are given below. Further, the index is divided into three categories viz., low, medium and high.

- Help wife in her household activities during pregnancy and soon after childbirth.
- Whether takes care of wife's reproductive health related problem.
- Restrict himself in going to workplace during illness of wife.
- Whether discuses with the wife regarding her treatment and health care.
- Perception like whether he should be at the side of his wife during delivery.
- Whether took care or not at the time of pregnancy of his wife.
- Whether helped his wife in her household chores.
- Accompanies his wife during medical check up.

Analysis of the Data and Findings

It is observed from the analysis presented in Table 1 that most of the husbands (43%) were middle aged (30–44), whereas 52 per cent wives, were at young age group (18–29 years). The mean ages for husbands and wives were 34 and 29 years respectively.

Approximately 41 per cent husbands and 39 per cent wives were having one child to two children followed by 34 per cent husbands and 38 per cent wives with three to four children. Majority of the respondent was Hindu (96%); further, predominantly they were from other backward caste (roughly 49%).

Table 1

Background Characteristics of the Respondents

Background characteristics	*Husbands (N=419)*	*Wives (N=417)*
A. Demographic Characteristics	(%)	
1. Age in Years		
18–29	38.9 (163)	51.5 (214)
30–44	43.2 (181)	39.3 (164z)
45+	17.9 (75)	9.2 (39)
2. Children Ever Born		
No Child	19.6 (82)	19.9 (83)
1–2	40.8 (171)	38.8 (162)
3–4	33.7 (141)	37.8 (158)
4+	6.0 (25)	3.5 (14)
B. Socio-economic Characteristics		
1. Religion		
Hindu	95.9 (402)	95.9 (400)
Others	4.1 (17)	4.1 (17)
2. Caste		
SC/ST	28.4 (119)	28.4 (119)
OBC	48.7 (204)	48.7 (204)
Others	22.9 (96)	22.9 (96)
3. Education		
Illiterate	23.2 (97)	62.6 (261)
Up to Middle	43.0 (180)	26.4 (110)
9 Years+	33.9 (142)	11.0 (46)
4. Occupation		
Agriculture	52.5 (220)	35.9 (150)
Service	22.9 (96)	5.0 (21)
Business	8.8 (37)	2.87 (12)
5. Monthly Family Income (in Rs)		
0–1000	16.7 (70)	30.9 (129)
1001–5000	48.7 (204)	12.9 (54)
5000+	34.6 (145)	0.0 (0)

Around 43 per cent of the husbands had studied up to middle standard, while, majority of the wives, about 63 per cent were illiterate. Most of the husbands were involved in agricultural activities (52%) followed by service sector (23%). Approximately 56 per cent wives were economically inactive.

The distribution of the husbands according to their knowledge regarding their wives reproductive health problems is shown in Table 2. It was observed that around 80 per cent of the husbands in the young age group (18–29 years) were having knowledge regarding their wives' reproductive health problem. Approximately 81 per cent husbands without any child had the same knowledge. Roughly 75 per cent Hindu husbands were aware about the reproductive health problem of their wives whereas the corresponding value for the same is around 52 per cent in case of husbands belonging to other religion. Knowledge on the subject of reproductive health problem of their wives was found highest (78%) among the husbands of other backward castes, while it is lowest (68%) among the

Table 2

Distribution of the Husbands According to their Knowledge Regarding Wife's Reproductive Health Problems.

Background characteristics	*Husbands (N=419) (%)*
A. Demographic Characteristics	
1. *Age*	
18–29	79.8
30–44	68.0
45+	74.7
2. *Children Ever Born*	
No Child	80.5
1–2	70.8
3–4	74.5
4+	68.0
B. Socio-economic Characteristics	
1. *Religion*	
Hindu	74.6
Others	52.9
2. *Caste*	
SC/ST	68.1
OBC	77.9
Others	71.9
3. *Education*	
Illiterate	72.2
Up to Middle	76.1
9 Years+	71.8
4. *Occupation*	
Agriculture	75.0
Service	80.0
Business	75.6
5. *Monthly Family Income (in Rs)*	
0–1,000	71.4
1,001–5,000	72.5
5,000+	76.6

husbands of Scheduled Castes and Scheduled Tribes. Majority (80%) of the service holder were aware about reproductive health problems of their wives. Also it is found that husbands with middle standard of schooling were aware more (76%) about their wives reproductive health problems than their counterparts. Around 77 per cent husbands of the highest income group were conscious about their wives' reproductive health problem.

The results based on Table 3 describe perception of the husbands "whether they should take part in the reproductive health related matters of their wives or not?" Approximately 44 per cent of the middle aged husbands (30–44 years) have reported in affirmative, while only 16 per cent husbands with 45 or more years of age were in agreement for the same.

Further, the data analysed for husbands' perception according to number of children ever born revealed that around 41 per cent husbands with one to two children reported that they should take part in reproductive health related matters

Table 3

Distribution of the Husbands According to their Perception 'Whether they should Take Part in the Reproductive Health Related Matters of their Wives?'

Background characteristics	*Husbands (N=419)*
A. Demographic Characteristics	Yes (%)
1. Age	
18–29	40.0
30–44	44.0
45+	16.0
2. Children Ever Born	
No Child	19.3
1–2	41.1
3–4	33.3
4+	6.3
B. Socio-economic Characteristics	
1. Religion	
Hindu	94.7
Others	5.3
2. Caste	
SC/ST	29.3
OBC	49.3
Others	21.4
3. Education	
Illiterate	24.0
Up to Middle	43.0
9 Years+	33.0
4. Occupation	
Agriculture	34.8
Service	44.0
Business	21.2
5. Monthly Family Income (in Rs)	
0–1,000	16.0
1,001–5,000	47.0
5000+	37.0

of their wives. In contrast to that only six per cent husbands with four or more children were found having the same opinion. The data analysed for husbands' perception according to their religion and caste affiliation showed that nearly 95 per cent among Hindus and five per cent husbands belonging to the other religions perceived that they should take part in reproductive health related matters of their wives. Further, around 49 per cent husbands from the other backward castes opined alike.

The husbands' perception pertaining to the above mentioned subject according to their occupation suggests that 44 per cent of the service holder agreed that they should take part in reproductive health related matter of their wives. Nearly 43 per cent husbands educated up to middle standard replied in an affirmative way.

The distribution of the husbands according to their perception regarding their wives' reproductive health problems is presented in Table 4. Specific questions were asked to the husbands to know their perception

Table 4

Distribution of Husbands according to their Perception Regarding Reproductive Health Problems of their Wives

Background characteristics	*Husbands (N=419)*
A. Demographic Characteristics	Yes %
1. Age	
18–29	42.8
30–44	41.7
45+	15.5
2. Children Ever Born	
No Child	21.4
1–2	42.4
3–4	31.9
4+	4.3
B. Socio-economic Characteristics	
1. Religion	
Hindu	95.7
Others	4.3
2. Caste	
SC/ST	30.1
OBC	43.5
Others	26.4
3. Education	
Illiterate	20.7
Up to Middle	44.2
9 Years+	35.1
4. Occupation	
Agriculture	33.7
Service	33.5
Business	32.8
5. Monthly Family Income (in Rs)	
0–1,000	14.9
1,001–5,000	44.9
5,000+	40.2

regarding their wives reproductive health problems viz., heavy bleeding during menstruation, prolonged menstruation, painful menstruation, burning sensation during urination, pain in lower abdomen and any other RTI related problem. In case of all the above mentioned symptoms the middle aged husbands (30–44 years) perceived more than that of younger husbands aged (18–29 years) as well as those husbands aged 45 or more years. The corresponding values for different RTI stretch out between around 42 per cent in case of any other RTI to 69 per cent for burning sensation during urination. Husbands with one to two children were found more concerned about their wives' reproductive health problems. The values for the same, ranges between approximately 42 per cent for burning sensation during urination to 52 per cent for prolonged menstruation, whereas, around 35 per cent of the husbands of younger age group (18–29 years) reported lower abdominal pain of their wives. Hindu husbands perceived more than the husbands with other religion for all the values relating to the same. Barring the perception about painful menstruation, burning sensation during urination and feeling of heavy down below the husbands of the category of other backward caste perceived most regarding their wives' reproductive health problems. Also it is depicted that pain in lower abdomen was perceived by around 53 per cent of the husbands of other backward caste. Besides the husbands with other caste perceived more in case of painful menstruation, burning sensation during urination and feeling of heavy down below and the respective values were around 43, 39 and 64 per cent. Husband's perception regarding wives' reproductive health problem was found more among educated husbands compared with their illiterate counterparts. Further, husbands with 9 or more years of education showed relatively higher percentages in case of heavy bleeding during menstruation, prolonged menstruation, painful menstruation, burning sensation during urination. Also husbands educated up to middle standard had better perception for feeling of heavy down below, pain in lower abdomen and any other RTI as compared with those who were illiterate. Except the perception about any other RTI, the husbands with monthly family income between Rs 1,001 to Rs 5,000 were more concerned regarding their wives' reproductive health problems.

Table 5

Distribution of the Husbands According to their Perception whether in their Culture they are Allowed to Help their Wives During or after Pregnancy?

Background characteristics	Husbands (N=419) (%)							
	Heavy bleeding during menst-ruation (N=40)	Prolonged menst-ruation (N=46)	Pain full menst-ruation (N=65)	Burning sensation during urination (N=26)	Feeling of heavy down below (N=14)	Pain in Lower abdomen (N=20)	Any other RTI (N=12)	None (N=290)
A. Demographic Characteristics								
1. Age								
18–29	27.5	26.1	27.7	23.1	14.3	34.1	25.0	42.1
30–44	60.0	52.2	61.5	69.2	57.1	45.3	41.7	39.3
45+	12.5	21.7	10.8	7.7	28.6	20.6	33.3	18.6
2. Children Ever Born								
No Child	7.5	13.0	13.8	11.5	14.3	35.2	33.3	21.7
1–2	50.0	52.2	49.2	42.3	42.9	25.8	33.3	39.0
3–4	37.5	23.9	33.8	38.5	35.7	29.0	25.0	33.8
4+	5.0	10.9	3.2	7.7	7.1	10.6	8.4	5.5
B. Socio-economic Characteristics								
1. Religion								
Hindu	92.5	93.5	92.3	96.2	100.0	100.0	83.3	97.9
Others	7.5	6.5	7.7	3.8	0.0	0.0	16.7	2.1
2. Caste								
SC/ST	42.5	28.3	23.1	23.1	14.3	20.3	24.9	22.1
OBC	42.5	47.8	33.8	38.4	21.4	54.5	40.6	26.5
Others	15.0	23.9	43.1	38.5	64.3	25.2	34.5	51.4
3. Education								
Illiterate	25.0	28.3	29.2	30.5	35.7	23.1	25.0	23.8
Up to Middle	30.0	32.6	33.8	30.7	35.7	42.4	39.8	42.8
9 Years+	45.0	39.1	37.0	38.8	28.6	34.5	35.2	33.4
4. Occupation								
Agriculture	42.3	53.5	52.0	48.2	44.5	49.1	45.2	52.4
Service	32.1	22.9	22.0	29.4	30.3	22.5	21.5	19.7
Business	25.6	24.6	26.0	22.4	25.2	28.4	33.3	27.9
5. Monthly Family Income (in Rs)								
0–1,000	7.5	15.2	21.5	23.1	21.4	30.0	32.3	16.6
1,001–5,000	50.0	58.7	49.2	53.8	57.1	50.0	25.8	48.3
5,000+	42.5	26.1	29.3	23.1	21.5	20.0	41.9	35.1

The husbands' perception regarding "whether their culture allows them to help their wives' during their pregnancy and after childbirth", 43 per cent husbands in the age group 18–29 years replied in affirmative. Another 42 per cent husbands with one to two children were found in agreement on the subject matter. In contrast to that only four per cent husbands with four or more children responded in positive. The analysis of the data by religion showed that nearly 96 per cent Hindu husbands answered that they are allowed to help their wives in such circumstances, whereas the same is only around four per cent for the husbands with other religious affiliation. Nearly 43 per cent husbands belonging to other backward caste approved that their culture allows them to help their wives during pregnancy as well as after childbirth. The corresponding percentage for the husbands belonging to other castes was 26. Further it was observed that nearly 44 per cent husbands educated up to middle confirmed that they could help their wives during the same period, where as only about 21 per cent illiterate husbands perceived the same.

As far the husbands monthly family income and their perception regarding the above subject matter is concerned nearly 45 per cent husbands with monthly income between Rs 1,001 to Rs 5,000 perceived that they could help their wives during their pregnancy and after childbirth. On the contrary nearly 15 per cent husbands with monthly family income up to Rs 1,000 replied in positive. Level of husbands' education showed positive relation with the same viewpoint as 44 per cent husbands educated up to Middle level and 35 per cent educated up to 9 years schooling and above were found having positive attitude while in case of the illiterate husbands the corresponding value was 21 per cent.

In response to a question posed to the husbands "why they should help their wives during pregnancy and after childbirth", various reasons were given viz., she is my wife, she should take rest, I consider it to be my duty, it's a female affair (not helping), both mother and child should be healthy, it is necessary, etc.

Further, the analysis was done with different socio economic and demographic characteristics of husbands and presented in Table 6. A glance at the analysis of the data revealed that among the younger husbands (18–29 years) the feeling that she is my wife and both mother and child should be healthy were observed more around 44 and 45 per cent respectively. Whereas, 47 and 44 per cent among the middle aged husbands (30–44 years) replied that 'she should take rest' and 'I consider it to be my duty' respectively. Husbands with one child to two

Table 6

Distribution of the Husbands According to Reason for Helping their Wives during Pregnancy or after Childbirth

Background Characteristics	Husbands (N=419) %							
	She is my wife (N=133)	She should take rest (N=45)	I consider it to be my duty (N=71)	It's a female affair (N=121)	Both mother and child should be healthy (N=133)	It is neces-sary (N=5)	Do not know (N=10)	Due to shyness (N=7)
A. Demographic Characteristics								
1. Age								
18–29	43.6	42.2	42.3	31.4	45.4	40.0	60.0	14.3
30–44	36.8	46.7	43.7	47.9	31.5	40.0	20.0	57.1
45+	19.6	11.1	14.0	20.7	23.1	20.0	20.0	28.6
2. Children Ever Born								
No Child	24.1	15.6	19.7	15.7	20.0	19.1	50.0	0.0
1–2	39.1	53.3	42.3	38.0	46.2	35.6	20.0	42.9
3–4	32.3	31.1	32.4	35.5	33.8	35.3	30.0	42.9
4+	04.5	00.0	05.6	10.8	00.0	10.0	00.0	14.2
B. Socio-economic Characteristics								
1. Religion								
Hindu	96.3	97.8	94.4	96.7	84.6	100.0	100.0	100.0
Others	03.7	02.2	05.6	03.3	15.4	00.0	00.0	00.0
2. Caste								
SC/ST	28.5	26.7	31.0	24.8	15.4	80.0	60.0	0.0
OBC	41.4	44.4	49.3	55.4	53.8	20.0	40.0	100.0
Others	30.1	28.9	19.7	19.8	30.8	00.0	00.0	00.0
3. Education								
Illiterate	18.8	15.6	28.2	28.1	15.4	40.0	40.0	14.3
Up to Middle	44.4	35.5	26.1	41.3	38.2	20.0	50.0	42.9
9 Years+	36.8	48.9	45.7	30.6	46.4	40.0	10.0	42.8
4. Occupation								
Agriculture	48.6	38.9	39.0	45.1	31.1	36.4	60.9	29.5
Service	26.3	35.9	29.4	25.4	37.1	32.7	0.0	21.5
Business	25.1	25.2	31.6	29.5	31.8	30.9	39.1	49.0
5. Monthly Family Income (in Rs)								
0–1,000	22.6	6.7	8.5	19.0	7.7	20.0	40.0	0.0
1,001–5,000	42.9	44.4	49.3	54.5	30.8	40.0	50.0	71.4
5,000+	34.5	48.9	42.2	26.5	61.5	40.0	10.0	28.6

children were found more in case of reasons for helping their wives in all the above stated categories. The respective value for the same ranged between nearly 36 per cent in case of 'it is necessary' to 53 per cent for the reason 'she should take rest'. Husbands with other religion were found relatively lesser able to give reasons for helping their wives during the process of childbearing and after childbirth than their Hindu counterpart. Interestingly husbands belonging to the other backward castes (OBC) have explained the reasons better than their counterparts. The corresponding value for the same ranged between 20 per cent for 'it is necessary' to almost 54 per cent for 'both mother and child should be healthy'. Except the reason that 'she is my wife' for all other reasons related to help their wives during pregnancy and childbirth the husbands with 9 or more years of schooling represented highest percentages. The values were 49, 46, 46 and 40 per cent for the reasons 'she should take rest', 'I consider it to be my duty', 'both mother and child should be healthy' and ' it is necessary' respectively. Almost 62 per cent husbands with monthly family income of more than Rs 5,000 agreed that they could help their wives as both mother and child should be healthy. Whereas all other reasons for helping their wives were observed more for the husbands whose monthly income were between Rs 1,001 to Rs 5,000. The corresponding value ranged between 40 per cent in case of 'it is necessary' to almost 49 per cent for 'I consider it to be my duty'.

Table 7 presents perception of the husbands pertaining to a question "whether they should restrict themselves in going to workplace if their wife is seriously ill?" In response to the same around 43 per cent middle aged husbands (30–44 years) said 'yes', whereas the figure stood at only 17 per cent for the husbands with 45 or more years of age. Nearly 41 per cent husbands with one child to two children perceived that they should not go to their workplace while their wives are seriously ill. However, only five per cent husbands with four or more children said 'yes'. Hindu husbands and those belonging to other backward castes (OBC) showed relatively higher percentage values as compared with their other counterparts when they were asked the same question.

Nearly 43 per cent husbands who had completed Middle School education have opined in affirmative. Another nearly 54 per cent husbands, whose occupation was agriculture perceived the same, whereas only around 19 per cent service holders believed to do so.

Index of husbands' involvement in their wives' reproductive health problems suggested that around 5 per cent of husbands were found

Table 7

Distribution of the Husbands According to their Perception whether they Restrict Themselves in Going to Workplace if their Wife is Suffering from Serious Disease?

Background characteristics	*Husbands (N=419)*
A. Demographic Characteristics	Yes %
1. Age	
18–29	39.6
30–44	42.9
45+	17.5
2. Children Ever Born	
No Child	19.7
1–2	41.4
3–4	33.6
4+	5.3
B. Socio-economic Characteristics	
1. Religion	
Hindu	96.2
Others	3.8
2. Caste	
SC/ST	27.8
OBC	48.7
Others	23.5
3. Education	
Illiterate	23.7
Up to Middle	42.7
9 Years+	33.6
4. Occupation	
Agriculture	53.9
Service	18.6
Business	27.5
5. Monthly Family Income (in Rs)	
0–1,000	16.7
1,001–5,000	48.7
5,000+	34.6

having low involvement, while 73 per cent husband had medium involvement and around 22 per cent husbands were found highly involved in their wives' reproductive health problems (Table 8).

Factors influencing involvement of the husbands in their wives' reproductive health problems showed high involvement (around 28%) in case of middle aged (30–44 years) husbands in comparison to the husbands of other age groups. Approximately 24 per cent husbands having one to two children were found highly involved in their wives' reproductive health problems. High involvement was around 21 per cent for the husbands belonging Hindu religion. Further the study revealed that nearly 27 per cent Scheduled Caste and Scheduled Tribe husbands were highly involved in the issues related to reproductive health of their wives. Almost 22 per cent husbands who have attended middle school were found highly involved regarding the same issue. With regard husbands' occupation and their involvement is concerned, 23 per cent of the service holders were found to be highly involved, followed by agriculturists (around 21%). Economically well-off husbands (monthly income Rs 1,001 to 5,000 and more) were found to be highly involved in the reproductive health related matters of their wives as compared to the husbands with relatively low income.

To accomplish the qualitative technique the relevant data was collected through observation method, case study approach and conducting focus group discussions (FGDs). In all six FGDs each was conducted for husbands and wives separately. Some of the thrust issues emerged out of the FGDs are given below.

By and large husbands were aware about the reproductive health problems of their wives, like irregular menstrual cycle, acute bleeding, burning sensation in urination, etc. Besides, they had some knowledge concerning RTI/STD and HIV/AIDS. Almost all FGDs suggested that for the majority the meaning of HIV/AIDS is a sexually transmitted disease also for some amongst them it is an infectious disease. Surprisingly some respondents were of the opinion that this is a fatal disease.

Though a majority of the husbands opined that it is their prime responsibility to take care of their wives and some openly said that they helped their wives with regard their reproductive health problems—during menstruation, childbearing period, antenatal and postnatal care but because of shame and cultural pressure people usually hesitate in accepting their responsibility openly.

Table 8

Index of Husbands' Involvement in Wives' Reproductive Health

Low Involvement	4.8
Medium Involvement	73.0
High Involvement	22.2

*All the values are in percentages of the respective category.

Table 9

Factors Governing Husbands' Involvement in their Wives' Reproductive Health Issues

Background characteristics	*Low*	*Medium*	*High*
A. Demographic Characteristics		(%)	
1. Age			
18–29	4.3	78.5	17.2
30–44	4.4	68.0	27.6
45+	6.7	73.3	20.0
2. Children Ever Born			
No Child	3.7	76.8	19.5
1–2	5.7	70.2	24.1
3–4	3.5	74.9	21.6
4+	12.0	64.0	24.0
B. Socio-economic Characteristics			
1. Religion			
Hindu	4.7	73.9	21.4
Others	5.9	52.9	41.2
2. Caste			
SC/ST	4.2	68.9	26.9
OBC	6.4	76.0	17.6
Others	2.1	71.9	26.0
3. Education			
Illiterate	3.1	76.3	20.6
Up to Middle	4.4	73.3	22.2
9 Years+	6.3	70.4	23.2
4. Occupation			
Agriculture	3.6	75.0	21.4
Service	0.0	80.0	20.0
Business	3.5	79.1	17.4
5. Monthly Family Income (in Rs)			
0–1,000	4.3	77.1	18.6
1,001–5,000	4.4	72.5	23.0
5,000+	5.5	71.7	22.8

* All the values are in percentages of the respective category.

Government of India launched a National Plan of Action (NPA) for children in 1992, in response to the world submit for children held at New York in September 1990. The Plan of Action set itself the task of achieving the intermediate and long-term goals of reducing several of the maternal and child health indicators, for example the reduction of the infant mortality rate to 60 per thousand live births by 1995 and to 40 by 2000; under-five mortality to 80 per 1000 live births by 1995 and 60 by 2000; maternal mortality to 250 by 1995 and 200 by 2000; controlling childhood diseases through the eradication of polio in 50 per cent of the districts by 1995 and all districts by 2000; elimination of neonatal tetanus by 1995; reduction in the deaths due to measles to 45 per cent by 1995 and eradication of all such deaths due to measles by 2000; reduction of deaths due to diarrhoeal diseases by 30 per cent by 1995 and 70 per cent by 2000; reduction of deaths due to Acute Respiratory Infection (ARI) by 20 per cent by 1995 and 40 per cent by the year 2000; and reduction of severe and moderate malnutrition among children of 0 to 6 years of age to less than half of the 1990 level by the year 2000. However, even after six years (2006) of the deadline date of achievement of these goals, the set goals for the year 2000 have not been achieved.

The achievement of the above goals depend on various indicators of child and maternal health scenarios in various states and union territories of the country, and also the differential levels of these indicators by rural-urban characteristic of the population. Further, the MCH indicators in the urban slums (where relatively poor people stay) are expected to be poorer than that in the rest of the urban population. This paper presents a comparative study of the MCH parameters in the rural and urban slum populations of Gujarat state.

Methodology

Two multi-indicator cluster surveys (MICS) were conducted, one for the entire rural population of Gujarat state as the universe and the other for the urban poor with the known urban slum population in the six municipal corporations of the state as the universe.

The sample population in MICS is chosen based on a two-stage cluster sampling technique. A cluster in MICS is a randomly selected habitation, i.e., a census village in rural area and a slum settlement in the six municipal corporation areas of the state. Fifteen clusters from each of the two universes i.e., 15 villages and 15 urban slum settlements were selected by using systematic PPS (probability proportional to the size) sampling procedure.

Within each cluster (i.e., selected village or urban slum settlement), first a street lane, basti or falia was selected on a random basis. For this selection, information on the number of streets, lanes, bastis or falias which exists in the given cluster was collected. Then, by using a random number, a street, lane, basti or falia was selected randomly. After having selected the street/lane/basti/falia the total number of households was quickly ascertained. And by using a number on a currency note or a random number, a household was selected in the selected street/lane/basti/falia randomly and was taken as first sample household. Subsequent selection was made from the nearest house. This selection process was repeated till the target sample of twenty children of 12–23 months of age and twenty mothers who had a delivery within 12 months prior to the date of survey, were collected in each cluster. In the process, the total number of households surveyed were 1,898 in urban slums and 2,196 in rural areas of Gujarat. Further, requisite information on childhood diseases from all under-five children in the households surveyed in the course of covering samples of 12–23 month old children and mothers who had a childbirth within the 12 months prior to survey was obtained.

Child Health

This section deals with the immunization coverage of children by sex in the age group 12–23 months and coverage of Vitamin A prophylaxes to these children. It provides the information on the incidence of diarrhoea and the treatment received (indicating the use of Oral Rehydration Salts-ORS). It also gives information on mother's knowledge regarding symptoms of Acute Respiratory Infection (ARI).

Immunization of Children

Immunization of children against the six serious but preventable diseases viz., diphtheria, tuberculosis, pertussis, tetanus, polio and measles has been one of the important programme of childcare health system initiated by Government of India way back in 1978 with the objective of reducing morbidity, mortality and disabilities due to those six childhood diseases. In this section an effort is made to assess the extent of coverage of children in the age group 12–23 months who were immunized against these diseases. The relevant information on immunization and vitamin A prophylaxis was collected from the mothers of 300 children, age 12–23 months each, from urban slums and rural areas of Gujarat.

Table 1 reveals that immunization card was available for 44 per cent of the cases in the rural areas as against 33 per cent of cases in urban slums. Further, in both urban slums and rural areas, the presence of immunization card was found more when the child was male than female (about 6 and 11 percentage points more availability of immunization card for male as compared to female children in rural areas and urban slums respectively). This implies that mothers in rural areas are relatively more conscious in preserving the card and that too when the child is male, thereby reflecting the possibility of a gender bias in favour of male child.

Table 1

Immunization Coverage of Children (12–23 months) in Urban Slums and Rural Areas by Sex, Gujarat, 1996

Vaccination status	*Percentage of children*					
	Urban slums			*Rural*		
	Male	*Female*	*Total*	*Male*	*Female*	*Total*
Immunization card available	36.2	30.2	33.0	49.0	38.1	43.7
Children immunized BCG	63.8	62.9	63.3	86.3	83.0	84.7
DPT						
1 dose	73.8	66.7	70.0	88.9	85.7	87.3
2 dose	67.4	61.0	64.0	85.6	80.3	83.0
3 dose	58.2	56.6	57.3	82.4	72.1	77.3
OPV						
1 dose	84.4	76.7	80.3	94.1	90.5	92.3
2 dose	74.5	66.7	70.3	86.9	79.6	83.3
3 dose	63.1	57.9	60.3	81.7	72.1	77.0
Measles	41.1	38.4	39.7	69.9	61.9	66.0
Completely immunized	37.6	32.1	34.7	67.3	58.5	62.9
Partially immunized	53.2	56.0	54.7	29.4	34.7	32.0
Not immunized	9.2	11.9	10.6	3.3	6.8	5.1
Total number of children (12–23 months)	141	159	300	153	147	300

Analysis of antigen-specific coverage data showed that as against 85 per cent of the children in the rural areas only 63 per cent of the children in the urban slums were immunized with BCG. This means that 22 percentage points more rural children had taken BCG immunization as compared to urban slum children. Similarly, the coverage of DPT3 and OPV3 was much higher in the case of rural children (77% each) as compared to urban slum children (57 and 60% respectively). DPT3 and OPV3 coverage is 20 and 17 percentage points more among rural children compared to urban slum children respectively. Further, measles coverage among the rural children (66%) is 26 percentage points more than the urban slum (40%) children.

The table clearly delineates that as compared to 63 per cent of children in rural areas of Gujarat, only 35 per cent of children in urban slums were completely immunized from all the six dreaded childhood diseases. Not immunized children in the urban slum population (11%) was almost double than the rural population (5%). Further, partially immunized children (those who were supposed to take three doses of vaccine and took just one or two or else did not get immunized from all the six diseases) among the urban slum population (55%) are 23 percentage points-higher than that of rural population (32%) in Gujarat.

This calls for further need to lay more emphasis in converting partially immunized children to fully immunized children, on the one hand, and motivating parents about the need for getting their children immunized from the six childhood diseases, on the other, especially when such services are readily available at the doorsteps in their respective community.

It, thus, seems to be difficult to attain the set goals of achieving 100 per cent immunization coverage of children against the six preventable diseases even by 2010, unless special efforts are made by the government to gear up its immunization programme, in general, and especially in the urban slums of the state. Special efforts are also called for raising immunization coverage of female children as the coverage of this group is relatively lower than that of male children.

Vitamin-A Prophylaxis

Table 2 presents the vitamin-A prophylaxis by sex in both urban slums and rural areas of Gujarat. The coverage of vitamin-A received with measles or other times is found to be 49 per cent in the rural areas and only 28 per cent in the urban slums, illustrating thereby that urban slums again lagged behind in the coverage of vitamin-A to the children.

It has further been observed that though the measles coverage in the urban slums and rural areas of Gujarat has been 40 and 66 per cent respectively, vitamin-A coverage in these areas have been only 28 and 49 per cent respectively. This illustrates that the gap between measles vaccination and first vitamin-A dose was relatively higher (17% points) in rural areas as compared to urban slums (12% points). The table further reveals that the coverage of vitamin-A was relatively higher for male children compared to female children and this was found to be true in both urban slums and rural areas.

Table 2

Percentage of Children who Received Vitamin-A Prophylaxis in Urban Slums and Rural Areas by Sex, Gujarat, 1996

Vitamin-A received	*Percentage of children*					
	Urban slums			*Rural*		
	Male	*Female*	*Total*	*Male*	*Female*	*Total*
Received with Measles	29.1	26.4	27.7	51.0	44.9	48.0
Received other times	0.0	0.6	0.3	2.0	0.0	1.0
Not received	66.0	72.4	69.3	44.4	54.4	49.3
Do not know	4.9	0.6	2.7	2.6	0.7	1.7
Total	146	154	300	171	129	300

Incidence of Diarrhoea

The incidence of occurrence of diarrhoea during the last two weeks prior to the date of survey, among children under 5 years of age was reported to be 28 per cent in urban slums and 24 per cent in the rural areas of Gujarat (Table 3). Here too, the incidence of diarrhoea in the urban slums was slightly higher than that in the rural areas of the state. However, the difference in the extent of diarrhoea among the male and female children was found to be marginal in both urban slums as well as rural areas.

Treatment of Diarrhoea and its Source

Table 3 illustrates that among children who suffered from diarrhoea, 73 per cent in the urban slums and 74 per cent in the rural areas sought treatment outside the home. The difference between male and female children seeking treatment outside the home for diarrhoea was marginal in both the areas.

Table 3

Percentage of Children (under 5 years of age) who Suffered from Diarrhoea in Last Two Weeks in Urban Slums and Rural Areas of Gujarat, 1996

	Percentage of children					
	Urban slums			Rural		
	Male	Female	Total	Male	Female	Total
Children suffered from diarrhoea	27.7	28.6	28.2	23.7	23.2	23.5
Treatment received outside the home	73.4	72.5	73.0	72.3	76.6	74.3
Source of treatment government doctor/health worker	7.3	17.3	12.3	24.2	33.9	28.9
Private doctor	84.9	79.4	82.1	71.9	61.2	66.7
Chemist	5.9	3.3	4.6	—	—	—
Others	1.9	—	1.0	3.9	4.9	4.4
Children advised to ORS packets	20.4	12.7	16.6	43.8	32.2	38.2
Children who received ORS	19.1	12.0	15.6	39.8	28.9	34.5
Total number of children <5 years	746	724	1470	748	680	1428

The table clearly indicates that among the children who suffered from diarrhoea, majority (82% in the urban slums and 67% in the rural areas) got treatment from private doctors. It is, however, interesting to note that relatively higher percentage of female children compared to male children (17% female children compared to 7% male children in urban slums; 34% female children compared to 24% male children in rural areas) received treatment for diarrhoea from government doctors/hospitals in both urban slums and rural areas of Gujarat.

Thus, certain bias seems to be evident among the parents to give better health services of private doctors to their male children as compared to female children and this bias of son preferences has been clearly evident in both urban slums and rural population under study.

Table 3 further reveals that while 38 per cent of the children, who suffered from diarrhoea in the rural areas were advised to take ORS packets (of which 35% received ORS) only 17 per cent of such children were advised ORS packets (of which 16% received ORS) in the urban slums. Thus, the situation of urban slums children in this respect is much worse than that in the rural areas of Gujarat.

Knowledge of Acute Respiratory Infection (ARI)

Information on mother's knowledge regarding symptoms of acute respiratory infection for which immediate treatment has to be sought for a child was obtained from mothers of all children under 5 years of age and the data are presented in Table 4.

Table 4

Perceived ARI Symptoms Among Mothers for which a Child is Taken to a Health Provider in Urban Slums and Rural Areas of Gujarat, 1996

ARI symptoms for which a child is taken to a health provider	*Percentage*	
	Knowledge of ARI symptoms among	
	Urban slums	*Rural*
Fever	52.9	70.3
Breathing fast	38.4	45.9
Difficulty in breathing	44.0	50.8
Blocked nose	31.5	43.0
Trouble in sleeping/eating	14.8	18.4
Cough	68.8	76.1
Other	4.8	7.0
Do not know	16.4	7.2
Total number of mothers contacted	1118	1016

The table reveals 'cough' and 'fever', were the most common symptoms perceived by mothers as danger signs in both the areas under study (53–69% mothers in urban slums and 70–76% mothers in rural areas). It was, however, heartening to note that the important danger signals like 'fast breathing' and 'difficulty in breathing' were perceived as life threatening by as high as 38 to 44 per cent in the urban slums and 46 to 51 per cent of mothers in the rural areas of Gujarat. This illustrates that even in the knowledge of acute respiratory infection, rural area mothers have an edge over the mothers in the urban slum area.

Safe Motherhood

The health of mothers is inextricably bound up with the health of the children born. So mothers' health care during pregnancy is essential to ensure that she may carry the pregnancy to full term without risk. This section deals with the information on antenatal care, consumption of iron and folic acid tablets, TT immunization received by women, place of delivery and assistance during delivery and mother's age at first pregnancy. This data was collected from 300 women each from urban slums and rural areas of Gujarat.

Antenatal (ANC) Check-up and Number of ANC Visits

It is encouraging to observe that more than three-fourths of surveyed women (77% in urban slums as against 82% in rural areas) had gone for antenatal check-up (Table 5). However, among those who had gone for antenatal check-up about 50 per cent of mothers in the urban slums and 46 per cent in the rural areas had undergone three or more antenatal check-ups. Further, 22 per cent of the mothers in the urban slums and 18 per cent in the rural areas did not go for any antenatal check-up during their pregnancy period.

Table 5

Type of Essential Maternal Care Received by those who had a Live Birth in Last One Year in Urban Slums and Rural Areas of Gujarat, 1996

Type of services	*Percentage*	
	Urban slums	*Rural*
Women who underwent check-up	77.4	82.0
Number of ANC visits		
Once	8.0	11.0
Twice	19.4	24.6
Thrice	23.0	20.7
Four or more	27.0	25.7
None	22.3	17.7
Don't remember	0.3	0.3
TT immunization received	75.3	90.4
Once	9.3	10.7
Twice	64.0	75.0
Booster	2.0	4.7
None	24.3	9.6
Don't remember	0.3	0.0
Total number of women who had a live birth in last 12 moths	300	300

The above discussion clearly points to the fact that urban slum mothers are lagging far behind the rural mothers in receiving ANC check-up during their pregnancies.

TT Immunization and Receipt of IFA Tablets

Seventy-five per cent of the mothers in the urban slums and 90 per cent of them in the rural areas had received TT immunization. Thus, rural mothers had an edge over urban slum population even in terms of the receipt of the TT immunization services.

It can be seen from the Table 6 that 84 per cent of pregnant women in urban slums and 82 per cent in rural areas received iron folic acid tablets but majority of the women in both areas (73% in urban areas 69% in rural areas) did not receive the recommended number of 100 tablets. It was also observed that though 84 and 82 per cent of the mothers in urban slums and rural areas respectively received IFA tablets, only 76 per cent in urban area and 77 per cent in the rural area actually consumed these IFA tablets.

Table 6

Supplementation and Use of Iron Folic Tablets in Pregnancy in Urban Slums and Rural Areas of Gujarat, 1996

IFA supplements during pregnancy	*Percentage*	
	Urban slums	*Rural*
IFA supplements received		
< 50	30.7	26.3
51–100	42.6	42.7
>100	10.7	12.7
No IFA supplements received	16.0	18.3
IFA supplements consumed		
< 50	42.6	39.3
51–100	29.1	31.3
>100	4.5	6.7
No IFA supplements consumed	23.8	22.7
Total number of women who had a live birth in last 12 months	300	300

Place of Delivery and Assistance during Delivery

It was observed that more than one half of the deliveries (55% in slums and 60% in rural areas) are still conducted at home. The percentage of institutional deliveries was 45 in slum population and 40 in rural areas (Table 7).

Regarding the type of attendance at the time of delivery, for one half of slum mothers (50%) the deliveries were attended by untrained personnel (untrained dai, family member, neighbour etc.) while among the rural mothers this percentage was far less (35%) (Figure 1). This indicates that compared to slum population, rural population have been more conscious to utilize the services of trained personnel to conduct safe delivery.

Table 7

Place of Delivery and Assistance During Delivery in Urban Slums and Rural Areas of Gujarat, 1996

Place of delivery	*Percentage*	
	Urban slums	*Rural*
Institutional delivery	44.7	40.0
Government hospital/PHC/SC	23.0	7.6
Private hospital	21.7	32.4
Home	55.3	60.0
Total number of women who had a live birth in last 12 months	300	300

Mother's Age at First Pregnancy

Becoming pregnant at too young age (before age of 18 years) increases the health risks for both mother and child. In societies where many girls marry at an early age, couples should delay the first pregnancy until at least the age of 18, as the girls are not physically fit for childbearing at the tender age. Also babies born to these younger mothers are more likely to be premature babies (born too early) or with very low weight at birth. Table 8 presents the distribution of women by age at first pregnancy. It illustrates that 22 per cent of women in urban slums and 11 per cent of women in rural areas had their first pregnancy before the age of 18. However, women whose age at first pregnancy was 19 or more were found to be as high as 72 per cent in rural areas and 61 per cent in urban slums. Thus, substantially higher proportion of urban slum girls are having pregnancy before the age 18 when they are not mature enough to bear the burden of pregnancy as compared to the girls in the rural areas.

Figure 1

Assistance During the Delivery in Urban Slums and Rural Areas of Gujarat, 2006

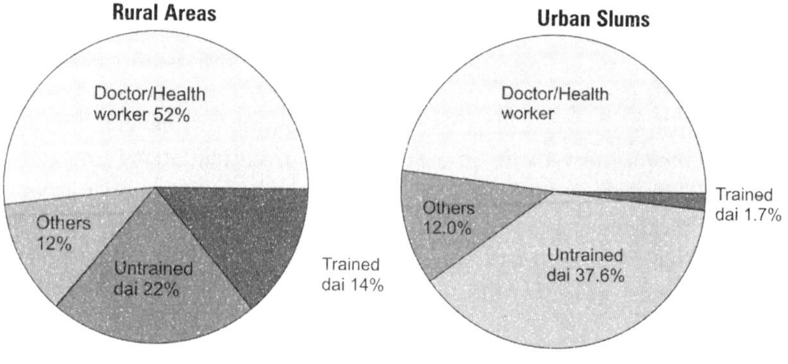

Table 8

Age at First Pregnancy in Urban Slums and Rural Areas of Gujarat, 1996

Age at first pregnancy in years	*Percentage*	
	Urban slums	*Rural*
<13	0.3	0.0
13–17	21.3	10.7
18	17.0	17.7
19–20	37.4	36.0
21+	24.0	35.6
Total number of women who had a live birth in last 12 months	300	300

Conclusion

The study clearly delineates that both in terms of child health as well as maternal health parameters urban slum population is far behind the rural population. Further, high risk pregnancies especially at the young age (lower than 18) are much more in the urban slum population as compared to the rural population. This calls for an urgent need to take necessary measures in improving the MCH situation in the urban slum population as compared to the rural population, if the overall infant and maternal mortality is to be curbed within a stipulated timeframe.

References

Bhat Mari, P.N., K. Navneetham and S. Irudya Rajan. 1992. *Maternal Mortality in India: Estimates from an Econometric Model Studies in Family Planning* 26, 4.

Bhatia, J.C. and J. Clealand. 1995. Determinants of Maternal Care in a Region of South India. *Health Transition Review* 5(2), 127–42.

International Institute for Population Sciences (IIPS). 1995. *National Family Health Survey (MCH and Family Planning), India, 1992–93*. IIPS, Bombay

—— and ORC Macro, 2000. *National Family Health Survey (NFHS-2), 1998–99*. India, IIPS, Mumbai.

Ministry of Health and Family Welfare (MOHFW) 1991. *Family Welfare Programme in India, Year Book 1989–90*. Department of Family Welfare, New Delhi, MOHFW.

UNFPA. 1995. *The State of World Population*. United Nations Population Fund, New York.

CHAPTER 14

Abortion in Nepal

Knowledge and Attitudes of Married and Unmarried Men

Sona Sethi, Anand Tamang and Dinesh Dhungel

Nepal made a historical achievement in reproductive health and rights of women in September 2002 when abortion was legalized in the country. The law grants women the right to control over, and decide on, their unintended pregnancies. It allows women to seek abortion during the first 12 weeks of pregnancy for any reason, up to 18 weeks of pregnancy in case of rape or incest, and up to any gestational period in case of fetal deformity or disability or risk to woman's life or health. Nepal began providing comprehensive abortion care (CAC) services from March 2004, seventeen months after abortion was legalized in the country.

Data for this paper was derived from a larger study conducted from August to October 2005 by the Centre for Research on Environment Health and Population Activities (CREHPA) in six out of sixteen programme districts, where four rights-based non-governmental organizations are implementing a three-year innovative programme "Network for Addressing Women's Reproductive Rights in Nepal" (NAWRN), supported by the Planned Parenthood Federation of America International. A total of 526 married men and 128 single men, also referred to in this paper as male youth (15–24 years of age), were interviewed using a multi-stage systematic random sampling technique.

Objective of the Study

To explore the extent to which Nepalese men especially those residing in rural areas are aware of women's right to abortion and analyse their attitudes.

Table 1

Percentage Distribution of Respondents According to Age

Age	*Married Men*	*Unmarried Men*
15–24	14.7	100.0
25–34	31.2	
35–44	26.8	
45+	27.3	
Total	100.0	100.0
N	526	128

Characteristics of the Study Population

Age Distribution

The respondents' age ranged from 15 to 45+ years for married and 15 to 24 years for unmarried. As evident from Table 1, one-third (31%) of the married respondents were 25–34 years old. The median age was 35 years for the married men and 18 years for the unmarried men.

Education Level

As shown in Table 2, one-fifth of the married (22%) and less than one-tenth (6%) of the unmarried men were illiterate. More than one quarter of the married (26%) and over one-third of the unmarried (32%) had some secondary education. Likewise, less than a fifth of the respondents had passed high school. About one-third of the married (10%) and less than one-fifth of the unmarried men (19%) had completed high school.

Table 2

Percentage Distribution of Respondents According to Highest Level of Education

Level of education	*Married men*	*Unmarried men*
Illiterate	21.9	5.5
Non-formal education	7.8	1.6
Primary (1–5) incomplete	18.6	16.4
Primary completed	8.0	7.8
Lower secondary (6–8) complete	12.7	21.9
Secondary (8–10) complete	13.7	18.0
High school	9.9	18.7
Intermediate and above	7.2	10.1
Madrasa (Muslim education)	0.2	—
Total	100	100
N	526	128

Caste/Ethnicity Composition

As shown in Table 3, the Brahmin/Chhetri caste was dominant; over one-third of the married (34%) and unmarried men (39%) belonged to this group. The proportion of hill-marginalized caste such as Kami/Damai/Sarki was more represented than the Terai marginalized caste among both married (10%) and unmarried (15%) groups.

Hill ethnic communities (Rai/Magar/Gurung/Tamang) and Terai ethnic communities (Muslim) and general caste were represented considerably in both married and unmarried men groups.

Table 3

Percentage Distribution of Respondents According to Caste/Ethnicity

Caste/ethnicity	*Married men*	*Unmarried men*
Hill ethnicity		
Brahmin/Chhetri	33.8	39.1
Newar	3.0	2.3
Rai/Magar/Gurung/Tamang	10.5	7.0
Gharti	1.5	1.6
KDS (Kami/Damai/ Sarki)	10.1	14.8
Terai ethnicity		
Terai Brahmin	0.4	—
Tharu	1.9	1.6
Yadav	11.8	10.1
Terai other general caste	12.0	5.5
Marginalized caste (Terai)	4.0	5.5
Muslim	11.0	12.5
Total	100	100
N	526	128

Main Occupation

As shown in Table 4, a large percentage of the married men (61%) mentioned 'agriculture' as their main occupation and majority (60%) of the unmarried men were students.

Table 4

Percentage Distribution of the Respondents According to Their Occupation

Main occupation	*Married men*	*Unmarried men*
Agriculture	58.3	15.6
Agriculture labour	2.3	—
Teacher	4.2	—
Government service holder	3.8	—
Business	9.9	4.7
Employed in Factory	2.1	0.8
Student	1.3	60.1
Unemployed	0.8	10.9
Skilled labourer	6.1	—
Unskilled labourer	6.8	6.3
Others	4.4	1.6
Total	100	100
N	526	128

Percentage total may exceed 100 due to multiple responses.

Knowledge About the Abortion Law

Knowledge on Legalization of Abortion

Abortion was legalized in Nepal to improve the health status and condition of women. Previous laws did not allow abortion under any circumstances and many women who had had an abortion were imprisoned. Despite this, abortion was rampant in the country, and women with unintended pregnancy were compelled to seek unsafe and clandestine abortions, often risking their lives and health. In order to assess knowledge on abortion law, the respondents were asked, "Is abortion legal in our country?" As evident from Figure 1, a large proportion of unmarried men (36%) tagged as 'Youth Male' were more knowledgeable about legalization of abortion than married male respondents of whom less than one-third (28%) were aware about it. Similarly, a quarter of married men (27%) had the mistaken notion that abortion was illegal in Nepal. In contrast, about a third of unmarried men (32%) mentioned that abortion is illegal. Almost half of the married men (45%) and a third (32%) of the unmarried men did not know whether abortion was legal or not in the country. This demonstrates that a significant number of Nepalese men are still unaware about the legalization of abortion in the country.

Both bi-variate (chi-square test) and multi-variate analysis (binary logistic regression) techniques were applied to identify the factors associated with the likelihood of being aware about the abortion law. As shown in Table 5, the variables caste/ethnicity, level of education, religion and occupation had statistically significant association with knowledge about the abortion law. Higher proportions of men from Brahmin/Chhetri caste (49%) were aware about the law compared with men from other castes. Similarly, more than two-fifths of the

Figure 1

Awareness about Legal Reform: Is Abortion Legal in Our Country?

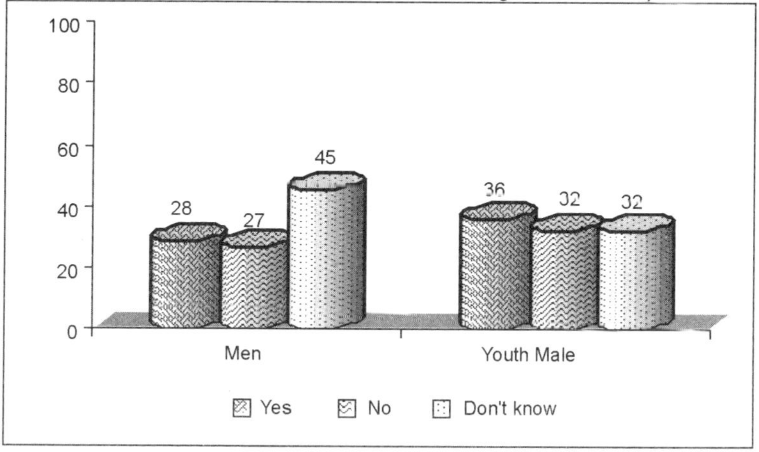

respondents who had some secondary level of education (44%) were aware about the legal situation while the proportion was very low (9%) among those who were illiterate. Likewise, respondents whose occupation was non-agriculture (34%) were more likely to be aware compared to those who relied on agriculture (26%). Likewise, one-third of the respondents who were Hindus (33%) compared to only one out of seven non-Hindus (15%) were aware about the abortion law.

Table 5

Percentage Distribution of Respondents by Selected Demographic and Socio-economic Characteristics

Demographic and socio-economic characteristics	*Is abortion legal in Nepal?*		*Chi-square*	*N*
	Yes	*No/DK*		
Age Group				
15–24 year	32.7	67.3	—	205
25–39 year	29.1	70.9	(1.3) ns	237
40 or above	27.8	72.2	—	212
Marital Status				
Unmarried	35.9	64.1	—	128
Married	28.3	71.7	(2.8) ns	526
Family Structure				
Nuclear	31.0	69.0	(0.4) ns	313
Joint/Extended	28.7	71.3	—	341
Caste/Ethnicity				
Brahmin/Chhetri	49.1	50.9	—	230
Marginalized caste	20.0	80.0	(63.3)***	100
Other	19.1	80.9	—	324
Level of Education				
Illiterate	9.0	91.0	—	122
Primary or below	20.5	79.5	(65.3)***	215
Some secondary	44.2	55.8	—	317
Religion				
Non-Hindu	15.0	85.0	(13.5)***	107
Hindu	32.7	67.3	—	547
Occupation				
Agriculture	25.7	74.3	(5.8)*	339
Non-agriculture	34.3	65.7	—	315
Total	29.8	70.2		654

Note: ***=p<.001, **=p<.01, *=p<.05, ns=not significant.

DK: Don't know

Logistic regression revealed that level of education and caste/ethnicity were significant predictors. Respondents from other castes in comparison to Brahmin/Chhetri were less likely to be aware about the law. A strong positive relation was observed between level of

Table 6

Odd Ratio (OR) and 95 per cent Confidence Interval for having Awareness about Legalization of Abortion Law among Men in Nepal

	OR	*95% CI*
Age Group		
15–24 year (Ref.)	1.0	—
25–39 year	1.24	0.65–2.33
40 or above	1.15	0.59–2.25
Marital Status		
Unmarried (Ref.)	1.0	—
Married	0.95	0.47–1.96
Caste/Ethnicity		
Brahmin/Chhetri (Ref.)	1.0	—
Marginalized caste	0.39**	0.21–0.69
Other	0.36***	0.23–0.55
Level of Education		
Illiterate (Ref.)	1.0	—
Primary or below	2.07*	1.01–4.26
Some secondary	5.27***	2.61–10.64
Religion		
Non-Hindu (Ref.)	1.0	—
Hindu	1.19	0.62–2.28
Family Structure		
Nuclear (Ref.)	1.0	—
Joint/Extended	0.86	0.59–1.27
Occupation		
Agriculture (Ref.)	1.0	—
Non-agriculture	1.24	0.83–1.86
–2 Log likelihood	692.5	
Cox & Snell R^2	0.148	

Note: *=p<.05, **=p<.01, ***=p<.001.

education and awareness about the abortion law; respondents who had primary or below and some secondary level of education were two times and five times more likely to be aware about the abortion law. No significant difference was found between the socio-demographic variables—age group, martial status, religion, family structure, occupation and awareness about legalization of the abortion law (Table 6).

Knowledge on the Conditions of the Abortion Law

Regarding the conditions permitted by the law, the unmarried male respondents were again more knowledgeable than their married counterparts. As shown in Figure 2, around 16 per cent of the unmarried men and only 10 per cent of the married men knew of at least one of the three conditions under which abortion is permitted by the law. Further, a negligible number of married male respondents could cite two or three legal conditions for abortion. The same is true for unmarried men. It was surprising to learn that a large majority of the married (90%) and unmarried men (84%) could not cite even one legal condition.

Figure 2

Extent of Knowledge about Legal Conditions

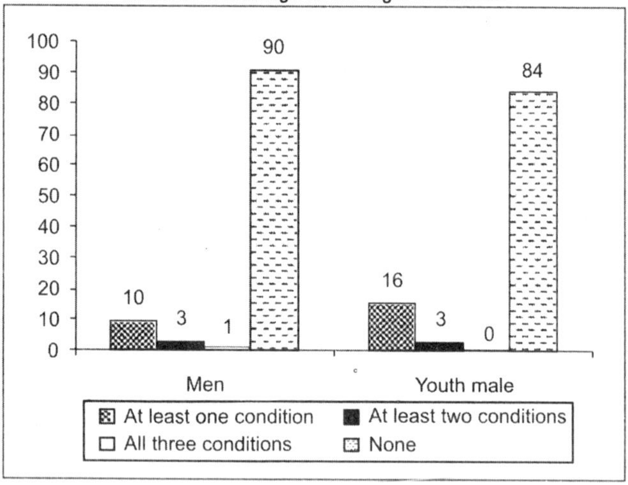

Perception on Women's Rights to Abortion

Although the law grants women absolute right to abortion, more than half (52%) of the married male respondents were against it. In contrast, the majority of unmarried men (58%) agreed with it and only a little over a third (37%) disagreed. Some of the respondents did not reveal their view on abortion right (Figure 3).

Figure 3

Do You think that a Woman should have the Right to Abortion?

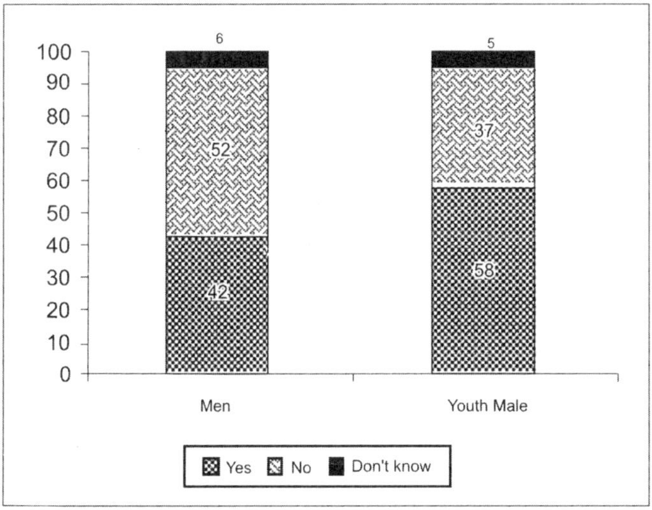

Perception on Abortion Rights for Unmarried Women

As shown in Table 7, on this issue, there was an apparent unanimity of belief for both the married and unmarried men. For every 10 men in both groups, there were 8.4 married and 7 unmarried men who were opposed to abortion rights for unmarried women. Only 14 per cent of the married and 25 per cent of the unmarried men supported an unmarried woman's right to abortion.

Both bi-variate (chi-square test) and multi-variate analysis (binary logistic regression) techniques were applied to identify the factors associated with positive attitudes on abortion rights for unmarried women. As shown in Table 8, the variables marital status,

Table 7

Percentage Distribution of the Respondents according to Perception on Abortion Rights for Unmarried Women

Perception on abortion rights for unmarried women	*Married men*	*Unmarried men*
Yes	14.1	25.8
No	84.4	71.1
Don't know	1.5	3.1
Total	100	100
N	526	128

caste/ethnicity, level of education had significant association with attitude towards abortion rights for unmarried women. Unmarried respondents had more positive attitudes towards this issue; more than a fourth unmarried respondent (26%) while only one out of seven married men (14%) agreed about abortion rights for unmarried women.

Table 8

Perception on Abortion Rights for Unmarried Women by Socio-economic and Demographic Characteristics

	Agree	*Disagree/DK*	*Chi-square*	*Total N*
Age Group				
15–24	21.0	79.0	—	205
25–39	13.9	86.1	(4.7) ns	237
40 or above	14.6	85.4	—	212
Marital Status				
Unmarried	25.8	74.2	—	128
Married	14.1	85.9	(10.3)**	526
Caste/Ethnicity				
Brahmin/Chhetri	23.0	77.0	—	230
Marginalized caste	12.0	88.0	—	100
Other	13.0	87.0	(11.6)***	324
Level of Education				
Illiterate	5.7	94.3	—	122
Primary and below	13.5	86.5	—	215
Some secondary	22.4	77.6	(19.8)***	317
Religion				
Non-Hindu	10.3	89.7	—	107
Hindu	17.6	82.4	(3.5) ns	547
Family Structure				
Nuclear	16.9	83.1	—	313
Joint/Extended	15.8	84.2	(0.1) ns	341
Occupation				
Agriculture	14.7	85.3	—	339
Non-agriculture	18.1	81.9	(1.3) ns	315
Total	16.4	83.6	—	654

Note: ***=p<.001, **=p<.01, *=p<.05, ns=not significant.

In regard to caste/ethnicity, male from Brahmin/Chhetri (23%) had more positive attitudes towards abortion rights than male from other castes (13%). The impact of education on perception regarding abortion rights was positive; more than a fifth of the male with some secondary level of education while only one out of twenty illiterate respondents had agreed about abortion rights for unmarried women.

Table 9

Odd Ratio and 95 per cent CI for having Positive Attitude Towards Abortion Rights for Unmarried Women

	OR	*95% CI*
Age Group		
15–24 year (Ref.)	1.0	—
25–39 year	1.17	0.53–2.57
40 or above	1.25	0.55–2.85
Marital Status		
Unmarried (Ref.)	1.0	—
Married	0.46	0.19–1.07
Caste/Ethnicity		
Brahmin/Chhetri (Ref.)	1.0	—
Marginalized caste	0.58	0.28–1.18
Other	0.71	0.43–1.19
Level of Education		
Illiterate (Ref.)	1.0	—
Primary or below	2.16	0.90–5.15
Some secondary	3.44**	1.46–8.10
Religion		
Non-Hindu (Ref.)	1.0	—
Hindu	1.28	0.60–2.73
Family Structure		
Nuclear (Ref.)	1.0	—
Joint/Extended	0.96	0.61–1.50
Occupation		
Agriculture (Ref.)	1.0	—
Non-agriculture	0.91	0.56–1.47
–2 Log likelihood	550.98	—
Cox & Snell R Square	0.048	—

Note: ***=p<.001, **=p<.01, *=p<.05.

Logistic regression model showed that only level of education was a strong predictor for having positive attitude towards abortion rights for unmarried women. As shown in Table 9, men who had some secondary level of education were 3.4 times more likely for having positive attitude towards abortion right for unmarried girls compared to illiterate men.

Although statistically not significant, married men were less likely for having positive attitude towards abortion rights for unmarried women.

CAC Facility

All the project districts have at least one government approved comprehensive abortion care (CAC) facility and some districts (Banke, Rupendehi and Kaski) have three (government and NGO). In the present study, the extent of awareness regarding the presence of government approved CAC facilities in the district was assessed. As shown in Figure 4, the awareness was almost equal among married (35%) and unmarried men (41%).

Figure 4

Knowledge about CAC

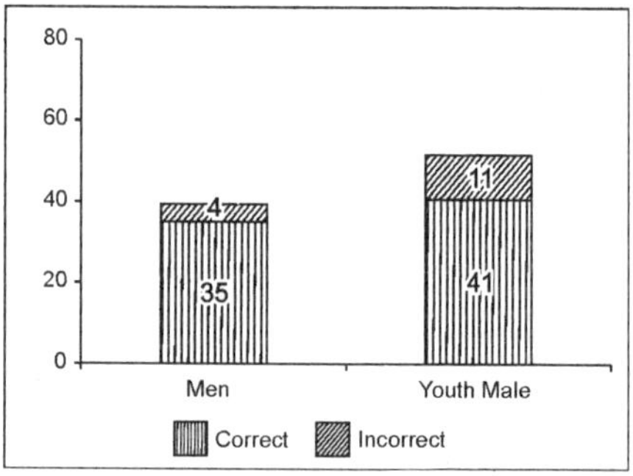

Places where Abortion was Obtained

About one-third married men (33%) revealed that they had visited India for obtaining an abortion for their spouse and the same proportion (33%) mentioned they had visited private clinic/nursing home. Only one-fourth of married men (25%) mentioned they had visited government hospital. Among the unmarried group, only one male mentioned that his spouse had obtained an abortion.

Table 10

Percentage Distribution of the Respondents According to the Places Visited for Terminating the Last Pregnancy

Places where pregnancy terminated	*Married men*	*Unmarried men*
Government hospital	25.0	100
Private clinic/Nursing home	33.3	—
Marie Stopes clinic	—	—
FPAN clinic	—	—
Visited India	33.3	—
Bought medicine from chemist	—	—
Health post	8.4	—
Medical college	—	—
Total	100	100
N	12	1

Conclusion

Knowledge about legalization of abortion, women's right to abortion and the presence of an approved comprehensive abortion care facility in the district was higher among unmarried than married men. Regarding the conditions in which abortion is permitted by law, knowledge was disappointingly low for both the groups. Only a few were aware of at least one of the three conditions for which law permits abortion.

Although the law grants women absolute right to abortion up to 12 weeks, majority of the married men and about two-fifths of the unmarried male youths were skeptical about women's absolute right to abortion. Most of the married and unmarried males also disagreed on the right of unmarried women to have an abortion.

Majority of the married men whose wives terminated an unintended pregnancy had visited India for the abortion service.

Recommendations

To expand women's access to safe abortion services, the study suggests that the programme should focus on creating positive attitudes among rural men toward women's abortion rights. Like in many cultures, men either facilitate or impede women's access to reproductive health information and services. It is therefore important to get the men's support on this issue.

Further, the study recommends the involvement of community-based health providers and volunteers to establish referral linkages between women and approved CAC service providers to expand women's access to safe abortion service. Women should be encouraged to seek safe abortion services from government-approved CAC service centres.

Acknowledgement

The authors gratefully acknowledge the assistance of CREHPA in administering the baseline survey which provided the springboard for this paper. The completion of the survey was made possible through the cooperation of PPFA International's three other partners in Nepal: The Family Planning Association of Nepal; Forum for Women, Law and Development and the Safe Motherhood Network Federation. Dr Seerat Nasir, former Programme Officer of PPFA International APRO helped put together the final baseline report.

Reference

Planned Parenthood Federation of America International, 2005. *Knowledge and Perspectives of Nepalese Married and Unmarried Men and Women on the Abortion Law and Safe Abortion Services Baseline Survey.* Asia Regional Office.

CHAPTER 15

Fertility Behaviour and Women's Reproductive Health and Reproductive Rights

Study of Ajmer

Laxmi Thakur

Fertility is the social character of human life and of human reproduction that differentiates human societies from those of animals. It is a very important demographic process, which is largely responsible for the replacement of population for the continuation of society. Fertility refers to biological procreation, i.e., the birth of a child as the result of a man impregnating a woman and the latter delivering an infant after the gestation period. Fertility behaviour refers to the processes of bearing and rearing children in the context of the household and the wider society. It covers the processes including institutional mechanism, leading directly or indirectly to childbirth and other demographic outcomes, like child survival and mortality.

As McKintosh (1981) states, "fertility behaviour refers not merely to the bearing of children but also to their care and socialization and the maintenance of adult individuals through their lives, processes which create individuals to fit more or less into social structure of society and so ensure the continuation of that society in the next generation". Besides childbearing, childcare and provision of domestic and other services to adults also constitute the entire complex of fertility behaviour.

Social practices are at the root of objective conditions and their perceptions. As Giddens (1984) states that the concept of structuration, seeks to relate the category of action and meaning to that of rules, resources and institutional framework. Fertility behaviour (FB) here is to be located neither in the experience of the individual actor nor in the existence of any form of societal totality, but in social practices occurring routinely. The various social practices associated with fertility are recursive-repetitive activities undertaken in a like manner day after day.

To see how fertility behaviour goes on recursively over time, the developmental process of the household is useful. Just as the household goes through a developmental process, the husband-wife couple also follow a socially expected and regulated 'fertility career'. Fertility behaviour is the process in which we observe the functions of various processes in the life of a couple which influence the developmental phases of their fertility career. Relevant to our understanding is the knowledge ability of couple, which is always present in recursive social practices associated with fertility behaviour. People are not ignorant of what they do and which behaviour is expected from them or which is not. Continuity of practices presumes reflectivity i.e., continuous monitoring of fertility behaviour which couples perform and expect others to perform. Whatever couples know about their fertility behaviour is not restricted to reasons and rationalizations in their verbal expression but is also embedded in mutual knowledge. This is traceable in people's behaviour carried on routinely in a taken-for-granted fashion. Thus, the emphasis here is on the analysis of fertility behaviour as grounded in the activities of couple which draw upon social structure.

Government programmes generally transgress the fact that reproduction takes places through sexual relations. To date, most reproductive health programmes including family planning programme target women and their fertility goals. Feudalistic structure of the society and the distorted traditions in delineating women's activities, which may be, in general, referred to as the PURDAH on women. The emphasis of a culture is a rationale for contraceptive behaviour operating at the family and interspousal level which has an immediate appeal but diverts attentions from the deep rooted social and economic inequalities at the family level as well as at the societal level. This may lead to gender differentials, so far as contraceptive behaviour is concerned within a household and society. Moreover, reproductive goals and contraceptive behaviour occur at individual level and hence consideration of its determinants also demands a micro-level perspective.

Reproductive health refers to a condition in which reproductive process is accomplished in a state of complete physical, mental and social well-being and is not merely the absence of any disease in the reproductive organs or in the reproductive system. The concept of women's reproductive health was developed by the World Health Organization, International Women's Health Movement Groups and International Family Planning Network in contrast to bio-medical approaches to women health.

World Health Organization's definition of reproductive health further enhanced at the International Conference on Population and Development (Cairo, 1994) makes explicit what reproductive health means, "Reproductive health is a state of complete physical, mental and social well-being and not merely the absence of disease or infirmity, in all matters relating to the reproductive system and its functions and processes. Reproductive health therefore, implies that people are able to have a satisfying and safe sex life and that they have the capacity to reproduce with the freedom to decide it, when and how often to do so". In other words, reproductive health implies that women can go safely through pregnancy and childbirth, that fertility regulation can be achieved without health hazards and that people are safe in having sex (Fathalla, 1992). On health seeking, the limited evidence available suggests that symptoms are often dismissed as being normal aspects of womanhood. Where symptoms are recognized, embarrassment and shame often constrain health seeking, and when care is sought, it often follows a sequence of options ranging from self-treatment using home remedies, to visiting traditional healers and allopathic providers. Whether or not a woman receives prompt treatment appears to be linked, moreover, to the involvement of her husband and the extent of inter-spousal communications.

Adolescent girls (15–19 years) and older women (35 years and above) are more likely to experience morbidity and mortality than women in the intervening ages. In our country early onset of marriage and childbearing is one of the main causes of deterioration in reproductive health of women. The median age at marriage is about 16 years, and cultural pressures make adolescent marriage synonymous with adolescent childbearing. Over one in six women in India aged 13–19 years had already commenced childbearing, often before full physical maturity is attained (IIPS, 1995). As a result there are multiple negative effects with major consequences are short average maternal height, competition for nutrients between the mother's growth needs and the growth needs of the foetus in the womb, and the poorer placental function of adolescent mothers. As Leslie (1991) has also emphasized that adolescent mothers are at high risk so far as their physical and reproductive health is concerned.

Addressing the world's most serious problem is dependent on behaviour change at every level at individuals families, communities organizations and at policy making bodies. Fertility behaviour is very effective aspects which directly influence the reproductive health of the person. Reproductive illness is not only due to unhealthy or unhygienic behaviour of women only, but it is also because of unhealthy behaviour of their sexual partners.

In India, vast majority of research studies on women's reproductive health are based on hospital facilities, health facilities and community-based studies. A fair proportion of these researches cover issues of maternity mortality risks, their causes and trends. Some of the sections deal with morbidity related to pregnancies, gynecological morbidity, sexually transmitted infections, abnormal menstrual bleeding, infertility and causes of the reproductive tract. But the reasons and causes of all the above diseases are lying somewhere in behaviour of woman and attitude and behaviour of their sexual partners, who are also associated with the fertility processes and reproductive health of the women.

The purpose of this study is to assess women's reproductive health and rights in the present era when sex selective abortions are also taking place in the society. The data for the study are collected using a well-structured schedule through personal interview of women covering all aspects of reproductive health and their fertility behaviour. To obtain general information and to know respondent's socio-economic conditions, a small questionnaire was prepared. This questionnaire first begins with the preliminary information about respondents, then the general information such as caste, religion, age, family type, occupation of husband and available health services in the area.

For the present study, 500 respondents were chosen from the rural areas of Ajmer district. Ajmer has eight Panchayat Samities comprising of 1,061 villages, out of which 1,044 villages are inhabited with a population of 10 lakh in 1991 and 13 lakh in 2001. Two villages named Ghooghra and Kayad nearby to M.D.S. University, Ajmer have been selected for the present study. Approximately, 3,000 people live in Ghooghra village and 4,000 people live in Kayad village. Total 500 women aged 15–49 have been selected randomly, 50 per cent each from both the villages. The life of rural people is governed by their socio-cultural systems. Their social customs and beliefs influence their social institutions. The norms about fertility in rural societies are different from the urban population. Their social and cultural norms regarding the marriage pattern, age at marriage, ideal number of children, value of children and specially the status of women are very rigid and fixed. The household structure is of joint family type where three generations live together.

Main Objective of the Study

The study is a micro-level investigation dealing with family's size, fertility behaviours and women's reproductive health. The main objective of the study is to find out different aspects and variables of reproduction with women's health which consists of women's physical as well as psychological health and their quality of life. Some more relevant objectives of the study are:

- To find out the various socio-cultural factors related to fertility behaviour and reproductive health of the respondents of Ghooghra and Kayad villages.
- To explore the structure of cultural practices and belief system of the people in relation to fertility behaviour.
- To study the fertility behaviour of two villages of Ajmer district and accessibility of health and family welfare services/programmes.
- To study the trends of maternal mortality and social determinants affecting fertility behaviour of the women of Ghooghra and Kayad villages.
- To seek out the level of awareness regarding health aspects of reproduction, sexually transmitted diseases and AIDS.

Findings of the study are revealing that generally, after marriage every woman wants children, but it is not a planned procedure; most of the respondents were not aware regarding their reproductive health and their planning for the family size.

It is revealed from the Table 1 that approximately half of the respondents (47%) do not have much interaction regarding family welfare aspects. Only 4.2 per cent of the respondents discuss all the matters with their husbands so far as health and family welfare matters are concerned. It is also observed that one-fifth of the respondents had never discussed family planning matters with each other.

It is also found from the results that the respondents who had a continuous interaction with spouse about the number of children, they have planned their life better as compared to those who did not. In order to assess the level of communication between the respondents and their husbands they were asked whether they have ever discussed family welfare aspects with their husband. These findings are in the support of the study by Bhatia and Newman (1980), which concludes that inter-spousal communication is a very strong variable in influencing the decision to accept family planning. It is also believed that a traditional joint family stands in the way of effective inter-spousal communication, which in turn has a barrier in the acceptance of contraception and hence on fertility career.

Table 1

Interaction among Spouses Regarding Family Welfare Aspects

Level of inter-spousal interaction	*Respondents of Ghooghra village*		*Respondents of Kayad village*		*Total respondents*	
	Freq.	*%*	*Freq.*	*%*	*Freq.*	*%*
90–100%	13	5.2	08	3.2	21	4.2
50–60%	76	30.4	66	26.4	142	28.4
20–30%	98	39.2	137	54.8	235	47.0
Nil	63	25.2	39	15.6	102	20.4
Total	250	100.0	250	100.0	500	100.0

Management of Birth Interval

A new couple follows social norms regarding the onset of fertility. A socially prescribed fertility career also prevails which regulates the couple's initiation into the reproductive career, the long drawn process of bearing the socially optimum number of children and putting an end to procreation. An important mode of indigenous fertility regulation is the prevalence of social practices that favour a certain interval between births. An attempt is made to study the desirable spacing between children. The respondents are asked what should be the gap between two children?

Table 2 reveals that 131 of the total respondents do not have any desire about the spacing between two children. A lion's share of the respondents (more than 60%),are of the opinion that there should be 2–3 years gap between two children. Only 12.4 per cent women said that there should be more than 3 years gap to maintain the health of child and mother. It can be observed the difference in the opinion of the respondents of both the villages, but there is not any remarkable difference of opinions.

Table 2

Desirable Space among Children

Desirable space (in years)	Respondents of Ghooghra village		Respondents of Kayad village		Total respondents	
	Freq.	%	Freq.	%	Freq.	%
1	Nil	—	Nil	—	Nil	—
2	89	35.6	96	38.4	185	37.0
3	68	27.2	54	21.6	122	24.4
3+	21	08.4	41	16.4	62	12.4
Uncertain	72	28.8	59	23.6	131	26.2
Total	250	100	250	100	500	100

Table 3

Preference to Family Planning Method

S. No.	Family planning methods	Respondents of Ghooghra village		Respondents of Kayad village		Total respondents	
		Freq.	%	Freq.	%	Freq.	%
1.	Female sterilization	110	44.0	140	56.0	250	50
2.	Male sterilization	20	08.0	35	14.0	55	11
3.	Copper-T	35	14.0	22	8.8	57	11.4
4.	Oral pills	18	7.2	05	2.0	23	04.6
5.	Condom/Nirodh	52	20.8	46	18.4	98	19.6
6.	Others	15	6.0	02	0.8	17	3.4
	Total	250	100	250	100	500	100

The use of contraceptives reduces the fertility and can keep desirable gap in between two pregnancies. The use of them is very well known, when the respondents are asked about the best method of family planning they have adopted. The above table reveals that half of the respondents are in favour of female sterilization. Whereas, only 11 per cent of the women told that their husbands are interested to go for the vasectomy. In this context, when enquired most of them replied that husband does not want to go for it, because if something happen to the wife or if she dies than how he will reproduce children from the second wife. Other than sterilization the second preference is given to condom. People can get it easily from any family planning centre or any shop. Sterilization is the first preference to control the fertility.

In people's experience contraceptives threaten whatever little privacy they have. To handle and to keep it safe for the nights is very difficult because most of the respondents do not have sufficient personal space. In case of pills it is extremely difficult for a woman to maintain a specific time schedule. Condoms are a perpetual source of embarrassment for both husband and wife. They restrict freedom of sex outside the house in the fields or any other hideout. Disposing them of is also not an easy task. They are not easily perishable and consequently they are to be buried carefully to avoid children playing with them.

In the words of some of the respondents in rural areas, all household members have an almost equal claim and access to rooms in the house. It is not easy to escape children's vigil and take the contraceptives away. The sense of individual privacy is discouraged. It is rare for a person to have a room exclusively to oneself. The newly married couples have a separate room exclusively to themselves only at night. During that period generally people do not use contraceptives as they are not afraid of conceiving and most of them are unaware about the consequences of adolescent pregnancy. After some time of marriage, the couple begins to use a shed or such other site away from the courtyard where most of the household members sleep at night.

It may be concluded from the above table that generally couples try contraception with a desire to stop fertility, their regular use confronts them with a series of pain and discomfort, which in turn, results in discarding the use of modern contraceptives and preference to go for sterilization. But they go for it after completion of their desirable size of family.

Table 4

Relationship between Behaviour of Pregnant Women and Gender of her Child

Village	*Opinion of the respondents*				
	Yes	*%*	*No*	*%*	*Total*
Ghooghra	239	95.6	11	10.8	250
Kayad	207	82.8	43	17.2	250
Total	446	89.2	54	10.8	500

There are many beliefs related to behaviour and appearance of the pregnant woman suggesting the gender of the wombed child. An access to this belief is made by asking the respondents that does the behaviour and physical appearance of the pregnant woman reveal the sex of the child. The analysis of Table 4 reveals that in both the village people think that behaviour and physical appearance of the pregnant women denotes the sex of the child.

Child Delivery Practices: Child delivery is exclusively a women's affair, so every care is taken to see that men should not participate either by knowing or by being present near the woman who is in the labour pain. Child delivery is usually conducted by some elderly women, relatives or neighbours who are considered as the experienced women so far as deliveries are concerned. Sometimes a Dai may also be called in difficult cases; when the mother's life is in danger, a professionally trained nurse is summoned. Rural people's attitudes are 'wait and watch' and go to hospitals in rare cases when they think that now there is risk on the lives of child and mother. Some of the cases are very difficult and complicated when the rural people reach to the hospital for the delivery.

A Dai is preferred in comparison to a trained nurse or a doctor because she is available nearby the residence and one can call her, even at odd hours. Her services and medicines are less expensive than the nurse. A Dai offers several additional services such as cleaning the effluvia and placenta, burying the placenta, cleaning the place and purifying it with dung paste, bathing the baby, sponging the mother, making her bed, washing her clothes, giving post-natal massage etc., whereas, a nurse does the main work of delivery only. A Dai accepts payment in cash and kind. She is given meals, food grains, old garments, a piece of new cloth, balls of herbal sweets prepared for the parturient mother. A Dai accepts payment in instalments which a nurse does not.

Table 5

Place of First Delivery

Place of first delivery	*Respondents of Ghooghra village*		*Respondents of Kayad village*		*Total respondents*	
	Frequency	*%*	*Frequency*	*%*	*Frequency*	*%*
House	230	92.0	222	88.8	455	90.4
Hospital	17	6.8	23	9.2	40	8.0
Other places	3	1.2	5	2.0	8	1.6
Total	250	100	250	100	500	100

In the urban areas, a small cut or bruise might be considered a serious matter, with an associated fear of tetanus needing quick medical attention such as a bandage, ointment or an injection. In contrast, such cuts and bruises are overlooked in the rural areas. A little sand on a cut is all that the remedy consists of. The attitude towards pregnancy and child delivery in the rural areas should not mean that there is no fear of maternal mortality.

Table 6

Distribution of Maternal Mortality in the Household

Maternal mortality	*Respondents of Ghooghra village*		*Respondents of Kayad village*		*Total respondents*	
	Frequency	*%*	*Frequency*	*%*	*Frequency*	*%*
Yes	16	6.4	23	9.2	39	7.8
No	234	93.6	227	90.8	461	92.2
Total	250	100	250	100	500	100

The analysis of data reveals that in the Ghooghra village, women died during delivery are 6.4 per cent while in the Kayad village it is 9.2 per cent. Out of total 500 respondents the combined percentage of maternal mortality is 7.8 per cent. In this matter, respondents told that when they take pregnant women to the hospitals she generally dies. But the reason of maternal mortality is perhaps because they take the patient to the hospitals when she is in a critical conditions.

Table 7

Respondent's Awareness Regarding AIDS and Diseases in Reproductive Organs

Awareness regarding	*Respondents of Ghooghra village*		*Respondents of Kayad village*		*Total respondents*	
	Frequency	*%*	*Frequency*	*%*	*Frequency*	*%*
AIDS/HIV	12	4.8	17	6.8	29	5.8
STD	39	15.6	47	18.8	86	17.2
Infections in reproductive organs	168	67.2	153	61.2	321	64.2
All diseases	3	1.2	5	2.0	8	1.6

It is very strange to see the awareness of rural people regarding sexually transmitted diseases and AIDS is very low. Only 1.6 per cent of the total respondents know about infections in reproductive organs or

STDs or about AIDS. There were very few people who have sufficient knowledge of reproductive diseases; most of them are social workers or key persons of the area. But here one thing is clear, not a single respondent out of 500 was able to make out the difference between HIV positive and AIDS.

Table 8

Visit to Doctors During Illness

Visit to doctor	Respondents of Ghooghra village		Respondents of Kayad village		Total respondents	
	Frequency	%	Frequency	%	Frequency	%
Always	Nil	00	Nil	00	Nil	00
75%	29	11.6	20	8.0	55	11.0
50%	54	21.6	44	17.6	98	19.6
25%	165	66.0	181	72.4	346	69.2
Never	02	40.8	05	2.0	07	1.4
Total	250	100	250	100	500	100

When enquired about the health seeking behaviour in the context of physical as well as reproductive health of the respondents, they do not go to the doctor always when they are ill. A general statement of the respondents was that they go to the doctors only, when there is serious illness or high fever which cannot be controlled through domestic medicines. Maximum number of rural people avoid going to the doctor when they have the symptoms of disease. It was explained that they can-not afford the doctor frequently.

Table 9

Illness in Reproductive System or Organ

Illness in reproductive system/organ	Respondents of Ghooghra village		Respondents of Kayad village		Total respondents	
	Frequency	%	Frequency	%	Frequency	%
Yes	123	49.2	147	58.8	270	54
No	127	50.8	103	41.2	230	46

So far as reproductive health is concerned 54 per cent women are victims of sexually transmitted diseases and other infections. After getting symptoms they had consulted the physicians. In the beginning of the symptoms, because of shyness and social stigma they did not go to

It is also revealed that 39 per cent of the respondents are being forced for having sex with their partners; 90 per cent of them told that if they say no, husband beats them, and sometimes some of the pregnant women got aborted because of forced sex with some of the respondents are having pain and ruptures also. On the other side it is also revealed that during the ill-health or after the beating and giving injuries by the husband, not a single member of the family pays proper attention or supports for medical care.

Summary and Discussion

Constantly subjected to physical abuse, women lose their sense of dignity in the face of violence, shame and humiliation with their identities having been completely submerged. The value attached to the family system, supports and justifies domestic violence and such victims would be further condemned, if they dared to oppose this violence. Unable to bear this hardship some of these respondents have psychological problems which in turn give physical symptoms especially in the reproductive system when they do not want to maintain a sexual life with their partners.

Psychological pain followed by sexual violence is the next hardship women face in the marital relationship. Respondents of this study were reluctant to address the issue of sexual violence in the behaviour of their partner, which is responsible for injuries and pains in the reproductive organs. Some of the respondents pointed out that they do not have the right to ask regarding extramarital relationship of their husbands. So far as condom is concerned, spouse does not want to use it even when they have extramarital relation sometime with sexual workers.

Human behaviour plays a key role in the leading causes of death and disability with their prevention or mitigation. The leading preventable causes of death and disease include behaviour such as unhealthy or inadequate diets, smoking, drinking, and drug use, sedentary lifestyles, and unsafe sexual practices. Health experts estimate that life expectancy could be increased measurably if health promoting decisions have been taken by individuals, communities, health systems, and governments. Normal and proper fertility behaviour reduces risks in reproductive system and maintains the reproductive health, but this risk reduction will require that public health and other professionals better integrate behaviour-change strategies into their programmes and policies at every level. Improving health will depend on changing the behaviour not only of individuals but also of community leaders, health system officials, and policy makers.

Recommendations

- To improve the reproductive health some new approaches should be adopted by using effective tools which are bolstered by political and religious will.
- Social workers and NGOs should recognize reciprocal consultation between individuals and their environment because, fertility behaviour influences and is influenced by the social environment in which we live.
- NGOs and activists should use identified communication channel to reach key audience with coordinated, mutually reinforcing message and opportunities for community discussions.
- All forms of discrimination against the girl child and violation of her rights shall be eliminated by undertaking strong measures within and outside the family. These measures should relate specifically to strict enforcement of laws against prenatal sex selection and the practice of female foeticide, female infanticide, child marriage, child abuse and child prostitution, etc.
- There will be special emphasis on the basic needs of women and earmarking of substantial investments in the areas relating to food and nutrition, health and education, etc.
- Personal space for day-to-day needs and toilet facilities should be made available to women for improving the quality of their reproductive health.
- Media will be used to portray images consistent with human dignity of women. The policy will specially strive to remove demanding, degrading conventional, stereotypical images of women and violence against women.

References

Arora, C. 1983. Socio-economic Determinants of Fertility. *The Journal of Family Welfare*. Vol. XXIX, No. 3, 39–52.

——. 1985. Caste, Socio-economic Status and Fertility: A Study of Proximate Determinants of Fertility in Village Ruvasa. *Guru Nanak Journal of Sociology*. Vol. 6, No. 2, 81–6.

——. 1990. *Social Structure and Fertility.* National Book Organisation, New Delhi.

Bhatia, J.C. and A.K. Newman. 1980. Inter-Spousal Communication and Practice of Contraception in India. *The Journal of Family Welfare*. Vol. XXVI, No. 4, 18–30.

Fathalla, M. 1992. Reproductive Health: A Global Overview. *Early Human Development* 29. 3542.

Giddens, A. 1984. *The Constitution of Society*. Polity Press, Cambridge.

International Institute of Population Sciences (IIPS). 1995. *National Family Health Survey (MCH and Family Planning), India 1992–93*. IIPS, Mumbai.

Leslie, J. 1991. Women's Nutrition: The Key to Improving Health in Developing Countries. *Health Policy and Planning* 6, 1, 1–19.

McKintosh, M. 1981. "The Sexual Division of Labour and the Subordination of Women" in K. Yong, C. Wolkowitz and R. McCullagh (eds.), *Of Marriage and the Market*. CSE Books Publication, London.

Patel, T. 1994. *Fertility Behaviour: Population and Society in a Rajasthan Village.* Oxford University Press, New Delhi.

Singh, K.P. 1986. *Correlates of Fertility Behaviour: A Study of Rural Communities in Punjab and Haryana*. Concept Publishing Co., New Delhi.

Section IV

Adolescent Health

CHAPTER 16

Determinants of Risky Behaviour Among Young Men Hosiery Workers in an Urban Setting of South India

Narayanaswamy Audinarayana

In the recent past, engaging one in risk-taking behaviour (in the present context used as risky behaviour) has become a common phenomenon among young generation and such tendency appears to be high especially among the industrial workers. Risk may be defined as an action that jeopardizes something of value. The object that is threatened may be a physical object, or a socially or culturally valued psychological entity. In the present context, the risks are those lifestyles, viz., playing cards for gambling, chewing tobacco/panparag and smoking beedies/cigarettes, drinking alcohol, reading pornographic literature, watching blue films and browsing pornographic sites and taking drugs, which physically, socially and psychologically affect the person concerned.

The recent writings in newspapers, magazines, and other media clearly establish that a lot of changes are taking place in Indian cultural values, reflecting the ever increasing impact of the opening up of Indian markets, continued onslaughts of foreign movies and television, the strong influence of tourism as well as the increased number of Indian nationals living abroad. Such changes, though taken place initially in urban areas, very recently, with the outreach of media influences (TV, movies, etc.) and other agents, have spread to rural hinterlands. In fact, cable television is now ubiquitous in urban places and is reportedly reaching the distant rural areas; so also is the case with the Internet connections. These changes have been made possible with the dynamics of open economy and globalization and in turn tremendous increase in transportation and communication. In these processes, youth, especially adolescent and young working in industrial establishments, are more attracted for such ultra-modern lifestyles, mostly western in nature. With this backdrop, in this paper, an attempt is made to understand the magnitude of risky behaviour (lifestyles) and the major determinants of engaging themselves in such lifestyles among young men hosiery workers in an urban setting of Tamil Nadu, India.

Influences on Taking up of Risky Lifestyles

Taking up risky lifestyles, first of all, would be influenced by their background characteristics. Among these, age, as a biological variable, would play a positive role in embracing risky lifestyles because of the transition from childhood to adulthood, exhibiting their masculinity, physical maturity and psychological factors associated with age. Education of young men, on the one side, increases the curiosity to participate in risky lifestyles so as to experience their taste; on the other hand, higher education may discourage the young boys from such behaviour since they would become knowledgeable about the disadvantages of such lifestyles and engaging themselves in a productive manner. Type of work/occupation also plays an important role in influencing the tendency of taking up risky lifestyles. In a setting like hosiery establishment, supervisors and other white collar workers who have greater opportunities to take up risky behaviour since they are earning higher incomes, believe that such behaviour would reduce fatigue, mental tension and in addition to larger social interaction with friends and peers of whom many may have already engaged in such risky behaviour for relaxation. Moreover, earning higher income influences the young boys to embrace risky lifestyles due to multiple reasons, viz., (i) availability of money and thereby, they are capable of spending on various items for different lifestyles, (ii) trying to be more social or to have fun, and (iii) inculcating the tendency of having more peers who in turn motivate them to indulge in such risky behaviour.

Within India, people from Tamil Nadu are most religious and God fearing, and thereby, young ones believe that embracing risky lifestyles would be a considered as stigmatized one in anybody's life. Moreover, through socialization process such contention is transmitted to younger ones through parents, who are, by and large, more religious, from childhood. Interestingly, youth who wants to come up in life by setting up a goal and career option would try to be away from these risky lifestyles, since they would spend most of their leisure time in a fruitful manner to achieve their goal. Besides all these, in Indian context, the influence of peer groups is particularly strong upon the young workers to embrace risky lifestyles as well as pre marital sex. For instance, first of all, those workers who have large number of colleagues and friends of same age who are experienced in risk-taking behaviour would naturally persuade/lure them to take up such lifestyles with a curiosity to learn and experience. Secondly, hosiery workers would be greatly influenced by peers during their social interaction while staying in the same room (and also in the work place) as well as during leisure time activities (viewing Television/movies and playing cards). Finally, younger boys who have migrated to the city for work may try to engage themselves more in risky lifestyles than non-migrants. This is mainly because of the lack of parents' control or supervision. In addition to this, conducive environment like staying in rooms, having more peers' interaction by spending a lot of leisure time with them and/or earning more money by working in double shifts or over time are also reasons for these sorry state of affairs. Empirically, very few studies have examined these propositions, that too, mostly in relation to smoking, tobacco/substance use and alcohol use, but customarily with cross-tabular analysis (Kadri et al., 2003; Sinha et al., 2003; Naskar et al., 2004; Kumar, 2004; Mukherjee and Hadaye, 2006; Bala et al., 2006; Priyanka, 2006). On the other hand, several studies have examined the role of engaging in these risky lifestyles on risky sexual behaviour (for details see Audinarayana, 2005).

Methods and Materials

The Setting

Tirupur, one of the fastest growing cities in Coimbatore district, Tamil Nadu state, India, is the study area for this research. According to 2001 census, the population of Tirupur municipal area (core urban) was 3,44,543, with a sex ratio of 915 females per 1,000 males. The surrounding urban areas have a population of 1,96,202 (Directorate of Census Operations, Chennai, 2004). The city is well known for hosiery industry and manufacturing of hosiery goods, and thereby, as a centre for export of hosiery products. It houses more than 5,000 hosiery units and about 85 per cent of its products are sold in other states of India and in other countries. The city's changing status as an export oriented power loom centre is going to overtake shortly its cotton hosiery industry.

In most of the industrial establishments of this city, children and youth, both boys and girls, are in great demand as workers. To meet the demand for labour, young people, especially boys and even at times girls, migrate in considerable numbers from other districts of Tamil Nadu and also from other states of India. Daily commuters from nearby villages and natives of the city also work in the local industries. Most of the workers are temporarily out of schools and/or dropouts. Some have studied till higher/higher secondary school and a few have completed undergraduate or postgraduate courses. The migrant workers usually leave behind their family in the villages/towns and live in small rented rooms, mostly with peers. Initially, they work for daily wages, at times in two shifts, and earn reasonably well. As most of the workers in Tirupur city earn comparatively high income at young age, naturally they are more susceptible to risky behaviour including risky sexual behaviour.

Sample and Data

Data for the present study were collected from 995 never-married young male workers of Tirupur city, Tamil Nadu during 2003–04 as part of a research project entitled "Youth Sexuality Project". The sample young men were in the age group of 15–24 years, working in hosiery establishments and had working experience of at least one year (or more). They were selected (on census basis) from 5 clusters (streets or part of streets) of 52 wards (smaller administrative units in the city), which were selected on the basis of simple random sampling technique (Audinarayana, 2005).

Data Analysis

The results section presents three types of analyses. In the first sub-section, some descriptive statistics about the sample workers, the patterns of participation in risky behaviour and the level of participation in risky behaviour (summary measure constructed based on the involvement of workers in individual risky lifestyles) are provided with the help of uni-variate analysis. The second sub-section examines the bi-variate relationships between the background variables and the level of participation in risky behaviour based on cross-tabular analysis and chi-square test of significance. Finally, in the third sub-section, the results of the multinomial logistic regression models examining the influence of background characteristics of the workers on the level of participation in risky behaviour are presented. The variables used in the present paper are mostly self-explanatory, which have been provided in Table 1 and in the sections concerned. However, for those variables computed as indexes the description is provided in Appendix.

Results

Background Characteristics of the Sample

Among the sample young hosiery workers (Table 1), a large percentage belongs to 20–24 years, completed middle school and high school education and above, working as supervisors and other white collar workers and thereby, earning reasonably high income (Rs 2,000 and above per month). Majority of them and their parents can said to be as more religious, whereas some of them only have a better career (other than the present one) option in the near future. A substantial per cent of the workers have five or more peers (close friends/room-mates/ colleagues) who are engaged in one or the other high risky lifestyles and even have the habit of more frequently viewing TV/movies and playing cards during leisure time. Though the percentage of workers who came as migrants to the city for work is little higher, a large majority are living in family environment rather than with peers in rooms.

Patterns of Risk-Behaviour and Level of Risky Behaviour

Among the sample young hosiery workers, about 38 per cent are reported to have the habit of smoking beedis/cigarettes during the last one year, whereas 17 per cent and 12 per cent, respectively used to participate in risky activities like playing cards for gambling and chewing tobacco/*gutaka* (Table 2). On the other hand, it is remarkable to note that a large per cent of the young workers participate in risky lifestyles such as browsing pornographic sites and watching blue films closely followed by reading pornographic literature and drinking alcohol, however, the use of drugs among them is very minimal. When enquired about the age at which they started to involve themselves in the risky lifestyles (Table 2), participation in activities like smoking closely followed by playing cards and reading pornographic literature appears to be somewhat ahead (about 17 years) than those taking part of other lifestyles (18 years).

In the present context, taking part in the former three activities, by and large, can be said as less risky for one's own health, but may stimulate the young boys to try/go for the latter five risky life styles. Moreover, there is ample evidence that participating in the latter lifestyles would trigger off the young boys to premarital sexual activities, mostly without condom, which in turn result in contracting of RTIs/STDs as well as HIV/AIDS. Keeping this in mind, in the present paper an attempt has been made to construct a single variable of level of

Table 1

Background Characteristics of the Respondents

Variables used in the study	*Percentage*	*Frequency*
Age of the Respondent (in Years)		
15–19	39.0	388
20–24	61.0	607
Education of the Respondent		
Up to Primary School	22.5	224
Middle School	43.6	434
High School and above	33.9	337
Type of Work of the Respondent		
Tailoring and related works	25.1	250
Supervisory and White Collar Works	74.9	745
Respondent's Monthly Income (in Rs)		
< 2000	24.3	242
2000–2999	46.9	467
3000 +	28.7	286
Respondent's Religiosity		
Less Religious	26.6	265
Moderate Religious	53.7	534
Highly Religious	19.7	196
Parents' Religiosity		
Less Religious	42.5	423
More Religious	57.5	572
Career Option in Near Future		
No Specific Career Option	80.9	805
Have Some Specific Career Option	19.1	190
No. of Peers Participating in Higher Risky Life Styles		
2	39.4	392
3–5	35.6	354
6 +	25.0	249
Frequency of Viewing TV/Movie/Playing Cards during Leisure Time (Index)		
Lesser extent	38.2	380
Higher extent	61.8	615
Migration Status		
Non-migrants	45.2	452
Migrants	54.6	543
Place of Stay		
With family in a home	69.2	689
With peer in a room	30.8	306
Total	100.0	995

risky behaviour so as to examine its principle determinants. In the present context, all those who are taking part in any of the lifestyles such as playing cards for gambling, chewing tobacco/*gutaka* and smoking beedies/cigarettes have been categorized as 'participating in lesser risky lifestyles' and all those who used to engage themselves in any of the five latter activities have been designated as 'participating in higher risky lifestyles'; and the remaining as 'not participating at any risky activity'. As is evident from the last panel of Table 1, about 48 per cent of the young hosiery workers are at risky behaviour to a lesser extent and about one-third are participating in risky lifestyles at a higher extent.

Table 2

Percentage Distribution of the Respondents by their Participation in Risky Lifestyles (N = 995)

Risky Lifestyles	*%*	*Mean age of starting*	*N*
Playing Cards for Gambling	16.6	17.58	165
Chewing Tobacco/*gutaka*	11.6	18.15	115
Smoking Beedies/Cigarettes	38.1	17.37	379
Drinking Alcohol/Liquors	52.0	18.49	517
Use the Drugs	2.3	18.78	23
Watching Blue Films	63.0	18.00	627
Reading Pornographic Literature	55.3	17.66	550
Browsing Pornographic Sites	64.3	18.00	640
Level of Participation in Risky Lifestyles (Index)			
Not Participating in any Risky Lifestyle	18.9		188
Participating in any Lifestyles that are Less Risky	47.7		475
Participating in any Lifestyles that are Highly Risky	33.4		332

Bi-variate Analysis Results on the Level of Risky Behaviour

Table 3 shows the percentage of young hosiery workers' level of risky-behaviour across their background characteristics. On the whole, the percentage of workers reported to be participating in risky lifestyles at a lower extent appears to be higher among those aged 20–24 years, who are engaged in supervisory and other white collar works, viewing TV/movie and playing cards during leisure time, migrant workers and living with peer in a room than their counterparts. Likewise, such proportion appears to be increasing with an increase in their educational status, monthly income, and number of peers participating in higher risky lifestyles. On the other hand, such proportion is noted to be lower and/or decreasing with young workers' religiosity, whose parents are more religious.

Table 3

Per cent Distribution of the Respondents by their Level of Risky Behaviour across their Background Characteristics

Background characteristics of the respondents	Level of risky behaviour			
	Not risky	Less risky	Highly risky	Total
Age of the Respondent (in Years)				
15–19	34.5	33.2	32.2	388
20–24	8.9	57.0	34.1	607
	χ^2=110.586; p<0.000			
Education of the Respondent				
Up to Primary School	23.2	45.5	31.3	224
Middle School	20.5	47.5	32.0	434
High School and above	13.9	49.6	36.5	337
	χ^2=9.168; p<0.05			
Type of Work of the Respondent				
Tailoring and Related Works	21.9	44.6	33.6	250
Supervisory and White Collar Works	10.0	57.2	32.8	745
	χ^2=20.273; p<000			
Respondent's Monthly Income (in Rs)				
< 2000	38.4	37.2	24.4	242
2000–2999	16.5	45.8	37.7	467
3000 +	6.3	59.8	33.9	286
	χ^2=97.540; p<0.000			
Respondent's Degree of Religiosity				
Less Religious	12.1	53.6	34.3	265
Moderate Religious	21.0	45.9	33.1	534
Highly Religious	22.4	44.9	32.7	196
	χ^2=11.872; p<0.01			
Career Option in Near Future				
No Specific Career Option	20.2	46.3	33.4	805
Have Some Specific Career Option	13.2	53.7	33.2	190
	χ^2=5.832; p<0.05			

Cont'd...

Table 4

Multinomial Logistic Regression Results on Respondents' Level of Risky Behaviour

Background characteristics of the respondents	*Any less risky vs not risky*		*Any high risky vs not risky*	
Current Age (15–19 Years—Ref.)	1.000		1.000	0.000
20–24	4.586	0.000	2.652	
Education (Up to Primary School—Ref.)	1.000		1.000	
Middle School	1.036	0.889	0.999	0.997
High School and above	0.782	0.421	1.121	0.713
Type of Work (Tailoring & Related Works—Ref.)	1.000		1.000	
Supervisory & Other White Collar Works	1.587	0.100	1.164	0.598
Monthly Income (Rs< 2000—Ref.)	1.000		1.000	
2000–2999	1.957	0.003	2.959	0.000
3000+	4.533	0.000	4.933	0.000
Respondent's Religiosity (Less Religious—Ref.)	1.000		1.000	
Moderate Religious	0.473	0.005	0.603	0.060
Highly Religious	0.456	0.013	0.561	0.071
Career Option in Near Future				
(No Specific Career Option—Ref.)	1.000		0.000	
Have Some Specific Career Option	1.641	0.069	1.291	0.362
Parent's Religiosity (Less Religious—Ref.)	1.000		1.000	
More Religious	0.571	0.008	0.530	0.003
No. of Peers Participating in Higher Risky	1.000		1.000	
Life Styles (≤ 2—Ref.)	2.820	0.000	2.233	0.001
3–5, 6 +	3.121	0.000	2.277	0.002
Frequency of Viewing TV/Movie/Playing Cards during Leisure Time (Index)				
(Lesser Extent—Ref.)	1.000		1.000	
Higher Extent	1.720	0.011	0.863	0.488
Migrant Status (Non-Migrant—Ref.)	1.000		1.000	
Migrant	1.196	0.447	1.156	0.549
Place of Stay (With Family in a Home—Ref.)	1.000		1.000	
With Peer in a Room	1.578	0.103	1.402	0.238
–2 Log-likelihood	1586.883			
Chi-square Value (d.f.)	248.498 (30)			
Level of Significance	0.000			
N	995			

exist in this city and hiring CDs and television sets to watch blue films in rooms with peers is also common on Sundays. All these suggest that though mass media and information technology revolution would be beneficial to the social and economic development of the nation, we can not avoid these types of adverse effects too.

As expected, taking up of less as well as high risky lifestyles is found to be significantly more among those young workers, who are higher in their age, earning comparatively better income per month and having contact with large number of peers who participate in higher risky lifestyles, whereas engaging in such risky behaviour is observed as much less among those workers whose degree of religiosity is higher and also whose parents are said to be more religious. It is also interesting to note that those workers who are more frequently watching TV/movies and playing cards, and living with peers in rooms, to some extent, participate in risky behaviour (lesser health risks). All these findings suggest that, on the one side, physiological and psychological properties of young age combining with availability of resources (money) and peer's social interaction play an important role in luring the workers to engage themselves in risky behaviour; on the other side, religious faiths influence them in not refraining from such lifestyles.

The findings of this analysis also suggest that engaging in less risky lifestyles is found to be significantly high among those working as 'supervisors and other white collar workers' (as compared to tailors and related workers) and among those who determine to have a (better) career option in the near future. The former association is justified in the context of earning higher monthly incomes and large peer interaction, since majority of them are migrant workers who work mostly more than one shift. Of course, these workers are comparatively better educated than their counterparts, but the effect of education on embracing risky lifestyles appears to be inconsistent and insignificant in this study. The latter association to a certain extent is possible because those who are currently working in moderate and better positioned jobs (supervisors and other white collar workers in the present case among whom participation in risky lifestyles is high) mostly aspire for the good jobs in the near future as they have the experience and avenues to achieve them.

The associations between the workers' levels of education and participation in risky behaviour, in the present study, are noted to be neither consistent nor significant. This could be, on the one hand, the differentials in levels of education of young men are not that much (mostly varied between primary school to high school and above), and on the other hand, the education would have multifarious associations with several other variables. However, migrant status per se exhibited a net positive effect on young workers' risky behaviour, it did not turn out to be significant. The possible reasons could be its close association with their living arrangements (most of them live in rooms with peers), earning better incomes and having large number of peers who are engaged in risky behaviour.

Limitations

This study has certain limitations. Firstly, as noted earlier, the data is from young workers of hosiery establishments of an urban centre wherein migrants are outnumbered by the natives (in work participation). Data from young workers of other establishments also need to be looked into. Secondly, information is self-reported, and thus contains all of the problems inherent to self-report measures. However, care is taken to train the field investigators so as to get reliable information by informing the young workers about the confidentiality of data, by encouraging the voluntary participation and allowing them to withdraw from the interviews at any point of time if they wish, etc. Another major limitation of this paper is that it did not consider the family environment of young boys like parents' background characteristics (except religious background) and monitoring/supervision of young ones, which are said to be the major determinants of risky behaviour of younger people. Of course, such data have been collected as part of this major study; the preliminary bi-variate analysis did not show any associations and thereby, they have not been considered for analysis here.

Implications

Health care planners and health educators need to build prevention messages that stress the specific relationships between risky lifestyles and various health risks like occurrences of diseases, psychological illnesses and interrelationships with other major risky outcomes like premarital sex, STDs and HIV/AIDS and such messages to be imparted to the adolescents and young people through various mass media and inter-personal channels.

Young workers, in general, and young risk takers, in particular, have to be educated and counselled in an effective manner about the potential dangers of all these risky lifestyles, in addition to designing specific messages and coping mechanisms of such risks for this group.

Legislations/strategies against the use of tobacco, *panparag* (*gutka*), gambling, pornography, video piracy, etc., have to be implemented effectively by the government administration, so as to discourage the present youngsters from taking up such risky lifestyles.

Acknowledgements

The author would like to thank The Ford Foundation, USA for providing financial support under the Youth Sexuality Project, through Dr TK Sundari Ravindran, Honorary Professor, AMCHSS, SCTIMST, Thiruvananthapuram, from which this paper is being prepared.

References

Audinarayana, N. 2005. Correlates of High-Risk Sexual Behaviour among Never-Married Male Industrial Workers in Tirupur City, Tamil Nadu. AMCHSS, SCTIMST, Trivandrum.

Bala, D.V., Ila N. Bodiwala, D.D. Patel and P.M. Shah. 2006. Epidemiological Determinants of Tobacco Use in Gujarat State, India. *Indian Journal of Community Medicine* 31(3): 173–6.

Director of Census Operations, Chennai. 2004. *Primary Census Abstract, 2001, Coimbatore district – Data on CD.* Office of the Director of Census Operations, Chennai.

Kadri, A.M., A. Bhagyalaxmi and Geeta Kedia. 2003. A Study of Socio-Demographic Profile of Substance Abusers Attending a De-addiction Centre in Ahmedabad City. *Indian Journal of Community Medicine* 28(2): 74–6.

Kumar, Anil K. 2004. Economic Aspects of Sex Work: Can Employment Dissuade Women from Entering into and Continuing Sex Work? *The Journal of Family Welfare* 50 (Spl. Issue): 79–82.

Mukherjee, K. and R.S. Hadaye. 2006. Gutka Consumption and its Determinants among Secondary School Male Students. *Indian Journal of Community Medicine* 31(3): 177.

Naskar, N.N., M. Roy and S.K. Bhattacharya. 2004. A Study of Some Socio-economic Factors on Drug Abuse among the Undergraduate Medical Students in Calcutta. *Indian Journal of Community Medicine* 29(2): 69–71 and 76.

Priyanka, P.D. 2006. A Cross-Cultural Epidemiological Study of Substance Users in an Urban Field Practice Area in Mumbai, India. *Indian Journal of Preventive and Social Medicine* 37(1 and 2): 44–8.

Sinha, D.N., P.C. Gupta and M.S. Pednekar. 2003. Tobacco Use in Rural Areas of Bihar, India. *Indian Journal of Community Medicine* 28(4): 167–70.

Appendix

Respondents' Religiosity (Index): Pooled scores of young boys' responses to three of the following religious activities: Performing *puja* at home (scores of '0', '1' and '2' for No, Sometimes and Regularly, respectively); frequency of visiting place of worship (scores of '0' '1' and '2' for Not at all, Occasionally and Weekly/Daily, respectively); and observing religious fasting (scores of '0', '1' and '2' for Never, Rare and Often, respectively). Based on the pooled scores for each respondent, they have been classified into three groups: Less Religious (scores 0–1), Moderate Religious (2–4) and Highly Religious (5–6).

Frequency of Viewing TV/Movie/Playing Cards during Leisure Time (Index): Pooled scores of young workers' responses to three of the following leisure time activities: Viewing television, watching movies and playing cards for time pass (scores of '0', '1' and '2' for Never, Occasionally and Frequently). From these pooled scores respondents have been grouped into two categories: Lesser Extent (scores 0–2) and Higher Extent (3–6).

No. of Peers Participating in Higher Risky Lifestyles: Cumulative number of peers participating in the following activities: Drinking alcohol, use of drugs, reading pornographic literature, browsing pornographic sites and watching pornographic films. From these cumulative numbers, all the respondents have been categorized into three groups: Few (0–2), Some (3–5) and Large (6–13).

CHAPTER 17

Emerging Sexual Vulnerability Among Adolescents and Youth in Sri Lanka

W. Indralal De Silva and K. Karunathilake

The changing demographic and socio-economic scenarios throughout the world have unfolded many important issues that demand, the immediate focus of all the relevant members of the world community. Among these, the sexual and reproductive health of the population is an important issue to be addressed immediately, throughout the countries in the developing world where the quality of health has a major impact on the development process.

The entry into reproductive phase of the lifecycle is an important threshold in a person's life in which, the choice and the behavioural patterns acquired during early adolescence will determine the subsequent life course (United Nations, 1989). Important steps in this transitional process are several critical life events such as puberty, initiation to sexuality, marriage and childbearing. The timing, as well as the sequence and context in which these events take place have immediate and long-term repercussions for a particular individuals' sexual and reproductive health. Generally, the commencement of adolescence is with a period of rapid physical growth, in which a gradual development of reproductive organs occur, along with the appearance of gender specific secondary sex characteristics and menarche in girls (De Silva et al., 2003).

In almost all the developing countries, two distinctive demographic trends, having strong implications for the sexual and reproductive health of adolescents and youth[1] are apparent. First, is the decline of average age at menarche, primarily related to variety of environmental, genetic and socio-economic factors, such as improved nutrition and more importantly to change in the cultural norms (Bongaarts and

Cohen, 1998). Second, is the trend towards increasing average age at marriage of both males and females causing the proportion of unmarried adolescents to increase (De Silva, 1997). As a result of the above trends the period of potential premarital sex, a phase of risk-taking behaviour among adolescents and youth had lengthened (United Nations, 2001).

Sri Lanka has been identified as "the Ireland of Asia" because of the long delay in entry into marriage, where male and female average age at marriage has now increased to over 25 and 28 years of age respectively. Caldwell et al. (1989) identified Sri Lanka as the leader in Third World Asia's change in marriage patterns; by mid-1970s Sri Lankan females were marrying not at puberty but a decade after puberty. Consequent to this trend many Sri Lankans experience an extended period of adolescence during which their sexual vulnerability has increased significantly. Thus the general objective of this paper is to understand the level of sexual awareness, behaviour, and vulnerability experienced by adolescents and youth in the changing socio-economic and cultural environment in Sri Lanka.

Methodology

Although multi-layered data collection approach, including focus group discussions, key informant interviews and observations, was adopted as the overall methodology of the study, the present paper primarily depends on the data collected in an island-wide field survey. In the survey, out of the total 25 districts in Sri Lanka, nine districts were selected randomly to represent the sub-national (urban, rural and estate sectors) variations in sexual vulnerability with a target sample of 4,000 adolescents and youth of age 10–24 years. When deciding the sample for the field survey the adequacy and reliability of the sample to represent the urban, rural and estate sectors, and three age groups namely 10–14, 15–17 and 18–24 years[2] are considered.

Our initial investigations about the population composition of the selected nine districts, showed that, it will enable the study of an adequate and representative sample of urban, rural and estate sectors.

As the Primary Sampling Unit (PSU)[3] of this survey, the Census Block Frame of 2001 Census of Population and Census Block (CB), was used. Each district in which the survey was conducted was divided by the sector of residence, namely urban, rural and estate, into three strata. With an intension of having 4,000 adolescents and youth of age 10–24 years as the ultimate target sample, a sample of 42 CBs were initially selected at the primary stage and these 42 CBs were allocated among the nine districts by the sector of residence. The PSUs so allocated have been selected using the systematic sampling method with a probability-proportionate to size (PPS) in each stratum of each district. In other words the number of housing units was used as the size measure in the selection procedure.[4]

Six questionnaires were developed for different segments (age, sex and marital status categories) of the eligible population to facilitate the collection of data in the island-wide field survey. A number of ethical factors were given consideration in great detail, when these questionnaires were developed. Depending on the targeted sub-group, the application of different questionnaire modules were intended to gather the basic background information of the respondents, and their knowledge, attitudes and behaviour pertaining to sexual and reproductive health.

Adolescents and youth of age 10–24 living in the selected clusters were called at centres for canvassing questionnaires. The survey, adopting self-completion type of interview approach, gathered information from 3,996 eligible respondents, however only 3,749 were found to be complete with all main sections of the questionnaire. Thus, completed questionnaires of 3,322 unmarried adolescents aged 10–24 and another 427 married adolescents aged 18–24 from nine districts of Sri Lanka were used for the final analysis.

Self-Completion Approach

A large number of studies have attempted to collect information on sexual behaviour of adolescent and youth in Sri Lanka by interviewing adolescents and/or youth at their respective households. In almost all South Asian and many other cultures, this approach had not yielded the expected results. The possibility of knowing the true level of sexual behaviour if they are interviewed at the household level is less. Adolescents and youth who are away from their respective households would respond more genuinely, to report their attitudes, knowledge and sexual behaviour when requested using appropriate survey techniques. Therefore, consequent to the introduction of the questionnaire tc the group, as the survey technique to collect reliable information from the target group of adolescents and youth in Sri Lanka located at different centres of the selected clusters, it was decided to administer a self-completion type of questionnaire.

Eligible adolescents and youth of the selected clusters were first identified through the householder list or/and with the assistance of the relevant Grama Niladari (GN) of the area. Thereafter, the eligible respondents were requested to arrive at the particular centres for the self-reporting of the survey modules. There were seven selected NGOs, who possesses health related experiences, collaborating in the data collection exercise.

Results

Sex is exclusively a biological function, defined on the basis of individuality and socio-cultural background of that individual. It is biologically associated with male and female reproductive organs such as genitals and the reproductive maturity of individuals indicated by gender specific secondary characteristics such as facial and body hair, pelvic size, musculature, etc. Most persons are in a well defined sex category, although there are occasional hormonal imbalances. Generally, almost all cases where a person's genitals are partly of one sex, partly of other. Sex is inclusive of behaviour related to eroticism and procreation.

Sex is a difficult subject to study, because it touches upon so many different complex aspects related to human experience. There are four major characteristics of sex frequently focussed by many researchers, namely sexual acts, sexual partners, sexual meanings, and, sexual desire and pleasure. Though all four of these elements are important, the first two deserves more attention. As they are the most personal, activities that may occur in an individuals life. Sexual desire and pleasure are aspects more difficult to capture which makes the study of that aspect of sex rather problematic. Human behaviour is difficult to comprehend, and drawing inferences about the study of sexuality is further complicated by issues such as privacy, acceptability, appropriateness. Thus, sexuality is a subject difficult to define.

Sexuality

Sexuality is often simplified to sexual behaviour but it is a very complex issue which exceeds mere sexual behaviour. It encompasses eroticism, sexual behaviour, social and gender roles and identity, relationships, and the personal, social and cultural meanings that each of these might contain. The study of sexual behaviour itself is important, but is incomplete if divorced from personal, social and cultural context in which it occurs. Views about sexuality are specific to a particular place, time and group of people. They keep on changing, as do also the factors that govern the regulation of sexuality. Especially, age, attitudes and beliefs, education level, locality, exposure to the modern world, influence of mass media, etc., are some factors governing this situation. This study is focussed on several important issues related to the sexuality of adolescents and youth in Sri Lanka.

Awareness on Sexuality

It is important to create a gradual awareness on human sexuality, among all adolescents and youth in the society, through the formal education system. For any formal organization, there are obstacles that prevent launching such awareness activities. From a group who are totally ignorant about human sexuality, such as those in early stage of adolescence, it is ethically and culturally unsuitable to inquire about sex, though it is vital that they should possess such knowledge on human sexuality.

Despite all these barriers, we have examined the awareness on sexual behaviour[5] found among adolescents in the 10–14 age group using indirect questioning method, by which the answers given may reflect the knowledge of one's own activities. The figures given in Table 1 indicate that most of the males and females of 10–14 age group adolescents in all sectors do not have such exposure. On gender basis, male adolescents are more exposed to sex than the females. Place of residence (sector) comparison show that, females in the estate sector represent the highest percentage (80.5%); who did not possess any awareness on sexual activities.

Table 1

Knowledge on Sexual Behaviour among 10–14 Age Group

Sector	*Answer*	*Male*		*Female*	
		%	*(N)*	%	*(N)*
Rural	Yes	33.4	132	26.8	165
	No	66.6	263	73.2	451
	Total	100.0	395	100.0	616
Urban	Yes	32.4	36	28.7	52
	No	67.6	75	71.3	129
	Total	100.0	111	100.0	181
Estate	Yes	35.0	14	19.5	8
	No	65.0	26	80.5	33
	Total	100.0	40	100.0	41

In all three sectors the proportion of males who had awareness in sexual behaviour was more than that of females while males in the estate sector indicated the highest proportion. The implication is that majority of the young adolescents do not have sufficient knowledge on sexual behaviour or hesitate to acknowledge awareness, due to cultural barriers, especially in an atmosphere that impedes discussion of such matters openly.

Homosexual behaviour consists of choosing a partner of the same sex for sexual interaction. The term homosexual is used to characterize individuals who prefer romantic attachments and sexual interaction with the same sex and typically are maximally aroused by same-sex erotic imagery. The term is used for both sexes, although female homosexuality is often referred to as lesbianism. Homosexuality is one way by which they satisfy their sexual needs and adults also tend to use adolescents for such activities. The more pronounced tendency in this regard is peer related sexual activity.

In the survey, a few questions were asked related to premarital sex of the respondents itself and their peers. Experience of the respondents in the 10–14 age group on homosexual activities was not directly inquired due to ethical matters. They were only questioned about their knowledge on peer homosexual activities. The situation prevailing among the 10–14 segments in each sector illustrated in Table 2 shows that males are more knowledgeable and aware than the females on homosexual activities among their peers, but the percentage is relatively low. There is a substantial percentage who responded that they did not have an idea or who were not knowledgeable about their peers behaviour on this issue. Those who do not have such knowledge represented a high percentage. Young urban adolescent males have a high involvement in homosexual activities than their rural counterparts, while estate males showed the highest percentage, and estate females a relatively low involvement.

The general expectation was that the investigated age groups above 15 years of age of all marital statuses, should possess a clear understanding about human sexuality. As age progresses they may have the opportunity of learning through formal education system as well as through other ways such as media, communication, and experience.

The study revealed that the interviewees of age group 15–17 even do not have a sound understanding about sexuality. Nevertheless, 36 per cent of both males and females in the rural sector have a scientific understanding on sexuality (Table 3). The males in estate sector were more vulnerable as most of them (63%) did not have any idea about the theme. The highest percentage (39%) among the urban females of aged 15–17 reported to have a sound understanding about sexuality.

Table 2

Knowledge on Peer's Homosexual Activity among 10–14 Age Group

Sector	Answer	Male		Female	
		%	(N)	%	(N)
Rural	Yes	5.3	21	4.5	28
	No	41.0	162	38.3	236
	Can't say/Don't know	53.7	212	57.2	352
	Total	100.0	395	100.0	616
Urban	Yes	8.1	9	6.1	11
	No	44.1	49	44.2	80
	Can't say/Don't know	47.8	53	49.7	90
	Total	100.0	111	100.0	181
Estate	Yes	20.0	8	2.4	1
	No	44.6	18	41.5	17
	Can't say/Don't know	35.4	14	56.1	23
	Total	100.0	40	100.0	41

In general, most of the rural and urban adolescents have a clearer and more scientific understanding about human sexuality than the estate sector respondents who indicated a substantially lesser understanding (Table 3). For instance among the 18–24 unmarried estate females only 17 per cent possess the correct knowledge on sexuality while the corresponding level among their urban counterparts are at high as 57 per cent. Evidently, most of the interviewees in the estate sector had very poor knowledge on sexuality. According to their traditional way of thinking, sexuality is confined to having sexual intercourse and procreation. They have received a significantly low level of sex education through the formal education system.

Interestingly, the 18–24 age group unmarried males displayed a higher knowledge than the married group on human sexuality. This may be due to the better educational background they had than others. The process of giving priority to sex education and emphasis on reproductive and sexual health at school level may have contributed to this improvement. This fact can be verified by studying the curricula and examining the steps taken by the government agencies in introducing

Table 3

Knowledge on Human Sexuality among the Different Age Categories

Sector	*Knowledge*	*15–17 (UM)*		*18–24 (UM)*		*18–24 (M)*	
		Male	*Female*	*Male*	*Female*	*Male*	*Female*
Rural	Knowledge and understanding on human sexual behaviour	35.8	35.0	64.6	53.1	46.2	48.6
	Ability to bear children	20.1	13.2	9.6	7.8	10.8	18.4
	Engaging in sexual activities	10.4	9.2	14.5	10.7	18.3	11.9
	Not anything of mentioned here	3.3	3.5	5.4	3.9	4.3	3.7
	No idea	30.4	39.1	5.9	24.5	20.4	17.4
	Total	100.0	100.0	100.0	100.0	100.0	100.0
Urban	Knowledge and understanding on human sexual behaviour	34.7	39.3	56.8	57.3	50.0	56.2
	Ability to bear children	9.7	10.3	9.9	10.1	15.8	12.3
	Engaging in sexual activities	9.7	6.8	14.6	6.2	10.5	8.2
	Not anything of mentioned here	9.7	5.1	1.0	6.2	5.3	2.7
	No idea	36.2	38.5	17.7	20.2	18.4	20.6
	Total	100.0	100.0	100.0	100.0	100.0	100.0
Estate	Knowledge and understanding on human sexual behaviour	29.5	36.8	48.7	16.8	25.0	21.7
	Ability to bear children	0.0	0.0	8.1	6.7	16.6	0.0
	Engaging in sexual activities	0.0	0.0	5.4	3.3	16.7	21.7
	Not anything of mentioned here	7.6	15.8	10.8	13.2	0.0	0.0
	No idea	62.9	47.4	27.0	60.0	41.7	34.8
	Total	100.0	100.0	100.0	100.0	100.0	78.2

UM = Unmarried; M = Married

health education in Sri Lanka. This improvement in knowledge was observed in the three sectors examined. On the basis of this situation, one can argue that 15–17 age group possessed a better knowledge. Additionally though, not reflected in the material presented, discussions with the focussed groups, revealed that urban adolescents possessed a better knowledge on human sexuality.

Nature of Communication on Sexual Problems and Other Matters

Many adolescents and youth would be very keen to be more aware of human sexual behaviour, particularly, aspects such as knowledge, attitudes, and practices related to sex, which have a direct bearing on them. Biologically and psychologically the period of adolescence in the life cycle is a very crucial stage that transform the child into a more responsible social being (Jejeebhoy, 1996). Therefore, it is worthwhile to identify how adolescents and youth can be educated in human sexuality. Generally it is assumed that pertaining to matters on sex, most of them communicate among themselves. Thus when socializing such a group, peer groups can be used to influence the development of their knowledge, attitudes, and practice. The level of communication among peers on sexual activities is set out in the Table 4.

Table 4

The Existing Level of Communication among Peers on Sexual Behaviour

Sector	*Type*	*15–17 (UM)*		*18–24 (UM)*	
		Male	*Female*	*Male*	*Female*
Rural	Yes	39.8	29.1	66.1	47.4
	No	60.2	70.9	33.9	52.6
	Total	100.0	100.0	100.0	100.0
Urban	Yes	43.1	28.2	65.6	53.4
	No	56.9	71.9	34.4	46.6
	Total	100.0	100.0	100.0	100.0
Estate	Yes	33.3	36.8	68.4	33.3
	No	66.7	63.2	31.6	66.7
	Total	100.0	100.0	100.0	100.0

UM = Unmarried; M = Married

The analysis indicated that, 15–17 age group did not have a thorough communication with peers while unmarried 18–24 age group had a substantial communication amongst themselves. In contrast to males, females have a limited communication in this respect (Table 4). Compared with the 18–24 unmarried males, females of the same group indicated a significant variation in the level of communication by place of residence. The estate females again reported the lowest level of communication while the urban females the highest. Therefore, there is a need to identify the source of authentic knowledge. Unless they gained scientific knowledge from the school, it is positive, that they will face many difficulties when they engage in sexual behaviour. For instance, unmarried males of 18–24 show an average of 66 percentage communication on sexual behaviour among themselves. For further analysis, the few more questions to be addressed are, why unmarried males and females are having a tendency to communicate with peers more than the 15–17 age groups; why 15–17 age group does not have high tendency to communicate with peers, etc. Generally all groups indicate a low tendency to communicate with peers on sexual behaviour.

The most important issue is to find out the subjects that they discus with their friends regarding human sexuality. Several important issues were highlighted in the questions asked in the main survey. Almost all respondents have paid more attention to genital organs, sexual intercourse, and family planning (Table 5). It reveals that only a small percentage has paid attention to the incidence of conception, and abortion. This implies that there are certain number of adolescents and youth who have faced or have experienced such issues or they are interested in gaining knowledge in these areas that have a direct bearing on their life or someone close to them.

Table 5

The Matters Discussed with Peers Among Unmarried

Sector	*The matters discussed*	*15–17*		*18–24*	
		Male	*Female*	*Male*	*Female*
Rural	Genital organ	24.2	32.5	23.3	25.4
	Sexual intercourse	34.3	19.1	33.2	20.3
	Family planning	15.3	18.4	17.2	22.3
	The incidence of conception	14.8	14.4	14.2	20.5
	Abortion	6.2	9.3	10.1	8.1
	Other	5.2	6.3	2.0	3.4
	Total	100.0	100.0	100.0	100.0
Urban	Genital organ	25.1	36.7	20.2	24.3
	Sexual intercourse	30.2	21.5	35.1	16.5
	Family planning	12.7	11.0	16.3	20.4
	The incidence of conception	15.2	19.2	15.3	24.3
	Abortion	11.5	3.4	11.4	12.4
	Other	5.3	8.2	1.7	2.1
	Total	100.0	100.0	100.0	100.0
Estate	Genital organ	43.1	29.3	17.2	37.5
	Sexual intercourse	31.3	49.1	29.5	12.1
	Family planning	19.5	7.2	32.7	18.0
	The incidence of conception	6.1	7.2	10.1	13.0
	Abortion	0.0	7.2	7.4	6.4
	Other	0.0	0.0	3.1	13.0
	Total	100.0	100.0	100.0	100.0

In general, among adolescents, matters discussed with their peers changed significantly according to the gender of the respondent. For instance matters discussed among the males of 15–17 and 18–24, the sexual intercourse rank the top of the list, while among the female respondents it is the genital organs that received the highest attention. Presumably the items discussed among the peers indicate, to some extent, their present sexual behaviour or future intentions. The gender difference highlights the likelihood of more males to engage in sexual intercourse earlier in their life than their female counterparts thereby acquiring the sexual vulnerability sooner than the females.

Sexual Behaviour

As was mentioned at the beginning of the paper, to draw universal patterns or an all encompassing definition on human sexuality is a complex issue as it is a multifaceted phenomenon. These different types of sexual patterns may have links with age, gender, and marital status of individuals in the particular society that they belong. An attempt has been made to identify different types of sexual activities among the adolescents and youth in each sector and age group in Sri Lanka.

Undoubtedly, adolescence is also a time when young persons look beyond their relationships with their parents and families and begin to form more intense relationships with their peers and adults in their communities. During this period they experiment with new behaviours and emotional relationships, which may give rise to new experiences such as masturbation, homosexual and, heterosexual relationships.

Homosexuality and Heterosexuality

As defined above, homosexuality is the behaviour of a person who is sexually attracted to a member of the same sex or gender. However, the sexual activities of homosexual members can take different forms, for instance, anal sex, oral sex, etc. These activities can be engaged by any person who is interested in homosexuality, heterosexuality, or even bisexuality.

Heterosexuality is a behaviour of a person who is sexually attracted to the member of the opposite sex or gender. This condition is not too complex because, most of married or unmarried people are attracted to the opposite sex by natural instinct. When they indulge in love play, they make penetrative sex or sexual intercourse with the member of opposite sex.

The study is purported to investigate the knowledge possessed by the adolescents and youth regarding different sexual activities. Table 6 shows detailed knowledge on different sexual behaviours of adolescents and youth in different age categories and in three main sectors. The investigated sexual behaviours are homosexuality, masturbation, anal sex, and oral sex. Those who experience certain sexual activities such as anal and oral sex could develop vulnerable conditions in their lifestyle.

As shown in Table 6, majority of the respondents in the sample population had knowledge on homosexuality, with no marked difference between males and females, except in case of urban females in the 15–17 age group. The urban females had higher knowledge (51.3%) than the male counterparts. Rural males in the 15–17 age group, had higher knowledge of masturbation than males in other two sectors.

Most males and females in all sectors and age groups did not have a sound understanding of anal sex. Nevertheless, males, in the 18–24 age category, in rural and urban sectors, irrespective of their marital status, possessed reasonably good level of knowledge on oral sex. Many males in rural and urban sectors irrespective of their marital status displayed better knowledge on all types of sexual activity, while females did not show that they were knowledgeable except on homosexuality and masturbation. In general, knowledge on masturbation is relatively high among males than the females in all three sectors investigated.

Comparison of the estate sector with the other two show that there are few distinctive features. In this sector, males, both unmarried and married, have indicated having a good knowledge on homosexuality (65.8% of unmarried males aged 18–24) and masturbation (55.6% of married males). When analysed further, both married males and females of 18–24 age group did possess knowledge on masturbation. In contrast to other sectors, most of estate adolescents and youth did not have good understanding on various sexual activities that the others were knowledgeable. This has been disclosed at the focussed group discussions with the estate sector members. Seemingly, the estate sector adolescents and youth need to be exposed to comprehensive awareness programmes to enlighten them on human sexual activities.

These findings can be verified further through the information collected on particular sexual behaviours, such as homosexuality and masturbation. Most adolescents had clearly identified the nature of homosexuality. On the average, 33 per cent of males and females in the 15–17 age group in the rural sector believe that homosexuality is a form of sexual behaviour between two males and 31 per cent of them believed that it happened between females, while 38 per cent of the same categories in urban sector believed that this type of sex activity is either

Table 6

Knowledge on Different Sexual Behaviours

Sector	Gender	Knowledge	Sexual behaviour											
			15 – 17 (UM)				18 –24 (UM)				18 –24 (M)			
			H	*M*	*Anal sex*	*Oral sex*	*H*	*M*	*Anal sex*	*Oral sex*	*H*	*M*	*Anal sex*	*Oral sex*
Rural	Male	Yes	47.5	55.2	29.8	37.1	79.9	72.0	49.5	54.0	80.7	69.2	57.0	54.8
		No	52.5	44.8	70.2	62.9	20.1	28.0	50.5	46.0	19.4	30.8	43.0	45.2
	Female	Yes	44.4	14.6	11.3	20.6	68.2	18.4	21.9	26.0	72.5	39.7	33.5	44.0
		No	55.6	85.4	88.8	79.4	31.8	81.6	78.1	74.0	27.5	60.3	66.5	56.0
Urban	Male	Yes	45.8	45.3	30.6	37.5	79.7	72.5	49.0	53.7	86.8	56.3	71.1	65.8
		No	54.2	54.7	69.4	62.5	20.3	27.5	51.0	46.4	13.2	43.8	29.0	34.2
	Female	Yes	51.3	19.2	10.3	15.4	75.8	15.8	31.5	38.8	71.2	37.0	39.7	37.0
		No	48.7	80.8	89.7	84.6	24.2	84.2	68.5	61.2	28.8	63.0	60.3	63.0
Estate	Male	Yes	25.9	6.7	14.8	22.2	65.8	43.8	29.0	23.7	33.3	55.6	16.7	25.0
		No	74.1	93.3	85.2	77.8	34.2	56.3	71.1	76.3	66.7	44.4	83.3	75.0
	Female	Yes	42.1	22.2	21.1	31.6	46.7	14.3	13.3	23.3	47.8	55.6	21.7	13.0
		No	57.9	77.8	79.0	68.4	53.3	85.7	86.7	76.7	52.2	44.4	78.3	87.0

Note: H = Homosexuality; M = Masturbation; UM = Unmarried; M = Married

between a male and a male or between a female and a female (table not shown). Almost 45 per cent of the respondents in the 18–24 age category, irrespective of the marital status, also agreed with this opinion. Many adolescents in the estate sector believe that homosexuality is mainly a sexual union confined to a male with another male (average 53%). At least a quarter of married females in the 18–24 age group thought that, homosexuality happened between two males. Around 31 per cent of them believed that it is between two females or between a male and a female. This understanding of male and female union is based on the assumption that such sexual behaviour is not penetrative sex activity.

Premarital Sex

As a consequence to the increase in age at marriage of males and females, the risk-taking period has increased significantly. For instance female average age at marriage has increased from 21 years in 1967 to 25 years in 2001. Apart from the postponement of marriage, average age at menarche have also dropped during the last couple of decades. The combined effect of these trends resulted in a lengthening of the risk-taking period among adolescents and youth thus enormously increasing the period of premarital sexual vulnerability of adolescents (De Silva, 1998).

It is plausible that some adolescents and youth in all sectors in Sri Lanka may have had premarital sex in their life, which would have involved certain risks, as far as their future life is concerned. In this study the focus is on experience of sexual intercourse among peers. However, the respondents were not asked directly how they gained their experience, nevertheless it is assumed that the knowledge of the experience of others would reflect a persons own attitude.

Naturally, with a high mean age at marriage the trend could be developed to a habit formation that is keen to satisfy their sexual drives through any of aforesaid sexual behaviour and there is a high risk of contracting HIV/AIDS. A verification of their knowledge and understanding on the use of contraceptive methods when they engage in premarital sex is desirable. Table 7 shows the knowledge on peer's sexual intercourse among the unmarried adolescents and youth. These figures reveal that there is a substantial percentage among adolescents and youth who have had premarital sex.

Table 7

Knowledge on Peer's Sexual Intercourse Among Unmarried

Sector	Experience	15–17		18–24	
		Male	Female	Male	Female
Rural	Have experience	26.8	11.0	40.7	19.5
	No experience	30.4	35.0	24.9	39.6
	Don't know	42.8	54.0	34.5	40.9
	Total	100.0	100.0	100.0	100.0
Urban	Have experience	30.6	12.0	46.9	19.2
	No experience	26.4	34.2	22.4	44.6
	Don't know	43.1	53.9	30.7	36.2
	Total	100.0	100.0	100.0	100.0
Estate	Have experience	14.8	10.5	23.7	13.3
	No experience	44.4	31.6	44.7	33.3
	Don't know	40.7	57.9	31.6	53.3
	Total	100.0	100.0	100.0	100.0

Compared with males, females show a low tendency in engaging in premarital sex. Among the 18–24 unmarried male respondents in the urban sector nearly one-half (47%) believe that their peers already had experience on sexual intercourse, while corresponding estimate among females was only 19% (Table 7). Supporting the proposition on the extended period of risk-taking, 18–24 old group reported higher level of experience on sexual intercourse than the 15–17 age group.

When compared with the rural or estate sectors there is a higher tendency of such sexual behaviour in the urban sector. Availability of opportunities and motivation by various seductive means are higher in the urban set-up.

The counter partner with whom the sexual intercourse was made was basically confined to two categories. The main category was lovers, the other category being someone else other than the lover (Table 8). The second category especially, was at high risk, if commercial sex workers or prostitutes and others (refers to the type of partners) were hired for the purpose. This situation generally, could lead to a negative impact on the individual, and to the society in particular. For instance the increase in demand for prostitution may create an environment where adolescents and youth had a high risk of contacting STIs, including HIV/AIDS. Potential increase in the prostitution would also create a major threat for the family, its basic functions and related issues in the society.

Table 8

Partners with whom their Peers had Sexual Intercourse Among Unmarried

Sector	*Partner*	*15–17*		*18–24*	
		Male	*Female*	*Male*	*Female*
Rural	With lover	30.7	13.9	38.1	40.4
	With sex worker	11.5	2.2	22.2	2.2
	Unidentified person	4.2	3.3	6.3	3.3
	With relative	5.7	2.8	4.7	3.8
	Other	2.6	1.1	24.8	47.5
	Don't know	45.3	76.7	3.9	2.7
	Total	100.0	100.0	100.0	100.0
Urban	With lover	28.6	34.6	38.9	45.5
	With sex worker	28.6	15.4	29.6	1.3
	Unidentified person	3.6	11.5	7.4	3.9
	With relative	3.6	11.5	9.9	1.3
	Other	0.0	3.9	10.5	46.8
	Don't know	35.7	23.1	3.7	1.3
	Total	100.0	100.0	100.0	100.0
Estate	With lover	13.3	9.1	36.8	33.3
	With sex worker	0.0	9.1	15.8	0.0
	Unidentified person	6.7	9.1	10.5	6.7
	With relative	13.3	9.1	21.1	6.7
	Other	6.7	9.1	0.0	53.3
	Don't know	60.0	54.6	15.8	0.0
	Total	100.0	100.0	100.0	100.0

Urban males of age 15–17 had close connection (28%) with commercial sex workers much more than their rural or estate counterparts. In the 18–24 age group too, urban males tended to be highly associated with sex workers (30%). However, males in the 18–24 age group in each sector were noted to be having sexual intercourse with the lover much more than with others. The types of partners indicated by females of the 15–17 age group suggested that they were in a very vulnerable position as they had made connection with relatives and unidentified persons on the sex than with other categories. Thus, they were exposed to a constant risk condition than the others.

Attitudes on Premarital and Extramarital Sex

With the diffusion of visual media, labour migration, changes in attitudes in the recent decades of Sri Lankan society there is a motivation of sex in human social life. It is obvious that there are more incidents of premarital and extramarital sex in the modern Sri Lankan society. The survey as well as focussed group interviews gathered information related to attitudes on pre and extramarital sexual behaviour from adolescents and youth aged 15–24.

An average of 20 per cent of males in all categories investigate have responded in favour of premarital sex. While an average 60 per cent male were disagreed and the balance 20 per cent do not have precise attitude on premarital sex. Of females nearly 5 per cent approved of premarital sex, while 65 per cent disapproved it in the rural sector. However, females of age category 15–17 in urban sector have shown a remarkable response in favour of having premarital sex, with one-half agreeing. As usual, the estate sector showed a different picture than the other two sectors. In the estate sector, both unmarried and married females have favourable response on premarital sex, 15.8 per cent and 16.7 per cent respectively (table not shown).

In all three sectors, there is a tendency in accepting the extramarital sex by both genders creating a subsequent norm in the society. Just over one-half of the unmarried male respondents of age 18–24 process attitude towards accepting extramarital sex, while among their female counterparts the corresponding figure is 40 per cent (table not shown). It is interesting to note that among the unmarried females of age 18–24 in the urban sector accepts extramarital sexual behaviour more than their counterparts in rural and estate sectors. The married category of both genders indicate similar patterns of behaviour specially those who are not much satisfied in their sexual life.

Other Risk Factors

Adolescents and youth are always facing different risks in terms of sexuality. They are among the minority groups in any society marginalized and exploited by adults, knowingly or unknowingly. As a result, some of them have experienced sexual exploitation by others. On the other hand, they have to meet their goals of individual life that prompted them to engage in gainful employment, travel extensively, stay in a strange place, and meet known and unknown people in their everyday life. This type of life circle exposes individuals, specially the adolescents to risk factors. They are still in the process of socializing in the society and do not have a thorough understanding and experience on different events and the people who they are confronted in their day-to-day life. Failing to meet the needs of adolescents and youth is a main reason for frustration, engendering self-destructive behaviours, including drug dependence, suicide, and engaging in crime and violence.

Discussion and Conclusions

The current generation of adolescents and youth in Sri Lanka, face many challenges compared to their predecessors, due to the rapid socio-economic and cultural changes in the Sri Lankan society, since the late 1970s. The protracted ethnic conflict, the disintegration of the extended family, unemployment, threat of HIV/AIDS, adolescent behavioural patterns leaning towards premarital sex, unwanted pregnancies and abortions are some of the main risks and challenges faced by this generation of adolescents and youth. Globally the rights based approach adopted at the International Conference on Population and Development in 1994 and subsequent conferences recognized the need to define and address adolescent health needs as a right of adolescents and youth in a rapidly changing world.

The survey results indicate the level of sexual awareness, attitudes and practices of adolescents and youth in different age categories and sectors in Sri Lanka. Although different survey modules were used to gather information from 10–14, 15–17 and 18–24 age respondents, the sexual experience of the 10–14 age group was not directly inquired due to ethical reasons, instead an attempt has been made to examine the awareness on sexual behaviour of their peers. Majority of these young adolescents do not have a sufficient knowledge on sexual behaviour or hesitate to acknowledge awareness due to cultural barriers. A survey conducted by the UNICEF (2004), revealed that more than 70 per cent of the school going children aged 10–13 were in need of reproductive health information. They were not aware of physiological changes and processes taking place in their own bodies.

In general, males in all sectors were more aware than the females on homosexual activities among their peers. Peer's homosexual activity among the 10–14 age group indicate a relatively low incidence (males 5–20%; females 2–6%). Attanayake (2001), also find a relatively low level of homosexual activity among school going children. Even though

Basnayake (1996) found a relatively higher level of homosexual activities among 16–29 age group, as comparable with present study, the males tend to have a high incidence than females. However, the present Sri Lankan adolescents and youth are experiencing 'sex tourism' in which particularly young boys are exploited to satisfy paedophilic desire of tourists (Silva et al., 1997; Amarasinghe, 2002).

In general, respondents of the 15–17 age group also do not possess a sound knowledge about sexuality. Only the urban sector reports the best knowledge on sexuality while the estate sector males were least knowledgeable about the theme. Interestingly, the 18–24 aged unmarried males displayed a better knowledge than the married group on human sexuality. This difference could be due to the better educational background they had than the others. The findings revealed that certain sectors and age groups need to be more knowledgeable on sexual behaviour and it is the responsibility of the government and other agencies in Sri Lanka to conduct comprehensive awareness programmes on sexual health for adolescents and youth.

In the urban sector, almost one-half of the 18–24 age group unmarried males reported that among peers there was experience in sexual intercourse. The reported incidence of the same event among rural sector adolescents was not far behind. However, compared with males, females show a low tendency of engaging in premarital penetrative sex. Basnayake (1996), investigating the experience of sexual intercourse among the 16–29 age group, found that 43 per cent and 6 per cent of urban males and females respectively had such experience, while the same experience among their rural counterparts was significantly lower. Also the UNICEF (2004) study reports that among the in-school male adolescents of age 14–19 almost 14 per cent ever having had sexual intercourse while the corresponding estimate for females was only 2 per cent. However, when asked the respondents of same age category, who had friends having sexual intercourse, almost 40 per cent of males and 11 per cent females reported positively (UNICEF, 2004).

Though there is an incidence of premarital sex with different partners, most of them disapproved of such sexual activity. This could be recognized as a type of contradictory behaviour, where the actual sexual behaviour of adolescents disagrees with their own attitude. When societies are in transition their behavioural changes may occur at a much faster rate than the transitional changes in attitudes. There are certain changes that have pervaded the sexual life of the adolescents and youth in Sri Lanka, largely due to the external influences. Seemingly, the current behaviour of many adolescents have been sexually motivated. In the current Sri Lankan society, they, have different ways and means to gratify their sexual needs. There is a high incidence of premarital sex with their lovers or some other partners including commercial sex workers. In fact, considerable number of participants in the focussed group discussions claimed their own experience on premarital sexual intercourse, which is fairly matched with the responses given by respondents referring to their peers.

Most of respondents in rural and urban sectors could categorically indicate their sex partners, while clear identification of the partner was not possible in the estate sector. Even, the category 'other' could not indicate it precisely. It means that there is an undisclosed area which needs further research. However, the incidence of incest can be assumed, when media and police reports on incest are considered. These incidents take place in families with males who are addicted to alcohol, or when the wife has migrated for employment, or among broken families. It is difficult to gather these types of critical and qualitative data from a survey. Therefore, there is a need of further research based on further probing and in-depth analysis of adolescent sexual behaviour.

Sexual activities among the unmarried adolescents and youth are often sporadic, unplanned, infrequent. Thus, the use of contraception is less likely. Despite that, most of the health clinics in Sri Lanka are not designed to provide sexual and reproductive health services for the unmarried people. Even though unmarried people may refrain from obtaining contraceptives and related knowledge from health clinics, the present trend indicate that many unmarried adolescents and youth who are engaged in sexual intercourse rely on *Postino* (emergency contraception), which is readily available in almost all pharmacies island-wide. One could also argue that with the wide availability of *Postino* and induced abortion facility in contemporary Sri Lanka, the sexual vulnerability among the adolescents and youth in Sri Lanka could increase (Ban et al., 2003).

In general, adolescents and youth who engage in premarital sexual activities would encounter with a host of social and behavioural problems such as family conflicts, educational problems and school dropping-out, pregnancy, abortion, STDs etc. Pregnancies and live births that occur during early adolescence (say below 17 years of age) could also have a significant impact on the birth weight, morbid conditions and also the very survival of the baby.

As the study revealed, acceptance of the extramarital sex by both genders may create new subsequent norms in the society. As a consequence of complicated social life experienced by unmarried aged 18–24 males and females in the urban sector, approve this behaviour much more than their counterparts in the other sectors. Most of married people have a more complex social life, as they are struggling to make both ends meet. As mentioned above, they have very dynamic and more accessible means to achieve their goals in their daily life. Therefore, it is evident that sex has become an instrument to achieve many things, such as pleasure or satisfaction, or desired end in their life. It was revealed that many married adolescents were not content with their married life and they did not adhere seriously to the etiquettes governed by the society and culture.

This situation will lead to a sexual behavioural condition in the Sri Lankan society. There is an urgent requirement for a system of family counselling which would help them to gain knowledge as well as treatment. It is a positive step towards controlling of domestic violence and divorce among marital unions. The other new trend of behaviour exposed is the 'living together' pattern of behaviour observed among both married and unmarried members of the society. An almost a similar pattern without much distinction, was observed which could be applied equally to married and unmarried groups.

Along with an increasing occurrence of sexual and reproductive health problems in many countries of the developing world, formal teaching on reproductive health at the secondary school level has begun and the success has already been noted. For instance India has shown that reproductive health education at the secondary school level have had a positive impact on knowledge, attitudes and practices of adolescents (Anand, 1993). On the other hand improving the knowledge and skills of school children's own health and well-being via school education programmes is noted to be strongly related with the development of that nation. Thus, promoting health education among school children is a simple innovative approach but noted to be relatively new approach in many developing countries including Sri Lanka.

One of the early attempts to provide reproductive health education in schools in Sri Lanka dates back to 1973, when the Department of Education embarked on a population education programme funded by the UNFPA. However, teaching on population and family life education and reproductive health at the secondary school level was initiated in Sri Lanka in 1996. Subsequently, reproductive health curriculum at Grade

8 level was further expanded by adding a new areas related to adolescents and youth introduced to Grades 8–11.

Parallel to the introduction of reproductive health curriculum, a programme of training for school teachers has been initiated by the National Institute for Education (NIE) with the support of UNFPA to provide information and guidance on reproductive health issues to students in schools. The Health Education Bureau (HEB) provided the necessary inputs for school based sexual and reproductive health education. Also the aim of the peer education programme, which has been implemented in universities in Sri Lanka, is to raise awareness among the peer groups. The main objective of the peer education programme is to improve the awareness of first-year university students on issues related to reproductive health, as well as making reproductive health counselling available to them when needed.

In 1998, the Family Planning Association of Sri Lanka (FPASL) launched a series of projects to provide reproductive health information, counselling and services to adolescents. They were funded by EC/UNFPA under an initiative to enhance reproductive health in Asia. FPASL selected 156 midwife areas in 13 districts (with a total population around 5,00,000) to implement the project. One objective of the project was to provide the community-based sexual and reproductive health information services to adolescents and youth, with a special focus on those living in vulnerable or under-served areas.

Although sexual and reproductive health needs of adolescents and unmarried youth are beginning to be recognized, their needs are still unmet. The above stated projects and activities are largely pilot in nature and hardly touched the out-of-school adolescents and youth. As a result, the usual channels of information on safe sex, reproductive health, and encountering peer pressure are not available to many adolescents and youth. The same cultural taboos that have inhibited open discussion on adolescent reproductive issues have also hampered the marketing campaigns to promote contraceptives. Promotional campaigns had to be sensitized by local cultural and religious beliefs. The challenge that Sri Lanka is facing is a means to initiate a change in the approach to adolescent and youth reproductive and sexual rights and the provision of appropriate and accessible services to youth and adolescents in a rapidly changing society (De Silva et al., 2006).

There are certain changes that exist in the sexual life among the adolescents and youth in Sri Lanka. Especially, it is influenced by the external factors and it seems that many adolescents are sexually motivated and vulnerable. They have different ways and means to satisfy their sexual needs. Hence, there is a need for increased prompt attention to rectify such behavioural patterns. If not addressed immediately, this situation would become more vulnerable and would affect the adolescents in Sri Lanka more adversely. Therefore, preventive measures by the responsible organizations to arrest this situation have become the need of the hour.

Notes

1. The World Health Organization (WHO, 1975) defines adolescents as persons between (10–19 years) of age, youth as those between (15–24 years) and young people as those between (10–24 years). Many studies throughout the world have adopted these age ranges though overlapping, as appropriate to their cultures. Defining adolescence and youth by a particular age range may defy standardization since different terms and age ranges are commonly encountered in the literature. Sociologically or biologically, there is no universally accepted beginning or end of adolescence. Experience in many countries also indicates that age definition should be culture-specific. Therefore, in line with WHO definitions, the present study unless otherwise stated, specifically will conform to the age range of (10–24 years) when referring to adolescents and youth.
2. The broader group (10–24 years) is subdivided into three categories, namely age 10–14, 15–17 and 18–24 years for analytical purposes. In fact as noted by Elliott and Feldman (1990), the first period (age 10–14) is particularly marked with profound physical and social changes that occur with puberty at which maturation begins. Middle period (age 15–17) is a period of increasing independence. The last category (age 18–24) is marked with educational goals or other social factors, delay their entry into the adult role. In fact in most countries, these subdivisions have been incorporated into the educational structure, junior high or secondary school, senior high school and college.
3. The entire Sri Lanka is geographically divided into enumeration areas called Census Blocks and the Department of Census and Statistics updates the household listings at the Census Block level on a regular basis. The last update of the Census Blocks was made at the 2001 Population and Housing Census. The auxiliary information that could be used for the sample selection purpose of the present study is available in the Census Block Frame of 2001 Census of Population. Thus, it was decided to use the latest available Census Block Frame and the Census Block (CB) as the Primary Sampling Unit (PSU) for the survey.

4. The important design decision centred on the discussion of the number of PSUs to include in the study and thus, how geographically dispersed the sample PSUs would be. The sample selection and allocation of the sample was modified in ways which maintain its scientific validity while reflecting the particular goals and resources available for the entire study. For practical convenience, it was decided to expand the initially selected PSUs into clusters by amalgamating the adjacent CBs, if the estimated number of persons in each selected Census Block at the primary stage is less than the expected number. Thus, the sample of 42 clusters was used for the entire design and 11, 27 and 4 clusters represented urban, rural and estate sector respectively. These 42 clusters were used for final enumeration and the persons in the age group (10–24 years) living in the selected clusters were called at centres for canvassing the questionnaire.
5. Any sexual activity, among males and females, that may occur before marriage is referred to as premarital sex and includes several sexual behaviours such as masturbation, homosexuality, prostitution, etc. and even is related to penetrative and non-penetrative sex. Premarital sex is more common among adolescents in developed countries, and among men, premarital experience was nearly universal – 95 percent.

References

Amarasinghe, S.W. 2002. *The Commercial Sexual Exploitation of Children: A Rapid Assessment – Sri Lanka*. International Labour Office, Geneva.

Anand, A. 1993. India: Introduction of Sex Education. *Lancet*, Vol. 341, No: 8854, pp. 1207.

Attanayake, C. 2001. The Terminal Survey Report on Knowledge, Attitudes and Practices of Secondary School Students in Sri Lanka on Reproductive Health Education and Reproductive Issues, UNFPA, Colombo.

Ban, D.J., J. Kim and W.I. De Silva. 2003. Induced Abortion in Sri Lanka: Who goes to providers for Pregnancy Termination? *Journal of Biosocial Science* 34: 303–15.

Basnayake, S. 1996. *Sri Lankan Youth: Survey on Reproductive Health Knowledge, Attitudes and Practices*. Family Planning Association of Sri Lanka, Colombo.

Bongaarts, J. and B. Cohen. 1998. Introduction and Overview. *Studies in Family Planning* 29(2): 99–105.

Caldwell, J.C., I. Gajanayake, B. Caldwell and P. Caldwell. 1989. Is Marriage Delay a Multiphasic Response to Pressures for Fertility Decline? The Case of Sri Lanka. *Journal of Marriage and Family* 51: 337–51.

De Silva, W.I. 1998. "Socio-economic Changes and Adolescent Issues in the Asian and Pacific Region" in *Report and Recommendations of the Expert Group Meeting on Adolescents: Implications of Population Trends, Environment and Development*. Asian Population Studies Series No. 149, United Nations, New York, 46–81.

——. 1997. The Ireland of Asia: Trends in Marriage Timing in Sri Lanka. *Asia-Pacific Population Journal* 12(2): 3–24.

De Silva, W.I., R.A. Dayananda and N.W.P.D.B.N. Perera. 2006. Contraceptive Behaviour of Abortion Seekers in Sri Lanka. *Asian Population Studies* 2(1): 3–418.

De Silva, W.I., A. Somanathan and V. Eriyagama. 2003. *Adolescent and Youth Reproductive Health in Sri Lanka: Status, Issues, Policies and Programs.* POLICY Project, Future Group International, Washington D.C.

Elliot, G.R. and S.S. Feldman. 1990. *At the Threshold: The Developing Adolescent*. Harvard University Press, Cambridge, Massachusetts.

Hettiarachchy, T. and S. Schensul. 2001. The Risks of Pregnancy and the Consequences among Young Unmarried Women Working in a Free Trade Zone in Sri Lanka. *Asia-Pacific Population Journal* 16(2): 125–40.

Jejeebhoy, S.J. 1996. *Adolescent Sexual and Reproductive Behaviour: A Review of the Evidence from India.* International Centre for Research on Women (ICRW), Washington D.C.

Silva, K.T., C. Sivayoganathan and S. Schensul. 1998. Peer Culture and the Social Context of Love and Sex in a Sample of University Students in Sri Lanka. *Sri Lanka Journal of Social Sciences* 21(1 and 2): 59–82.

Silva, K.T., S.L. Schensul, J.J. Schensul, B. Nastasi, M.W.A. De Silva, C. Sivayoganathan, P. Rathnayake, P. Wedsinghe, J. Lewis, M. Eisenberg and H. Aponso. 1997. *Youth and Sexual Risk in Sri Lanka*. Women and AIDS Research Program, ICRW, Washington D.C.

UNICEF. 2004. *National Survey on Emerging Issues among Adolescents in Sri Lanka*. UNICEF, Colombo.

United Nations. 2001. *Adolescent Reproductive Health in the Asian and Pacific Region*. Asian Population Studies, Series No. 156, New York.

——. 1989. *Adolescent Reproductive Behaviour: Evidence from Developing Countries.* United Nations, New York.

World Health Organization (WHO). 1975. *Pregnancies and Abortion in Adolescence: Report of a WHO Meeting*. Technical Report Series 583, World Health Organization, Geneva.

Section V

Health Care and HIV/AIDS

CHAPTER 18

HIV/AIDS Knowledge of Hmong Youth in Thailand

A Gendered Tale of the Tapes

Romeo Arca, Jr. and Sona Sethi

The Hmong people of northern Thailand are ethnic minorities affected by HIV/AIDS at much higher rates than any other group (UNESCO, 2005). This could be attributed to low educational status, poverty, increased mobility, and non-traditional drug use (UNESCO, 2005). The HIV prevalence among this group is estimated to be 2.22 per cent for women and 2.04 per cent for men (Beyrer et al., 1997). In a culture where polygamy or sexual promiscuity among men is an accepted practice, it may be easy to pinpoint what makes this hill tribe population vulnerable to HIV/AIDS. But apart from traditional sexual practices, the link may be found in the level of awareness and perceptions of risk among this group.

To shed light on the matter, a baseline survey was conducted for the Planned Parenthood Federation of America-International supported project—"Mainstreaming STI/HIV and Family Planning Services for the Hmong Population", implemented by the Planned Parenthood Association of Thailand. The survey was conducted from October to December 2005. Data are culled from interviews in 13 Hmong communities in Chiang Mai, a province in northern Thailand located 696 km from the capital city of Bangkok. Information was gathered from a sample population of 300 households obtained through proportional sampling method. Findings of the baseline were intended to inform the planning and implementation of the project.

This paper relies upon a subset of data from the baseline survey. The analysis focussed on information provided by 91 youth respondents aged 15–24 years old which included 55 male and 36 female, almost a third or 30 per cent of the total baseline sample population. The majority of the youth were unmarried. More than two-thirds (71–75% respectively) of the male youth respondents were between 20–24 years old and had completed junior or senior high school, while approximately half of the female youth were between 15–19 years old and had completed junior or senior high school (Table 1).

Table 1

Profile of Youth Respondents

Description	Male (n=55)	Female (n=36)
Age		
15–19	16 (29%)	19 (53%)
20–24	39 (71%)	17 (47%)
Marital Status		
Married	24 (44%)	11 (31%)
Unmarried	31 (56%)	25 (69%)
Mean age of marriage	18 years	18 years
Education		
Did not complete primary school	2 (4%)	6 (17%)
Completed primary school	12 (21%)	12 (33%)
Completed junior high school	19 (35%)	14 (40%)
Completed senior high school or above	22 (40%)	4 (10%)

In addition, three-fourths (75%) of the youth respondents were Buddhists while the rest were Christians or from other religions.

Objective of the Study

To determine the knowledge level of male and female Hmong youth regarding HIV/AIDS.

Discussion

This paper compares the level of knowledge between Hmong male and female youth in northern Thailand regarding modes of HIV/AIDS transmission and prevention, and condom. Some recommendations are put forward in light of the conclusion.

Knowledge on Modes of HIV/AIDS Transmission

Living in a country with one of the highest rates of HIV infection, almost every Thai knows or has heard about AIDS. But when it comes to the mode of transmission, many people including those in hill tribe communities are still not fully aware of the bare facts. For this analysis, respondents were classified as follows: (i) knows one mode of transmission; (ii) knows two modes; (iii) knows three modes; (iv) complete knowledge (knows all four modes: sexual, blood transfusion, needle sharing, mother-to-child). Data showed that more male youth (63%) had complete knowledge about transmission compared to female youth (46%) but the difference is offset by the fact that twice the number of male youth (19%) had knowledge on only one mode of transmission compared to female youth (9%); and less number of male youth (19%) knew about 2–3 modes of transmission compared to female youth (46%). Figure 1 elaborates this.

With more male youth knowing only one correct mode of transmission, it is not surprising that there were also more male youth who had incorrect notions about modes of transmission such as through kissing, hugging, eating from the same utensils or mosquito bites as indicated in Table 2. Further, the proportion of female youths who have correct knowledge of transmission modes was greater than that of the male youth.

Figure 1

Knowledge on Number of Correct Modes of HIV/AIDS Transmission (%)

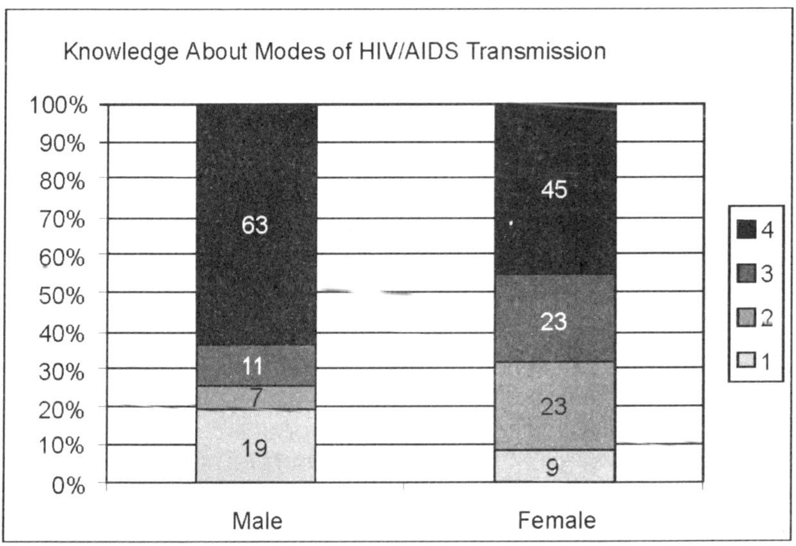

Table 2

Knowledge on HIV/AIDS modes of Transmission (%)

Transmission of HIV/AIDS	*Married*		*Unmarried*	
	Male (%)	*Female (%)*	*Male (%)*	*Female (%)*
Sexual contact	100.0	100.0	100.0	100.0
Sharing syringe/ needle	82.2	100.0	76.9	92.0
Mother-to-child	56.5	72.7	62.5	88.0
Blood transfusion	52.2	63.6	53.9	72.0
Kissing/hugging sharing utensils	4.4	9.1	15.4	4.0
Mosquito bites	4.4	0.0	11.5	12.0

Based on the foregoing data, there was still a significant proportion of Hmong youth who did not know correctly the routes of HIV/AIDS infection and this was clearly so for the male youth.

Knowledge About Condom

With condom (and abstinence) as the only available means of protection against HIV/AIDS for sexually active people, correct knowledge about this matter is critical. In this study, the respondents' knowledge about condom was measured based upon three important factors: having seen an actual condom, knowledge about its efficacy, and knowledge on proper use. Their level of knowledge was categorized as follows:

No knowledge (No Know)	had never seen a condom
	believes that a condom can be used more than once
	believes that condom is not an effective protection against HIV/AIDS
Low knowledge (Low Know)	1 correct response
Moderate knowledge (Mod Know)	2–3 correct responses
High Knowledge (High Know)	had seen a condom
	believes that a condom cannot be used more than once
	believes that condom is an effective protection against HIV/AIDS

Despite the condom being a male gadget, the study showed that proportionally more female youth (57%) had high knowledge about condom compared to males (30%). This may be a sign that these female

Figure 2

Knowledge About Condom

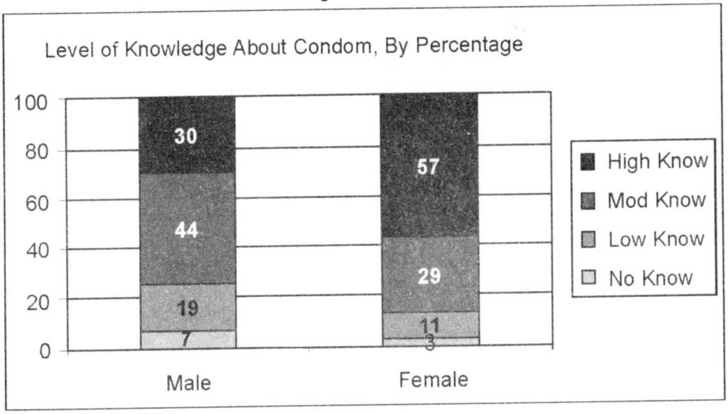

youth are living up to the common view in Thai society that contraception (including the use of condom) is the woman's responsibility (Saiprasert and Ford, 1993). In the same vein, only 3 per cent female youth compared to 7 per cent male youth had no knowledge of condom. Figure 2 shows further details.

When broken down into single pieces of information, the females consistently showed superior knowledge over their male counterparts as Table 3 manifests:

Table 3

Beliefs About Condom

Statement	*Agree*		*Disagree*		*Don't know*	
	Male (%)	*Female (%)*	*Male (%)*	*Female (%)*	*Male (%)*	*Female (%)*
Condom is an effective protection against HIV/AIDS	45	76	22	9	33	15
Condoms can be used more than once	11	0	74	94	15	6

Clearly, more than half of the male youth were still not yet convinced or may not have heard that condom is an effective protection, when used correctly, against HIV/AIDS. It is hard to imagine how the 11 per cent of male youth 'recycle' their condoms after the first use. An almost equal proportion of male (86%) and female (84%) youth had seen a condom.

Knowledge About Prevention

Knowledge about prevention of HIV is important not only for protecting oneself or one's partner but also in relating with those living with the virus. To measure the respondents' knowledge about this subject, they were asked to spontaneously enumerate ways of protecting themselves. These four important ways as abbreviated in Figure 3 are:

Abstinence	—	Abstaining from sex
Use condom	—	By using condom
One partner	—	Having only one sex partner
Avoid com sex	—	Avoid sex with commercial sex workers

An examination of this matter among the youth respondents revealed a high degree of vulnerability for male Hmong youth who were apparently not fully aware of the means of prevention. By looking at the respondents' knowledge about ways of prevention, some interesting information may be deduced. Figure 3 reveals the percentage of respondents who mentioned the four ways of prevention:

Figure 3

Knowledge About HIV Prevention (%)

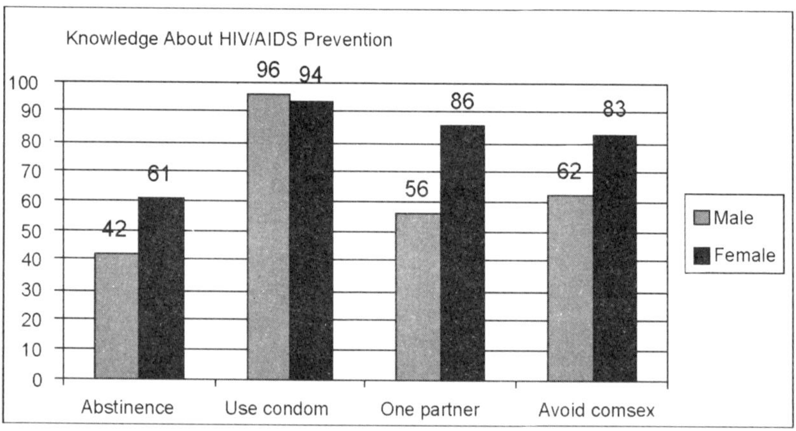

It is interesting to note that the use of condom was almost universally accepted by both male and female Hmong youth though a few were still not aware of its protective value. While abstaining from sex is an effective means of protecting oneself, the majority of male youth believed that it will not work, probably due to the perceived propensity of their peers to engage in sexual activity. Hence, less than half of the males cited it as a means of protection. In this case, abstinence had more believers among the females.

The next two factors present some gender-related issues pertinent to the Hmong culture. As Figure 3 illustrates, an almost equal number of female youth thought that having only one sex partner and avoiding sex with commercial sex workers are the most effective ways of protection next to condom. As mentioned in the beginning, the Hmong people accept polygamy as a practice and their culture allows a man to freely snatch any woman he fancies and as many as he likes. It is therefore not uncommon to see Hmong men with two or three wives (or just plain partners) at one time. By suggesting that their men stick to only one partner and not patronize commercial sex in order to avoid HIV, the female Hmong youth were subtly expressing a desire to raise the value of women. It could be interpreted as a subconscious effort to liberate Hmong women from being merely sex objects that the men collect. At the same time, it could be taken as a rejection of the practice of polygamy. Interestingly, the female youth had some allies among the ranks of males because more than half of the male youth also mentioned having only one partner as a means of protection. Somehow, this reflects the declining popularity of multiple sex partnerships among the current generation of Hmong youth. In addition, a significant number of male youth also believed that avoiding commercial sex can protect them from HIV infection which is a good sign for this vulnerable group.

Conclusion and Recommendations

The findings of the study suggest that in general, the female Hmong youth are more knowledgeable about HIV/AIDS than their male counterparts. Among others, the study reveals that:

1. Regarding transmission, more male than female youth knew correctly the four modes of infection, however, there were also more male youth who knew only one (sexual). In addition, more male than female youth had incorrect beliefs about the modes of transmission.
2. As for condom, the female youth have shown superior knowledge about its efficacy as a means of protection as well as its proper use.
3. While not all female youth demonstrated complete knowledge concerning prevention, there were still more females than males who understood the many ways of protecting oneself from HIV infection.

4. Finally, the study shows that the male Hmong youth were not fully armed with the knowledge and attitude needed to protect themselves and their partners against HIV/AIDS. The analysis exposes a high degree of vulnerability for this particular group.

Some practical and social factors may explain why the male youth appeared to have less knowledge on HIV/AIDS. Actual community experiences highlight the limited exposure of men to most Information Education and Communication (IEC) activities since adult men prioritize work more than these events. In the case of boys, they would be most likely in schools because they get first priority over girls for education. Hence, it is mostly the women or girls who are seen by health educators, talk to health providers, and therefore get more education on health issues including HIV/AIDS. It may also be a reflection of the perceived gender roles, where the baseline study showed that taking care of women's health, contraception, and treatment for sexual and reproductive health problems are the woman's responsibility (PPFA-International, 2006). Finally, the men's general aversion for condom use may also be a factor in not gaining enough knowledge about its use or confidence about its efficacy.

In light of these findings, the following recommendations are put forward:

1. Educate Hmong youth, both male and female, about the correct modes of transmission and clarify myths that are still prevalent.
2. Emphasize proper condom use as well as its protective value.
3. In developing IEC messages on HIV/AIDS for the Hmong youth, focus on the concept of risks and vulnerability and propose messages to overcome those risks.
4. Identify more gender issues pertinent to this cultural group in relation to condom use and sexual relationships and develop relevant behaviour change communication programmes.
5. Finally, reach out to the men. Go where the men are and deal with their myths, fears, doubts, and concept of pleasure.

Acknowledgements

The authors wish to thank the following for their important contributions to the development of this paper: Dr Chupensri Wongbuddha of Chiang Mai University Faculty of Science for her technical advice in the conduct of the baseline survey; Ms. Tassanee Srimongkol, former Director of the Planned Parenthood Association of Thailand (PPAT) Northern Office for her leadership in the project and the PPAT staff who diligently worked on the survey; and the staff of PPFA-International in Bangkok and New York for their technical and administrative support. Finally, the authors acknowledge the participation of Hmong youths in this study from whom this paper derives its substance and inspiration.

References

Beyrer, et al. 1997. Widely Varying HIV Prevalence and Risk Behaviours among the Ethnic Minority Peoples of Northern Thailand. AIDS CARE 9: 4, 427–39.

Planned Parenthood Federation of America-International. 2006. Baseline Survey of the Knowledge, Attitude and Practices Concerning Reproductive Health and Gender Perspectives of Men and Women in Selected Communities of Chiang Mai Province. Final Report, Bangkok, Thailand.

Saiprasert, S. and N. Ford. 1993. *Qualitative Methods for Population and Health Research.* Mahidol University, Nakhon Pathom, Thailand.

UNESCO. 2005. Review of Socio-Cultural Research on HIV/AIDS in Greater Mekong Subregion, HIV/AIDS Co-ordination and School Health Unit, UNESCO, Bangkok.

CHAPTER 19

Level of Prejudices Among Health Care Providers

Hemlata Sadhwani and M.E. Khan

AIDS is a disease long associated with fear. No other disease in recent history has generated so much concern, fear, anxiety, and prejudice, both among health care personnel and the general public, as has HIV/AIDS. Medical science till date has not been able to contain the virus, and HIV elicits a strong emotional response in most health care workers (HCWs) (Bhatnagar and Bhalwar, 2005).

Health care professionals, particularly those who frequently encounter HIV-positive people, can be insensitive to their patients' concerns. They are not always knowledgeable about appropriate procedures for maintaining patients' confidentiality (Herek and Capitanio, 1998). People expect health care providers to know all about the disease, but often the providers themselves experience the same fear, ignorance and prejudice as the general public. Knowledge and attitude of health care providers regarding HIV/AIDS still leaves much to be desired and even after almost two decades of sustained efforts to educate them, most continue to harbour a morbid fear of the disease.

"There is an almost hysterical kind of fear…at all levels, starting from the humblest, the sweeper or the ward boy, up to the heads of departments, which makes them pathologically scared of having to deal with an HIV-positive patient. Wherever they have an HIV patient, the responses are shameful." (UNAIDS, 2001, as cited by AVERT).

This reaction in turn creates anxiety and fear among many people living with HIV and AIDS. Many HIV-positive people keep their sero status secret. It is not surprising that among a majority of HIV positive people, AIDS-related fear and anxiety, and at times denial of their HIV status can be traced to their traumatic experiences in health care settings.

Providers' attitudes about HIV/AIDS are an important dimension in the delivery of quality health care services to persons with HIV/AIDS (Yadida et al., 1996; Heald, 1998). Timely treatment not only reduces suffering, improves health and productivity, but also benefits the individual and society (Chesney and Smith, 1999). However, accessing health care can be a challenge for people who are HIV positive, because the health care system itself is often a source of stigma. This may be expressed in a lesser standard of medical care or, in the worst instances, in a complete denial of treatment—often as a result of a misplaced fear of infection. Examples of the types of stigma and discrimination faced by HIV-positive people in health care setting are:

- excuses and explanations about why a person cannot be admitted to a hospital (without admission being directly refused);
- isolation, name-tagging or other methods of identifying someone as HIV-positive;
- breaches of confidentiality, negative attitudes of staff, use of negative verbal and body language by health care workers; conditional treatment (e.g., patients will only be treated if they sign up for medical trials);
- shunting of patients between wards, doctors or hospitals; and restricted access to hospital facilities (World AIDS Day Campaign on Stigma and Discrimination, 2002).

Studies from various parts of the world have brought out the discriminatory and negligent attitude of health care providers towards HIV-positive people. A survey of 1,000 physicians, nurses and midwives in four states of Nigeria, found that one in 10 doctors and nurses had refused to care for an HIV/AIDS patient or had denied HIV/AIDS patients admission to a hospital. Almost 40 per cent thought a person's appearance betrayed his or her HIV-positive status, and 20 per cent felt that people living with HIV/AIDS had behaved immorally and deserved their fate (as cited by AVERT). A study by AVERT carried out in India in 2006 found that 25 per cent of people living with HIV in India had been refused medical treatment on the basis of their HIV-positive status (Fredrikson and Kanabus, undated).

Lack of confidentiality has been repeatedly mentioned as a particular problem in health care settings. When surveyed recently, 29 per cent of persons living with HIV/AIDS in India, 38 per cent in Indonesia, and over 40 per cent in Thailand said their HIV-positive status had been revealed to someone else without their consent (As cited by AVERT). There are also reports of signs in some hospitals, where signs have been placed near people living with HIV/AIDS with words such as 'HIV-positive' and 'AIDS' written on them (ibid.).

The fear or exposure to HIV as a result of lack of protective equipment was an important source of stigma. There was also the frustration at not having medicines for treating HIV/AIDS patients, who therefore were seen as 'doomed' to die (ibid.).

However, the fear of exposure to the disease and contracting it is not the only factor fuelling stigma. Health care providers also may fear stigmatization of themselves because of their work with HIV-positive patients (Durham, 1994). Caregivers, whether professionals or volunteers, risk what Goffman (1963) called 'courtesy stigma', in which they are stigmatized as a result of their association with the diseases, in this case HIV/AIDS, and people living with the disease. That stigma may influence their willingness to work with people with HIV or may make their work more difficult (Snyder et al., 1999).

While several studies exist on stigma and discrimination against HIV-positive people by health care providers, and instruments have also been developed to measure general attitudes of health care providers and the general public towards HIV/AIDS, very few attempt has been made in India to develop a standardized instrument to measure the level of prejudices among the health care providers. The study measures the level of prejudice against HIV-positive people among health care providers in India. For the study a standardized scale to measure the prejudices among the health care provider towards the People Living with HIV/AIDS (PLHAs) was developed.

Objectives

The objective of the present study was to assess the level of prejudice among doctors and paramedics and to standardize the prejudice scale specially developed for this purpose.

Methods

The present study was carried out in Vadodara district, Gujarat. Fifty doctors, including both general physicians and specialists from the fields of gynecology, skin and venereal diseases, and surgery were selected. General physicians were selected as they are the first point of contact for treatment of common ailments. The rationale for selecting specialists was that the likelihood of their patients being tested for HIV when they come for antenatal care, treatment of sexually transmitted infections, or invasive surgical procedures respectively.

Besides doctors, 58 paramedics and 25 lab-technicians were interviewed from private and government facilities.

The doctors were selected from the directory of the Indian Medical Association. On the basis of their designation and specialization, a list of 65 doctors including their names and contact details was prepared. All the 65 doctors listed were contacted and briefed about the study, and those who gave their consent were interviewed. Further, all those who gave their consent were assured about the confidentiality of the information provided by them and were given the choice to terminate the interview at any point. Out of sixty-five doctors who were contacted, fifty gave their consent to participate in the study.

Nurses and ward boys of the selected clinics and hospitals were approached and interviewed with prior permission of the doctors or the hospital in-charge they worked for.

For the selection of the laboratory technicians, a list of the diagnostic laboratories in Vadodara was prepared with the help of the telephone directory. The in-charge of the laboratories were contacted and briefed about the study, and the lab-technicians suggested by them were interviewed.

Information was collected by four well-trained female investigators who were final year students of Master Degree in Psychology. They made at least two visits to each study participant to collect all the relevant information. The data collection was spread over two months (August and September, 2005).

Prejudice Scale

The study tool had three sections—(a) background information of the respondents and training received in HIV/AIDS, (b) structured questions and statements to measure the level of knowledge about HIV/AIDS, (c) a battery of 46 statements to measure prejudices,.

To measure the level of prejudices, a five-point Likert scale of 'strongly agree' to 'strongly disagree' was developed. Subjects were asked to express agreement or disagreement on a five-point scale. Each degree of agreement was given a numerical value from 1 to 5 and thereby allowing a total numerical value to be calculated from all the responses.

Prior to the actual interview the scale was prepared on the basis of the views of doctors and paramedics reflecting their attitude towards HIV/AIDS. Around 10–15 doctors and paramedics were visited. These doctors and paramedics were other than those selected for the actual interview. During the visits they were asked about their opinion towards people living with HIV/AIDS (PLHA), both as service providers and as members of society, i.e., how they view people living with HIV/AIDS, whether or not they should be provided services, where and what type of care and support should be provided to them. Based on their responses forty-six statements were formed for inclusion in the prejudices scale. These statements were grouped into three aspects namely:

- *Treatment/service* example—I am comfortable in treating PLHAs, My reputation will be at stake if I treat HIV/AIDS patient;
- *Family* example—PLHAs should be allowed to lead a normal life; Allowing HIV+ to live in a family could be dangerous for other family members; and
- *Social Interaction* example—I feel comfortable sitting and dinning with PLHAs; I feel aversion when I come across PLHAs, because I feel they have low moral values.

Since the scale was for health providers, there were more statements related to treatment/service provision than on family and community. Positive and negative statements were prepared and arranged in a random order to control habituation error and error of expectancy. 'Strongly agree' and 'agree' in a positive statement were considered as indication that the respondent does not have any prejudice for the PLHAs; whereas responses 'undecided' and 'no response' were considered as indicating a possibility of moderate prejudice because respondents are not sure of their own view; since 'disagree' and 'strongly disagree' show prejudice, responses in these two were categorized into high prejudice. The reverse was true in the case of negative statements, where responses with 'disagree' and 'strongly disagree' were categorized as 'low' prejudice and responses with 'strongly agree' and agree as high prejudices and undecided as moderate prejudice (See Annexure).

On completion of the scale it was reviewed by the psychologist to assess whether the statements were framed following the Likert Scale procedure to measure prejudices among the health care provider. After their review it was once again given to various experts in the fields of sociology, home science, preventive and social medicine, and social work to assess whether the statements were appropriate to measure the prejudices of the health care providers towards people living with HIV/AIDS. Based on their comments and suggestions the statements were reframed. Finally, the scale was administered on 133 respondents (doctors and paramedics) for its reliability and validity test.

Reliability and Validity of the Scale

Based on the responses elicited from 133 respondents, item analysis was carried out to assess whether the statements were appropriate to measure level of prejudice. For this, the mean value of all the 46 items for each of the 133 respondents (doctors and paramedics) was considered to be indicative of differential level of prejudice prevalent among the respondents. To assess whether there is a significant difference on each of the items, two extreme groups of first quartile (mean 2.24) and third quartile (mean 2.81) was derived on the basis of the mean scores. If there is a significant difference between the first and the third quartile on the given item then the item is considered to be valid, else it is not valid. Thus, respondents with mean value ranging from 1.31 to 2.24 were coded as '1', i.e., first quartile group/low prejudice group, 2.24–2.81 were coded as '2' as median group/moderate prejudice group and respondents with mean value ranging from 2.82 to 3.38 were coded '3', i.e., third quartile group/high prejudice group.

Subsequently, a t-test was carried out to find the difference between first and the third quartile groups on each of the 46 items. It was assumed that there is equal variance among the higher and the lower group. All the significant items ($p=0.05$) were retained and the rest were eliminated. Out of 46 items, item number 16, 29, 31, 37, 38, 40, 41 and 46 were found to be insignificant and were eliminated from the scale. Thus, the standardized scale consisted of 38 items.

The reliability analysis on the same data yielded Cronbach's Alpha Coefficient to be 0.88. The intrinsic validity based on Cronbach's Alpha Coefficient was 0.94.

Findings

Background of the Health Care Providers

The Table 1 reveals that majority of the doctors (58%) were 40 or more years of age, in contrast to two-thirds of the paramedics aged 40 years or less. The mean age of the doctors was 44 years and that of paramedics was 36 years. Majority (74%) of the doctors interviewed were male, while majority (82%) of the paramedics interviewed were female. With regard to the marital status, majority of the doctors (88%) and paramedics (66%) were married. However, about 31 per cent of the paramedics were unmarried.

On an average, doctors had 17 years of work experience while paramedics had approximately 14 to 15 years of work experience. Majority of the doctors (78%) and paramedics (59%) worked in private clinics or hospitals. However, about 41 per cent of the paramedics worked with the public health institutions.

Table 1

Background Characteristics of the Health Care Providers (Percentages)

Characteristics	*Doctors*	*Paramedics**	*All*
Age (in Years)			
21–30	6.0	41	27.8
31–40	36.0	33.7	34.6
41–50	34.0	14.5	21.8
51 and above	24.0	7.2	13.5
Sex			
Male	74.0	18.1	39.1
Female	26.0	81.9	60.9
Marital status			
Married	88.0	66.3	74.4
Unmarried	10.0	31.3	23.3
Others (widow/divorces)	2.0	2.4	2.3
Professional experience (in years)			
1–5	8.0	39.8	27.8
6–10	20.0	14.5	16.5
11–15	22.0	19.3	20.3
16–20	22.0	10.8	15.0
21 and above	28.0	15.7	20.3
Type of work place			
Public	22.0	41.0	33.8
Private	78.0	59.0	66.2
Total doctors	50	83	133

*Paramedics include nurse, ward boys, health worker and lab. technicians.

Level of Prejudices

The basic objective of this study was to measure the level of prejudices among the health care providers. As mentioned earlier, prejudice has been measured at three levels—low, moderate and high prejudices. Table 2 presents levels of prejudice among the health care providers. Around half (48%) of all the health care providers (doctors and paramedics) had moderate level of prejudice and 25 per cent had high level of prejudice and rest (27%) had low level of prejudice towards people living with HIV/AIDS (PLHAs).

Table 2

Levels of Prejudice among the Health Care Providers (Horizontal Percentage)

Respondents	*Prejudices*			*Total*
	High	*Moderate*	*Low*	
All	24.8	48.1	27.1	133
Doctors	14.0	56.0	30.0	50
Paramedics*	31.3	43.4	25.3	83

* Paramedics include nurses, ward boys, health worker, and lab. technicians.

High level of prejudice was more among the paramedics (31%) than among doctors (14%). Further, among the paramedics, prejudice was much higher among the lab-technicians (40%) than among health workers (28%).

Taking high and moderate level of prejudices together against PLHAs, health care providers had prejudices related to treatment/service than on aspects related to family and social interaction (Table 3). Majority of the health care providers had moderate to high level of prejudices related to treatment/services (74%) than social interaction (66%) and family relationships (62%).

Whereas doctors had moderate to low level of prejudices, however about 14 per cent of them had high prejudices related to treatment/services and less per cent on other aspects. On the other hand, relatively larger percentage of paramedics had high prejudices on all the three dimensions.

Since the health care providers had high prejudices related to treatment/services, an attempt was made to see on what particular statements they had prejudices on. There were 23 statements related to treatment services. Of these 23 statements, a diagnosis test of positive HIV status in patients was found to be one of the major factors for high

Table 3

Respondents Level of Prejudice in Different Aspects of Concern (Horizontal Percentage)

Respondents	Prejudices			Total
	High	Moderate	Low	
All health care providers				
Treatment/service	22.6	51.1	26.3	
Social interaction	24.8	41.1	33.8	133
Family	20.3	41.4	38.3	
Doctors				
Treatment/service	14.0	52.0	34.0	
Social interaction	10.0	44.0	46.0	50
Family	8.0	52.0	40.0	
*Paramedics**				
Treatment/service	27.7	50.6	21.7	
Social interaction	33.7	39.8	26.5	83
Family	27.7	34.9	37.3	

*Paramedics include nurses, ward boys, health worker, and lab. Technicians.

prejudices. Ninety-two per cent of the doctors and 72 per cent of the paramedics strongly agreed to the statement that they would withdraw services to individuals the moment they are diagnosed as being HIV positive. In the words of one of the doctors:

> I never deal with HIV/AIDS patients, when they come for treatment I just refer them to other hospital.

Concern for one's 'reputation' was yet another major factor where prejudice was found to be relatively high among the doctors and paramedics. Majority (92%) of the doctors and around three-fifths (59%) of the paramedics strongly felt that their reputation would be at stake if they treat HIV/AIDS patients. But 'reputation' was perceived differently by doctors and paramedics. While doctors perceived 'reputation' as loss of inflow of patients, paramedics equated loss of reputation with loss of employment as a result of low patient turnover. As a doctor stated:

> My hospital's reputation will be at stake the moment people will come to know that HIV positive (people) are treated here.

One of the paramedics expressing his insecurity of losing his job said:

> If people come to know that I treat HIV positive people then nobody will come and avail services from me, they would avoid me.

Further, 72 per cent of the doctors agreed to the fact that HIV/AIDS is given undue importance by government and international agencies at the cost of other serious life-threatening diseases. About 68 per cent of the doctors were also of the opinion that they have the right to demand high fees from HIV/AIDS patients. One of the doctors explained the reason why HIV/AIDS patients should be charged more money for treatment:

> If you see the cost of maintenance of the instruments, equipment once used (for HIV-positive patients) are to be disposed off and care of HIV/AIDS patients turns out to be very expensive compared to the cost of treatment of any other common disease. So to make-up this loss it is fair to charge high fees from such cases (HIV-positive patients).

However, a substantial proportion of the doctors also had a sympathetic view of people with HIV/AIDS, i.e., they had very low or no prejudices towards them. About 68 per cent of the doctors agreed that they feel bad and helpless when they come across PLHAs and another 60 per cent of them agreed that they dislike the idea of people dying of AIDS. One of the doctors voiced saying:

> It is our duty to treat the patients equally, but we cannot do anything for PLHAs, it is really bad to see them dying.

Other than treatment/services, doctors and paramedics also had strong prejudice on aspects related to family and social interaction. Ninety per cent of the doctors and 64 per cent of the paramedics believed that allowing HIV-positive people live in the family could be dangerous for other family members; another 88 per cent of the doctors and 66 per cent of the paramedics were of the view that PLHAs should be isolated. Further, on the aspect related to social interaction, majority felt that a person identified as HIV should be terminated from his/her job (94% doctors; 80% paramedics); HIV positive should not be allowed to continue his/her work for the safety of the other co-workers (86% doctors; 68% paramedics). Majority of the respondents also felt aversion for HIV-positive people because they felt that such people had low moral values (86% doctors; 70% paramedics).

Prejudices and Knowledge about HIV/AIDS

To assess provider's knowledge about HIV/AIDS, they were asked what is HIV and AIDS, three most common cause of HIV infection, gap between getting infected with HIV and getting AIDS, difference between HIV infection and AIDS, preventive measures against HIV infection, symptoms that indicates person having AIDS, condom as preventive measure against HIV/AIDS and that HIV/AIDS is curable or not. In order to know whether providers (doctors and paramedics) had correct knowledge about HIV/AIDS each of the questions mentioned was scored as '1' as having correct knowledge and '0' as having incorrect knowledge. In case of open ended question, if the providers had given two correct answer then they were given the score of 2, if five correct answer then they were given the score of 5 and so on. Based on the correct answer a total score was developed which ranged from 1 to 21. All the respondents with score less than 25 per cent (first quartile) was grouped as those with poor knowledge, 26–74 per cent as those with average knowledge and those above 75 per cent (fourth quartile) were considered to be having good or high knowledge (See Annexure 4).

Based on these groups, the data is presented in Figure 1. The figure depicts that only 11 per cent of the providers had very good knowledge about HIV/AIDS, majority (59%) had average knowledge

Figure 1

Level of Knowledge about HIV/AIDS

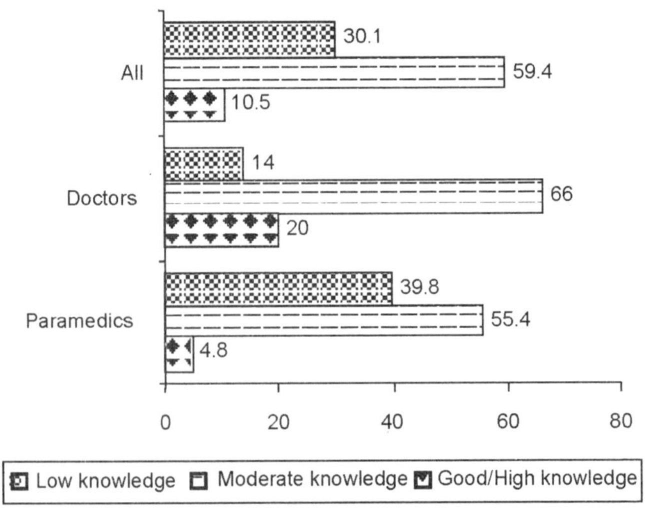

and the rest 30 per cent had very poor knowledge. The level of knowledge remained more or less the same among doctors and paramedics. Only 14 per cent of the total doctors answered correctly on almost all the questions related to HIV/AIDS. As expected, the level of knowledge was found to be poor among the paramedics as two-fifths of them had poor knowledge about it. Among paramedics the knowledge was again found to be very poor among the lab. technicians (60%) than nurse/ward boys (31%).

Table 4 shows a negative association between correct knowledge of HIV/AIDS and prejudices against PLHAs. As the level of knowledge about HIV/AIDS decreases personal prejudices increases among the health care providers. More than half (54%) of the providers with high prejudices had poor knowledge about HIV/AIDS (See Table 4). Measuring association between level of knowledge and level of prejudices was found to be highly significant (P<0.006).

Table 4

Health Care Providers Level of Prejudices by Level of Knowledge about HIV/AIDS

Level of knowledge	*Prejudices*		
	High	*Moderate*	*Low*
All*			
High	2 (6.1)	6 (9.4)	6 (16.7)
Moderate	13 (39.4)	45 (70.3)	21 (58.3)
Low	18 (54.5)	13 (20.3)	9 (25.0)
Total Providers	33	64	36

* Pearson Chi-square—significant at 0.006.

Prejudices and Training on HIV/AIDS

Figure 2, presents the percentage of providers who had attended any training on HIV/AIDS. As can be seen from Figure 2, only 29 per cent of the total providers had received any training on HIV/AIDS. More or less equal percentage of the doctors (30%) and paramedics (29%) had received training related to HIV/AIDS through workshops. In case of doctors, it needs to be mentioned that doctors who had not received any training reported that HIV/AIDS was one of the topics taught as part of their curriculum, and that they had never considered it important to receive such training. Efforts were made to see if training is associated with prejudices, Chi-square test was used to find such an association.

Figure 2

Training on HIV/AIDS received by Health Care Providers

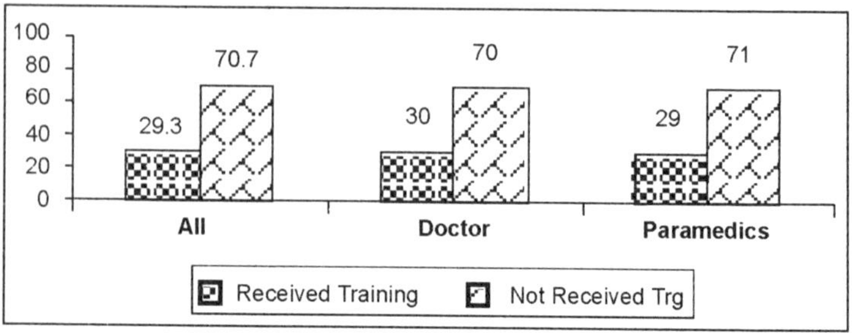

As can be see from Table 5, training had impact on prejudices (significant at 0.001 level). Almost all (94%) the providers with high prejudices were those who had not received training on HIV/AIDS.

Table 5

Providers Level of Prejudices by Training (Horizontal Percentage)

Respondents/Training Received	*Prejudices*		
	High	*Moderate*	*Low*
All*			
Received Training	6.1 (2)	31.3 (20)	47.2 (17)
Not received	93.9 (31)	68.8 (44)	52.8 (19)
Total	33	64	36

*Pearson Chi-square test—significant at 0.001.

Logit Regression Model

In order to assess which factors contribute to the prejudices, logit analysis was carried out. Before analysis the variables were recoded in binary. Prejudices was taken as dependent variable and coded as 0 for no or low prejudice and 1 for average and high prejudice. The independent variables included in the model were: sex of the providers (0 for male and 1 for female), training status in HIV/AIDS (0 if no training, 1 if had received training), work affiliation (0 for public, 1 for private), years of professional experience (0 for less than 4 years and 1 for more than 4 years of experience) and level of HIV/AIDS knowledge (0 if low or no knowledge, 1 if average or high knowledge). The results of the analysis are presented in Table 6.

Table 6

Logit Regression Analysis

Particulars	*df*	*Sig.*	*Exp(B) Odd Ratio*
Intercept (coeff.)	1	0.07	6.00
Female	1	0.041	2.67
Received Training	1	0.009	0.30
Private	1	0.328	1.64
4+ years of work experience	1	0.901	1.08
Average/Good knowledge about HIV/AIDS	1	0.005	0.17

As the table shows that the variables which are highly significant include sex of providers, training status and knowledge about HIV/AIDS. The odds ratios show that female providers have 2.7 times more prejudices compared to the male providers. It was also observed that the training does contribute to reduce the prejudice. The odds ratio indicates that the prejudice was 70 per cent less in the case of those providers who had undergone any training compared to those who had no training. It also illustrates that the providers who had knowledge about HIV/AIDS had 82 per cent less prejudices compared to those who had no or some knowledge.

Conclusion and Discussion

The study has contributed in developing a standardized scale for measuring prejudice of the health care providers against PLHA. Further, the study demonstrated that in majority of the cases the health care providers hold prejudice against PLHA. Indeed there is considerable variation in the level of prejudice among the providers—the doctors exhibit less strong prejudice than the paramedics. Among paramedics the lab technicians showed highest prejudice, may be because they do pathological testing including managing bloods test thus they perceive themselves more vulnerable to infection and hence develop stronger prejudice against PLHA. Interestingly, significantly more female providers were found holding prejudice against PLHA than males. Further, the providers having training and knowledge had relatively less prejudices against PLHA as compared to those who had no training and no or some knowledge about HIV/AIDS. Finally Logit regression model strongly suggests that training in HIV/AIDS contributes significantly in reducing prejudice against PLHA. Analysis also shows that increase in knowledge about the disease reduces prejudice against PLHA.

All these findings are significant and have programmatic implications. To reduce prejudice against PLHA and improve care and support for them, intervention to improve knowledge of providers (true for other also) should be taken seriously. Short training courses to the health providers about the disease and in the management and counselling of HIV/AIDS patients could go a long way in reducing their prejudice against PLHA and making the hospital environment more conducive for the HIV/AIDS patients for seeking care and treatment.

The paper has its own limitation because of small sample size and hence the findings though significant, should be taken as tentative. The prejudice scale developed here is useful and should be tested in other setting also to make it robust in Indian setting. The findings that female providers and those working in public sectors exhibits more prejudice against PLHA than male providers and those working in private clinic, need attention and further study to understand for the causes of such differentials and appropriate intervention to manage it.

Acknowledgements

This paper has been made possible due to the efforts of postgraduate trainees, namely Ms Grishma Simon, Ms Asmani, Ms Veena Gupta, Ms Kiran Lakhani, Ms Prajakta Sarpotdar and Ms Priyanka Kacker of the Department of Psychology, M.S. University, Vadodara. My sincere thanks to Dr Rashmin Sompura, Placement In-charge, Psychology Department, M.S. University, Vadodara, a great motivator for students, for helping us standardize the scale developed to measure prejudices. Last but not the least; I also thank Ms. Yamini Venkatachalam for her help in copy-editing.

References

Baron, R. and D. Byrne. 2003. *Social Psychology* (10th edition). Prentice Hall, New Delhi.

Bhatnagar, A. and R. Bhalwar. 2005. The Curse of HIV: How well prepared is our Paramedical Forces? *MJAFI*, 61: 230–3.

Chesney, M.A. and A.W. Smith. 1999. Critical Delays in HIV Testing and Care: The Potential Role of Stigma. *Am. Behavioural Scientist* 42(7): 1162–74.

Durham, J.D. 1994. The Changing HIV/AIDS Epidemic: Emerging Psychosocial Challenges for Nurses. *Nurs Clin North Am.* 29, 9–18.

Fredriksson, J. and A. Kanabus (eds.), (n.d.). 2006. HIV and AIDS Stigma and Discrimination. Retrieved on 13 November 2006, from http://www.avert.org/aidsstigma.htm

Goffman, E. 1963. *Stigma: Notes on the Management of Spoiled Identity.* Englewood Cliffs, Prentice Hall, New Jersey.

Heald, R.B. 1988. Physicians' Attitudes about AIDS Vary, MSMS Survey Reveals. *Mich Med* 87(12): 763–5.

Herek, G.M. and J.P. Capitanio. 1998. Symbolic Prejudice or Fear of Infection? A Functional Analysis of AIDS-related Stigma among Heterosexual Adults. *Basic App Soc Psychol.* 20(3): 230–41.

Link, B.G., J. Mirotznik and F.T. Cullen. 1991. The Effectiveness of Stigma Coping Orientations: Can Negative Consequences of Mental Illness Labeling be Avoided? *Journal of Health and Social Behaviour* 32: 302–20.

Snyder, M., A.M. Omoto and A.L. Crain. 1999. Punished for their Good Deeds: Stigmatization for AIDS Volunteers. *Am. Behav Scientist* 42(7): 1175–92.

UNAIDS. 2001. *India: HIV and AIDS-related Discrimination, Stigmatization and Denial*, cited in AVERT.org. Retrieved on 13 November 2006, from http://www.avert.org/aidsindia.htm

UNDP. 2006. *The Socio Economic Impact of HIV and AIDS in India*, cited in AVERT.org. Retrieved on 13 November 2006, from http://www.avert.org/aidsindia.htm

World AIDS Day Campaign on Stigma and Discrimination. 2002. Retrieved on 13 November 2006, from http://www.psgaidsinfo.org/2000wac.htm

Yadida, M.J., C.A. Berry and J.K. Barr. 1996. Changes in Physicians' Attitudes toward AIDS during Residency Training: A Longitudinal Study of Medical School Graduates. *Journal of Health and Social Behaviour* 37(2): 179–91.

Annexure

Categorization of the Statements Treatment and Services

Positive Statements:

- I am comfortable in treating PLHA
- A doctor with HIV/AIDS should be allowed to continue his practice
- A paramedic with HIV/AIDS should be allowed to continue delivering services to patients.
- I have no reservations in treating and assisting PLHAs.
- Lab-technicians with HIV/AIDS should be allowed to continue with their profession.
- As a health provider it is my duty to provide extra care and support to PLHA.
- I am happy that the government has started providing free ART (Anti Retroviral Therapy) to AIDS patients.
- I feel I am inadequately skilled when it comes to treating PLHAs.
- I respect a health provider more who works with and treats PLHAs than those who work with general patients.
- AIDS patients need at least the same, if not more, care and support as any other serious disease like kidney or cancer patients.
- With the invention of PEP and ART I feel more capable of handling PLHAs.

Negative Statements

- I feel more sympathetic towards leprosy patients than those who suffer from HIV/AIDS.
- Drug users who contract HIV/AIDS through infected needles should not get treatment.
- I would not treat a person if I came to know that he/she is HIV-positive.
- I will feel more satisfied to treat cancer patients than HIV-infected patients
- My reputation will be at stake if I treat HIV/AIDS patients.
- As a health provider I am duty bound to treat PLHA, but personally I do not like this.
- I feel helpless and sad when I come across PLHAs, as I think there is not much I can do for them.
- Doctors have a right to demand high fees from HIV/AIDS patients.
- I would prefer patients dying of cancer rather than AIDS.
- I feel afraid when I come across PLHA.
- To treat HIV patients there should be separate hospitals.

- In hospitals; waiting place, examination place and indoor ward of HIV patients should be separate from other general patients attending clinic/hospital.
- Health providers' refusal to treat HIV+ patients is justified if they do it for their own safety.
- In spite of PEP (post exposure prophylaxis) I will feel worried in treating or attending PLHAs.
- I am angry that HIV/AIDS is given importance by government and international agencies at the cost of other serious life threatening diseases.
- It is a matter of professional pride to be identified as AIDS specialist.
- I will treat PLHA only when I am sure of my safety.

Family Relation

Positive Statements

- PLHAs should be allowed to lead their normal family life.

Negative Statements

- Allowing HIV+ person to live in a family could be dangerous for other family members.
- The spouse of a HIV+ person should have legal right to divorce his/her partner.
- PLHA should be made to stay in an isolated place/home.
- PLHAs should be legally barred from marrying.
- Women living with HIV/AIDS should be discouraged from having children.

Social Interaction

Positive Statements

- I do not feel uncomfortable sitting and dinning with PLHAs.
- Calling all HIV patients immoral is wrong.
- I would not mind my child to study in school where HIV + children are also studying.
- I feel sad when I see an increasing number of people dying of AIDS.

Negative Statements

- Homosexuals are more to be blamed than heterosexuals, if they get HIV/AIDS.
- I have no sympathy for PLHAs who have contracted the infection due to multiple sex partners.

- I am more sympathetic to those HIV+ patients who are infected due to blood transfusion than to those who acquired HIV from multiple sexual partners or from homosexual relations.
- For the safety of co-workers HIV+ persons should not be allowed to continue their work.
- I feel aversion when I come across PLHA, because I feel they have low moral values.
- Any person identified with HIV/AIDS in an organization/institution should be terminated immediately.
- TB patients deserve more care and sympathy than HIV patient who suffer because of their immorality.

Chapter 20

High Risk Behaviour among Injecting Drug Users in Mumbai, India

Time to Upscale Interventions

Jayanta Kumar Basu

An estimated 13 million people worldwide inject drugs. Of those, 78 per cent live in developing and transitional countries (Gable et al., 2006). The sharing of contaminated injecting equipment has become a major driving force of the global AIDS pandemic, and is the primary mode of HIV transmission in many countries. In some cases, HIV is spreading rapidly from the injecting drug users to their partners through sexual transmission, and from injecting drug users and their partners to the newborns.

Injecting drug use contributes significantly to the spread of HIV epidemic in India. The sharing of injection equipment among drug users represents one of the highest risk of HIV transmission and the prevalence is higher among Injecting Drug Users (IDUs) than other groups. In India it was found to be above 10 per cent of drug users tested in sentinel sites in 2006 (Ambekar et al., 2008). Until recently, it was believed that injecting drug use was mostly confined to the north-eastern states of the country. However, a growing number of reports from the researchers, educators, social workers and civil society organizations mentioned that this practice was spreading even to the other States and metropolitan cities.

Injecting Drug Users are considered as one of the Most at Risk Population (MARP) groups for HIV/AIDS transmission and are one of the key target groups for any intervention programme under National AIDS Control Programme (NACP) third phase. They are most vulnerable groups due to high partner exchange, lack of knowledge about HIV transmission, low condom usage with commercial and non-regular sex partners, lack of exposure to intervention and relatively high needle sharing behaviour.

Injecting drug users are operationally defined here as:

> Men or women aged between 18–49 years identified to have injected addictive drugs in the past three months for intoxication without medical advice.

In spite of some existing interventions among IDUs in the State of Maharashtra, there is no significant positive impact over a period of time. In Mumbai, HIV prevalence rate among the IDUs was 20.40 in 2006 (HSS, NACO, 2006). The present paper attempts to analyse the gaps in the programme over a period of time and suggests up scaling of the intervention activities among the IDUs.

Methods and Materials

The necessary data for this paper was gathered from the second and third waves of Behavioural Surveillance Survey (BSS) in Maharashtra (BSS Wave II, 2004–05; BSS Wave III, 2005–06) conducted by Avert Society.[1] The conceptual premise of Behavioural Surveillance Survey (BSS) is based on the classical HIV and Sexually Transmitted Infection (STI) serologic surveillance methods that comprise of repeated cross-sectional sentinel surveys of key population groups that affect the spread of HIV. As the behaviour change is the best remedy and the only way to change the scenario of the current HIV pandemic, it is very important to understand the trends of behavioural indicators. While the Behavioural Surveillance Survey is basically evolved from the classical STI and HIV serologic surveillance, its methodology has been consolidated through the experience of conducting the survey in many developing countries during the past decade. The purpose of this survey is to systematically monitor trends in behavioural indicators over time that helps the programme implementers to understand the outcome of interventions being carried out among the select population sub-groups who are vulnerable to HIV/AIDS. Looking into the vulnerability and needs for systematic intervention, the information regarding the IDUs was gathered from the second and third waves of Behavioural Surveillance Survey in Mumbai during 2004–05 and 2005–06. Altogether 568 IDUs (298 in Wave II and 270 in Wave III) were contacted in both the waves at their cruising sites. The respondents were selected by two stage time location cluster sampling approach. Follow up qualitative study (4 In-depth Interviews) was also carried out to answer some of the 'whys' identified in the quantitative study. To conduct BSS among the injecting drug users, the core questionnaire on IDUs, designed by

Family Health International (FHI) was adopted and necessary socio-cultural adjuncts were added.

Data were entered using package with inbuilt features for inter-record checks and intra-record checks. All possible care was taken in terms of errors and inconsistencies to avoid any difficulty at the stage of data processing. Firstly, the accuracy of the data entry was checked by verifying a sample of filled-in questionnaires. Range and consistency checks were carried out later for values of all the variables. Data were also checked for 'missing items' prior to beginning of the data processing. The analysis was carried out using Statistical Package for Social Sciences (SPSS).

In addition to the calculation of core behavioural indicators, tables were generated for other key variables. Weighted analysis was carried out applying sampling weights to the data. Standardized weights were calculated based on the sampling probabilities generated from the cluster information sheets. To understand the significance of the difference from wave II and III, relevant statistical tests of significance (Z-test) were carried out.

Findings

Profile of the IDUs

The mean age of the injecting drug users surveyed in Wave III was 29 years, while the median age was 27 years. Whereas, mean and median age of those surveyed in Wave II was 30 years and 29 years respectively (Table 1). Literacy level is not that high among the IDUs as one-fourth of them are illiterates. The literacy rates remain the same in Wave II and Wave III. In both the waves only three-fourth were found to be literate. Footpath/railway station/bus terminus/other public places emerge as the major place of stay for the IDUs.

Table 1

Profile of the Injecting Drug Users (IDUs)

A. Age Distribution of IDUs (%)

Age Group	*Wave II*	*Wave III*
19 and less	3	14
20–25	28	30
25–35	48	36
36–45	16	17
46+	6	3

Cont'd...

Cont'd...

Mean (Years)	30	29
Median (Years)	29	27
Total N	298	270

B. Distribution of IDUs by Educational Attainment (%)

Education	*Wave II*	*Wave III*
Illiterate	27	26
Literate without formal education	8	19
Middle (5–7)	16	37
Secondary (8–10)	12	14
Higher Secondary (11–12)	6	3
Total N	298	270

C. Distribution of IDUs by Marital Status and Age at Marriage (%)

Marital Status	*Wave II*	*Wave III*
Ever married	39	40
Not married	61	60
Age at marriage (years)		
Less than 19 years	10	17
20–22	24	37
23–25	38	36
26+	27	10
Mean (in years)	24	22
Median (in years)	23	22
SD	6	2.6
Total N	115	270

D. Distribution of IDUs by Occupation (%)

Occupation	*Wave II*	*Wave III*
Casual labour	13	36
Garbage collection	0	29
Unemployed/not working	46	8
Petty business/small shop owner	6	7
Coolie	0	5
Pick pocketing	0	4
Transport worker/driver	2	3
Others	9	8
Total N	298	270

About one-fifth of the injecting drug users are working as casual labourers in Wave III, while about half were unemployed/not working in Wave II. Slightly more than one-fourth of them is garbage collectors. About one tenth each is unemployed/not working and having petty business in wave III.

All the injecting drug users were also asked whether they are married or living with a person with whom they have a sexual relationship. The findings indicate that about three fifths of the injecting drug users reported to be not married and living alone in both Waves II and III. Two fifths of the injecting drug users were ever married with mean as well as median age at marriage being 22 years. Less than one tenth of the married and unmarried injecting drug users reported to be living with (other) sex partner. This indicates that the proportion of IDUs who are married and living with spouse increased since Wave II (from 15% to 28%) while the proportion of single IDUs increased substantially since Wave II (from 19% to 61%).

Drug Use

The details pertaining to the usage of addictive drugs and injecting drug in terms of age at which started, duration of addiction, frequency of injecting drugs and the type of drugs injected were asked to the respondents.

It was observed that while only about one tenth reported to have started using the addictive drugs when they were less than 20 years in Wave II, more than half of the IDUs reported so in Wave III. The mean age at which the IDUs started injecting addictive drugs is 21 years with median being 19 years in Wave III, while the same for Wave II are 28 years and 29 years respectively. This indicates more and younger people started injecting drugs.

More than half of the injecting drug users interviewed reported to be using addictive drugs for more than 60 months (i.e., 5 years).

The frequency of injecting drugs in Wave III increased compared to Wave II as about four fifths of the IDUs reported to have injected drugs 1–3 times a day in the past one month in Wave III while about one-third reported so in Wave II. While one tenth reported to have injected drugs 4–6 times a week, less than one tenth reported to have injected more than 4 times a day in the past one month (Table 2).

Heroin without cocaine emerges as the major drug injected in the past one month.

Table 2

Distribution of IDUs by Frequency of Injecting Drugs in the Past One Month (%)

Frequency	*Wave II*	*Wave III*
Only once a month	4	1
2–3 times a month	15	1
2–3 times a week	21	2
4–6 times a week	13	10
About once a day	15	22
2–3 times a day	16	58
4 or more times a day	7	6
Total N	298	270

Needle Sharing Behaviour

The behaviour of IDUs in terms of needle sharing, cleaning, awareness of availability of new/unused needles/syringes and other sharing behaviour, usage of pre-filled syringes, squirting from one needle to another, sharing utensils for cleaning, sharing utensils for drawing drugs and the drug related treatment status were investigated.

The results indicate that about two fifths of the injecting drug users reported to have shared the equipment last time when they injected drugs. This proportion slightly increased since Wave II. More than one tenth of the IDUs reported to have shared the needle/syringe every time and most of the times. About one-third of the injecting drug users reported to have never shared the injecting equipment in the past one month. This proportion has increased in Wave III compared to Wave II.

About one-fifths of the IDUs reported that they clean every time, same proportion reported that they clean most of the times and slight less proportion was of those who reported that they clean half of the times and occasionally, the needle/syringe that was used previously. The proportion of IDUs reporting to clean the shared needles/syringes decreased in the Wave III compared to Wave II. Similarly, while none in Wave II reported to have never cleaned the shared needle, 7 per cent reported so in Wave III. About three fifths and majority of IDUs reported use of cold water to clean the used syringe/needle.

About two fifth and one-third each of the IDUs reported to have used unused/clean needles/syringes every time in Wave II and Wave III. Proportion of IDUs reporting to have used unused/clean needles/syringes most of the times almost increased 3 times in Wave III.

While about one tenth reported to have never used the unused/clean needles/syringes in the past one month before the survey in Wave II, only 4 per cent reported so in Wave III.

The above discussions indicate that though almost all the IDUs (99%) reported accessibility to the sterile needles, majority of them (74%) reported to have shared needles in high equipment sharing situation. This proportion increased since Wave II. Two fifths of the IDUs shared needles/syringe the last time in spite of reduction (69%) in sharing of needles/syringe in the last one month (Figure 1).

Figure 1

Needle/Syringe Sharing Behaviour

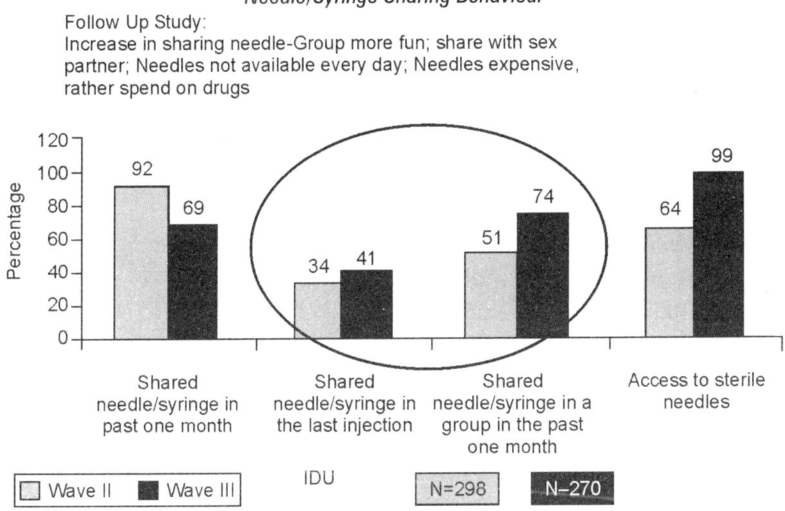

The foremost reason for sharing needles cited by the IDUs is that they like sharing their needles with a group of friends. Since injecting drugs is a group activity rather than an individual specific activity, sharing drugs and needles is perceived to be a pleasurable and enjoyable activity. With this feeling of camaraderie that leads them to share needles.

The follow up qualitative study reveals that many times injecting of drugs is followed by engaging in sexual activity and vice versa, as they are on a high after they end up sharing needles with their sex partner. According to one male IDU:

> I like having sex and doing drugs at the same time. My partner and I always have drugs after we have had sex. If I don't have extra needles then I share those (needles) with her.

The follow up qualitative study also reveals that one of the major reasons for needle sharing is non-availability of needles at the time of use. It was reported that even though they are fully aware of the implications and risk involved in needle sharing, and the fact that some NGOs even provide them with needles, the needles are made available to them only after 10–15 days. As they cannot always procure the needle at the time they are injecting themselves, they end up sharing needles.

Lack of financial resources to purchase needles was the other major reason cited for needle sharing. Spending money on the purchase of needles is not one of the chief priorities. They would rather spend money on purchasing drugs.

All the IDUs were asked whether they know the source of obtaining and whether they can obtain sterile, unused needles/syringes. All the IDUs reported that they are aware of a source where they can obtain sterile/unused needles/syringes. While about two-thirds reported access to new/unused needles/syringes in Wave II, almost all reported so in Wave III.

Sexual Behaviour

The results pertaining to the sexual behaviour of the injecting drug users in terms of number and type of heterosexual partners and condom usage pattern are discussed here.

Majority of the IDUs interviewed reported to be sexually active, as more than three-fourths and four fifths of them reported to have ever had sex in Wave II and Wave III respectively. More than one-fourth of the injecting drug users who ever had sex reported to have had first sex experience in their teen age with the mean and median age at first sex being 21 years in Wave II and 20 years in Wave III.

The injecting drug users were asked about the different types of sexual partners[2] they had in the past 12 months. About two fifths of the IDUs reported to have ever had commercial sex in the past 12 months while about 30 per cent each reported sex with regular and non-paying/non-commercial partners in Wave III (Figure 2). Though the proportion of IDUs reported having commercial sex and sex with non-paying/non-commercial partner have increased in Wave III compared to Wave II, the average number of commercial and non-paying/non-commercial partners has reduced. On an average, the IDUs reported to have had 3 commercial and 2 non-commercial partners in Wave II while the average number in Wave III is 2 commercial and 1 non-commercial partners.

Figure 2

Sexual Activity in Previous 12 Months by Type of Partners

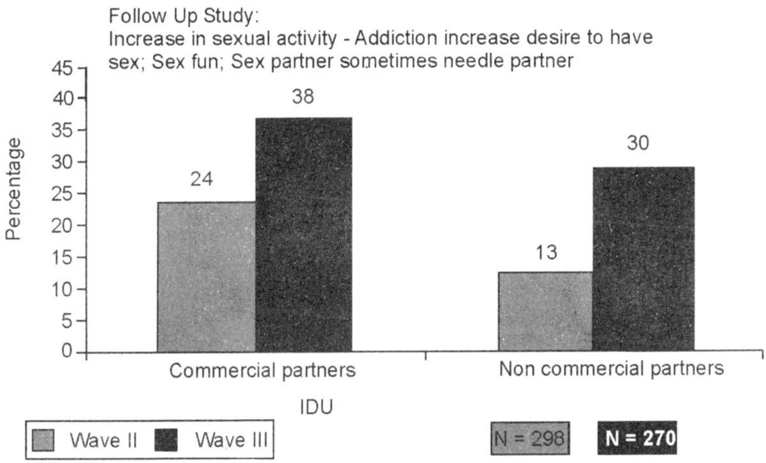

The significant increase in sex with commercial (24 to 38%) and non regular (non spouse)/non commercial (13 to 30%) partners across the waves indicate that along with needle sharing, sex with multiple partner is also common among the IDUs. The study among IDUs in Nepal also showed high level of multi-partner sex without condom (Shrestha and Sharma, 2006).

Condom Use

The extent of condom use at the last sex increased since Wave II across the three types of partners but a declining trend is observed in case of consistent use of condom (use of condom during every sexual act during last 12 months). More than four fifths of the IDUs used condom at the last sex (85%) but only one-third used condom consistently with their commercial partners. The same scenario is observed in case of their non-regular/non-commercial and regular partners (Figures 3 and 4). Decline in consistent condom use with the commercial [46% (95% CI 31.4, 60.2) to 34% (95% CI 31.5, 36.5)] and non-regular/non-commercial [37 (95% CI 17.1, 56.5) to 22% (95% CI 19.7, 24.2)] partners are of serious concern.

IDUs largely attributed the inconsistent use of condoms to their being under the influence of drugs. They said that once they were high they were not conscious of their actions and this leads them not to use condoms with their sex partners.

Figure 3

Condom Use Last Time and Consistent Use with Commercial Partners

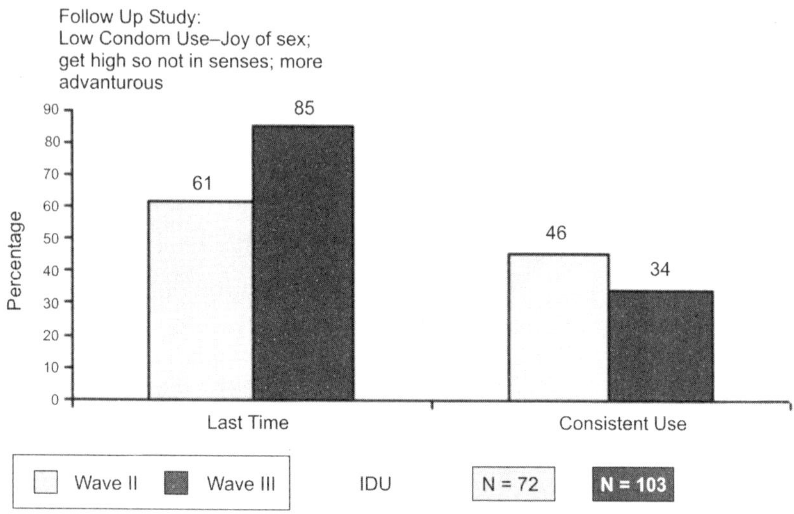

Figure 4

Condom Use Last Time and Consistent Use with Non Commercial Partners

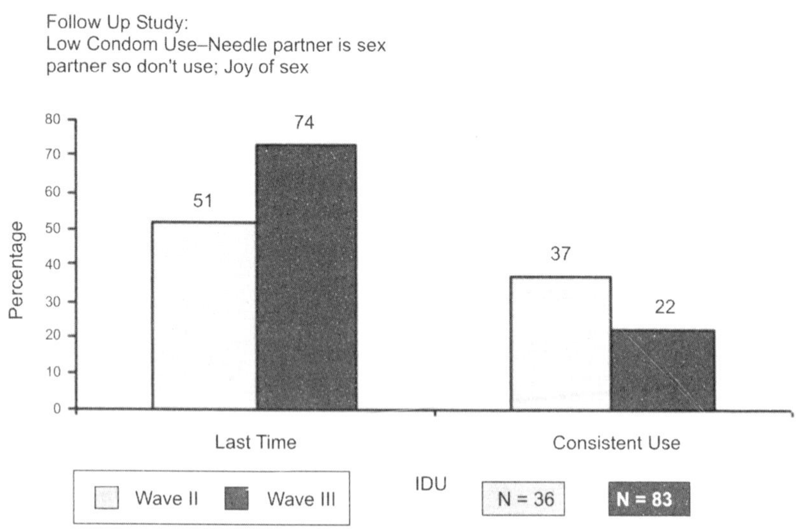

According to one young male IDU:

> We enjoy sex without the condom. We don't get pleasure when we use condom after injecting drug.

Sexually Transmitted Infection

All the IDUs were asked about STI symptoms they had in the past 12 months. Overall, two fifths of the injecting drug users reported to have had some STI (40%) in wave III. About one-fourth each of the injecting drug users reported to have suffered from burning pain during urination in Wave II and III respectively. The reported symptoms of STI among IDUs have increased from 27 per cent to 40 per cent across the Waves.

About half of the IDUs (who had STI symptoms) in Wave II and II respectively did not seek any treatment from a qualified medical practitioner. One-fifth of them approached NGO peer educator, while one tenth each approached government hospital and purchased medicine from chemist shop.

Knowledge of HIV

The following paragraphs deal with knowledge of the IDUs on HIV/AIDS. The questions pertaining to 'knowledge' emphasized upon mode of transmission and methods of prevention. Besides knowledge and attitude, an attempt has been made to measure the misconceptions about spread of HIV/AIDS.

On being asked whether they have ever heard of HIV/AIDS, almost all replied in affirmative (98%). More than one-third of the IDUs

Figure 5

Knowledge of ABC as Methods of HIV Prevention (Composite Index) by District

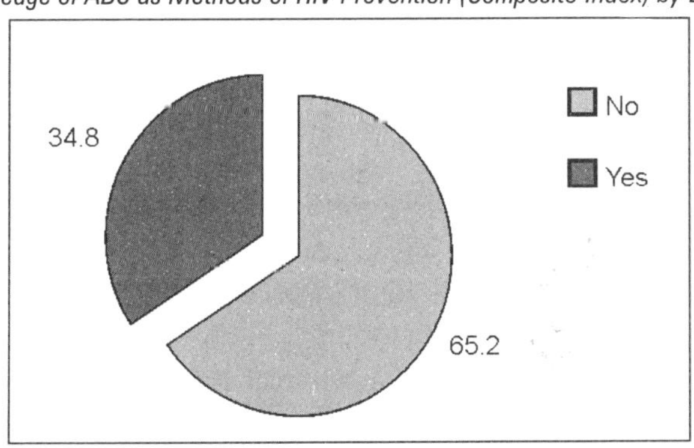

reported switching to non-injecting drugs and avoiding sharing of injecting equipment as a method to prevent HIV. This proportion has slightly increased since the Wave II.

To measure correct knowledge of HIV prevention, a composite index derived on the basis of awareness of HIV prevention through (i) abstinence from sex (ii) being faithful to one uninfected partner and (iii) consistent use of condom was also used. About three fifths of the IDUs reported to have correct knowledge about HIV/AIDS transmission (Figure 5). However, the correct knowledge of HIV prevention had increased only marginally (30 to 36%) from Wave II to Wave III.

Exposure to Interventions

In order to understand the extent of exposure to HIV/AIDS messages/interventions, all the injecting drug users were asked the relevant questions. About two fifths of the IDUs reported that they were educated on STI/HIV/AIDS by someone while one-third reported to have participated in the meeting/campaign. Only 60 per cent of the IDUs had exposure to any interventions related HIV/AIDS (Figure 6).

Figure 6

Exposure to Intervention

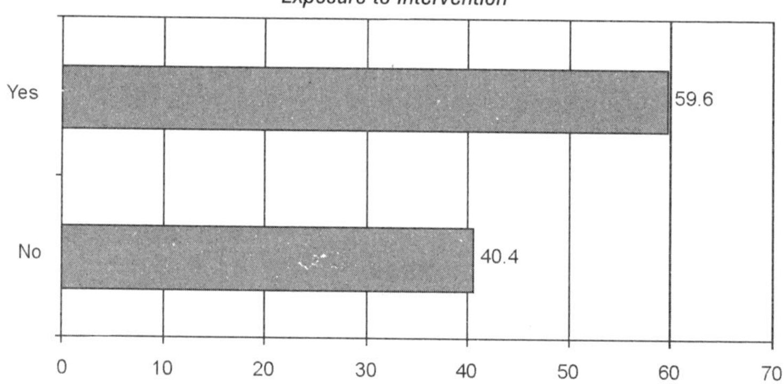

Concluding Remarks

The present paper highlights the following findings:

Two fifth [41% (95% CI 38.04, 43.35)] in Wave III as against 34 per cent (95% CI 24.34, 42.86) in Wave II of the injecting drug users reported to have shared injecting equipment, the last time they had injected the drugs. Around three-fourths [74% (95% CI 71.7, 76.5)] of the IDUs reportedly shared the equipment in high-equipment sharing situations.

Irrespective of partner, the percentage of injecting drug users reporting consistent condom use with paying clients and non-paying/non-regular/non commercial partners has decreased since the Wave II.

The proportion of IDUs reporting STI incidence during the past one year increased from 27 per cent in Wave II to 40 per cent in Wave III.

The exposure to interventions among the IDUs is limited.

Based on the findings of this paper, it is recommended:

Intervention efforts must address the casual approach of this high-risk group towards use of condoms. It is only when they are made familiar with the ramifications of their actions that they may lead to a proactive approach on their part.

IDUs being the most vulnerable group in Mumbai, due to both high needle sharing and partner exchange, need immediate programmatic attention for up scaling. To achieve impact the programme needs to understand their dynamics and emphasize more on life skill development as alternative to drug use. The risk perceptions among the IDUs need to be changed by creating awareness through interpersonal communication.

Finally, this is the high time to scale up interventions among IDUs with focus on sexual activity and the sharing of equipment

Notes

1. Avert Society, established in November 2001 to combat HIV/AIDS in the State of Maharashtra aims to increase the use of effective and sustainable responses to reduce the transmission and mitigate the impact of STI, HIV and related infectious diseases in Maharashtra. Avert Society, a joint project of NACO and USAID, has been entrusted with the responsibility of conducting Behavioural Surveillance Survey in the Avert targeted intervention districts of Maharashtra. (www.avertsociety.org)
2. Commercial partners are the sexual partners with whom the injecting drug users had sex in exchange for money. Non-paying/non-commercial partners are the sexual partners whom the injecting drug user was not married to or had never lived with and did not pay money in exchange for having sex. Spouse or live-in partner is defined as regular partner.

References

Ambekar, Atul and B.M. Tripathi. 2008. Size Estimation of Injecting Drug Use in Punjab and Haryana. UNAIDS, January.

Behavioural Surveillance Survey (BSS) – Wave II in Maharashtra, 2004–05. Summary Report, Avert Society, Mumbai.

Behavioural Surveillance Survey (BSS) – Wave III in Maharashtra, 2005–06. Summary Report, Avert Society, Mumbai.

Gable, Alicia R., Schwaber Alyson and Lawoyin Sheyi. 2006. Preventing HIV Infections among Injecting Drug Users in High Risk Countries. Institute of Medicines of the National Academics.

HIV Sentinel Surveillance Report (HSS). National AIDS Control Organization (NACO). 2005. New Delhi.

HIV/AIDS Country Profile – India. 2003. USAID, March.

L. Sherstha and N. Sharma. 2006. "Assessment Study on Harm Reduction Program Activities among Injection Drug Users (IDUs) in Two Districts of Nepal". Paper presented at XVI International AIDS Conference, Toronto, 13–18 August.

N. Razaki et al. 2006. "High Risk Behaviour and Harm Reduction among IDUs in Tehran, Iran". Paper presented at XVI International AIDS Conference, Toronto, 13–18 August.

National AIDS Prevention and Control Policy (UNPAN), National AIDS Control Organization (NACO). 2003. New Delhi.

CHAPTER 21

Household Health Spending Characteristics in India

Evidence from World Health Survey, India 2003

P. Arokiasamy, H. Lhungdim and M. Guruswamy

Health expenditure comprises of: (i) government and private sector expenditure and (ii) household expenditure. In India, the government provides major allocation of funds to provide health services to the people irrespective of their capacity to pay for the services. In addition, there is substantial investment on health by the private sector also. On the other hand, households and individuals spend a certain amount of money from their pockets for treatment known as out-of-pocket health expenditure. The evidence on health spending characteristics is first reviewed from other studies as a background before presenting the results from the World Health Survey.

In an economy as a whole, public spending on health forms only a minuscule proportion of the total spending on health, with very high levels of out-of-pocket expenditure. Out-of-pocket health expenditure refers to the payments made by households at the point they receive health services that includes doctor's consultation fees, purchase of medicines and hospital bills. Traditional medicine is included in out-of-pocket payments, but expenditure on health related transportation and special nutrition are excluded. Out-of-pocket payments are net of any insurance reimbursement. The household expenditure on health accounts for a major share of about 70–80 per cent of the total health expenditure in India. Rural households in India bear the maximum burden as they account for about 85 per cent of the total household expenditure on health (Sanyal, 1996). The lack of appropriate and consistent information on out-of-pocket expenditure is found to be the prime reason for the exclusion of this important category from health policy planning in India (Selvaraju, 2000).

As a percentage of income, households spend about 5.4 per cent while government spends only 1.09 per cent in rural India according to 1993–94 data (Selvaraju, 2003). In India, households on an average spent nearly 9.9 per cent of their income on curative health care. Rural households bear the largest burden to the extent of 5.3 per cent of their income compared to their urban counterparts with 4.3 per cent (Shariff, 1995). Health subsidies are not particularly well targeted towards the poor in India, especially those living in rural areas and in the poorer states.

States in South India, such as Kerala and Tamil Nadu, do considerably better in this regard than their poorer counterparts in the north such as Uttar Pradesh, Bihar and Orissa. These differences are most apparent when we consider subsidies as a portion of consumption expenditure by quintile (Selvaraju, 2000).

Indeed, it is remarkable that all the south Indian states show a progressive distribution of subsidies in that ratio of subsidies to per capita consumption expenditure falls with expenditure, whereas the poor states (more recently referred to as empowered action group states) have a regressive distribution of public subsidies on health (NCAER, 2000). The poorest states also had the most unequal distributions of inpatient day utilization in public facilities—most notably the backward states in health transition. The states performing particularly well with regard to distribution of total inpatient days are Kerala, Tamil Nadu, Gujarat and Maharashtra. The poorer groups tend to rely more on public facilities for hospital-based care, relative to richer ones (Shariff, 1995). During 1995–96, of the total estimated 14.6 million hospitalizations, nearly 56 per cent were in private facilities, although the share of public and private facilities in total inpatient days utilized was about equal (ibid.). The poor tend to rely on public sector for inpatient care and the rich mostly on private care measured in terms of proportions of inpatient days consumed. A substantial proportion of poorer households in rural India depend on public health facilities for treatment of short duration and major morbidity.

All-India rural health expenditure for all types of categories together has averaged out to 56 rupees per episode of treatment during a 30-day reference period. Expenditure on non-hospitalized treatment was considerably lower than the hospitalized care and the expenditure in seeking public health care were much less than in private facilities. For non-hospitalized treatment, it is interesting to note that the expenditures were substantially lower when treatment was sought in public extension facilities compared to public hospitals. Similarly, the expenditures were much lower when treatment was sought in public clinics rather than private hospitals. The mean expenditure only on fees and medicines is worked out to be 78 rupees for the country as a whole. Poor households spend 7–8 per cent of their annual household income on health care. Relatively, richer households spend 2–3 per cent of their household income on health care. This suggests that the adverse effect of ill-health and sickness have been disproportionately higher on the poorer section in India. The benefits of public health care investment and free provision of primary health care appears to have not reached those who deserve them most (NCAER, 2000).

Studies have shown that on an average, inpatient visits cost about four to 10 times as much as an outpatient visit, though the exact ratio depends on quality of care, capacity utilization, case mix of the inpatient services, level of facility and the actual number of visits and inpatient days (Drummond et al., 1997; Castro-Leal et al., 1999; World Bank, 1997; NCAER, 2000).

Also, patients in India, Indonesia and Vietnam had to pay 2–3 times the official fees for each visit in terms of indirect costs such as transport expenses, the opportunity cost of time spent etc., for availing the health services (World Bank, 1993). It is however, not clearly known that the decline in public spending on health may have increased the household out-of-pocket expenditure on health, because a clear link between the public and private shares of health expenditure and the proportion of income devoted to health is not sufficiently established.

Given the above background on health spending, we use health financing data collected in WHS, 2003. This paper examines the household health spending characteristics using World Health Survey (WHS) data, 2003 collected from six states.

Data and Methods

The WHS collected household expenditure on various services of health such as inpatient fees, outpatient fees, drugs, traditional medicinal practitioners, and other services for one month prior to the survey. The survey also gathered information on sources of household health financing such as current income, savings, insurance, sale of assets, family members/friends outside the household, borrowed and others.

The sampling distribution of households and individual respondents covered in the survey in six states and India is shown in the Table 1. A total of 10,279 households were covered with a population of

58,343. Information on individual health modules was collected from 9,994 individual respondents based on KISH grid tables.

Table 1

Number of Households and Individual Respondents in the World Health Survey in States and India, 2003

States	*Household covered*	*Household population*
Assam	1,141	6,157
Karnataka	1,451	7,883
Maharashtra	2,051	10,674
Rajasthan	1,882	11,662
Uttar Pradesh	2,035	13,138
West Bengal	1,719	8,874
India (six states pooled)	10,279	58,343

This paper explores: (a) the differentials in household health financing and sources of household health financing, and (b) the extent of catastrophic health expenditure and its impact on impoverishment. Evidences of household health expenditure and their sources are presented for the six states by residence and household permanent income quintiles. The paper also presents the distribution of out-of-pocket health expenditure as a share of capacity to pay and the estimates of percentage of households with catastrophic health payments and households impoverished by catastrophic health payments.

Health Expenditure by Type of Services

Total expenditure on health treatment incurred by households in the six states and for India is presented in Table 2. Overall, a household on an average spent Rs 117 in a month for health treatment, which works out to Rs 1,404 in a year. Similarly, a household on an average spent Rs 52 per month for drugs, seven rupees for traditional medicines and Rs 18 for other expenses related to health treatment. The pattern of maximum spending on drugs indicates that there is more reliance on drugs than payments for health services consultation. Inter-state variations in total health spending range from Rs 90 in Karnataka to Rs 203 in Maharashtra. Household health expenditure on inpatient, outpatient, traditional medicines, drugs and other related health purpose is highest in Maharashtra. In the high health spending state of Maharashtra, a large share of expenditure is on both outpatient fees and drugs.

Comparatively, in the states of Rajasthan and Uttar Pradesh the major share of health spending is on drugs.

Household spending on health treatment shows systematic increase with increasing household income quintiles. In the highest income quintile, a household spent 221 rupees compared to 136 rupees in the lowest income quintile. Household health expenditure on each services of inpatient, outpatient treatment, drugs and other related expenditure also show systematic increase with increasing income quintiles. However, health spending on traditional medical treatment does not vary across the income quintile. The health spending on drugs ranges from 80 rupees in the highest income quintile to the low of 47 rupees in the lowest income quintile.

The health spending for outpatient treatment for respondents in the lowest income quintile is 44 rupees, which increases to 80 rupees in the highest income quintile. Health spending on drugs ranges between 47 and 80 rupees from low to high-income quintile households. Other medical related expenses are about three times higher in the highest income quintile (29 rupees) compared to lowest income quintile (eight rupees).

Table 2

Household Health Expenditure in Rupees by Types of Services and Income[1] in India, 2003

States	Total health spending (Rs)	Inpatient fees (Rs)	Outpatient fees (Rs)	Traditional medicine practitioners (Rs)	Drugs (Rs)	Other (Rs)	No. of households
Assam	105.3	2.0	29.5	5.0	57.5	11.2	1141
Karnataka	90.2	3.2	30.8	1.7	34.0	20.4	1451
Maharashtra	203.3	13.8	70.8	24.1	73.1	21.5	2051
Rajasthan	125.7	5.8	25.4	6.1	71.3	17.1	1882
Uttar Pradesh	122.6	9.6	19.9	17.7	63.6	11.9	2035
West Bengal	138.2	2.1	44.0	4.4	70.9	16.7	1719
India (Pooled)	116.7	5.2	34.7	7.0	51.8	18.0	10279
Household income quintiles							
Q1	65.3	1.3	17.9	8.0	30.5	7.6	2037
Q2	80.7	2.4	24.0	6.7	39.1	8.5	2062
Q3	127.6	5.2	37.9	5.9	60.0	18.6	2066
Q4	148.2	4.9	45.2	6.9	60.9	30.3	2019
Q5	148.0	12.0	43.6	7.8	62.4	22.2	2095

Note: 1. Reference period for household health expenditure is last one month

Previous studies have indicated similar trends (Selvaraju, 2003). First, expenditure on treatment of both short duration and long duration illness by various income levels clearly indicates that the expenditure on health care also increases with income quintiles. Expenditure on indigenous medicines also declines with the rise in the income of the patients.

Sources of Health Financing

The percentages shown on the source of financing by income categories on health expenditures (Table 3) are based on multiple responses. Eighty per cent of the households reported they paid their health expenditure through current income followed by 16 per cent from borrowed sources. Nine per cent of households paid their health expenditure through savings (bank account) and 11 per cent of households paid through income from outside the family (family members or outside). About seven per cent of the households financed their health spending by selling household assets such as furniture, cattle, jewellery etc. Less than one per cent of households relied on health insurance to meet their health payments.

Table 3

Percentage of Households by Source of Health Financing[1] in States and India, 2003

States	Current Income	Savings[2]	Insurance[3]	Sold assets[4]	Family outside[5]	Borrowed[6]	Other	No. of house-holds
Assam	76.9	10.8	4.6	16.5	17.8	15.8	3.2	1141
Karnataka	76.1	0.2	0.1	0.4	2.0	4.7	4.0	1451
Maharashtra	87.5	12.8	0.6	4.9	12.2	15.2	2.0	2051
Rajasthan	80.9	12.7	1.1	14.4	27.1	35.2	17.7	1882
Uttar Pradesh	79.8	24.9	0.7	15.3	20.0	30.5	6.1	2035
West Bengal	83.9	12.6	1.4	8.2	14.3	22.4	1.6	1719
India (Pooled)	79.6	8.9	0.8	6.6	11.3	16.1	5.4	10279

Note: 1. Reference period for household expenditure is last one year; percentages are based on multiple responses;
2. Savings (bank account etc.);
3. Payment from a health insurance plan;
4. Sold assets like furniture, animals, jewellery, etc.;
5. Family members or friends from outside the household;
6. Borrowed from someone other than a friend or family.

The percentage of households depending on current income varies between 76 per cent in Karnataka and 88 per cent in Maharashtra. Less than one per cent of households in Karnataka use savings to meet the health expenditure compared to 25 per cent in Uttar Pradesh. About 15 per cent of the households in Uttar Pradesh, Rajasthan and Assam sold their household assets to meet their health payments.

Differences in health spending are very small by current income as source of health treatment. Households with overall expenditure of 2,500 rupees and above spent six times higher amounts (38%) on health treatment paid through savings compared to households with overall expenditure of less than 500 rupees. Those households that paid their health expenditure through insurance coverage and sale of household assets increases with increasing health-spending categories. Also, there is a systematic increase in the percentage of households meeting their health expenditure through borrowings from different sources at the

Table 4

Percentage of Households by Source of Health Expenditures[1] in by Expenditure Categories and Income Quintiles in India, 2003

Characteristics	*Current income*	*Savings[2]*	*Insurance[3]*	*Sold assets[4]*	*Family outside[5]*	*Borrowed[6]*	*Other*	*No. of households*
Health spending categories								
0–500	76.0	6.2	0.6	4.9	7.9	10.7	4.1	7436
501–1000	92.2	14.8	1.1	10.2	18.5	30.7	8.7	2192
1001–2500	82.9	21.4	1.1	18.2	30.2	37.6	12.0	369
2501–105150	86.6	37.2	4.6	18.3	38.0	45.5	13.8	282
Expenditure quintiles[7]								
Q1	74.4	1.7	0.03	10.4	17.0	26.1	5.2	2037
Q2	80.9	7.4	0.1	15.0	18.1	30.5	6.6	2062
Q3	81.3	7.2	0.2	9.4	17.9	20.6	9.0	2066
Q4	70.4	7.5	0.5	3.2	6.7	10.7	5.3	2019
Q5	89.7	16.0	2.1	2.1	5.1	6.3	2.9	2095
Total (six states pooled)	79.6	8.9	0.8	6.6	11.3	16.1	5.4	10279

Note: 1. Reference period for household expenditure is last one year and percentages are for multiple responses;
2. Savings (Bank account etc.);
3. Payment from a health insurance plan;
4. Sold assets like furniture, animals, jewellery etc.;
5. Family members or friends from outside the household;
6. Borrowed from someone other than a friend or family;
7. Expenditure quintiles are based on health spending range from 1 to 105150 rupees.
– No cases reported

higher health-spending category compared to lower health-spending category. Households depending on income from outside the families is about five times and borrowings is about four times higher at the higher health-spending categories compared to those in the lower health-spending categories (Table 4).

Household's expenditure on health from current income, savings and insurance increases at highest income quintiles. Households that sold their household assets and borrowed from someone other than the family members and others to pay their health expenditure are mostly in the lower income quintiles compared to higher income quintiles. This pattern suggests that those who are at the higher end income scale were able to manage their health spending through current income and savings and those at the end of low-income scale depended on selling their own household items or borrowed from outside family sources.

Out-of-Pocket Expenditure on Health

Table 5 presents that in about 63 per cent of households, out-of-pocket expenditure as a share of households' capacity to pay (OOPCTP) is less than 10 per cent. In 16 per cent of households, out-of-pocket expenditure as a share of household capacity to pay range between 10 and 20 per cent and in 12 per cent of households out-of-pocket expenditure as a share of capacity to pay is between 20 and 40 per cent. In eight per cent of the households out-of-pocket expenditure share of capacity to pay is equal to or above 40 per cent, which by definition constitutes catastrophic payments. The percentage of households with out-of-pocket expenditure greater than 40 per cent as a share of capacity to pay is the highest (11%) in Uttar Pradesh.

Table 5

Percentage of Out-of-Pocket Expenditure as a Share of Capacity to Pay in States and India, 2003

	OOPCTP <10%	*10%>OOPCTP <20%*	*20%>OOPCTP <40%*	*OOPCTP >40%*
Assam	75.1	13.1	7.2	4.6
Karnataka	67.2	14.5	11.3	7.0
Maharashtra	68.0	15.6	9.3	7.1
Rajasthan	56.5	18.2	15.7	9.6
Uttar Pradesh	60.8	15.8	12.6	10.8
West Bengal	60.4	19.5	14.5	5.7
India (six states pooled)	63.4	16.4	12.2	7.9

Table 6 shows the structure of out-of-pocket health payment of households to different health services in six states and India. In India the highest proportion of out-of-pocket health payment is for drugs (44.4%), 29.7 per cent for outpatient treatment, 15.4 per cent in other category and six per cent for traditional medicines. The lowest of four per cent of out-of-pocket expenditure on health is for inpatient care. The overall structure of out-of-pocket expenditure also indicates the major outgo of health payments is on drugs and outpatient care.

Table 6

Structure of Out-of-Pocket Expenditure on Health Payments in Six States, 2003

	Out Patient	*In Patient*	*Traditional*	*Drugs*	*Other*
Assam	28.0	1.9	4.8	54.7	10.6
Karnataka	34.2	3.6	1.9	37.7	22.6
Maharashtra	34.8	6.8	11.9	36.0	10.6
Rajasthan	20.2	4.6	4.9	56.7	13.6
Uttar Pradesh	16.2	7.8	14.4	51.8	9.7
West Bengal	31.9	1.5	3.2	51.3	12.1
India (six states pooled)	29.7	4.5	6.0	44.4	15.4

Catastrophic Spending on Health

Catastrophic spending on health occurs when a household must reduce its basic expenses over a certain period of time in order to cope with medical bills of one or more of its members. Insurance coverage is low in India, as a result, households tend to spend a larger share of their income on health care.

Also poor and middle households borrow from other sources when there is an incidence of major morbidity and get into a debt trap. Morbidity and expenditure incurred are found to be major causes for indebtedness among rural households (Selvaraju, 2003). Even households with higher levels of income resort to other sources, like borrowing for financing the treatment of major illness, however marginally, as the level of income increases. This implies that poor households bear a heavy financial burden on account of illness (Selvaraju, 2000). From the 52nd round of the National Sample Survey Organisation (1998) the estimated loss of household income per hospitalization episode in rural areas was 13.5 per cent of mean per capita expenditure for the lowest income quintile, somewhat smaller than 11.7 per cent for the highest. Taken as a proportion of mean expenditures per capita, these income losses were substantially higher for rural than for urban respondents (NCAER, 2000).

The World Health Survey in India identified 12 per cent of households (1,229) in the catastrophic health-spending category. Table 7 presents the distribution of households with catastrophic expenditure. The households with catastrophic spending on health on an average spent 202 rupees for health treatment in the last one month. This is nearly twice higher than the average health expenditure of all households. Of this, the expenditure on drugs amounted to highest of 77 rupees followed by outpatient fees of 49 rupees. Health spending for inpatient fees is 22 rupees, other treatment 40 rupees, and for traditional medicines 14 rupees. Expenditure on different services of health are also higher for households with catastrophic health spending. However, the expenditure on inpatient care is four times higher for households with catastrophic health spending than the average inpatient fees for all households.

Table 7

Households with Catastrophic Health Spending by Types of Services and Income[1] in India (Pooled), 2003

Characteristics	*Total health spending (Rs)*	*Inpatient fees (Rs)*	*Outpatient fees (Rs)*	*Traditional medicine practitioners (Rs)*	*Drugs (Rs)*	*Other (Rs)*	*No. of households*
Household income quintiles							
Q1	151.2	3.3	40.1	15.7	69.9	22.2	250
Q2	188.7	8.5	53.3	17.5	76.2	33.2	183
Q3	222.9	28.0	51.1	25.2	86.3	32.3	209
Q4	178.6	10.5	46.1	9.4	69.2	43.4	254
Q5	260.4	53.2	56.6	9.1	88.1	53.4	333
Total	201.7	22.1	49.1	13.8	77.2	39.5	1229

Note: 1. Reference period for Household health expenditure is last one month.

Total catastrophic health expenditures tend to increase with higher income quintiles. In the lowest income quintiles, on average, the catastrophic health expenditure is 151 rupees compared to 202 rupees in the highest income quintile. The highest income quintile households on an average spent 12 times higher for inpatient treatment compared with the low-income quintile households.

The amount spent on traditional medical practitioners is 16 rupees in the lowest income quintile and nine rupees in the highest income quintile. The lowest income quintile household spent 70 rupees on drugs compared to 88 rupees by the highest income quintile households. The very high spending on drugs and outpatient by lower income quintile households with catastrophic expenditure suggests a greater dependence on drugs and public health spending and avoidance of payments for private consultation. The expenditure on other items is 22 rupees in the lowest income quintile and 53 rupees at the highest household income quintile.

Impoverishment Due to Health Spending (IMPOOR)

A non-poor household is impoverished by health payment when it becomes poor after paying for health services. The household is pushed into poverty due to health payments, in the absence of insurance coverage and lack of protectional measures by other health reimbursement schemes.

Table 8 presents the percentage of households with catastrophic expenditure and the percentage of households impoverished by health spending by expenditure deciles in six states and India. The proportion of households with catastrophic expenditure in the first and second deciles is 13 per cent and 23 per cent respectively. About 30 per cent of the households incurred catastrophic expenditure in the third decile. A majority of households with catastrophic health spending are concentrated in the lower income deciles, indicating a higher burden of health spending for the poor households. As economic status improves, the catastrophic and impoverishment levels come down. Households in the fifth and sixth deciles experienced highest impoverishment. Most of the impoverished households are concentrated in the middle categories of health expenditure (fifth and sixth deciles). In sum, both catastrophic expenditure and impoverishment levels due to health payments are the highest in the middle health expenditure decile categories.

Insurance Coverage

The purpose of this section is to understand the extent of coverage by health insurance along with some characteristics of the insurance plans. The two major insurance schemes are mandatory and voluntary insurance. Mandatory health insurance would include any system or organization that covers a person's health costs on the condition that the person is formally registered or enrolled in the programme. The insurance voluntarily taken by an individual is known as voluntary insurance.

Table 8

Percentage of Households with Catastrophic Expenditure in Six States of India, 2003

	India		Assam		Karnataka		Maharashtra		Rajasthan		Uttar Pradesh		West Bengal	
Expenditure deciles	C	I	C	I	C	I	C	I	C	I	C	I	C	I
1.	12.24	—	6.63	—	1.75	—	29.94	—	53.96	—	25.41	—	17.79	—
2.	22.89	—	17.57	—	12.28	—	29.62	—	22.47	—	44.57	—	39.05	—
3.	30.19	—	5.19	—	27.63	—	48.61	—	33.54	—	45.18	—	34.19	—
4.	27.7	7.26	17.06	7.4	22.82	4.99	15.28	5.01	35.37	10.12	42.54	9.27	31.69	8.51
5.	27.34	10.85	16.64	8.53	24.26	15.06	27.52	14.21	35.88	21.45	38.85	27.4	23.85	15.23
6.	27.59	11.65	12.37	2.52	24.84	6.41	26.15	19.38	38.8	23.61	36.13	18.34	22.71	9.93
7.	23.71	7.3	19.48	9.83	19.23	2.16	20.64	12.58	28.73	13.6	40.71	21.33	23.6	1.71
8.	12.07	3.71	24.12	2.32	3.82	2.18	6.44	1.21	22.84	3.86	32.86	15.73	18.54	1.29
9.	12.69	2.73	12.47	3.86	6.04	0.27	4.52	0.72	28.7	7.75	25.59	6.93	10.79	0.21
10.	14.16	2	21.11	5.95	13.64	1.78	13.69	1.63	25.93	1.51	10.7	2.9	16.29	1.05

Note: No case or less than five cases.

C = Catastrophic; I = Impoverishment

In the World Health Survey, information was collected on the coverage of both mandatory and voluntary insurance. The mandatory insurance scheme in India consists of coverage by Employee State Insurance Scheme (ESIS), Central Government Health Scheme (CGHS) and medical reimbursements by employers (both government and private). Voluntary insurance consists of coverage by other personal insurances such as Mediclaim etc.

Table 9 presents the insurance coverage levels among the states of India. In India only two per cent of the individual respondents are reported to be covered by any insurance scheme and the rest are uninsured. The highest level of insurance coverage is in West Bengal (6%) followed by Rajasthan (5%) and Maharashtra (2%). Voluntary insurance is only one per cent in West Bengal and less than one per cent in the other states.

Table 9

Health Insurance Coverage in States and India (pooled), 2003

States	*Percentage of population with*			*No. of persons with insurance coverage*	*Total population size*
	Insurance coverage (Total)	*Mandatory insurance coverage*[1]	*Voluntary insurance coverage*[2]		
Assam	0.02	0.02	—	2	6,157
Karnataka	0.2	0.2	0.01	50	7,838
Maharashtra	2.3	1.6	0.7	146	10,674
Rajasthan	4.7	4.6	0.1	562	11,662
Uttar Pradesh	0.04	0.01	0.03	5	13,138
West Bengal	6.0	4.6	1.4	473	8,874
India (six states pooled)	1.6	1.4	0.4	1238	58,343

Note: No case reported

1. Includes coverage of individuals under ESIS, CGHS, medical reimbursements from employees.
2. Personal health insurance schemes voluntarily taken such as Mediclaim etc.

Table 10 presents the insurance status of respondents by their selected background characteristics such type of insurance, residence and economic status. In urban areas two per cent of respondents are insured compared with negligible coverage (0.7%) in rural areas. Both voluntary and mandatory insurance coverage exists at a minimum scale, but mainly in urban areas. All the individuals covered under insurance scheme are higher income quintile respondents; this is not surprising given that insurance prevalence is nil in the lower income quintile households.

Table 10

Health Insurance Coverage by Residence and Household Income Quintile in India (Pooled), 2003

Characteristics	Percentage of population			No. of persons with insurance coverage	Total household population size
	Insurance coverage (Mandatory + Voluntary)	Mandatory insurance coverage	Voluntary insurance coverage		
Residence					
Urban	2.2	1.9	0.3	731	15,108
Rural	0.7	0.6	0.1	507	43,235
Income quintiles					
Q1	0.2	0.2	—	23	10,308
Q2	0.4	0.3	0.1	72	11,544
Q3	0.7	0.6	0.1	115	12,092
Q4	1.4	1.3	0.1	355	12,406
Q5	3.6	2.9	0.7	673	11,993
Total (six states pooled)	1.6	1.4	0.4	1238	58,343

Note: No cases reported.

Conclusion

Eighty per cent of households reported that they paid their health expenditure through current income followed by 16 per cent from borrowed sources. Health expenditure paid through savings (bank account) is nine per cent and income from outside the family (family members or outside) constitutes about 11 per cent each. About seven per cent of the households financed their health expenditure through sale of assets such as furniture, cattles, jewellery etc. Less than one per cent of households relied on health insurance for their health payments.

In twelve per cent of the households, out-of-pocket expenditure as a share of capacity to pay is equal to or above 40 per cent, which by definition constitutes catastrophic payments. The highest proportion of out-of-pocket health payment is for drugs (45%) followed by 30 per cent for outpatient treatment, 15 per cent in other category and six per cent for traditional medicines. The lowest four per cent share of out-of-pocket expenditure on health is for inpatient care.

In all, the twelve per cent of households in India with catastrophic spending on health, on an average, spent 201 rupees for health treatment in the last one month. Of this, the amount spent on drugs was the highest of 77 rupees followed by 49 rupees for outpatient fees.

Households spent 22 rupees for inpatient fees, 40 rupees for other treatment and 14 rupees for traditional medicines.

Catastrophic health expenditures fend to rise with increasing levels of income quintiles. At the lower income quintiles, on average, the catastrophic health expenditure is 151 rupees compared to 260 rupees at the higher income quintile. Higher income quintile households on an average, spent 12 times higher for inpatient treatment compared to the low-income quintile households in India. Both catastrophic expenditure and impoverishment levels due to health payments are the highest in the middle health expenditure decile categories.

References

Bhat, Ramesh. 2000. "Health Care Financing: Goals of Health Care System". Paper presented at the conference on Health Insurance, Indian Institute of Management, Ahmedabad, 18–19, March.

Castro-Leal, Florencia, Julia Dayton, Lionel Demery and Kalpana Mehra. 1999. Public Social Spending in Africa: Do the Poor Benefit. *The World Bank Research Observer*, 14(1): 49–11.

Drummond, Michael, Bernie O' Brien, Greg Stoddart and George Torrance. 1997. Methods for Economic Evaluation of Health Care Programmes. Oxford Medical Publications, Second Edition, London.

National Council of Applied Economic Research. 2000. Who Benefits from Public Health Spending in India? NCAER, New Delhi.

National Sample Survey Organisation. 1998. Morbidity and Treatment of Ailments. Department of Statistics, Government of India, Report No. 441, New Delhi.

Sanyal, S.K. 1996. Household Financing of Health Care. *Economic and Political Weekly* 31(20): 1216–22.

Selvaraju, V. 2000. Government Expenditure in Health Sector, 1995–96. Draft Report, National Institute of Public Finance and Policy, New Delhi.

——. 2003. Health-Care Expenditure in Rural India. Working Paper Series No. 90, National Council of Applied Economic Research, New Delhi.

Shariff, A. 1995. Health Transition in India. Working Paper No. 57, National Council of Applied Economic Research, October, New Delhi.

World Bank. 1993. *World Development Report 1993*. Oxford University Press, New York.

——. 1997. Health, Nutrition and Population. Human Development Network, Washington D.C.

World Health Organization. 2000. *World Health Report 2000*. Geneva.

Contributors

Tavakkol Aghayari-Hir, Ph.D Student of Demography, University of Tehran, Iran. E-mail: aghayarih456+@yahoo.com

Aliyar Ahmadi, Ph.D Student of Demography, University of Tehran, Iran. E-mail: ahmadi_78@yahoo.com

Burhan Ali, Research Scholar, Centre for Religious and Cross-cultural Studies, Gadjah Mada University, Indonesia. E-mail: tuhan_kecil@yahoo.com

P. Arokiasamy, Professor, Department of Development Studies, International Institute for Population Sciences, Mumbai, India. E-mail: parokiasamy@iips.net

Romeo Arca Jr., Senior Programme Officer, Asia Regional Office of the Planned Parenthood Federation of America-International, Bangkok, Thailand. E-mail: romeo.arca@ppfa.org

Narayanaswamy Audinarayana, Professor, Department of Sociology and Population Studies, Bharathiar University, Coimbatore, India. E-mail: audi_bu@yahoo.co.in

Jayanta Kumar Basu, Manager, Monitoring & Evaluation, FPA India, Mumbai, India. E-mail: jayanta14@yahoo.com.

Chaiti Sharma Biswas, Researcher, Economic Research Unit, Indian Statistical Institute, Kolkata, India. E-mail : chaitisb@hotmail.com

H.R. Channakki, Research Fellow, Population Research Centre, JSS Institute of Economic Research, Dharwad, India. E-mail: hrchannakki@gmail.com

Susmita Das, Senior Lecturer, Department of Geography, St Mary's College, Shillong, Meghalaya, India. E-mail: susmita_7stm@yahoo.com

W. Indralal De Silva, Dean, Faculty of Arts & Senior Professor and Head, Department of Demography, University of Colombo, Colombo, Sri Lanka. E-mail: isilva84@mail.cmd.ac.uk

Devamoni Dey, Research Officer, Population Research Centre, M.S. University, Vadodara, India. E-mail:prcbaroda@yahoo.com

Dinesh Dhungel, Coordinator of Centre for Research on Environment, Health and Population Activities, Kathmandu, Nepal. E-mail: dinesh@crehpa.wink.com.np

M.M. Gandotra, Director, Centre for Operations Research and Training (CORT), Vadodara, India. E-mail: mmgandotra@cortindia.com

Bina Gubhaju, Post-doctoral Fellow, Asia Research Institute, National University of Singapore, Singapore. E-mail: aribg@nus.edu.sg.

Sunil Kumar Gulati, IAS, Director, Census Operations, Haryana, Chandigarh, India. E-mail: sunilaol@yahoo.com

M. Guruswamy, Professor and Head, Department of Development Studies, International Institute for Population Sciences, Mumbai, India. E-mail: gmadappa@iips.net

Mohammad Amirul Islam, Research Fellow, Southampton Statistical Sciences Research Institute, University of Southampton, UK, E-mail: m.aislam@soton.ac.uk.

K. Karunathilake, Senior Lecturer, Department of Sociology, University of Kelaniya, Kelaniya, Sri Lanka. E-mail: kkaru@kin.ac.lk

C.G. Hussain Khan, Professor of Anthropology and Coordinator, International Diploma in Reproductive Health Management, Karnatak University, Dharwad, India. E-mail: cghkhan2000@rediffmail.com

M.E. Khan, Senior Associate, Reproductive Health Programme, Population Council of India, New Delhi. E-mail: mekhan@popcouncil.org

H. Lhungdim, Associate Professor, Department of Public Health & Mortality Studies, International Institute for Population Sciences, Mumbai, India. E-mail: lhungdim.hem@iips.net

A.H. Mehryar, Former Director, Asia and Pacific Population Studies Centre, Ministry of Science and Technology, Tehran, Iran. E-mail: ahmehryar@gmail.com

Shekhar Mukherji, Former Professor, International Institute for Population Sciences, Mumbai, India. E-mail: spm631@vsnl.net

Abbas Askari Nadoushan, Ph.D Student of Demography, University of Tehran, Iran. E-mail: aaskarin@yahoo.com

Aswini Kumar Nanda, Professor and Director, Population Research Centre, Centre for Research in Rural and Industrial Development (CRRID), Chandigarh, India. E-mail: akn_aswini@yahoo.co.in

Sabu S. Padmadas, Senior Lecturer, Southampton Statistical Sciences Research Institute, University of Southampton, UK. E-mail: ssp@soton.ac.uk

Amita Pradhan, Associate Professor, Department of Community Medicine, KIST Medical College Teaching Hospital, Lalitpur, Nepal. E-mail: amiseason@yahoo.com

F. Ram, Director and Senior Professor, International Institute for Population Sciences, Mumbai, India. E-mail: director@iips.net

Hemlata Sadhwani, Manager (Projects), Centre for Operations Research and Training, Vadodara, India. E-mail: hsadhwani@cortindia.com

T.V. Sekher, Associate Professor, Department of Population Polices & Programmes, International Institute for Population Sciences, Mumbai, India. E-mail: tvsekher@gmail.com

Sona Sethi, Asia Regional Director of the PPFA International, Bangkok, Thailand. E-mail: sona.sethi@ppfa.org

Peter W.F. Smith, Professor, Southampton Statistical Sciences Research Institute, University of Southampton, UK. E-mail: P.W.Smith@soton.ac.uk

H.C. Srivastava, Former Professor, International Institute for Population Sciences, Mumbai, India. E-mail: harish_srivastava@hotmail.com

Anand Tamang, Director of the Centre for Research on Environment, Health, and Population Activities, Kathmandu, Nepal. E-mail: anand@crehpa.wlink.com.np

Laxmi Thakur, Professor, Department of Population Studies, Maharshi Dayananad Saraswati University, Ajmer India. E-mail: drlaxmithakur@gmail.com

A.K.M. Ahsan Ullah, Assistant Professor, International Development Studies, Saint Mary's University, Halifax, Canada. E-mail: ahsan722000@yahoo.com

Sayeed Unisa, Professor, Department of Mathematical Demography & Statistics, International Institute for Population Sciences, Mumbai, India. E-mail: unisa@iips.net